Bali: *Sekala and Niskala*

Volume II: *Essays on Society, Tradition, and Craft*

D1572240

BALI: SEKALA AND NISKALA

VOLUME II:
ESSAYS ON SOCIETY, TRADITION, AND CRAFT

Fred B. Eiseman, Jr.

PERIPLUS EDITIONS
BERKELEY - SINGAPORE

A version of the material in this book appeared in
Bali: Sekala & Niskala Volumes I, II, and III
published by Fred B. Eiseman, Jr. in Bali.

Edited by David Pickell
Designed by David Pickell and Peter Ivey
Cover by Peter Ivey
Cover painting by I Made Budi, Batuan

Published by Periplus Editions, Inc.
1442A Walnut Street # 206
Berkeley, California 94709
Publisher Eric M. Oey

Printed in the Republic of Singapore

ISBN 0-945971-05-2

The drawings appearing throughout this volume are by I Nyoman Sukartha

TO MY WIFE MAGGIE, whose encouragement, patience, and interest kept me going. I thank her for enduring all the months that I had to spend away from home. But she knew very well that if she had not allowed me to do this I would have been even harder to get along with than usual. And I thank her for helping me, both in the field and at home, with the gathering of information and photographs, and in the preparation of the text. In a very real sense, this book is not mine, but ours.

AND TO I WAYAN BUDIASA, of Jimbaran, Bali, my good friend and assistant. There is literally not a paragraph in this book that is not a direct result of Budi's help. His valuable, loyal, and efficient assistance is hereby recognized. Budi and I have worked together for more than ten years now, and our relationship has become more like that of father and son than of worker and employer. He has helped me learn to understand his culture as I have helped him learn to understand mine. We have both grown wiser and, I think, have become better human beings as a result of such mutual understanding.

Contents

Introduction

M<small>Y WIFE</small> M<small>AGGIE AND</small> I first came to Bali in 1961. At that time my only knowledge of the place was from the film *South Pacific*. As a former professional musician, Maggie insisted that we visit Bali because she had heard that its pentatonic music had influenced some important modern Western composers. That was when the summit of Gunung Agung was still pointed; when no motorbikes intruded among the bicycles and *dokars*; when there was no Hotel Bali Beach; no jets landing at the airport; no "Barong Show" at Batubulan; no cassettes; plenty of fried chicken, but not from Kentucky; no gigantic tourist buses; no traffic jams.

Much has intervened between that first glimpse of Bali and the present edition of *Bali: Sekala and Niskala*. After almost annual visits to Bali in the course of world travels, the island grew to be one of the principal destinations of our trips, and we extended our stays to several weeks, a month, several months. Soon Bali became the only destination.

Fortunately the first person we met on that first visit was Njoman Oka, *primus inter pares* of the small group of professional Balinese guides. We had been told about him before our arrival, and during our two-week visit he kept us busy night and day with adventures and information. He has remained our close friend and advisor ever since. Then, quite by chance, we met I Wayan Budiasa, "Budi," a young taxi and *bemo* driver who spoke almost no English. His desire to learn English and become a licensed guide was as great as our desire to learn about Bali. His friends became our friends. And his village, Jimbaran, became our adopted village. We gained new insights and perspectives. Bali's attractions, initially geographical, began to include and then concentrate upon cultural phenomena and personal relationships.

As former teachers, we started to feel the urge to share some of our experiences with others. Even then there was no dearth of books about Bali. But they were either written in Dutch or were intended for the in-and-out visitor who had little time to spend on the island and no particular urge to probe the inner workings of this complex culture. I saw a gap. And I began by researching and writing magazine articles. Perhaps the most important of these was one on the great 1979 Eka Dasa Rudra ceremonies for *National Geographic*. I followed this with a series of articles for the in-flight magazines of various airlines—Qantas, Singapore Airlines,

Philippine Airlines, Garuda, and others—plus articles in other publications devoted to Asian matters.

Then one day several years ago I happened to run across my friend Andy Toth. Andy—Dr. Toth—is an expert on music theory who now teaches at ASTI in Denpasar. Andy said he had seen some of my pieces and they interested him and his friends. But the magazines were no longer available. He suggested I round up all the articles and make them available under one cover. What you have here is the result of Andy's suggestion.

Over the course of four years I wrote three long volumes of *Bali: Sekala and Niskala*. I did not limit myself to the articles that had already appeared, but as new topics suggested themselves, I followed them up. The first volume, with 35 chapters, was published in Denpasar in 1985. In it Maggie wrote chapters on *wayang kulit* and traditional *gamelan*, since that is her specialty. The second volume came out in 1986, with 24 more chapters. A small run of plain-vanilla editions of these two volumes met with modest sales in the hotels and book stores of Denpasar, Kuta, and Sanur. I had the materials ready for a third volume when I was asked by Eric Oey if his press, Periplus Editions, could publish these books and three others I was then working on. Of course, I agreed at once.

I completed the 28 chapters of Volume III in the spring of 1988, but it was never offered for sale in anything other than a photocopied edition for a few friends and scholars. Rather, Eric determined to put all three volumes into the hands of a capable editor who would try to transform what was essentially a series of unconnected essays into a coherent and organized whole. David Pickell has done this job extremely well, I think.

We decided to enliven the newly edited and revised series by commissioning an artist to prepare illustrations. By good fortune, Budi and I located Drs. I Nyoman Sukartha, a well-known Denpasar artist who has taught at the Sekolah Menengah Seni Rupa Bali since 1973. In addition to his teaching, Drs. Sukartha is a painter, sculptor, mapmaker, and a creator of *wayang kulit* puppets. His work has been exhibited at art festivals and exhibitions in Bali as well as Europe.

Drs. Sukartha, 37, is from Ulakan in the district of Karangasem in northeastern Bali, although he makes his home in Denpasar. He graduated in 1968 from the Sekolah Teknologi Negeri in Denpasar, and completed his high school work in 1971 at the Sekolah Seni Rupa Indonesia in Denpasar. He entered the Faculty of Technology at Universitas Udayana in Bali in 1972 and received his Doctorandus degree in Art in 1983. While at the university he taught art at SSRI and, after graduating, taught at the university. Drs. Sukartha is married to Ni Putu Ariasih, from Manggis in Karangasem, and they have two boys and a girl.

As indicated above, this book had its origins in a series of independent essays, written at different times and for different audiences. Even when the articles are collected and edited to provide as much coherence as possible, they are still, to a considerable degree, independent. Each chapter can be understood without reference to the others, which makes for a certain amount of repetition. And although all the essays are about the same culture, there is no theme or story line. The editor has wisely decided not to try to change the basic structure of the original essays. No apologies need be made for that fact.

It will be useful to the reader to understand how and why the material in this book was gathered and written. The reader is always at the mercy of the prejudices, methods, and special points of view of the writer, and should be provided with a caveat lector right from the start. I am not a trained anthropologist and neither my method nor my writing style strictly follows the accepted norms of the profession. This has its advantages and disadvantages. It probably means that some of my conclusions could not withstand the harsh light of professional criticism. But it also means that my style can be more relaxed, informal, and therefore readable by one who himself is not a trained anthropologist.

My home in Bali, where I spend six months of each year, is in the house compound of my close friend and associate Budi. The story of my long relationship with Budi, a guide by profession, need not be recounted here. Budi's house compound is in Jimbaran, a village of some 12,000 people on the narrowest part of the isthmus connecting the Bukit Peninsula to the main part of the island. I am the only foreign resident of Jimbaran. Recently two small hotels have been built in the village, but visitors have little contact with the villagers. Other than Budi, who spent two years at my house in Scottsdale, Arizona perfecting his English, nobody in the village can speak English. Most of the villagers are fishermen, tailors, salt makers, truckers, drivers, or are engaged in various other forms of small business. Jimbaran, and the dry limestone Bukit in general, is not "typical" of the Bali seen by most visitors. There is no handicraft industry other than a few small shell jewelry factories. There is no irrigation water and therefore no rice cultivation. It is a world away from the tourist meccas of Ubud, Kuta, Sanur, and Nusa Dua.

When I first came to Jimbaran I was a novelty, of course; an unfamiliar unintelligibility. As the years passed I have made the transition to a familiar unintelligibility to some and a familiar intelligibility to many. I have entered freely into village activities, dancing at temple festivals, chopping up food for feasts, participating in the *barong* society's activities, helping at temple festivals, teaching English to high school students, and, in short, trying to become as much a part of Jimbaran life as possible.

The reader may suspect that I have somehow worked my way into Jimbaran society in order to learn its secrets with the purpose of writing about them—not an unknown practice among anthropologists. This is not my intent. I live in Jimbaran because I like it there. It is very much my home—perhaps even more my home than the one in Scottsdale. Many of the villagers are my close friends. We have learned from each other, but I value them foremost as people, not informants. I have begun to learn to live in their cultural setting and within their set of values. And I think that my neighbors recognize that my effort is to be as much a part of their culture as possible—not to gather information on interesting "phenomena." At least they pay me the compliment of ignoring my presence. When they started doing that, I felt that we had arrived at a condition of mutual respect and understanding.

I have adopted Balinese Hinduism. I was not converted to Hinduism. Quite the contrary, I was like the character in Molière's *Le Bourgeois Gentilhomme* who realized that he had been speaking prose all his life and didn't know it. I had been practicing a philosophical form of Hinduism since adolescence and never realized that my beliefs were consistent with a large, organized body of religion.

I investigate and write about Bali for the sheer joy of learning new things and to help others understand what I have learned. More than a little of this imperative can be traced to my 20-plus years as a schoolteacher. And my talents in investigation, such as they are, are perhaps the result of my education as a chemical engineer and the subject of my teaching—physics and chemistry.

There are a few important points the reader of this series must keep firmly in mind. Anyone who purports to write about "the way it is in Bali" is either ignorant or a liar. One would think that local variations in culture on such a tiny island would be insignificant. That is not the case. One of the first things a careful investigator learns is the principle of *desa kala patra:* that whatever one learns in Bali is largely determined by *where* he is, *when* he is there, and the *circumstances* under which the learning occurs.

Since I live about six months of each year in Jimbaran, my observations are strongly influenced by practice in that particular village. In effect, this book is really about Jimbaran and should be entitled *Jimbaran: Sekala & Niskala*. Years ago I set out to learn as much as I could about Indonesia. A decade of experience later, I decided to narrow my field to just Bali. Another decade later I thought I had better concentrate upon South Bali. A couple of years ago the field narrowed to Jimbaran. It is now becoming apparent that I had better focus only upon South Jimbaran. I have tried to gather information from as wide a variety of places as possible. My informants have been sought from Gilimanuk to Nusa Penida, Pecatu to Singaraja. But I make no apologies for the probable deviations of that which I report from what one might find elsewhere on the island.

There are many people I would like to thank. Budi, of course, makes countless contributions to my work. But his greatest assets are his ability to find informants, and his enthusiasm for extracting information from them. Our sources vary from university professors to *balians*, rice farmers to engineers; heads of government offices to sellers of *jamu;* master craftsmen, peddlers, waiters, builders, philosophers, *pedandas*, and housewives. The only requirement is that the people are willing to share their information. And Budi has a knack for prying out information without coloring it with his own preconceptions. This did not come naturally to him; it is not a common Balinese trait.

Budi's importance to me cannot be overestimated. But his wife Ni Wayan Lidawati also has been extremely important in my education. She is my dance teacher, and has been an invaluable source of information on a great variety of subjects. Wati works at the Rumah Sakit Umum Pusat, the public hospital in Denpasar. She is also a part-time seller, an accomplished cook, an expert maker of offerings, a former professional classical dancer, a dance instructor, and a mother. Since I have known her and her large family since before she and Budi married, I have had a good opportunity to see how matches are made. And since her own family lives in Denpasar, I have had a chance to compare life in the big city to that in Jimbaran.

When one's subject of study is people and their ideas, every person becomes a subject of study and a source of information—whether the contact is a formal interview or idle gossip over a cup of coffee. It would be impossible for me to acknowlege my debt to the thousands of people who have helped me since my arrival in 1961. If any of them should read these lines, I can only offer my sincere thanks. However, my most valuable contacts and sources have been the ordinary people of Jimbaran—not the professors and specialists and experts, just the sorts of people you might meet in your own town. They run the market, cure the sick, clean up the garbage, harvest the fish, make the salt, hoe the fields, sew the clothes, dance in the temples, sell cakes and coffee in the *warungs*, drive the trucks and bemos, bury the dead, and usher the newly born into the world. They are kind to me and share their lives with me. They discuss their problems and their joys with me. This is how I have learned.

The one area where Budi's help has been other than a complete boon is in my mastery of the Balinese language. Were it not for Budi I would probably be much more fluent than I am—his command of English and his skill at translation has somewhat spoiled me in this regard. I regularly study Balinese for one or two hours every day with Budi. But his ability to help me in my work has made it unnecessary for me to learn to speak Balinese really well, and his acting as a translator has made my work so much more efficient that—without him—it would have taken several lifetimes to do what I have done.

Finally, I would like to single out Maggie and Budi once again for thanks. Maggie has had almost as great a role in the writing of these books as I. She read all of the manuscripts, criticized, corrected, and offered suggestions. And, as mentioned above, she wrote two of the chapters herself. As for Budi, my feelings toward him are evident in the dedication of this book and in frequent remarks in the text. Except in the most technical interpretation of the term, the authorship of this work is ours—Maggie's, Budi's, and mine.

Fred B. Eiseman, Jr.
Jimbaran, Bali

A NOTE ON SPELLING. Balinese spelling varies widely. One reason is that there are almost no works written in Balinese using the Roman alphabet. Budi and I searched all of the principal bookstores in Denpasar—our harvest was a handful of paperbacks on specialized subjects, plus a few books for elementary and junior high school students. And most Balinese writers do not use a dictionary, but rather spell words as they hear them. Another source of variation is that many Balinese words come from Sanskrit, which can be accurately romanized only by using diacritical marks. The Balinese, who never use the special sounds represented by the diacritics in the spoken language, do not bother with the marks in their written works. (In this volume, I will stick to the Balinese spelling—closer to the true sound in Balinese—using, for example, *Siwa* instead of *Shiva* or *Siva*.)

Thus the few authoritative dictionaries of the Balinese language must serve as standards. I recommend to the interested reader the following three dictionaries, which I have constantly used as references: *Kamus Bali-Indonesia*, published in 1978 by the Balinese Office of Education; Father J. Kersten's *Bahasa Bali* (Balinese-Indonesian) published by Penerbit Nusa Indah in Ende, Flores, in 1984; and *Dictionary of Balinese-English* by Dr. C.C. Barber, Aberdeen University, 1979.

PART I

Geography

CHAPTER 1

Island of Bali

VOLCANOES, MONSOONS, AND TIDES

BALI IS A TINY VOLCANIC ISLAND, about the size of the state of Delaware, tucked between Java and Lombok in the middle of the 3,400 mile long Indonesian archipelago. The island's mild and steady climate, fertile volcanic soil, many and fast-moving rivers, and plentiful and consistent rains combine to create, in the eyes of most travelers, a physical paradise. The balmy, paradisiacal conditions that Bali's 2.5 million inhabitants and many visitors enjoy are a product of the climactic patterns and geology of the Indonesian region.

The island, roughly mushroom shaped, covers about 5,000 square kilometers (2,100 sq. mi.)—150 kilometers (90 mi.) east–west and 80 kilometers (50 mi.) north–south. The southern extension of the island, a rocky and arid peninsula called the Bukit, is kept from being an island in its own right by a tiny isthmus. The island of Nusa Penida, geologically similar to the Bukit, lies off Bali's southeast coast.

Bali is just 600 miles south of the equator, latitude 8° 4' to 8° 52' south, and at longitude 114° 26' to 115° 42' east, is about one-third of the way around the globe from Greenwich. Bali's proximity to the equator keeps the island consistently warm year-round, with a mean temperature of 27.2° C (81.0° F). Nor is there much daily fluctuation in temperature—in Denpasar, the greatest daily temperature fluctuation takes place in April, and the range is a mere 6.9° C (12° F). Being in the Southern Hemisphere, December is Bali's warmest month, but the average December temperature is only 2.2° C (4.0° F) warmer than that of the coolest month, July. Bali has a remarkably pleasant and steady temperature.

A number of factors conspire to keep Bali's temperature constant. Since it is so close to the equator the days vary little in length—the longest, in late December, has 12 hours and 38 minutes of daylight, only about an hour more than the shortest day, in late June, with 11 hours and 37 minutes of daylight. The island's humidity, a product of rainfall patterns, geography, and the steady, warm temperature, is monotonously constant at about 75 percent. Again, relative humidity varies less than 3 percent from the dampest to the driest months. This steady, relatively high humidity further attenuates any variation in temperature.

The only variation of temperature and humidity on Bali is geographic, the mountainous central regions being significantly colder and damper than the tableland and coast. The mountains average 4-5° C (7-9° F) colder with about 10 percent greater relative humidity than the rest of the island. Lightly clad motorcyclists visiting misty, mountainous Kintamani are quickly made aware of the effect of altitude upon temperature and rainfall.

The somewhat more rugged climate in the higher altitudes affects the culture there—different crops are grown, and clothing and house construction differ. The influence of foreigners has been less felt in the mountain areas and practices, terminology, calendars, and crafts in several of the more remote villages still differ significantly from the rest of Bali.

Bali is one of more than 13,000 islands in the Republic of Indonesia, fewer than half of which are even large enough to have names, and just over 900 of which are inhabited. The nation's territorial boundaries enclose 10 million square kilometers (4 million sq. mi.), of which only about 15 percent is land. The Greater Sunda Islands—Sumatra, Java, Borneo, and Sulawesi—dominate the northern and western part of the archipelago. Most of Borneo—Kalimantan—is part of the republic, but Sarawak and Sabah along the north coast are part of Malaysia, and the tiny, but oil-rich country of Brunei sandwiched between the two East Malaysian states is an independent sultanate. Stretching along the Indian Ocean from Java's eastern tip along the area south of Kalimantan and Sulawesi, north of Australia, and almost to New Guinea are the numerous Lesser Sunda Islands. Bali is the westernmost of the Lesser Sundas.

GEOLOGICALLY, THE ISLAND OF BALI is a succession of volcanoes with intervening saddles and alluvial slopes covered with rich ash. Bali, and in fact, most of Indonesia, lies along a large arc where two of the earth's seven tectonic plates meet. The meeting of these plates is one of the ways volcanoes and islands are formed. Bali's volcanic mountains are located in the north of the island, as the zone of seismographic and volcanic activity, where the plates meet, slopes north in the area where Bali is located.

The coastal plain on the north is thin while that on the south, the island's principal faming and population center, is broad. The south coastal plain was formed by the alluvial fans spreading downward and outward from a number of volcanic peaks, including Batukau (or Watukau), 2,276 meters (7,467 ft.); Abang, 2,152 meters (7,060 ft.); and Batur,

1,717 meters (5,633 ft.), and Bali's highest mountain, Gunung Agung, 3,142 meters (10,308 ft.).

The volcanoes of Bali are all young, meaning that, although they may have formed before the Recent (Holocene) epoch, all have been active more or less continuously since their birth, right up to the present. Indonesia overall has more active volcanoes than any other nation in the world. During the last 10,000 years at least 132 volcanoes have erupted in the archipelago—17 percent of the total known number of historic eruptions. Of these, 76 have been recorded.

The geography of the Indonesian archipelago is a product of the convergence of three major tectonic plates: the Eurasian, the Pacific, and the Indian-Australian. The Pacific plate does not reach west to Bali, but the island's volcanic activity and geology is determined by the interactions between the Indian Ocean floor, part of the Indian-Australian plate, and the continent of Eurasia. The floor of the Indian Ocean is sliding northward beneath the islands of Sumatra, Java, and the Lesser Sundas at a rate of about six centimeters a year, an average rate of plate movement. Under Bali, the plate moves about as fast as a human fingernail grows, which seems negligible, but is quite significant in geological terms. Every million years, the Indian-Australian plate shifts some 60 kilometers (37 mi.) further north.

As the Indian-Australian plate creeps northward it meets the Eurasian plate, and the energy generated by this encounter forces the Indian-Australian plate to slide beneath the Eurasian plate, a phenomenon called subduction. This zone of subduction forms a giant arc beginning at the Bay of Bengal, following the sweep of the Malay Peninsula, through the west coast of Sumatra and the south coasts of Java and Bali, and on through the Lesser Sunda Islands. The subduction zone then bends into a tight and geologically complex curve, the Banda Arc, between the southern part of Sulawesi and New Guinea, north of Australia. In the Indonesian region, the area of greatest subduction is at the Java Trench.

Subduction results in a characteristic series of geological land and ocean forms. The subducting plate moves from the comparatively thin, cool crust of the earth, a mere few dozen miles thick, down into the hotter, denser, and chemically very different mantle, where solid matter loses its rigidity, plastic flow is the rule, and heat and pressure cause and accelerate chemical changes in the materials of the subducting plate. The results of these changes in the environment of the subducting plate and the enormous shearing stresses are seen at the surface as a characteristic pattern. This pattern is nowhere more "classical," in the sense that it is newly created, clearly formed, and typical, than along the Java Trench and the arc of islands to its north.

The zone between the two plates, called the Benioff Seismic Zone, is the place of maximum shear and, not surprisingly, is the focus of the many

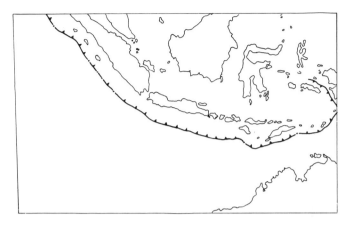

THE JAVA TRENCH

earthquakes. The point at which the two plates begin to overlap is called the mélange wedge, for the mélange of debris and material there that has been scraped off the subducting plate. After sloping gently beneath the mélange wedge to a depth of about 60 miles, the Benioff zone dips abruptly, and plunges, beneath the islands, to a traceable depth of 650 kilometers (400 mi.). Earthquakes are more frequent and violent along the upper, cooler, and more brittle section of the subducting slab, which becomes more plastic and less subject to sudden fracturing as it is heated in the mantle. In Bali, the Benioff Zone is about 100 kilometers (60 mi.) below the surface in the south part of the island, dipping to about 200 kilometers (120 mi.) in the north. Thus the earthquakes of South Bali tend to have more shallow foci than those of the north.

As ocean floor is carried down into the mantle, enormous chemical changes occur within the rocks and sediments carried by the plate. Under great heat and pressure, parts of the subducting plate melt to form magma under great pressure. As the magma, or molten rock, is pushed upward through zones of weakness toward the surface, the pressure lessens, which also lowers the melting point of the rock, allowing the melting process to accelerate. Escaping to the surface, this magma forms the main body of the chain of volcanoes that mark the volcanic arc of Java, Bali and many, but not all, of the Lesser Sunda Islands.

Differently formed volcanoes produce different magmas. The shield volcanoes of Hawaii, for example, produce a very low-viscosity, flowing lava. When it reaches the surface it simply flows out of fissures, often in actual streams of liquid rock that may run for many miles. Such shield volcanoes are almost never explosive, since the vents are not plugged by solidified ejecta. The profiles of the mountains show very gentle, rounded domes, since the magma is fluid and does not build up into steep cones. Such magmas are generally basic in chemical composition, with high concentrations of magnesium and iron.

Subduction zone magmas, however, tend to have rather high melting points, very high viscosities and cool and solidify quickly. They are high in silica content, are lighter-colored than Hawaiian magmas, and are more acidic. These magmas cool so quickly that they block the vents, which builds up pressure below—until there is a series of sudden, violent explosions. The volcanoes of Bali usually spew solid materials—ash, pumice, and dust—glassy, siliceous, clastic materials that are collectively called tephrite. Much of the tephrite is carried away by the violent convectional storms that accompany the release of so much heat and gases in such a concentrated area. Some, however, is too heavy to be windborne and simply falls onto the slopes of the vent, producing the characteristic cones of the subduction zone volcanoes. These cones, representing the piled-up tephrite of successive eruptions, exhibit stratification lines, earning Bali's volcanoes, as a class, the term "stratovolcanoes."

The periods between eruption of stratovolcanoes are irregular and unpredictable. They generally lie dormant for much longer periods than do shield volcanoes of the Hawaii type, sometimes leading people to consider them extinct. This can have disastrous consequences. Because the volcanic ash enriches the soil and the volcano itself carries water down its slopes, the slopes of the volcanoes are excellent for farming and thus often densely settled. Bali's highest mountain, Gunung Agung, erupted violently in 1963, killing thousands of people and destroying temples and many hectares of valuable farm land. But people have short memories, and the land has already been reclaimed and resettled.

Some very large stratovolcanoes plug themselves up so effectively that enormous magma chambers accumulate below the vent before the explosions occur. The result, after the explosion clears the chamber, is a gigantic vacant hole. The surrounding rocks quickly collapse into this hole, leaving a steep-walled crater so large that it looks like a great, flat-floored valley. Such a structure is called a caldera, after the Spanish word for kettle. This is the origin of the Batur caldera in North Bali, visited daily by hundreds of tourists. The caldera is partly filled by a beautiful, crescent-shaped lake, Lake Batur, and a smaller, still-active volcanic cone that last erupted in 1963.

The most famous caldera in the region lies below the surface of the ocean—Krakatau (sometimes spelled Krakatoa) in the Sunda Strait between Java and Sumatra. Krakatau erupted with extreme violence in 1883, generating gigantic tsunami waves that killed tens of thousands of people living along the shores of the surrounding islands. Krakatau produced an estimated four cubic miles of eruption products and, presumably, left an empty magma chamber about that large behind.

One of the greatest explosions recorded was that of Tambora, on the island of Sumbawa, in 1815. Tambora is estimated to have produced five times as much tephrite as Krakatau, and its caldera is 6.5 kilometers (four mi.) wide and about 600 meters (2,000 ft.) deep. Other famous examples are the Tengger caldera of East Java that still contains the active cone Bromo; the even larger caldera just west of Gunung Merapi in East Java (not the Merapi near Yogyakarta) and the principal attraction of North Sumatra, the huge Toba caldera. Geologists estimate that the eruption that formed the Toba caldera, which took place in prehistoric times, produced 1,000 cubic kilometers (240 cubic miles) of tephrite.

THE VOLCANOES OF WHICH BALI IS LARGELY COMPOSED (but not entirely, as we shall see) have important effects upon the civilization and culture of Bali. Tropical soils, because of the heavy rainfall that leaches the nutrients out of the soil, are generally quite poor. The lush growth of tropical rainforests is misleading, as most of the nutrients are contained in a relatively thin top-layer of detritus. Clear away the jungle, and the resulting surface quickly hardens into an almost impenetrable and certainly unmanageable brick-like pavement called laterite. Bali is spared this fate because a continual succession of volcanic eruptions has spread fertile ash over the island. This ash not only forms a fine medium for growing crops, but also enriches the irrigation waters that pass through it on the way to the sea. Irrigation water is both water and a fertilizer in Bali.

The presence of mountains also leads to rainfall, usually confined to the upwind side of the mountains. This so-called orographic precipitation takes place because as prevailing winds push moisture-laden air up the slope of a mountain the air expands and cools, and if the temperature drops below the dew point, clouds form and rain falls. Without mountains, there is no rising air, no cooling, and no rain. Thus Bali is blessed, at least part of the year, with abundant rain and a fertile soil.

The island's many streams tend to have their headwaters near the mountain peaks and flow downhill, away from the central peaks to the sea. Since the soil over which these streams flow is largely ash, they have eroded deep, narrow gorges into the alluvial slopes. Before modern techniques of bridge construction allowed these gorges to be spanned by all-weather roads and bridges, travel "against the grain" of these gorges was at best difficult, and at worst impossible. It was simple to travel toward or away from the mountain peaks because one had no river gorges to span. To a certain extent this is still true today because only a very few of the principal east–west roads carry the main tourist traffic, and hence have been adequately bridged.

Mountains determine the precipitation pattern of Bali, and their lee forms a "rain shadow" on the northern coast. The monsoonal rains in Bali come from the southeast in the dry season and the southwest in the wet season. Thus, regardless of the season, any clouds that form dump their rain on Bali's southerly areas, and the narrow strip north of the mountain ranges is by far the most arid part of Bali.

The raw material for one of the island's most famous native industries, stone carving, comes from the volcanic mountains. The local stone, quarried from the gorges of South Bali, is called *paras*—a soft sandstone that contains a lot of volcanic ash. *Paras* is tuff, a material so soft and crumbly that it is almost as easy to carve as wood. This capability has allowed a very ornate style of ornamentation to develop, and temples are adorned with filigrees of vegetation, leering faces, and elaborate scenes from everyday life. *Paras* weathers badly in Bali's humid and fertile climate and the carvings are quickly eroded by vines and other plants that take root in their many crevices and cracks. A blackened and lichen-covered statue, which looks hundreds of years old, may have been carved just five or ten years before. This rapid destruction insures the longevity of the stone carving trade.

The ashy slopes of the mountains contribute enormous amounts of sediment to Bali's many rivers. Much of the sediment is deposited along the way, but a lot still finds its way into the sea. At the mouths of rivers the water is murky, and the coral reefs that flank most of the island stop at the river mouths. Reef-building corals require ample sunlight, and are choked out by silty water. This excellent drainage from high central mountain ranges has prevented the presence of the swampy areas that characterize the coastal areas of so many other islands. Swamps not only prevent effective land use, especially agriculture, but are also breeding grounds for insects and disease. Bali has some mangrove swamps bordering the Benoa harbor area, but these are small, and put to good use as commercial breeding grounds for fish.

THE TEAR-DROP SHAPED PENINSULA on the south end of the island is called the Bukit, Indonesian for "hill." When you drive from the lush, green, rice-terraced slopes of the volcanoes to the south coast, across the the tiny isthmus and up the long twisting road to the top of the Bukit, it is as if you have entered a different world. This is a limestone plateau without a trace of vulcanism. The massive white or creamy rock is sedimentary in origin. The sediments were raised perhaps by gentle doming caused by the violent shearing forces taking place 50 kilometers (30 mi.) below in the Benioff Zone. The limestone of the Bukit is some 20 million years older than the volcanic ash of Bali proper. It is likely that before the volcanoes, the rest of the island was the same as the Bukit. But the volcanic cover to the north is so thick that evidence of northern extensions of the limestone is totally hidden, or perhaps destroyed. There is, however, a limestone strip of the same age that borders the sea all along the western part of Bali—both the north and south coasts of the western projection that extends from the central mountains to Java.

The Bukit is connected to the main part of Bali by a slender isthmus, less than a mile wide at its narrowest, with Jimbaran Bay on the west side and Benoa harbor on the east. Just to the north of this isthmus is a small area of volcanic sediments, the same age as the recent volcanoes, but differing in that the rocks are volcanic sediments deposited in a coastal basin—the area around Denpasar—and are not primarily crystalline volcanic rock. This area extends to the isthmus, past which there is an abrupt change to the limestone plateau of the Bukit.

The Bukit receives about the same rainfall as the area around Kuta and the isthmus. Its aridity is a result of a lack of available ground water, a product of the limestone base. Surface waters containing dissolved carbon dioxide from the air are slightly acidic and react readily with limestone, weathering crevices, caves, and fissures into the surface, allowing the water table to fall far below. Limestone cannot hold acidic surface water because its porous nature allows water to seep through, weather channels in the rock, and flow to lower lying levels where it is unavailable for surface use. To provide water for the new hotels in the Nusa Dua area, the Indonesian government had to drill down 30 meters (100 ft.). In the isthmus, around Jimbaran, wells provide abundant fresh water at a depth of about 3 meters (10 ft.).

People live on the Bukit, but they must depend on cisterns for their water supply. As far as crops go, they can only grow those that do not need irrigation, such as manioc. They grow some rice, but the crop is only successful when the rainy season is at least normal. Limestone plateaus such as the Bukit tend to develop a topography that is called karst, after an area in southern Europe where this sort of development is characteristic. Karst topography displays caves with stalactites and stalagmites, sink holes, rugged valleys, and rocky surfaces. The soil horizon is very thin, and arid land plants such as succulents and cacti grow in abundance, an entirely different community of plants than is found growing in the volcanic soils of the main part of the island. This physical environment has, of course, drastically affected the living patterns of those who inhabit the Bukit—the lack of readily available surface water and the thin and poor soil being the principal causes.

The Bukit is just a few meters above sea level in the Nusa Dua area, where the new hotel developments are located, and at Tanjung Benoa, south of the harbor. But as soon as it crosses the isthmus just south of Jimbaran the road rises steeply, in two steps, to the top of the plateau—about 210 meters (700 ft.) above sea level. The plateau has numerous gullies and small canyons, none with permanent water. From the south end of Jimbaran Bay, all the way around the Bukit counterclockwise to Nusa Dua, the plateau terminates abruptly in a perpendicular, wave-cut cliff that drops 30 meters (100 ft.) straight into the Indian Ocean. The famous Pura Luhur Uluwatu temple is located on the very edge of a spur of the cliff at the southwest side.

There are very few beaches here. Waves and their erosive energy focus upon points of land and quickly erode them. The destruction of the beach at Sanur, near Tandjung Sari, is a good example of this. The salvation for many hotel owners has been the construction of groins, concrete piers that project into the sea, buffering the force of the waves and allowing sand that is drifting parallel to the beach to accumulate.

BALI HAS A TROPICAL MONSOON CLIMATE with distinct wet and dry seasons. The wet is called *masan ujan*, or *ujan-ujan*, and the dry, *masan panes.* The wettest month is January and the driest is August. From April through November rainfall at the Denpasar Airport averages less than 10 centimeters (3.9 in.) a month; In December, January, and February, the rainfall is close to 30 centimeters (12 in.) a month. At the airport, the average annual rainfall is about 175 centimeters (70 in.). At Besakih, because of its elevation, the total is almost double this, and there is only one month when less than 10 centimeters (3.9 in.) of rain falls. Denpasar averages 126 rainy days per year, two-thirds of them coming in the months from November through March. Besakih has 150 rainy days per year, with about the same percentage for the rainy season. Skys are clear over Denpasar 78 percent of the time; the same is true of Besakih only 31 percent of the time.

The winds come from the southeast during the dry season, about 100 to 130 degrees on the compass, and from the southwest to west during the wet season, 230 to 270 degrees. This wind shift is the principal cause for the two seasons. The prevailing winds of an area are a product of latitude, as there is a general movement of air toward the equator, and the relative position of large land and water areas nearby—the difference in relative heat-retaining ability of water and land produces winds.

The sun is nearly overhead most of the time in the equatorial regions, which makes the region much warmer than the areas toward the earth's poles. The heated surface of the earth in equatorial regions produces a more or less permanent low-pressure band at the equator, produced by the warm air rising. Thus the wind pattern of the equatorial belt is a narrow band, perhaps no more than five degrees of latitude north and south of the equator, within which the predominant motion of the air is convectively upward. This area is often called the doldrums, in which in the days of sailing boats, crews found themselves becalmed.

On each side of the doldrums belt are bands that extend to about 15 or 20 degrees latitude in which the air is moving from the poles over the surface of the earth toward the doldrums low-pressure area, where it then rises. These belts are called the Trade Winds, because they made for excellent sailing. The Trades do not blow due south from the Northern Hemisphere, or due north from the Southern Hemisphere. A phenomenon based on the rotation of the earth, the Coriolis Effect, bends the winds from the south to the "left," counterclockwise, hence they are the Southeast Trades (winds being always named for the direction from which they come, not toward which they blow). The effect does just the opposite to winds from the north in the northern hemisphere. The Coriolis effect produces the swirling tropical storms, typhoons and hurricanes that cause so much damage in other parts of the world. But Bali is too close to the equator to suffer such storms, because the spinning or bending effect of Coriolis' phenomenon diminishes as it spirals out over the fattest part of the globe.

Thus Bali's near equatorial position should produce gentle, southeasterly winds most of the year. But in fact the winds shift in the autumn months, and again in the spring. This is a result of the effect of the area's dominant land masses—Asia, Australia, and India (Indonesia itself is mostly water). As the sun moves north of the equator, in the spring, India and Asia heat up rapidly and Australia cools off rapidly—more rapidly than the masses of water that border these land masses. As a result, a high pressure area develops over Australia and lows develop over India and Asia. The winds blow from the high pressure cell over the continent of Australia outward toward the surrounding seas. And they blow from the surrounding seas inland toward the low pressure cells centered over India and Asia. The reverse occurs when the sun moves south of the equator in the fall. Then Australia develops a low, and winds blow toward the continent, and India and Asia develop highs, and the winds blow oceanward away from the continents.

Thus the entire Asian area, because of its large land masses, is subject to a seasonally reversing wind, a monsoon. Many people in the West use the word "monsoon" to refer to a rainy season, but the word is only correctly used when referring to seasonally reversing winds—toward the land in the period of high sun, away from the land during the period of low sun. High sun means hotter land than surrounding ocean and a corresponding low pressure area. Low sun means cooler land than water and a resulting high pressure area. Of course, low sun means local "winter"—the months around June, July for Australia, those around December, January for Asia and India.

The Coriolis Effect makes winds in the Southern Hemisphere bend to their left and those in the Northern Hemisphere to their right. The result is that winds spiral clockwise out of Asia and India during their period of low sun, peaking in December, and counter clockwise into Asia and India during their period of high sun, June. And winds spiral counterclockwise out of Australia during its period of low sun, and clockwise into Australia during its period of high sun, respectively June and December.

Since Bali is almost due north of the West Coast of Australia, and separated from it only by the relatively narrow Timor Sea, winds spiral out of the north and northwest of Australia, bend toward the west, cross the less

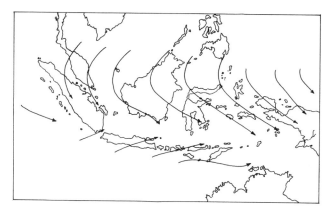

WIND PATTERN DURING THE WET SEASON

than 1,600-kilometer-wide (1,000 mi.) Timor Sea, and blow into Bali from the southeast and east. Since these winds have blown over the vast, dry, interior of Australia, and only a narrow band of ocean, they carry little moisture. This is *masan panes*—the "hot" and dry season.

Then the sun journeys southward again. Australia's land mass heats up, and Asia and India cool off. During the months of November through March, the winds that blow off the east coast of India and the south coast of Asia pass the equator and into the Southern Hemisphere, the Coriolis Effect reverses the direction of bending of these winds, and they begin bending to their left, towards Bali. Winds blowing from the east coast of India traverse the huge Indian Ocean, about 2,500 miles from Sri Lanka to Bali, at first blowing from the north, as they bend to their right, then becoming Westerlies as they enter the Southern Hemisphere. The same is true of the winds that sweep off the coasts of Southern Asia. They tend to be Northerlies as they leave Asia, then switch to Westerlies when they cross the equator. During these months, the prevailing winds sweep over the large expanse of the Indian Ocean and the other bodies of water before they reach Bali. As they cross these long expanses of warm water, the winds pick up a great deal of moisture, and, of course, dump it in large quantities upon any mountains, including Bali's, that they meet along the way. This is *masan ujan*—wet season.

The seasonal distribution of rain has major effects upon Bali's culture. The dry months of May through September prevent the growth anywhere in Bali of a true tropical rainforest, such as exists along the more equatorial parts of Indonesia, such as Kalimantan. The plant community of a tropical rainforest requires abundant rainfall every month of the year. Without a rainforest, communities of animals are absent in Bali and there are no large stands of the valuable hardwoods that are favored by year-round precipitation. But there are no malarial swamps, drainage problems, or dense and impenetrable jungles, and when Bali's forests are cleared, the rock-like laterite of tropical rainforest soil does not develop. Still, because of Bali's dry season, irrigation is a necessity for growing rice.

The necessity for irrigation in the main rice-growing parts of Bali determines the settlement patterns. And it determines the way people think about and organize their work and the structure of their society. Irrigation on steep mountain slopes and in valleys means carefully planned hydraulics and community effort directed toward maintenance of the irrigation systems. The irrigated fields must necessarily be located in a large group where the channels of the water supply are located. This, in turn, implies large open areas of rice, as well as small, compact, villages, where neighbors can work and plan together. This, of course, is precisely the pattern of both settlement and social interaction in Bali.

The alternate seasons have many other effects. The commercial fishing industry of Jimbaran Bay shuts down completely in November, as strong Westerlies sweep onshore, bringing huge waves that make it impossible to launch and control small boats. The salt makers who depend upon solar heat and lots of sunlight to evaporate the water from their salty coastal soils are temporarily out of business, as are the roof tile and brick makers, who must dry their products in the sun before firing. Motorcycles are the standard form of transportation for individuals in Bali, and it is no fun to ride a motorbike in the rain. Even the tourist industry slacks off, as those seeking a suntan go elsewhere.

BALI'S LOCATION AND GEOLOGICAL HISTORY has a great deal to do with its flora and fauna. Briton Alfred Russel Wallace, a naturalist and traveler, visited the Malayan Archipelago (Indonesia) in the middle 19th century. In the course of collecting and cataloging specimens in what is now Indonesia, Wallace noticed that the animals and plants of the

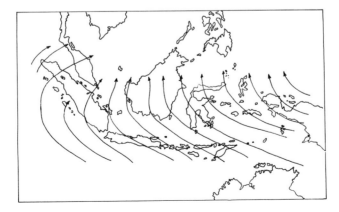

WIND PATTERN DURING THE DRY SEASON

archipelago undergo a very distinct transition as one travels from from one end of the string of islands to the other. Wallace eventually drew a line—to the west, the life forms were influenced by mainland Asia; to the east, the life forms were Australia and New Guinea influenced. The "Wallace Line" as it came to be known, passes between Bali and Lombok.

The Java Sea north and northwest of Bali is comparatively shallow and, starting in the Lombok Strait, the ocean floor, even between adjacent islands, is quite deep. There is a distinct possibility that, during the Quaternary period of glaciation, when a great deal of the oceans' waters were tied up in the form of ice that covered the northern parts of the continents, sea level was a hundred or more meters lower than it is now. This would have made Sumatra, Malaysia, Java and Bali a peninsula of the Asian continent and would have permitted Asian flora and fauna to disperse, uninterrupted by water, all the way to the Wallace Line.

In the course of his collecting, Wallace came up with a theory of evolution that turned on a principle very similar to Darwin's famous theory of "natural selection." In fact, it is possible that Wallace, who submitted his ideas on the matter well before Darwin published his *On the Origin of the Species,* was responsible for Darwin's great insight. Historians of science note that Wallace could not match Darwin's credibility. Wallace was a mere specimen collector (although his writings were always read with interest), and was not well connected in the English scientific establishment. His curiosity was such also that he dabbled in such taboo subjects as phrenology and mysticism. Darwin, on the other hand, was a credible and well-connected member of the gentlemen's network of British science.

ONE OF THE REASONS BALI WAS SO LITTLE AFFECTED by 300 years of Dutch rule is that it has no naturally protected harbors. Coral reefs line much of the island, allowing only small boats to penetrate the gaps where the murky river mouths inhibit the growth of coral. The pounding surf on the reef can be vicious, and many a ship has foundered, since the bottom drops off quickly and anchorage is poor. It was, in fact, the plundering of a wrecked ship on the Sanur coast that culminated in the infamous and bloody Dutch invasion in 1906.

The Dutch headquartered in the Singaraja area, because the northern city provided the only safe anchorage for their ships. Thus, Singaraja and the surrounding area, usually called Buleleng, was until the coming of air transportation the area most heavily influenced by foreigners, since trading ships from all over Southeast Asia came there to exchange goods. The mountain range separating Buleleng from South Bali prevented rapid spread of North Balinese culture to the South. Even today Buleleng harbors the vestiges of a melting pot of traditions that differ in many ways from the customs of South Bali.

Padang Bai on Bali's northeast coast, just south of Karangasem, is today the only harbor in Bali that can accommodate large ships. Most oil tankers and cruise ships anchor here, as does the Bali–Lombok ferry. But the large ships cannot come near the shore, as there is no satisfactory pier. Benoa harbor, south of Sanur on the east side of the isthmus, is a man-made harbor, but many larger ships cannot call here because the channel is too shallow, and the shifting, sandy bottom insures that efforts to dredge it any deeper are either futile or yield only temporary results.

The biggest fishing port in Bali is Pengambengan, on the Southwest coast, near Gilimanuk. There is really no harbor here. But the seas are rel-atively calm because of the proximity of Java, about 25 kilometers (16 mi.) to the west. Thus, Pengambengan is just a beach that is protected from the westerly winds of the rainy season by Java's large land mass. The remainder of Bali's coast is either coral-fringed beach, with a shallow lagoon between the reef and beach, or sheer, wave-cut cliffs, such as those in the Tanah Lot area and along the road from Antosari westward toward Gilimanuk and the Java ferry. Because harbors have always been scarce, and the land has always been fertile, Bali's chief activities have always been directed inward, never toward the sea. The Balinese were never an actively seafaring people. Trade, of course, did exist. But it was the Chinese, Indians, Arabs, Malays, Javanese, and Buginese, and later the Portuguese, English, and Dutch, who sailed the trade routes.

Almost all coastal areas on earth have two tidal cycles within a period of one lunar day, producing two low and two high tides. Tidal data for Bali are only available for Singaraja on the North Coast, and for Benoa, on the South. We can assume that there is not a very large difference between the tides at Sanur and Kuta and those of Benoa. The average range for spring tides at Benoa is a little over 2 meters (6.6 ft.), and for all tides, 1.6 meters (5.2 ft.). By world standards this is not a very great range. The ranges for Singaraja are even less than half of those at Benoa. South Bali tides tend to have a diurnal inequality. That is, there will be a high that is not very high, followed by a low that is not very low, and then a high that is considerably higher, followed by a low that is consider-ably lower than the norm.

Much of Bali is rimmed with coral reefs, with only a narrow, shallow lagoon between the reef and shore. In some areas of Bali the floor of the lagoon is completely exposed at low tide, leaving only puddles, and one can walk all the way out to the edge of the reef. A whole community of plants and animals has adapted itself to this periodic aeration and thrives in the intertidal zone. Fishermen must take account of the tides, for obvi-ous reasons. Tourists who come to Bali to swim in the ocean have to resort to the swimming pool at those hotels where the lagoon is too shal-low to permit swimming at low tide. The low tides of spring tide bring out the night fishermen in many shallow lagoons, and they roam to and fro with their kerosene lanterns to attract the fish.

WHY LUXURIANT BALI and why rocky, barren Nusa Penida, just an hour away by launch? Why is the architecture the way it is? Why is the settlement pattern the way it is? Why has Hinduism remained almost untouched by outside influence in Bali when it suffered virtual extinction in nearby Java? Why are the Balinese not seafarers and traders like the Buginese? Why can Bali produce more rice than it can use when islands like Ambon can produce almost no rice at all? Why the close family ties, the sense of mutual responsibility and obligation? The answer to many of these questions is: because of Bali's unique geology.

Geologists have long emphasized the effect of physical environment upon culture, perhaps the best known of these being the late A.K. Lobeck, professor of ecology at Columbia University, who makes his argument in *Geomorphology*. And the eminent French historian Fernand Braudel tirelessly advocated an approach to history that focuses to a large extent upon climate and geography and de-emphasizes the great men and political events that are the normal subject matter of historical studies.

When compared in importance to geography and climate, Braudel writes, the great men and politics are mere "surface disturbances, crests of foam that the tides of history carry on their backs."

CHAPTER 2

Touring the Bukit

THE ISLAND'S LITTLE KNOWN PENINSULA

EXCEPT FOR THE STRIP OF ROAD that crosses Bukit Badung to the famous Uluwatu temple, few tourists see much of this hilly, dry peninsula that hangs by a mere thread of land from south central Bali. *Bukit* means "hill" in Indonesian, and *badung* is the administrative district—including Denpasar, Sanur, Kuta and much of the tourist-frequented area of Bali. The Dutch called the Bukit the Tafelhoek, literally, "table corner." The tourist's first impression of the Bukit is likely to be one of desolation—rough, arid, barren. The Bukit does not offer stunning, lime-green vistas of terraced rice fields. Coconut trees do not line the roads. Nobody washes a cow or bathes in a roadside stream—there are no streams. The roads are lined with prickly pear cactus and euphorbia and the few open fields are small and rocky.

But the Bukit is by no means a desert. If the rainy season is good, the Bukit is in full glory from December to early April—the fields are green with rice, manioc, beans, sorghum, and a variety of both strange and familiar fruit trees. The recently-introduced trees along the road are loaded with flowers. The cows are fat. The barren, rocky hills contrast sharply with the pleasant little oases that one finds in low-lying drainages, where bananas and coconuts grow. No part of Bali shows a greater change from dry to rainy seasons. And the harsh environment certainly reflects in the attitudes of the people and the way they live.

Most of Bali's population lives on the alluvial slopes of the string of volcanoes that runs across the breadth of the island from east to west. These areas are well watered by mountain streams and the mineral-rich ash from frequent volcanic eruptions has made the land fertile. But the geology of the Bukit is sharply different. It is a high plateau of limestone without a single volcanic rock anywhere. There are no surface streams in the entire Bukit. Geologists call the the limestone topography of the Bukit "karst" from a type region on the Dalmation coast of Yugoslavia. Such landforms can be found many places in the world, including the American southeast. The Bukit has distinctive limestone phenomena like caves, caverns, disappearing streams, and sink holes, and the jagged landscape possesses only a thin veneer of topsoil—and this in just a few places —with no surface streams at all. Nusa Penida, lying off the coast of Bali just south of Klungkung and east of Sanur, shares a similar geography.

Limestone is calcium carbonate, and this carbonate is dissolved by the weak carbonic acid formed from the dissolved carbon dioxide in rainwater. Over the centuries natural cracks in the massive limestone are enlarged by this chemical reaction into larger channels. Ground water is channeled into the cracks and disappears into them instead of forming streams and rivers. The channels in the subterranean limestone enlarge further into caves. Further erosion may cause the caves to collapse, forming deep, open basins. Karst areas like the Bukit have no surface streams because there is very little runoff. The rainfall simply disappears into cracks in the surface rock and is unavailable for use. The level of the water table is far too deep to permit shallow wells. Along the isthmus the water table is a mere three meters down; on the Bukit it might lie ten times deeper.

People who live on the Bukit depend entirely upon cisterns for their water supply. These are usually large concrete tanks fed by a concrete-lined drainage area located right next to the tank. Such a cistern is called *bak yeh*. But some people just dig a pit in the ground or in the limestone bedrock—a *bang-bang*. The scarcity of water obviously has a profound effect upon the living patterns of the Bukit people. In many areas of Bali there are no wells, but there is invariably a stream or spring nearby where villagers can go to get water, and the supply is inexhaustible. In many villages the Government has now built large water tanks for public use, but not on the Bukit.

The rainy season brings very strong westerly winds to all of coastal Bali not shielded by Java. Jimbaran Bay, northwest of the Bukit, is 54 kilometers (33 mi.) east of the tip of Java and is thus open to the Indian Ocean. During the dry season, the easterlies are not nearly as strong as the wet season winds, and the ocean currents are correspondingly weaker. As a result, the two sides of the isthmus leading to the Bukit have developed distinct geographies: the west side is an open, sandy beach; the east side is protected mangrove swamp. The west and south sides of the Bukit are faced by sheer cliffs, testimony to the erosive action of the strong ocean currents from those directions.

Many foreigners refer to the entire peninsula south of the airport as the Bukit. But to the Balinese those low-lying areas of the peninsula on the north and especially on the east side are not part of the Bukit proper.

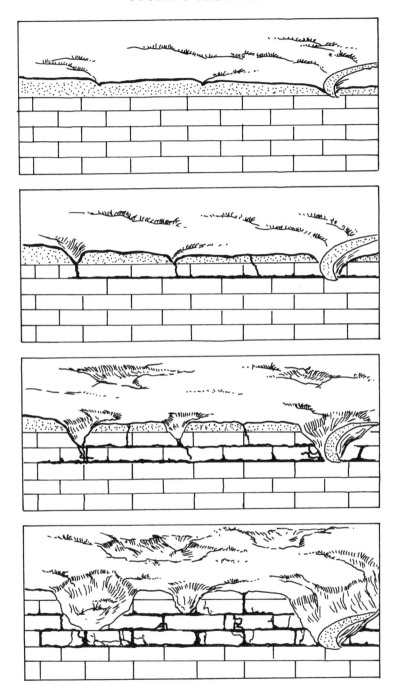

THE FORMATION OF KARST TOPOGRAPHY

Thus, the area traversed by the Nusa Dua by-pass highway is not really the Bukit, nor is the area around Bualu, Nusa Dua, and Tanjung Benoa.

BECAUSE OF THE LACK OF SURFACE WATER, the farming culture of the Bukit differs considerably from that of those areas of Bali where irrigation is possible. The Bukit farmers are utterly dependent upon rainy season rainfall for their major crops. The rice that is grown is a special strain, known locally as *padi gaga,* or, sometimes, *padi gogo.* It is related to, but stronger than, *padi* Bali, a variety that used to be the only one on the island. Both *padi* Bali, now rarely grown, and *padi gaga* have grains that are short and wide, in contrast to the long, thin grains of the dwarf rice that has now almost replaced *padi* Bali. *Padi gaga* is planted in the age-old way, called *matajuk*—a hole is poked in the ground with a stick, and in it a few seed grains of rice from last season's harvest are dropped. In many areas of the Bukit, rice planting cannot begin until after the completion of a special religious ceremony that is held to ask God for rain and to ask the soil for fertility. This usually insures that no crops will be planted before the start of the rainy season, which almost always results in crop failure. Indeed, the rainy season is so irregular that Bukit farmers are planting less rice than they did in the past.

In Kampial in the east central Bukit, rice farming had until recently almost disappeared. The farmers raised *kedele* (soybeans) instead. Soybeans produce a greater yield—eight to 12 *kwintal* per hectare, about three times that of rice (a *kwintal* is 100 kilograms [220 lbs.]). And the value of soybeans, U.S. 30¢ a kilo, is about 10 percent greater than that of rice. So the farmers of Kampial would sell their soybeans in the markets of Denpasar and buy *padi* Bali grown elsewhere. But *padi* Bali, considered to have a much better taste than the new long-grain rice, is now grown in so few places that it is becoming quite expensive. The people of Kampial were so used to the taste of short-grain rice that they decided to raise *padi gaga* once again, and it is catching on in the Bukit.

In addition to soybeans and rice, the principal Bukit crops are manioc, sorghum, corn, peanuts, sweet potatoes, beans of all varieties, mandarin oranges, and a variety of fruits, many of which are not abundant in other areas of Bali. Manioc, often called cassava, is called *ubi kayu* or just *ubi* by the Balinese. The ground root of this crop yields tapioca flour.

Manioc is a common source of starch for people who live in dry areas. It has little taste except when cooked imaginatively. The root must be cooked thoroughly because it contains considerable quantities of toxic cyanides that are only rendered harmless by heat. The roots are long and slender, 30-40 centimeters (12-16 in.) long and 4-5 centimeters (1.5-2 in.) in diameter. Manioc is a perennial, but since the root is eaten the plants last only one season. The plants are grown from cut-up sections of the stems. The large lobed leaves are eaten as a green or fed to cows, along with the stem. Manioc is drought resistant, and the roots keep indefinitely if dried.

Sorghum is well known in the West, but little is grown in Bali except on the Bukit, where it is called *jagung sangket*. *Jagung* means "corn" in Balinese. The sorghum plant is very similar to corn, except that it grows taller. When ripe, the seed-bearing head bends over like a hook—*sangket*. It is also known as *jagung bleleng* and *jagung gembal*. Sorghum is prepared by pounding the seeds with a *buntar*, an iron-tipped rice pounding stick. It is boiled or steamed, and is sometimes mixed with ground coconut, salt, and sugar. And it is also made into a cake, called *jaja jagung sangket*. The stalk of the plant, called *bleleng*, is sweet and is often chewed like sugar cane. Another crop, prepared and eaten much like manioc, is *suweg*, a 25-centimeter (10 in.), pumpkin-shaped, starchy root. Mandarin oranges, called *jok semaga* or *juwuk semaga*, are a relatively new crop on the Bukit. They grow well, but must be hand watered daily. And a recently discovered virus now threatens the island's entire crop.

THE MAP ON THE NEXT PAGE will provide a useful reference for a tour of the Bukit. Let us commence just south of the isthmus, on the main road from Kuta to Pura Luhur Uluwatu. This area is usually called **TEGEH SARI [1]**, but it is really just an extension of Jimbaran, 2 kilometers to the north. Tegeh Sari, as the map shows, can also be reached from the Nusa Dua By-Pass, by taking a paved, but pot-holed road. At Tegeh Sari there are two enormous limestone quarries, one on the west and one on the east side of the road that ascends the Bukit. The western-most one is not visible, but if you drive half a kilometer on up to the top of the first hill, an elevation of about 60 meters (200 ft.) above sea level, you can see the eastern quarry on the left side of the road. There is room here to pull off and drive right to the rim.

The eastern quarry was begun in 1965 as a source of fill for the Ngurah Rai International Airport. The rock was hauled on a special road that ran quite near the sea all the way north to the airport. The road is no longer in use, but vestiges of it can be seen here and there. While the airport was being constructed, the government rented the quarry, but it is now back in private hands. The owners, from Jimbaran, allow people to quarry the rock themselves and bill for the cubic meter of rock removed. The quarry on the west side is owned by the village of Jimbaran, but is rented by the public works department, the Bina Marga, which pays for the rock quarried. "Quarry" in Balinese is *kwari*, but most people call the quarry here *bongkaran batukarang* Bukit. A *bongkaran* is a place where things are in disorder and scattered about. The rock is massive, coarsely bedded, and, where freshly exposed, white to cream in color. It weathers to a black color, probably because of the growth of lichens on the surface. The limestone is not especially strong, but is adequate for fill and even

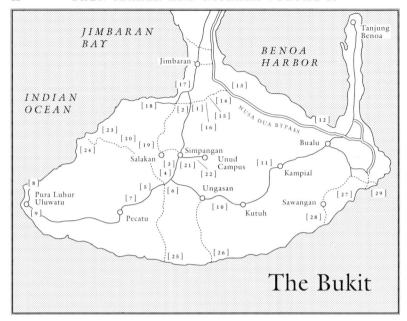

JIMBARAN BAY

BENOA HARBOR

Tanjung Benoa

Jimbaran

INDIAN OCEAN

Bualu

Simpangan
Salakan
Unud Campus
Kampial
Ungasan
Pura Luhur Uluwatu
Pecatu
Kutuh
Sawangan

The Bukit

[1] Tegeh Sari; quarry
[2] Pura Tegeh Sari; cave temple
[3] Tegeh Buu; wells
[4] Bongol village
[5] Gunung Ingas; 202 m.
[6] Bakung village
[7] Pecatu; temple
[8] Suluban; surfing
[9] Pura Uluwatu; temple
[10] Kutuh; temple and dance
[11] TVRI tower
[12] Mumbul village
[13] New road
[14] BULOG
[15] Pole factory
[16] Ice plant
[17] Pura Muaya; temple
[18] Pondok Wisata; youth hostel
[19] Pura Sarin Buana; temple
[20] Goa Peteng; cave
[21] Udayana University
[22] Pura Goa Gong; cave temple
[23] Cengliling village
[24] Pura Balangan; cave temple
[25] Pura Massuka; cliff temple
[26] Pura Batu Pageh; cave temple
[27] Pura Geger; temple
[28] Pura Karang Bhoma; temple
[29] Seaweed farming area

building. On top of the Bukit are other, much smaller, quarries where the outcrops are sawed into rectangular blocks and used for building all over South Bali.

Just past the quarry to your right is a small temple called **PURA TEGEH SARI [2]**, located in a cave a few dozen meters off the road. People from all over the area come to the anniversary celebration of this temple which, according to the Balinese ceremonial cycle, falls on Coma Landep (See "Balinese Calendars" *S&N Vol. I*). The cave is small, and one often has to wait over an hour to pray because of the limited space.

Twisting up the hill, the road tops out at about 100 meters (330 ft.). The north side of the Bukit really consists of a small plateau upon a larger one. There are two steep hills and a relatively flat area in between. We have just reached the top of the first hill. These two "steps" are still noticeable on the east side of the Bukit, but on the south and west sides the elevation changes rather gradually. Glance back toward the north here. You will get a spectacular view of the isthmus, Benoa Harbor, Jimbaran Bay, the airport, and on a clear day, even Mount Agung, some 60 kilometers (37 mi.) northeast.

Just under 2 kilometers from the start of our trip we reach the small village of Simpangan. This section of the road is destined, eventually, to become a superhighway because just to the east of Simpangan is the new 200 hectare (500 acre) campus of Universitas Udayana. The university is now still in South Denpasar. The new campus requires a side trip, so we will look at it on the way back. Just beyond Simpangan the road begins to ascend the second hill, and we begin to see some of the deep wells that furnish the water for the tourist hotels in Nusa Dua. They are in small, square concrete buildings on both sides of the road. This area is generally known as TEGEH BUU [3].

At almost the 4 kilometer (2.5 mi.) mark we reach the top of the second hill and the main intersection in the village of BONGOL [4]. Approaching the intersection, there are four radio towers visible on the west side of the road and an abandoned Omni station at Bongol. Here the main road branches east to Bualu. Due west of Bongol is the highest point of the Bukit, a peak known as GUNUNG INGAS [5], which reaches an elevation of 202 meters (663 ft.). At Bongol we are at about 175 meters (575 ft.) above sea level.

Taking the branch that heads west, we pass through BAKUNG [6], where a road leads northwest to Cengiling and south to Pura Massuka. We will return to these points later in the trip. Heading for Pecatu, the road passes through rocky land where many small outcrops of limestone are being worked as quarries. The fields have dark, rich-looking soil, but the layer is thin. Acacia trees line the road, and their long, fuzzy yellow flowers make a pleasant sight at the end of the dry season. The Badung government recently decided to spruce up the Bukit, and has planted many varieties of trees along the main roads, many of them exotic to Bali. Chosen for their rapid growth and suitability to the Bukit geography, many are legumes and help enrich the thin soil with nitrogen. Quite a few have beautiful flowers, most blooming at the end of the dry season, October or November. Here and there along the road you will notice the posting: *jalur hijau*. This means the area is a green strip, and any building there must be set back a specified distance from the road. This is an effective way to preserve the pleasant character of the roadside.

Fields along the road here are usually bordered and divided by living fences. *Gamal* and *tuwi* trees are usually planted as dividers in the fields because they are legumes and fertilize the soil. *Tuwi* are edible and also provide forage for animals. *Gamal* is easier to grow than *tuwi*, but it is only used for cattle food. *Gamal* will grow readily from a cutting, with no more effort than just sticking a branch in the ground. *Tuwi* must be grown from seed. Field and road borders are frequently made of living cactus and euphorbia. The cactus is what we call prickly pear, and the Balinese call it *belatung gepeng*. *Gepeng* means "flat," and *belatung* refers generally to any thorny plant. Birds, but not people, eat the fruit. Euphorbia here is called *belatung gada*, named after the club-like weapon of Bima, one of the heroes of the *Mahabharata*. Kapok trees, with their almost horizontal branches, also grow here in abundance. In season—October and November—the trees are loaded with pods full of seeds, each having a tuft of long white hair—the source of the kapok of industry, widely used in Bali for pillow and mattress stuffing.

Just before entering the village of **PECATU** [7], 7.4 kilometers (4.6 mi.) from our start, stands a tall microwave relay station and tower to the north. Then, at exactly 8 kilometers (5 mi.), we turn due south and enter the small village of Pecatu, elevation 175 meters (574 ft.), through a typical *candi bentar*, or split gate. Pecatu is important to the people of Jimbaran, the largest village in the area, because of the Pura Pererepan temple, which has a religious connection both with Pura Ulunsiwi in Jimbaran and the very important Pura Luhur Uluwatu. When the Jimbaran *barong* dance group makes its seasonal walk to Pura Luhur Uluwatu, it must stop at Pura Pererepan. And many of the offerings for the anniversary (*odalan*) at Pura Uluwatu are prepared at the Pecatu temple. The temple is on the right side of the road, about in the middle of the village, just south of the Pura Desa. Its *odalan* is the same day as that of Pura Luhur Uluwatu, Anggarkasih Medangsiya, week number 14 of the Pawukon calendar.

The political district of Pecatu extends from just south of Pura Balangan on the coast to Pura Massuka, and includes the western third of the Bukit. The district, or *desa,* is divided into three smaller districts, west, middle, and east, each with a population of approximately just under 2,000 people. The *desa* has a total population of 5,238 and an area of 2,674 hectares (6,607 acres). The village of Pecatu itself has a population of about 800. Pecatu is the site of two agricultural ceremonies, the *mami-ut,* a planting ceremony, in December, and the *ngusaba,* a harvest ceremony, in November.

The road turns abruptly to the west outside of Pecatu, and we continue over rolling countryside, with occasional quarries on both sides of the road. The Pecatu area has many mandarin orange orchards. At 12.6 kilometers (7.8 mi.) from the start, the sea appears as the road begins to

descend. At 13.3 kilometers (8.2 mi.) we pass a trail to the right that leads
to the surfing area at SULUBAN [8], and at 13.5 kilometers (8.4 mi.) we
enter the visitors parking lot of PURA LUHUR ULUWATU [9], the jewel
of the Bukit. The paved road continues to the temple steps, but those not
visiting the temple for religious purposes have to walk there. It takes only
a few minutes. The parking lot is full of the usual souvenir stalls and cold
drink stands. It is normally a busy place, because Pura Uluwatu is a very
sacred temple.

Pura Uluwatu is one of the Sad Kahyangan, the six temples of the
world—the most important temples in Bali. (See "Pura Uluwatu," S&N
Vol. I). It is dedicated to Rudra, the "howler," god as dissolver of life.
This temple is the one at which Pedanda Sakti Wawu Rauh, who according to legend came to Bali from Java on a keluwih tree leaf in A.D. 1546,
achieved Hindu liberation, moksa. Wawu Rauh, again according to legend, built the many padmasana shrines in temples across the island
including the very elaborate one at Pura Uluwatu. Until the end of the
last century, Uluwatu was the chief sanctuary of the kingdom of Mengwi.
Now it belongs to the people of Bali, and is administered chiefly by the
estate of the former royal family of Denpasar.

We must backtrack now on our journey to the junction at Bongol, this
time heading down the southeast fork. About two kilometers from the
junction is Ungasan, the administrative headquarters for the Ungasan
desa, which covers the south-central area of the Bukit. The desa has a population of 8,158 and an area of 2,384 hectares (5,891 acres), divided
administratively into four sections. Ungasan has a ceremony called mami-
ut ngadasa held in the village Pura Desa, before which no farmer can
plant rice. It is held either on Purnama (full moon) or Tilem (new moon)
in December. The leaders of the village wait for rain. Even if the rainy season apparently begins early they must wait until December. If the rain in
December comes late, the ceremony is held on Purnama; if early on
Tilem. There is also a ngusaba ceremony held in August in the Pura Desa,
after all the crops have been harvested. As in other areas, fewer people
plant rice now because there is less work and more income when one raises soybeans and the other common Bukit crops.

Just past Ungasan, in a little valley just to the right of the road, is the
huge satellite dish antenna of the Indonesian communication system.
About 1.5 kilometers further is the village of KUTUH [10], within the
jurisdiction of Ungasan. Both Ungasan and Kutuh are about 125 meters
(410 ft.) above sea level. Kutuh has a population of approximately 1,200.
There is a ngusaba ceremony held in the Pura Dalem on Purnama Kapat
of the Hindu Saka calendar, and the important rice-planting ceremony is
the odalan of Pura Melang, held on Purnama Kelima, after which the rice
may be planted. The odalan of the Pura Pengubengan in Kutuh, held on
Tumpek Wayang, offers a rare performance of sanghyang jaran. The name

of the dance refers to the symbolic horse (*jaran*) with which a solo male performer dances. He goes into trance and dances on the embers of glowing coconut husks that are put on the ground for that purpose. A similar dance, *sanghyang gadang*, is held at the Pura Puseh in Kutuh on its *odalan*, Purnama Kapat. The other important temple in Kutuh is Pura Pererepan Gunung Tedung, which has its *odalan* on the same day as does Pura Luhur Uluwatu.

Continuing eastward from Kutuh, the road turns toward the northeast. About two kilometers from Kutuh, off the road to the left, is the tall transmission tower of TELEVISI RADIO INDONESIA [11], or TVRI. One now begins the gradual descent, over three or four kilometers, from the upper hill of the Bukit to the lower terrace which begins at Kampial. There is a good view of Nusa Penida and the Benoa Harbor area from this point. Kampial has two *banjars,* village organizations, and a total population of 847. The Pura Desa here has a *ngusaba* on Purnama Ketiga, but it is unrelated to rice planting. The *odalan* of the Pura Desa is on Purnama Kelima. There is a ceremony called *pemendakan* given by the whole village on Tilem Kelima or Kajeng Keliwon in the middle of December. After the *pemendakan* of the whole village, each family has its own private ceremony, and then and only then can the rice be planted. *Pemendakan* is a welcoming ceremony that tells Dewi Sri, the rice goddess, that the celebrants hope to have a good crop. Generally the date is set for Tilem, but if there is a problem with sickness they use Kajeng Keliwon. After the harvest they have a *hari sukuran*, which is a ceremony of thanks to Dewi Sri.

On the right of the road, just past Kampial, is the first well that was drilled for the Nusa Dua complex. Continuing for about three kilometers, the road descends a short hill and takes us to the village of Bualu. The water treatment plant for the Nusa Dua complex is visible on the left. Bualu is a sprawling village, vastly changed since the Nusa Dua development. At the main intersection a road leads east to the hotel area. The road to the north leads 5 kilometers (3 mi.) to the village of Tanjung Benoa at the tip of the peninsula. A newly paved road leads south from the center of Bualu toward the village of Sawangan. The section of the Bukit on the east side is called Kelurahan Benoa, but the office is in Bualu, not in Tanjung Benoa. Bualu is divided into seven *banjars,* and has a population of about 5,500. The total population of the *kelurahan* is 12,809. The district covers 3,106 hectares (7,675 acres). Since Bualu, Nusa Dua, and Tanjung Benoa are not really part of the Bukit, they will not be described here.

Let us continue back to our starting point by turning left at the main intersection near Bualu, and take the By-Pass highway west towards the airport. Leaving the area of Benoa, the settlement of MUMBUL [12] is the first village. The coast to the north is the *suwung*, or mud flat, and the coastline is quite indefinite. The unattractive swamp has been beautified to some extent by planting mangrove trees. The highway passes over bridges when swampy land is encountered and must bend quite far westward to avoid the huge area of salt marsh southeast of Jimbaran. About 4.5 kilometers (2.8 mi.)from Mumbul is the large curve where the highway bends toward the north. At THE APEX OF THE CURVE [13] is a paved but rough road that leads back to our starting point. From here a new road is being built to the Unud campus on the hill. It leads due south, climbs the first terrace of the Bukit, then continues westward above the quarry, meeting the Jimbaran–Simpangan road south of the campus access road.

The short road back to our starting point passes first a sprawling complex of buildings on the left. The sign in front reads: "Badan Urusan Logistik, Komplex Pergudangan Beras Bali Di Jimbaran." The Badan Urusan Logistik, or BULOG, is the government agency of logistic affairs. The main office is in Jakarta and it is not really under any ministry. The job of BULOG is to collect and distribute—food mostly, particularly rice in its milled form, *baas*. The branch offices of BULOG, such as the one in the Niti Mandala government complex of Denpasar, are called DOLOG, meaning Depot Logistik. *Depot* refers to a branch establishment. The rice storage warehouses run by the DOLOG are popularly called DOLOG themselves. Rice, and such other products as soybeans and, in some areas, fish, are purchased from the farmers or fishermen by an organization in each populated area called KUD—Kooperasi Unit Desa. KUD is not a government agency, but it is supervised by the government. Farmers are not required to sell to KUD, and only do so if the price is right in their opinion. There is usually a KUD office or KUD representatives where crops are being harvested and fish brought in to buy whatever is offered.

The DOLOG warehouses are scattered over South Bali. There is one at Sempidi, Batubulan, Kediri, and this one at Jimbaran. The warehouse distributes only to agencies, not individuals. Rice is usually collected every six months, and no new rice is accepted until the old rice is distributed, preventing the handling of old and undesirable rice. Many agencies get rice from the warehouses. The complex in Jimbaran, built in 1984, consists of eight warehouses, with a total capacity of 12,800 tons.

The next large complex on the left is marked with a sign: "P.T. Wijayakarta Workshop Tiang Beton Jimbaran." This FACTORY [15] makes the concrete power poles that are appearing all over Bali, replacing the old steel and wooden poles that rust and rot so easily. The company that runs the plant is private, but the start-up was financed by the government. There are five similar plants in Java, owned by the same company, but none elsewhere. Production at the Jimbaran facility is 12,000 poles per year. The poles are reinforced with steel rod and are hollow, with 12-centimeter (5 in.) thick walls. Each of the poles, 8-13 meters (26-43 ft.)

long, weighs 6-8 tons. The plant was constructed in September of 1984.

The last stop on our circular tour is the small ICE PLANT [16], located just west of the concrete power pole factory. The plant produces 25-kilo (55 lb.) blocks of ice which are sold chiefly to fishermen in the Jimbaran–Kedonganan area. Every day the plant produces four tons of ice. Ammonia-cooled saltwater is used to freeze the water which comes from a well on the site. The factory is privately owned by a group, and sells its ice for Rp 500 per block. There are facilities for storing about 100 blocks, but this is just a shed, not a refrigerated storage area. A few hundred meters further and we are back at our starting point, on the road leading to Jimbaran.

SO FAR WE HAVE DESCRIBED SOME SIGHTS that are relatively close to the main roads. But the Bukit offers some other temples, caves, villages, and sights that are worth a visit if you don't mind straying from the beaten path. PURA MUAYA [17] in Jimbaran, is an important temple to farmers on the Bukit. An unprepossessing structure, right on the beach, it is considered the meeting place of mountains, sea, and fields. Pura Muaya can be reached by a smooth road that branches west off the main road to Jimbaran, just north of the junction where we started. Following the road past Pura Muaya, we ascend the hill that overlooks Jimbaran Bay from the south Here is a spectacular view of the bay, the airport, and much of South Bali. The paved road passes through a new housing development, P.T. Bukit Permai, and terminates at the PONDOK WISATA PEMUDA [18]. The Pondok, run by the ministry of youth and sports, Menteri Pemuda dan Olah Raga, is a youth hostel for Balinese and other Indonesians and is the center for the youth group, Pemuda, of Bali. The center boasts 19 buildings, including a kitchen, meeting room, recreation room, and dormitories, and can accommodate 60 people. Youth groups come here for recreation and study.

If instead of turning to the right through the new housing development you keep on going on foot straight up the hill, you will reach PURA SARIN BUANA [19], about an hour's walk from the beach. This temple is important to the people of Jimbaran and the surrounding Bukit area. The *odalan* is on Coma Ribek of the Pawukon cycle. The Jimbaran *barong* group sometimes walks to this temple. A short distance to the east is a huge sink hole, called GOA PETENG [20], or "Dark Cave." Sink holes are typical of karst areas, and this is a very large one. It is probably not a good idea to descend without a flashlight and care, because the sinkhole is home to many snakes. The bottom is jammed with rubble and boulders. There is undoubtedly a cave beyond the narrow, funnel-shaped bottom of the sink hole, but to my knowledge it has not been explored.

If you drive from the junction where we started, head up the hill once again to Simpangan and turn east along the newly paved road, you will

come, in about 1.5 kilometers, to the new site of the campus of
Universitas Udayana (21). The university, presently located on two
separate campuses in South Denpasar, bought the land in 1981 and has
begun a very ambitious development project. The campus area spans
some 2 kilometers east–west, and 1 kilometer north–south, for a total of
200 hectares (500 acres). The proposed student population is 18,000,
compared with the present enrollment of about 12,000. Only 10-15 percent of the student body will be housed on campus, the remainder finding
housing on the periphery provided by private developers and land owners.
The cost of the development is projected at Rp 100 billion. At the present
writing, the facility is only 5 percent complete and being budgeted at only
Rp 1 billion a year. The university is seeking bank loans to accelerate
development. The water supply will be from wells and a pipeline from
Denpasar. There is a model of the future campus in the foyer of the university main campus. It shows a lake, many trees, and a beautifully land-
scaped, green expanse of campus. The area, at least at the moment, is
nothing but rocks. The lake will be created by building two dams in the
dry stream bed that runs through the campus.

Continuing a bit east of the Unud campus, on a dirt trail, keep the
ridge of hills to your right, or south, in sight. At the bottom of the
hill—which has a tall tree on it—stop and climb the hill toward the tree.
There you will find a unique temple, **Pura Goa Gong [22]**. There is a
large cave in the north face of the top of the hill, inside of which hangs a
large stalactite. It gives the temple its name because, when struck with the
palm of the hand, the stalactite emits a booming, gong-like sound. The
entrance to the cave is blocked by a locked gate, so entrance can only be
gained at *odalan* time, which is Coma Ribek. The temple priest,
pemangku, hits the stalactite three times with his hand during the ceremony—the only time that it is ever heard. In the last five years considerable
concrete work has been done to the outer part of the cave, beyond the
gate, so that worshipers have a place to rest and sleep if necessary. A few
hundred meters west of Pura Gua Gong is yet another cave-temple, Pura
Kayu Sugih. According to legend, a snake lives here, under the soil, where
there is a sort of lump. But nobody has ever seen it. The *odalan* is the
same day as that of Pura Goa Gong, Coma Ribek. A nice view of the isthmus is available from the area in front of the cave. And many *kem* bushes
grow there, producing a locally favored red berry. The area here is called
Biingin, and the area to the east is called Batu Ngongkong, meaning
"stone dog's bark." There are a lot of sharp stones all around, looking,
apparently, like the teeth of a barking dog.

A motorcycle, *bemo,* or four-wheel-drive vehicle can make the interesting trip to the northwest coast of the Bukit. Turn right just 100 meters
past the junction at the top of the Bukit. The road is rough, rocky, and
steep, but you will be rewarded at the end. You pass the abandoned Omni

station to your right and then begin a gradual descent through a kind of rocky dry stream bed. At 2.2 kilometers (1.4 mi.) from the main road you'll reach a junction, at which you turn left. The "road" is relatively flat here. About one-half kilometer further a road branches off to the right, but you keep straight. Just 100 meters from this branch is the road to Pura Balangan, but keep going straight. A few hundred meters and you reach the quiet little settlement of CENGILING [23], about 3 kilometers from the original turnoff. About 800 people live in Cengiling. It is a *banjar* of Jimbaran, although most of the people are from Ungasan.

Cengiling is a shady, cool oasis in the midst of a barren land. There are coconut trees and bananas, and fertile, bottom-land fields that, in the rainy season, are as green and lush as any in Bali. Ninety-five percent of the villagers are farmers. They plant less rice than before, but they raise lots of beans, corn, and manioc. The only temple there is that of the *banjar*. The villagers generally observe the planting restrictions imposed by Pura Muaya in Jimbaran, and all attend the *odalan* at Pura Balangan. There are three private diesel generators for electricity. Lots of mandarin oranges are raised here and they normally ripen in March. The town boasts a small weaving industry and the women use the traditional *cagcag* back looms. The warp threads are kept taut by a kind of harness worn by the weaver such that when she leans backwards the structure tightens the threads. Most weavers make *sabuk*, a long belt of a solid color. There are three elementary schools in the Cengiling area. There are about 10 fishermen in the village, but the only access to the water is at Balangan to the west and at Batu Layah, just west of the Pondok Wisata Pemuda, where there are beaches. The rest of the coast is rocky.

Backtracking to the side road that took off to the west just before we entered Cengiling, we can drive a short distance farther to the trail to PURA BALANGAN [24], another cave temple, right on a lovely, quiet, sandy beach. The settlement of Balangan consists of just a few scattered houses. Not even a motorcycle can make it along the trail from the settlement to the cave, but it is not a long walk, maybe 15 minutes. The temple is quite important to the villagers of Cengiling and Jimbaran, and many even come by boat, although the waves may be quite rough and the landing dangerous. The *odalan* of the temple is held on Anggarkasih Medangsiya, the same as that of Pura Uluwatu. Many Jimbaran people spend the night here. A kitchen is set up, and there is plenty of room to stretch out. A small temple called Pura Konco is located in the rocks at the north end of the beach. It is said to be an old Chinese temple. Pura Balangan is in a lovely, quiet environment, and, although not a spectacular temple in any sense of the word, is interesting and colorful at *odalan* time. The beach itself is worth the visit.

A journey retracing our path to Pura Luhur Uluwatu will allow a side trip to the famous surfing area of Bali. The access road takes off from the main, paved road to Pura Uluwatu just a few hundred meters before one arrives at the temple parking lot at the bottom of the hill. There is a sign with an arrow pointing to the right "Bersilancar Pantai Suluban; Suluban Surfing Beach, 2 km." There will usually be a crowd of Balinese there, each eager to carry your surfboard the 2 kilometers to the end of the trail. It is a rough, rocky, narrow trail, only for foot or motorcycle. And only a very experienced motorcycle rider should try it carrying a surfboard. At the end there is a covered parking area for motorcycles, and from there a five minute walk down a long flight of concrete steps leads to the bottom of a dry, rocky wash. The entry point for surfers is down the wash where there is a small beach in a sort of cave.

The trail continues, slanting up the far side of the wash a few dozen meters to the edge of the cliff where one has a spectacular view of the huge breakers that roll in from the Indian Ocean. There are three *warungs* there to provide food and drink, but there is no water supply. There are no overnight facilities, and no one except the *warung* owners spends the night there. The nearest facilities of any sort are at Jimbaran or Kuta. Not even Pecatu has a homestay or losmen. I am not a surfer, but I am told that this spot offers world-class surfing. The best time for surfing at "Ulu," as the younger surfing set calls this place, is during the dry season, from March through September. During the wet season, the strong winds are onshore and make surfing very difficult or impossible. High tide during the surfing season is the best, and a steady stream of surfers, clad dangerously in nothing more than bathing suits, can be found streaming down the roads that converge upon the Bukit, surfboards slung over the shoulder, heading for Suluban. There are several newly developed surfing areas along the coast northeast of Suluban.

Again returning to the main road, we can drive straight south from a point just a bit west of where we detoured to Cengiling all the way to the south coast of the Bukit. The road is well marked with a sign directing us to Wana Giri, Sari Karya, Mendaet, and Pura Massuka. The sign is just one-half kilometer from the junction along the road to Pecatu. The main road turns west, and we proceed straight south. There are farmers' groups, called *kelompok tani*, in the area that help maintain the road. Pura Massuka, or, as it is often spelled, Masuka, has been recently renovated, and the governor of Bali visited the area when the temple was dedicated in August, 1985. The area has many weathered limestone boulders, which are harder than the quarried limestone and in demand for foundations. Drivers bring their sturdy trucks here to get the stone.

This is a very pleasant drive, although the road would be very hard on a regular automobile. We pass through relatively flat land as we descend gradually to the coast. There are large, fertile fields, and during the rainy season the area is a mass of green rice, bean crops, fruit trees, and vital living fences. There are many cows, occasional coconut trees, and even bananas. The area looks much more inviting than the part one sees from along the main paved road. The road dead ends, 5 kilometers (3 mi.) from the turnoff, at PURA MASSUKA [25], perched on a cliff overlooking the Indian Ocean. It is not a large temple, perhaps 12 meters (40 ft.) square, but the shrines in it are new, and the setting is superb.

Returning to the main road again, we can take an almost identical trip south from Ungasan to the south coast, just about 2 kilometers from where we were at Pura Massuka. The drive is almost identical, except here there are a number of large limestone block quarries, similar to, but larger than, those found in the Pecatu area. Again we end up on a cliff overlooking the Indian Ocean. There is a tall tower on the cliff here with a navigation and warning light on top for boats. A trail down over the edge of the cliff takes us to yet another of the many cave temples of the Bukit, PURA BATU PAGEH [26]. Again there are the usual stalactites, stalagmites, and dripping roof. The cave hangs on a cliff, with a dizzying descent straight to the narrow beach and sea below.

Another interesting area, complete with temples, can be reached from Bualu. A new paved road extends south from Bualu a few kilometers toward the beach. Unfortunately, this road soon ends and one encounters a series of very rocky hills while driving the remaining 2 kilometers to the small settlement of Sawangan, at the end of the road. There is one *banjar* here, and the total population is 1,227. At the main crossroads of the village are several huge *bunut* trees, close relations of the banyan, but without aerial roots. Nobody in the area has planted rice since 1965. The usual Bukit crops are in abundance: corn, sorghum, soybeans, manioc, peanuts, beans of all sorts, and sweet potatoes. There is no *ngusaba* ceremony for planting. The important temple, PURA GEGER [27], is nearby, on a cliff overlooking the sea, east of the village. There is a *ngusaba* held there, which used to signal the beginning of rice planting.

A 1.5 kilometer trail leads from Sawangan south, through fertile fields, to the cliff overlooking the sea, at the end of which is the important temple PURA KARANG BOMA [28]. This is a small temple perched on a cliff overlooking the sea. The nearby area is quite rocky, since fields end well before the edge of the cliff. The *odalan* of the temple is on Tumpek Landep, Saniscara Landep. Two *barongs*, a *barong ket* and a *barong landung,* come to the temple for the *odalan* and spend the night—one from Sesetan in South Denpasar, one from Bualu. There is a *gong,* and a large crowd of people always gathers to spend the night in prayer and to watch the *barong* performances. Nearby food stalls add to the color and noise.

Returning to the end of the paved road from Bualu, one can drive farther south on a sandy road to the beach, about 2 kilometers south of the Nusa Dua development. Here is one of Bali's most unusual industries, commercial SEAWEED FARMING [29]. (See CHAPTER 31.) Pura Geger can be seen on a rocky promontory from the seaweed farming area.

CHAPTER 3

Visiting Nusa Penida

A ROCKY ISLAND AND ITS STRANGE TEMPLE

TO THE MAINLAND BALINESE, Nusa Penida is virtually unknown except in legend. It is a place that is called *angker,* a term that is difficult to translate, but comes closest to "haunted." It is a fearful place, a source of disease, bad luck, and evil spirits—particularly the temple of the destructive and evil Ratu Gede Macaling, Pura Dalem Penataran Peed on the northwest corner of the main island. Another mark against the 200-square- kilometer (77 sq. mi.) island is that it served, until the early part of this century, as a penal colony for the rajadom of Klungkung.

Not only is Nusa Penida unloved by the Balinese, it is also generally ignored by tourists—or was, until recently when a few small hotels were built to accommodate surfers and divers who are attracted to the excellent reefs on nearby Nusa Lembongan. But 45,000 people live on Nusa Penida, suffering the dry karst geography and the power of Macaling, and the island makes an interesting stop on a tour of Bali.

Nusa Penida is a limestone plateau, just like the Bukit, without a trace of volcanic rock. The differences in geology between the island and the Bukit are in degree, with Nusa Penida possessing a thicker and rougher limestone base. The highest point on Nusa Penida is Bukit Mundi, which reaches 529 meters (1,736 ft.). In fact, the sheer white cliffs of the island, visible from Sanur, are themselves 200 meters (650 ft.) high in places. Because of its limestone platform, Nusa Penida has the same topography as the Bukit and the same problems with its water supply. Except for a few wells drilled along the low coastal regions, all local water is from cisterns, called *cubang,* made from concrete. There is generally a large, concrete-lined catchment area which leads to an underground storage tank.

The two islands off the northwest coast of the big island are Nusa

Lembongan and Nusa Ceningan. "Ceningan" comes from the Balinese *cenik,* or "small." Nusa Lembongan, the outer island, is for the most part a sand flat, although on the southeast side it rises to 44 meters (144 ft.). Ceningan has a distinct hump, some 100 meters (330 ft.) high, in the center. Lembongan is about 4 kilometers (2.5 mi.) along its long axis, and 2.5 kilometers (1.5 mi.) across its width. Ceningan is less than half as wide and considerably shorter. The two small islands are divided by a shallow channel that is only a hundred meters or so wide at its narrowest. Ceningan, the near island, lies only about a kilometer off the coast of Nusa Penida, but the channel separating the two is surprisingly deep, 122 meters (400 ft.) at its deepest spot.

Nusa Penida's shoreline is quite like that of the Bukit. The shores exposed to the full brunt of Indian Ocean waves, on the southwest and southeast sides, terminate abruptly in sheer cliffs, the highest more than 200 meters (650 ft.) above the surf. The shores facing Bali, on the northwest, north, and northeast, offer sandy beaches, protected by coral reefs everywhere except in the center of the north shore. But unlike the Bukit, the elevation of Nusa Penida rises rapidly from the shoreline. The island is separated from the Klungkung coast of Bali by the Badung Strait, which features swift currents, large waves, and a depth in places of more than 100 meters (330 ft.). Towards Sanur the water is only half as deep and on the Lombok side of the island, just four kilometers offshore, the water reaches 200 meters (650 ft.).

The crops and farming techniques on the island are almost the same as those found on the Bukit, although because Nusa Penida receives even less rain—and this very irregularly—no rice whatever is grown. There is plenty of rice available on the island, but it is all brought from the mainland. Beans of all sorts are cultivated, especially soybeans, peanuts, and the favorite snack *kacang hijau*—small green beans that are made into a kind of soup. Manioc (cassava) is the staple crop. Corn and sweet potatoes grow well. The government encouraged farmers to plant lots of sorghum, *jagung bleleng,* a few years ago and export it to the mainland. But there was little demand, and production has lately fallen off.

The fishing industry is confined to the north and northeast coasts, which are one long beach. Fishing is generally a small-scale, family-run operation. At last count there were 1,575 families engaged in fishing. The rest of the population is made up of farming families. Most of the fishing takes place in the Lombok Strait using long lines with hooks and lures. Almost all of the foodstuffs grown on Nusa Penida are consumed locally. A few mangos are exported to Bali, as are some fish, particularly *lemuru,* or sardines, and a small amount of fruit, usually in the form of the seldom-seen *sawo Bali,* a large, red, grape-like fruit that grows only on the island, in the Bukit, and in extreme West Bali.

The largest and most interesting export industry on Nusa Penida is the commercial growing of seaweed, which takes place all along the north-west coast of Nusa Lembongan, in the channel between the two small islands, and all along the north and northeast coats of Nusa Penida. Almost 900 families, some 2,700 people, farm seaweed on Nusa Penida. The beach-dried product is sent by small boat to the mainland and from there exported to either Japan or Denmark for processing into agar or carrageenan. (See CHAPTER 31.)

Politically, the 45,000 Nusa Penidans are members of the *kabupaten,* or district, of Klungkung. Nusa Penida all by itself consists of one *kecamatan,* with headquarters in the island's largest city, Sampalan. Sampalan is on the northeast coast. There are 13 municipalities, *desa dinas,* on Nusa Penida, each with an elected village head, *kepala desa.* There are 44 smaller religious/customary units, *desa adat.* Sampalan is really a cluster of several villages with a "capital," *ibukota desa,* called Batununggul, but they are all considered one village.

Radio telephone service was established between Klungkung and Sampalan in 1985, but other than boat traffic, this is the only means of communication with the mainland. The Sampalan area has electricity from a diesel generator stationed nearby. Color TV reception can be obtained from Klungkung, but there is no tower on the island. The island has three health clinics, a private high school and primary school, and two government run primary schools. A mosque serves about 50 Muslim families at Toyapakeh. There are a few wells scattered around, but cisterns are the standard water supply. There is a fair paved road from Toyapakeh to Sampalan, which continues southeast along the coast to Karangsari and south to to Klumpu. All the other roads are rocky and rough and suitable only for trucks, motorcycles or four-wheel-drive cars.

PERHAPS THE MOST DIFFICULT PART of a trip to Nusa Penida is getting there. The principal port for mainland boats, Toyapakeh (see map page 37), is 25 kilometers (16 mi.) from Sanur and 14 kilometers (9 mi.) from Kusamba. Most boats to Nusa Penida depart from Kusamba, a fishing village about 6 kilometers (3.7 mi.) from Klungkung that is populated mostly by Muslims. There are two "ports" in Kusamba. The older one, Kusamba Kampung, is reached by turning right at a junction near the Kusamba market and driving a few hundred meters to the beach, where you will find boats loading up. The boats wait their turn to fill up, and none leaves before it is full, so the wait may be about an hour or more. It is usually easier to find a boat to Nusa Penida in the afternoon than early in the morning. The trip from Kusamba to to Nusa Lembongan or to Toyapakeh—the only choices—will cost about Rp 1,500. Once on the island, *Bemos* ply the 9-kilometer (6 mi.) route between Toyapakeh and Sampalan, and their fare is Rp 1,000.

You can charter a small motorboat from Kusamba to Lembongan or

Toyapakeh for Rp 30,000, or to the port of Sampalan, called Sampalan Mentigi, for Rp 40,000, round trip. But the boat has to return no later than 3 P.M. because big waves on the Kusamba beach make landing in late afternoon dangerous. You can leave at 1 P.M. and spend the night at Lembongan, returning the next morning at 9 or 10 A.M. The boat cannot leave Nusa Penida any later than about 2 P.M. If you take the public boats you will find that it is easier to get a returning boat from Toyapakeh than from Nusa Lembongan. This is because the Nusa Penidans who want to come to the mainland to shop or trade leave there in the morning and go home late in the afternoon. And so there are only a few boats that go to Toyapakeh from Kusamba in the morning, because they are all in Toyapakeh, waiting to take the large numbers of people to the mainland.

The other point of embarkation is a new "harbor," actually just a stretch of beach at Kusamba Banjar Bias. From the junction at Kusamba, proceed one kilometer east along the main road to Amlapura. Here there is a small sign on the side of the road marked "Dermaga Penyebrangan Kusamba 200 m." that points to the right. Turn here and drive about 300 meters to the beach, along a road marked "Jalan Pasir Putih" (which, by the way, is a misnomer because the beach is black, not *putih*, white). Here boats depart for Sampalan. A regular one-way ticket is Rp 1,275. One boat carries 25 people, and it has to fill up before it leaves. A typical wait can be two hours. Chartering one of these big boats will cost Rp 30,000 one way or Rp 60,000 round trip. The boats begin leaving at 6 or 7 A.M. The trip takes 2 hours one way, maybe 3 if the weather is bad. The local boatmen say their large boats are safer than the smaller *prahus* that depart from Kusamba Kampung.

There is irregular and uncertain boat service from Sanur beach to Nusa Lembongan. To find a *prahu* that will take you to Lembongan, take the paved road that runs past the main entrance to the Hotel Bali Beach and leads to the beach. The *prahus* are usually parked a few dozen meters down the black sand beach. You must arrive in the morning, because the Badung Strait grows rough by the mid-afternoon. Prices are negotiable.

There is only one homestay on Nusa Penida, Bungalow Pemda at Sampalan. It has five bungalows, each with two rooms and bathroom, which rent for Rp 2,000 a night single, or Rp 3,000 twin. No meals are included, but there are plenty of *warungs* in Sampalan. No Western food is available. There are *bemos* to most of the villages, but service is slow and irregular. You can bring your rented motorbike from the mainland on a boat and use it. Or you can get someone on Nusa Penida to drive you around, an arrangement called *ojekan*. The accommodations at Bungalow Pemda are occasionally used by visiting government people, so it is not certain that there will be room for foreign visitors. Nusa Penida proper is not often visited by tourists.

Nusa Lembongan is the most popular spot because its sandy beach and

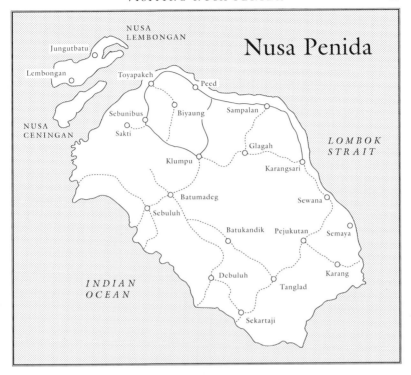

coral reef afford excellent snorkeling and scuba diving, and its coast has wonderful breakers for surfing. It is also a nice place just to sunbathe. There are about 30 rooms available on Lembongan, mostly at the village of Jungutbatu. The west coast of Nusa Lembongan forms a right angle, and Jungutbatu is right at the apex. The tourist accommodations are where the beach faces north. There is even a small bungalow-style hotel that serves Western food, or at least Western style food. The cost of accommodations vary from about Rp 1,000 per night to more than Rp 10,000 at the hotel, if meals are included. The accommodations are right on the beach, so there is no transportation problem. There are roads on Lembongan, but few motorcycles. One can walk from Jungutbatu to the other village, Lembongan, in a few minutes. In fact, the two run together. There are no villages on Ceningan, which can only be reached by boat from Nusa Lembongan. The people in Lembongan raise seaweed, fish, and make salt from seawater. Firewood is scarce, so coconut shells are used for fuel. There is a small temple on Lembongan, Pura Bakung, in addition to the three village temples, Pura Puseh, Pura Desa, and Pura Dalem.

THE INTERIOR OF NUSA PENIDA differs vastly from the low, sandy coast, where fishing and seaweed raising provide a fair income to most of the people. Inland, life is more difficult. The small Muslim village of

Toyapakeh—the name means "saltwater"—is the normal landing place for boats from Banjar Bias, Kusamba. There is a *warung* on the beach, and *bemos* are usually waiting to take passengers to the Sampalan area.The paved road from Toyapakeh to Sampalan, about 9 kilometers (6 mi.), runs along the beach past land that is noticeably more barren than the main island of Bali. There are, however, coconut trees and typical beach vegetation. Away from the beach, the topography is quite cut up and irregular. Sampalan is a medium-sized village, confined by hills to a narrow strip along the beach. The Bungalow Pemda is at the east end of town, and the boats from Banjar Bias land at Sampalan Mentigi, the port, only about 200 meters from this hotel. There is fair snorkeling along the coast here, but the best by far is along the northwest corner of Nusa Penida and off Nusa Lembongan, on each side of the channel separating the small islands from Nusa Penida. The water is calm, clear, and warm here, with superb visibility for diving.

Going south from Toyapakeh the road ascends a hill, and three kilometers from the landing is the village of Sebunibus. Just south of town a side road leads to Sakti, about 1.5 kilometers to the west, and at a junction here the main road turns east and crosses some rough country to Klumpu, about 5 kilometers (3 mi.) from the junction. Klumpu has an elevation of 225 meters (738 ft.) and the scenery here is stark, with small, rocky, terraced fields. All of the fields—most containing manioc—have rock walls. There are cisterns everywhere. About one-half kilometer east of Klumpu is a junction, the north branch heading back along the north coastal road, about 8 kilometers (5 mi.) back to Toyapakeh. That is the extent of pavement on Nusa Penida. The rest of the roads are rocky.

From Klumpu the stone road continues irregularly in a south and then southwest direction, passing close to Bukit Mundi, the highest point on the island. Another road from Klumpu leads north and east back to Sampalan. Passing Bukit Mundi you come to Batumadeg, where you can turn off and head southwest to Sebuluh, which is the end of the road. From here a 2-kilometer foot trail leads down a dry wash to the sea. The last few hundred meters is very steep, but the townspeople make the trip daily to reach a good spring at the foot of the cliff. Instead of proceeding down this draw to the sea, you can walk overland to the very edge of the cliffs, for a spectacular view of their size and sheer drop. Two kilometers southwest of this lookout is the steepest cliff along the coast, a sheer drop of 228 meters (748 ft.). You can see these cliffs from Sanur, but the close-up view is much more awe-inspiring. Rough roads connect the rest of villages of the island as can be seen from the map. At Suana there is an important temple, Pura Batu Madau, second only to Pura Dalem Penataran Peed in importance. There is a large cave at Karangsari.

There are few tourist articles on Nusa Penida. A kind of red weft *ikat* material is made here and there, but sold mostly on the main island.

A GREAT MANY "MAINLAND" BALINESE make the trip to Nusa Penida every 210 days for the *odalan* of Pura Peed, which, as my assistant and guide I Wayan Budiasa puts it in his mixed Balinese-English, is the "*angk-er*-est" place in all of Bali. The celebration is on Buda Cemeng Kelawu. The temple is the home of I Macaling, also known as Ratu Gede, Ratu Gede Nusa, or Ratu Gede Macaling. "Macaling" comes from *caling*, Balinese for "fang." Fangs are characteristic of animals and evil spirits and the masks of "coarse" or *keras* characters in any sort of Balinese drama are invariably fanged.

The shrine of I Macaling is only a small part of the temple complex of Pura Peed. But the temple is best known for this architecturally minor feature, and the name of the temple almost invariably evokes a feeling of trepidation in one who hears it. The temple is not one of the six important *sad kahyangan* directional temples, but in the minds of many Balinese it is of equal, or at least parallel, importance. The temple is not beautiful, or even attractive. The temple owns about 20 hectares (50 acres) of land on the hill nearby. Such temple-owned land is normally used to produce rental income to help maintain the temple. But the land owned by Pura Dalem Peed is barren rock. You will hear the names Pura Dalem Peed (or Ped), and Pura Penataran Peed. The official name combines them both, Pura Dalem Penataran Peed.

The temple is north of the main road, on the beach, about 50 meters from the sea. It is approximately 4 kilometers (2.5 mi.) from the village of Toyapakeh. The temple is not especially large, about 50 meters (150 ft.) square, and is surrounded by coconut trees. The temple faces a dry lime-stone hill to the south. Pura Peed has no secular, *jaba*, courtyard, just the *jaba tengah* and the sacred inner courtyard, the *jeroan*. There is a *candi bentar* gate at the entrance, and three small buildings in the *jaba tengah* courtyard. The entrance to the inner temple is on the north wall, and is decorated by a *kori agung*. The construction is of limestone block, with inset and carved *paras* stone. A Bhoma face leers down from its accus-tomed place over the gate. A gnarled frangipani tree leans over the entrance from the right. It is not a particularly beautiful gate. (For more on temple structure, see *S&N Vol. I.*)

A building called the *gedong pasimpenan pratima* dominates the *jeroan* courtyard. This building, storage for the sacred *pratima* statues, is quite ugly and reminds one of a lighthouse. Its two stories tower over the inner temple. The *gedong* is undecorated except for a large Hindu swastika set over the arched entrance and two guardian statues in front. The tower is stepped back so that it is in four sections. The entire building is plastered with lime-colored mortar, and the top two sections are painted yellow. In the southwest corner of the *jeroan*, is the *bale gong*, which here is con-structed in a Javanese, not Balinese, style. In the northeast corner is the tiered *padmasana* shrine, the empty seat for Sanghyang Widhi.

*Padmasana*s are usually set upon a carved Bedawang Nala, the world turtle, surrounded by the two sacred snakes, the Naga. But Bedawang and the snakes are lacking in Pura Dalem Peed. Perhaps this feature was omitted because, as the Balinese put it, the situation and conditions were not balanced. In the center of the east wall is the shrine to Dalem Peed, also known as Dalem Dukut, who overcame Ratu Gede Nusa and made him his minister. It is not large or impressive.

The shrine for Ratu Gede Nusa, or I Macaling, is not even in the *jeroan* proper. Passageways lead to it from both the *jeroan* and the *jaba tengah*. A small courtyard graces the front of the shrine, which faces south. This is the really *angker* part of the whole complex—the home of the dreaded Ratu Gede Nusa, spreader of disease, evil and, if you will, patron saint of the *leyaks* (witches) of Bali.

YOU MIGHT WELL WONDER why so many Balinese would visit such an *angker* spot. One would perhaps imagine that such a center of evil and sickness would be avoided. But the coexistence of opposites is a central thread of Hindu-Balinese thought. Good and evil are, if not equally desirable, equally necessary. And if a god or demon is powerful enough to bring evil and sickness, then surely he is equally capable of preventing and curing evil and sickness. According to legend, I Macaling does not indiscriminately bring people disease and death. He focuses upon those who have violated religious prescriptions and otherwise strayed beyond the bounds of accepted Hindu-Balinese behavior. Thus it is considered valid and worthwhile to visit the shrine of I Macaling to seek his power to ward off evil and sickness.

According to the late Ida Pedanda Made Sideman of Sanur, when Ida Bhatara Gunung Agung, Ida Bhatara Batukaru, and Ida Bhatara Rambut Siwi came to Bali from Java they brought 1,500 holy people called Wong Samar. This group was divided into three. Ratu Nusa Gede (I Macaling) meditated, got his power, and was chosen to be head of one group of 500 Wong Samar. About the time of Batu Renggong's kingdom, which occupied East Java, Timor, Lombok, Sumbawa, and Bali, the king decided that he wanted to control Nusa Penida, and sent one of his generals there to conquer the island.

But this general violated the important courtesy of announcing his presence and intent to the reigning king of Nusa Penida, Dalem Dukut. The latter became very angry and sent the forces of the holy men, the Wong Samar, against the general and killed him. Once again Dalem Batu Renggong picked a general, this time equipping him with a special sacred weapon, *ganja malela*. But the Wong Samar again resisted the attack, broke the weapon, and killed the general. A third general, however, had the ultimate weapon, *pencok sahang,* said to be the tooth of Naga Basuki, one of the two sacred snakes that are entwined around the world turtle,

Bedawang Nala, supporting the cosmos. And with this weapon, the general, Gusti Jelantik, conquered Dalem Dukut and killed him.

Jelantik was a gentleman, for he had approached Dalem Dukut before the battle and announced his intentions. Dalem Dukut, realizing that he could not oppose the tusk of Naga Basuki, gave the Wong Samar to Batu Renggong, and admonished the general to perform the necessary cremation rites after his death. Otherwise, said Dalem Dukut, the people of Nusa Penida will be constantly bothered by the Wong Samar as evil spirits. On the other hand, if the Wong Samar, including their leader I Macaling, were treated with respect and in the proper religious manner, the people would be helped to prevent or conquer disease and sickness. So Dalem Dukut was killed, cremated, and his is one of the principal shrines in Pura Dalem Penataran Peed. It is small and unpretentious, but it is his influence that was important—more important than that of I Macaling, who was only his minister. And so it is that people from far and wide come to the temple on the beach to seek protection from sickness from I Macaling, Ratu Gede Nusa. And so it is that this rather unattractive temple ranks almost with the Sad Kahyangan temples in importance to the Balinese people.

The *odalan* of Pura Dalem Penataran Peed takes place on Buda Cemeng, Wednesday of the week Kelawu, week number 28 of the Pawukon anniversary calendar. The ceremony usually lasts for three days. There are no accommodations, but people do not come here to sleep, just to pray and meditate. There are plenty of food stalls set up all around the temple, just as at the *odalans* of all major temples, and entertainment such as dances or *topeng* are offered.

CHAPTER 4

Stars in Bali

WHERE SCORPIUS IS A COCONUT TREE

BALI PRESENTS A VISITOR FROM THE NORTHERN HEMISPHERE with a whole new sky for stargazing. The island has little electric lighting and the stars shine brightly—the Southern Cross, the Pleiades, Centaurus. In addition, the near equatorial position of Bali provides for a brief twilight, and the sun drops straight and quickly at sunset. But perhaps more interesting than the constellations themselves, which are somewhat less dramatic than those northern dwellers are used to, is the unique Balinese twist on sidereal nomenclature—here the Southern Cross becomes Jaran, the horse, and familiar Scorpius is a coconut tree. And the local explanations for celestial phenomena, while probably leaving scientists unconvinced, provide some engaging folklore.

Stars and star lore are actually relatively unimportant to the majority of the Balinese. My assistant and friend Budi volunteered the fact that the Balinese used to call a pretty girl a *jegeg bulan,* meaning "pretty as the moon." But now that men have walked on the moon, he added, the colloquialism is no longer used. Putting one's feet on top of something is considered excessively bad manners. The multitude of religious offerings in Bali are made in countless shapes, but few are constructed as stars. Rice cake (*jaja*) offerings are sometimes made in the shape of the sun and moon, *jaja matanai* and *jaja bulan,* to be used at tooth filing ceremonies as well as at temple anniversaries. But *jaja* never represent stars, and, generally speaking, stars just don't play much of a role, either symbolically or otherwise, in Balinese Hinduism. But, as in many parts of the world, stars play an important practical role, helping fishermen navigate, and the Balinese have developed their own unique lore to explain, for example, eclipses and comets, and to give mythical form to the constellations.

MOST BALINESE KNOW THE CAUSE of eclipses, although their explanation is likely different from yours and mine. The story is taken from a famous section of the *Mahabharata* that describes how the gods obtained Tirtha Amertha, the elixir of life, holy water that conferred upon them their immortality (See "The Sea of Milk," *S&N Volume I*). This elixir was churned up out of the sea through the collective efforts of all the gods and demons, using a huge mountain, Mandara Giri, as the mixer. When, after truly epic labors, the Tirtha Amertha was produced, the demons immediately stole it. The gods fought with the demons and regained their elixir. But one of the demons—Kala Rahu—changed his shape and stole into the gods' camp to drink the holy water. The Sun and Moon, always on guard, saw this and alerted Wisnu, who hurled his lethal *cakra*, a discus-like weapon, which neatly sliced off Kala Rahu's head. His body fell lifeless, but because he was in the process of swallowing at the time, the Tirtha Amerta had already made his head immortal. Kala Rahu's head, angry at the Sun and Moon for reporting the theft, pursues them through the skies, occasionally swallowing one or the other.

An eclipse of the moon is called *bulan kepangan* or *kepaksa*, meaning that someone is eaten. Another term occasionally heard is *keleled*, which comes from *led*, "swallow." An eclipse of the sun is *kegera*, "a meeting," or *matanai* (the sun) *kepangan*. Other names for lunar and solar eclipses are, respectively, *kala ketemu* and *candra ketemu*—*ketemu* again coming from "meeting." Although I have never observed the practice, it is said that the Balinese used to beat the *kulkul* signal drums when there was an eclipse in order to scare Kala Rahu away.

One sometimes hears mention of a "star"—*bintang*—that the Balinese call *bintang kuskus*. *Kuskus* means "to steam rice," and the utensil for doing this (*kuskusan*) is a loosely woven, conical basket. The pointed end extends downward into the boiling pot, which has a flared rim to accept the pointed bottom of the *kuskusan*. The shape of this apparatus gives comets—*bintang kuskus*—their Balinese name. Comets are, of course, no good for navigational purposes, appearing irregularly and at long intervals. And when they do appear, they portend either something very good or something very bad in the world. One informant suggested that the appearance of a *bintang kuskus* meant the world was going to get "very hot, or bad." A *bintang kuskus* was reported in September 1965, at the time of the the *Gestapu*, the abortive Indonesian coup. Another was reported at the time of the death of Indonesia's first president, Sukarno.

THE SOUTHERN SKY is not quite as full as that in the Northern Hemisphere, but it offers a new group of constellations and, in equatorial Bali, an interesting phenomenon called zodiacal light. Just after sunset in the west, or just before sunrise in the east, the sky over Bali displays a tapering band of luminescence. Under ideal conditions, the zodiacal light may form a continuous band from eastern to western horizon. In northerly latitudes this light is only rarely visible, in evenings around the time of the Spring Equinox and in mornings around the time of the Fall Equinox, but in the tropics it can be seen all year long. Zodiacal light is a product of the reflection of sunlight off meteoric dust. The phenomenon is limited to the tropics because most of the dust and particulates near the earth lie in a fairly narrow plane that corresponds to the earth's orbit. This band of debris is thought to be left over from the time that the earth and moon formed. The Balinese rainy season often obscures the skies from November through April, and the best stargazing is in May through October, when the skies are seldom cloudy at night.

You can't see the familiar North Star from Bali, but the Big Dipper is visible at about 8 or 9 P.M. from about February through June, low in the northern sky. There is no equivalent "South Star" although the Southern Cross is a famous navigation tool. It is not very large, but it is prominent in the southern sky, reaching its highest point in the sky about 8 or 9 P.M. during May. At its zenith it is about 30 degrees above the horizon. It drops below the horizon at about 8 or 9 P.M. in August, and appears again in the east at the same time in the evening during December. Of course it is visible at other times of the year at different positions, and at different times of the night.

You should not need a star map to guide you to the Southern Cross. If you go stargazing at 8 or 9 P.M. between December and August, you can easily find it, but it is easier to find in the middle of this period when it is highest in the sky. Look toward the south. Look for two very bright stars in the constellation Centaurus. The brighter of the two is Alpha Centauri, often called Rigil Kentaurus or Rigil Kent. The other is Beta Centauri, known as Hadar. They are for the Southern Cross what the two pointers of the Big Dipper are for Polaris, the North Star. Start at Alpha Centauri and look along an imaginary line that goes through Beta—this will take you straight to Crux, as the astronomers call the Southern Cross. The line from Alpha to Beta and to Crux is more or less east to west parallel to the horizon when Crux is at its highest, in May. As the year proceeds, Crux, circling around the south celestial pole, appears lower and lower in the west each evening at the same time. It is almost lying on its side just before it disappears in August, and by then the guide stars, Alpha and Beta Centauri, form a line that is almost perpendicular to the horizon.

There are five bright stars in Crux. When it is at its highest point in the sky, crossing the meridian, and thus vertical, the brightest of the five, called Acrux, is nearest the horizon. The star marking the left end of the cross bar is the second brightest, Mimosa. The third brightest star, Gacrux, is at the top. The other two have no names except Delta and Epsilon Crucis. Delta is at the right, or west side, and epsilon is between Delta and Acrux.

SOUTHERN CROSS, POSITION AT 8-9 P.M., MID-MAY

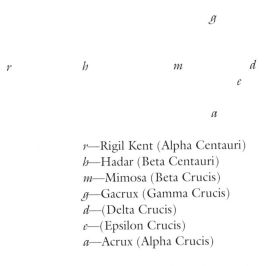

r—Rigil Kent (Alpha Centauri)
h—Hadar (Beta Centauri)
m—Mimosa (Beta Crucis)
g—Gacrux (Gamma Crucis)
d—(Delta Crucis)
e—(Epsilon Crucis)
a—Acrux (Alpha Crucis)

In the above diagram, you are looking due south, about 30 degrees above the horizon. East is to your left. And, as you watch, the stars will revolve clockwise about the south celestial pole, thirty degrees to the south of the diagram.

Westward from Crux, the principal constellations are two large, rambling, related groups: Vela, the sail of Jason's mythical ship, and directly below, or to the south, Carina, the keel of the ship. Together they measure about 30 degrees, north to south, and 45 degrees, east to west. The eastern-most stars of these two, Mu Velae and Theta Carinae, both of the third magnitude in brightness, rise about sunset in mid-February from a point in the sky are about 20 degrees west of Crux. There are several second magnitude stars in the western parts of these two constellations. But the brightest star, Canopus, still farther west, is the second brightest star in the entire sky.

The constellation Centaurus, the centaur, is a huge, rambling star group, only the top of which can be seen from the southern temperate zones. Centaurus covers 50 degrees of sky east to west, and 27 degrees north to south. The half-horse, half-man creature faces east and Alpha and Beta Centauri are his front feet. His body arches over Crux, and his hind feet are just west of Acrux. Centaurus has a very large, sweeping head, forming an arc, concave side down. The brightest star in the head is Menkent, due north of Hadar.

Northerners may see many of their old friends in the night skies of Bali, but they will be in different positions. The constellations of the zodiac, and those near them, which parade across the northern sky low in the

*DETAILS FROM THE BALINESE ASTROLOGICAL CALENDAR.
THE TOP IS THE STAR SIGN, BINTANG PUNYAN KELAPA,
OR COCONUT TREE. THE BOTTOM IS DUPA, OR INCENSE.*

south, here rise almost due east and are much higher above the horizon when they cross the meridian.

One of the most magnificent sights in the southern night sky is Scorpius. Even in the lower latitudes of the Northern Hemisphere, the long curving tail of this constellation tends to be obscured by horizon clouds or city lights. But in Bali the full sweep of this huge group is practically at the zenith, reaching its fullest height on the meridian at about 8 or 9 P.M. in July. Scorpius is 26 degrees from north to south and 28 degrees from east to west—enormous. Just east of Scorpius is the brilliant band of the Milky Way, and you will never see it so bright. Partially embedded in the east side of the Milky Way is the spout of the "teapot" of Sagittarius.

The familiar Northern Hemisphere winter constellations put in an appearance on the eastern horizon starting as early as July. The first to show up on the eastern horizon, farther north than you are used to seeing it, is the Great Square of Pegasus. Next on the 8 to 9 P.M. horizon is the small constellation Aries, the ram, which rises in Bali in late September. The brightest star in Aries, Hamal, has a magnitude of 2.2, and is 30 degrees east of Alpheratz, the brightest and most north-easterly star of a constellation called the Great Square. Hamal is 28 degrees west of the Pleiades, the famous group of "The Seven Sisters" that rises about 8 to 9 P.M. in early October. Then, in late October, fiery red Aldeberan rises about 8 to 9 P.M., in the constellation Taurus, the bull. It has a magnitude of 1.1 and is unmistakable because of its color. A few weeks later Orion appears for the first time, rising on his side out of the horizon almost due east, rather than more or less erect, as in the Northern latitudes.

Follow Orion's belt to the southeast to find the brightest star in the skies, Sirius, in the constellation of the Great Dog, Canis Major. Sirius is about 21 degrees from the nearest of the three belt stars. And in Bali you will also see the second brightest star in the sky, Canopus, in the constellation Carina, invisible in all but the most southerly part of the Northern Hemisphere. Canopus rises in the east about 8 or 9 P.M. during November and is highest in the sky, about 40 degrees above the southern horizon, in January. It sets in the west about 8 or 9 P.M. in May. Canopus is straight south from Sirius. It is quite a long distance from Sirius, but it is such a bright star that it is easy to see.

BALINESE FISHERMEN, LIKE THEIR COUNTERPARTS elsewhere in the world, use the stars for navigation. Although they never stray very far from home, since most of their boats lack even the most rudimentary navigational gear, the stars and waves—and sometimes the bright lights of Denpasar in the distance—are their only means of returning home safely. Most of the fishermen in my area put out at sunset because the fish can see their nets in the daytime. The names I give here are from my sources among the fishermen of Jimbaran, and they might not be the same as those used elsewhere on the island. But because Jimbaran is the second largest fishing area in Bali, and because many of the fishermen here are transients from Java, my suspicion is that the terminology is quite widespread.

The most widely known and used navigational constellation is the Pleiades. The Jimbaran area fishermen call it Bintang Muung, whereas it is often called Bintang Kartika in other places. One informant told me that *muung* means "group," but most Balinese are unfamiliar with the word. Kartika is, interestingly enough, derived from the Sanskrit *karttika*, meaning "the seventh month." The Indian calendar has undergone many changes and modifications, but according to one of the most ancient systems the year began in what we now call April, so that April-May was the first month, May-June the second, and so on, until the seventh month, October-November. The star group Pleiades, now considered to be part of the constellation Taurus, consists of seven medium-bright stars, around which there grew a legend, popular in classical Greek times, about the seven daughters of Atlas and Pleione. But for our purposes here, it is enough to observe that the Pleiades, or Bintang Muung, rises almost due east at about 8 or 9 P.M. in early October, the ancient Indian "seventh month." This also happens to be the beginning of the rainy season in Bali which, of course, has important implications for the planting of crops. *Bintang*, by the way, is used indiscriminately in Bali to mean a single star, a group of stars, or a constellation.

Our old friend Scorpius turns out to be, of all things, a coconut tree in Bali—Bintang Punyan Kelapa. The cross of the T, which we take to be the head of the animal, forms the tree's crown. Antares, the first magnitude star which we call the heart of the scorpion, is a squirrel, *semal,* climbing the tree. And bright Shaula, marking the end of the curled tail of the scorpion is *puuh,* or *puyuh,* a quail-like bird that always lives on the ground.

The Southern Cross is the head of a horse—*kuda* in High Balinese, *jaran* in Low Balinese—sometimes referred to as Jaran Gadang, "the green horse." The horse faces east, and his front feet are Mu Velae and Theta Carinae, and the rest of Vela and Carina make up his body. Balinese fishermen say that it is very bad to mention the names of animals when they are at sea fishing. So they refer to this constellation as Undakan, a euphemism meaning "something that you can ride." This idea of referring to an attribute of an object rather than the object itself is fairly widespread in Bali.

The curving head of our Centaurus strikes the Balinese as the helmet worn by the hero Arjuna, one of the five Pandawa brothers who are the heroes of the *Mahabharata*. In shadow puppet plays and other dramas, many of the male characters look so much alike that the only way you can tell them apart is by their distinctive headdresses. Thus, the characteristic backward sweep of the helmet of Arjuna is universally known in Bali. It is said that Arjuna is mad at the horse, Kuda, because, although he eats Bali's grass, he travels westward and thus leaves his "fertilizer" in Java. So Arjuna is shooting Kuda with Ru, the arrow—Alpha and Beta Centauri. Between Ru and Kuda are a few smaller stars in a rather shapeless mass which the Balinese call Punyan Kendal, the *kendal* tree. The arrow goes right through the tree, which explains why *kendal* trees always have holes in them (they do). Ru, Kuda, and Arjuna, when visible, make good south markers for the fishermen. Toward the north, the Big Dipper is Jong, the boat. Although it is a good indicator of north, is not visible during much of the year.

Rising after Punyan Kelapa is Merepat, the square, the same name we give this large part of Pegasus. Between Merepat and Muung is Bengkong, the curve. This is Aries. Rising after Muung is Suda Malung, which we call Aldeberan, the red eye of Taurus the bull. To the Balinese it is the eye of a pig, whose body extends toward the south and is not readily visible.

And the next major Bintang to rise is Tenggala, the plow, part of the constellation we call Orion. Standing straight up, as it does in the southern skies of the Northern Hemisphere, it is a bit difficult to make out any sort of plow in Orion. But in Bali Orion rises lying on his side, and it is easy to see the star group as a plow. The "blade" of the plow is Orion's belt. His sword is the horizontal handle of the plow, which attaches to the cow at the southwesterly star, Saiph. The farmer holds on to and leans on the top-most "belt" star. You kind of have to imagine a curve between the bottom of the "sword" and Saiph, and that makes the image complete. Tenggala is called Bintang Waluku by some people, which is just High Balinese for "plow."

One of the most useful star groups for fishermen rises shortly after Tenggala. A line drawn straight southeast from Orion's belt points right to Sirius, the brightest star in the sky, sometimes called Bintang Siagan by the Balinese. To the south of Sirius is Canopus, the second brightest star in the skies. And to the north of Canopus is the bright star Capella. The line from Capella to Sirius to Canopus describes a V with the tip pointing to the east. This is Bintang Lomba-Lomba, the porpoise, the star group most widely used by fishermen for determining the north-south direction. There is some local disagreement over the middle star in Lomba-Lomba, but Betelgeuse, the very bright red star in the northeast corner of Orion's shoulder, makes the most accurate north–south line.

PART II

Society

CHAPTER 5

Family life

DAY TO DAY LIVES IN JIMBARAN

BALI DRAWS THE VISITOR'S ATTENTION to large, spectacular events—cremations, dance performances, temple festivals, and the like. The religious celebrations of the Hindu Balinese are justly famous, and tour operators make every effort to guide their clients to these events. But life on the island is not all spectacle. People spend most of their time at home, doing the thousand-and-one trivial things that occupy families the world over. I live in Jimbaran, in the family compound of my good friend I Wayan Budiasa. The observations presented here are not drawn from Budi's family in particular, but are a kind of composite of Jimbaran family life. Since my experience of Balinese family life is for the most part based on one village, I won't suggest that the details apply to the entire island.

A typical Jimbaran family lives in a *pakarangan,* a walled-in house compound. One enters from the street or alley through a gate, which can range from an elaborate *kori,* almost like that of a temple, to a simple opening with a low wooden door. Most compounds house several nuclear families. The property itself was usually the home of a male ancestor, and the current male occupants are his descendants. On average, two to four brothers and their families share a *pakarangan.* If the family is too large for the compound, one or more of the brothers may have constructed his own *pakarangan,* usually nearby. But the main family temple, *sanggah* or *merajan,* remains in the original house compound and sons who have struck out on their own must still return here for all important ceremonies. It is here that his ancestral deities live.

The oldest brother is the patriarch of the house compound. The primacy of his birth automatically places responsibility for the entire family group upon his shoulders. He does the planning. He meets with the gov-

ernment employees in matters affecting his family. It is he outsiders must
see if they wish to have dealings with the family. It is he who must plan
for all of the religious activities of the family. It is he who must settle
problems that arise within the family, quash idle and destructive gossip,
and preserve the peace. That is not an easy job in a crowded enclave,
human nature being what it is.

Younger brothers, it is said, are like the tail of an animal. Having
grown up following the leader, they may never know what it is like to
have positions of responsibility and authority, and it is likely that their
childrens' attitudes will be affected by these feelings. The result is often
that the younger brothers, seldom having been in positions of authority,
seldom having had to make decisions, and always having had to depend
upon their oldest brother, are inexperienced—and may be indecisive and
subservient. They have never have exercised authority, and thrust occasionally into positions where decisions have to be made, they cannot handle the job.

According to tradition, the family of the oldest brother lives on the
kaja side of the house compound, that is, the privileged, mountainward
side. This practice is not often observed, however. The families may share
a kitchen, or, in some cases, to avoid conflict, there may be several
kitchens. These are usually located *kelod*—away from the sacred mountain, seaward—of the living area. The family temple, *sanggah*, is *kaja-kan-
gin*, northeast in South Bali. Buildings within the *pakarangan* are
arranged according to the Balinese sacred/profane directional axis. (See
"Kaja and Kelod," *S&N Vol. I.*) Animal pens, the most profane shelters,
are at the far *kelod* end of the compound. A rice storage barn, if there is
one, is also on the *kelod* side. The *pakarangan* usually features a traditional *bale*, or pavilion, in the middle of the area. Normally built of wood and
brick with a traditional thatch roof, the *bale* is the site of most family religious ceremonies. These days, the *bale* may be the only building in the
compound constructed in the traditional style.

Today, living and working quarters may be constructed in any of a
number of styles, and the trend is toward the use of more modern materials. Foundations are of concrete, often with commercial tile floors. Walls
are brick or precast concrete block, plastered and painted. Limestone
block is still used, but not as often as in the past. Rafters are hewn from
coconut logs. Concrete pillars are replacing traditional wooden ones.
Modern houses have ceilings of plywood or other commercially available
sheathing. Window and door frames are locally made by carpenters in the
traditional manner, but nowadays the doors and windows themselves are
usually purchased from a building supply company. Electricity is common.
Houses, gates, and walls in our village are very sparsely decorated, if at all.
There are almost no carvings of any sort inside or out. If the family temple structures are decorated, these are likely to be precast concrete rather

than the traditional hand-carved *paras* sandstone.

The interiors of houses are furnished very simply. Calendar art, photographs, and plastic flowers are about the extent of the usual ornamentation. People don't spend much time inside, except at night, or to watch TV. The living room often has a fancy wooden cabinet with glass doors that displays the best coffee cups and guest china, and there may be a few stuffed chairs and a table. Furniture tends to be rather heavy in appearance, with obvious Dutch colonial influence. Bedrooms are small and functional. One seldom sees built-in closets. Older people often prefer to sleep in the traditional open *bales,* their belongings stuffed here and there into boxes.

It is not at all unusual in our village for a man to have two, or even more than two wives. If he does, he normally maintains a separate house for each—in a separate house compound—so that the wives do not normally encounter each other. Polygamy is usually the result of the first wife not bearing children. Children do not have separate rooms, and they sleep with their parents. When they are older they crowd in with other children. It is not unusual to see several children piled up like puppies, all asleep on one small bed. Parents of the brothers may also live in the house compound. They are usually elderly and no longer have regular jobs. They help out around the house, look after the children, and take care of the cows. People live very close together within a house compound, and the compound itself is usually adjacent to another similar one. There is very little privacy. Although the entrance gate is always shut at night, it stands wide open during the day, and other villagers, even total strangers, wander in freely. If nobody is visible, manners require the stranger to call out several times to make his presence known. But he does so from within the compound, not outside the gate.

THE COMPOUND AWAKENS EARLY. Farmers want to get their work done before the hottest part of the day. The village market is in full swing by dawn, and the sellers' day may begin at 3:00 A.M. The best fruits and vegetables are gone by 8:00, so housewives must get the morning meal ready and the kids off to school well before then. Drivers, truckers, and those with business in Denpasar are on the road before dawn. Those who run their own businesses or work in the village can afford to be more leisurely. But children often must be at school before 7:00. Older children may have a dawn soccer game or go for a long jog on the streets before leaving for school. Just before civil holidays such as Independence Day, August 17th, there is marching practice, beginning at dawn, for all youngsters.

The women are up before anyone else, and rice is cooking in the kitchen by sunrise. Tiny pinches of the newly cooked foods are placed on small folded coconut leaf trays—*banten jotan*—and distributed to the various house shrines as offerings. One may be put on the stove and another

SWEEPING WITH A COCONUT SPINE BROOM, SAMPAT LIDI

on the pump or by the well. One of the women sweeps yesterday's trash from the compound using a bundle of coconut leaf spines as a broom. Sweepings are carried out to the street and put in the drainage ditch that parallels the street. Every now and then the debris is burned, giving off great clouds of very acrid smoke.

Everyone takes a bath before the daily routine commences. Most houses have bathrooms and electric water pumps, and elevated, gravity-fed water storage tanks are common in Jimbaran. But many people still have wells and haul the water up with buckets. If there is a storage tank, the bathroom may have a shower. Otherwise bathing consists of pouring a bucket of water over one's head, soaping down, and repeating. Some people use large water jars made of fired clay as shower baths. They are filled with water from the well. To take a bath, you just pull a wooden plug out of an opening near the bottom on one side, and water squirts out. There is no municipal water supply, but the government has installed several water faucets along the main road, supplied by pipeline from a reservoir north of Denpasar. Wells in our area are only 3-4 meters deep, and the water, although quite hard because of the limestone aquifer, is of excellent quality. Nearer the coast, well water becomes somewhat saline. Water for drinking is usually heated, although seldom actually boiled. Almost all houses have squat toilets.

Few homes have refrigerators. The food is purchased fresh and cooked immediately. Fresh *sambel* is prepared daily by mashing chili peppers, onion, garlic, salt, and a bit of oil on a *batu basa*, a mortar made of volcanic rock that has low sides and a flat bottom. Eating is quite a casual affair. Families almost never sit down together to any meal. Meal time is for eating, not for conversation. The wife prepares the food and puts it on a table in the kitchen, with a cover over the top. When anyone feels so moved he simply helps himself, putting whatever he wants on a plate and eating with his fingers, normally alone. A meal is over in minutes. Hot water is stored in a thermos, and anyone can make himself tea or coffee at any time, always loaded with sugar. Rice cakes of various kinds are always around. The same kinds of foods are eaten for breakfast, lunch, and dinner. Leftovers from breakfast constitute lunch. More rice may be cooked for dinner. The Balinese are very touchy about their rice and can detect variations that I could not possibly notice. Rice left overnight is considered fit only as animal food.

The diet is high in carbohydrates, of course, but there is almost always plenty of fish in our village, and usually some sort of soybeans. There is no fresh milk. Children drink canned evaporated milk or some sort of powdered commercial formula. Vegetables are cheap and plentiful, as is fruit. The Balinese do not eat leafy greens or salads, but often munch on raw cucumbers, or jicama, a juicy root the Balinese call *bangkwang*. The Balinese are compulsive snackers, and there are always little stands along the streets, push cart vendors that go from house to house, and stalls in the market where one can buy almost anything he wishes quite cheaply. If someone is away from home at lunch time he can buy *nasi bungkus,* cooked rice and bits of vegetable and meat wrapped up in a banana leaf, for Rp 500 in almost every village.

Children are bathed, dressed in their school uniforms, and sent off to school on foot or bicycle. Elementary and primary schools are always nearby. High schools may be farther away and require a bicycle or *bemo* ride. But a high school education is not common in our village.

Shopping at the village market is a daily chore for women who live within walking distance. For those who do not, there are always *warungs* nearby selling basic items. Many women make their own daily offerings, but the trend is toward buying them ready-made at the market. Activity at the market reaches a peak just after dawn and then tapers off to almost none by noon. The best meats and fruits and vegetables from Denpasar are quickly exhausted. But those who sell offerings, spices, staples such as rice and manioc, hardware, and clothes stay most of the day. In our village there are no special market days. In other parts of Bali there is usually a big market every three days, moving to nearby locations on the other two days. One or another important day falls almost weekly, and then more offerings than normal are required. On those days the market is especially busy, and prices rise with demand for items that are required for offerings, such as fruit and rice cakes. The market is always a good place to exchange gossip, have a snack, catch up on the latest news, and see what the rest of the village is doing.

IT IS INCREASINGLY COMMON FOR WOMEN TO WORK. This happens particularly in the villages near large cities or tourist areas, where employment in a shop or hotel is not hard to find. In such cases a grandparent or one of the older children looks after the house compound and the younger children while the mother is away. Schools in our area are on a double session program, so that those who leave early in the morning are back from school well before noon. Even university students go to school for only a couple of hours a day. In some areas women can supplement their husbands' income by sewing garments for exporters. They can go to the headquarters office once a week or so, pick up cloth that has already been cut and marked, take it home and sew it at their leisure, and return the finished goods to the factory when they pick up new material. In our village a large number of men are tailors and do sewing for garment manufacturers in Kuta for sale to tourists. Government offices open rather early in the morning, but close early as well. One with a government job can expect to be able to leave shortly after noon and either spend most of the afternoon at home or at a second job to supplement his income.

There is no theoretical discrimination between women and men, although in practice, the sexes usually assume traditional responsibilities. Women sell in the market, shop for food, and cook. Men attend to their *banjar* duties and participate in such activities as *gong* groups. Women make offerings, take care of the pigs, do the laundry. Men go to cockfights, *mebat*—prepare the spices and meats—for feasts, and attend to death rituals. There are no laws that say that these barriers cannot be broken. One often does see men helping with offerings, for example. But I have never seen a woman at a cockfight or, at least in our village, playing in a *gong*.

If the women of the household do not have jobs, they take care of family chores. Laundry can be a major chore where the water supply is meager. Then the clothes are hauled to nearby streams or ditches. But everyone has a well in our area, so that laundry is almost always done at home. Great care must be taken to pick an area for hanging up the wash so that nobody will accidentally walk underneath. This is an important taboo for the Balinese. Washing the dishes is not a major chore, since nobody uses knives or forks and usually there is only one plate or bowl, and one glass per person.

Clothing around the home is quite informal. Women may wear modern Western-style dresses from a store. Old-fashioned women wear the traditional *kamben*, a 2.5-meter sheet of *batik* or *endek* wrapped around their waists, and a blouse. Many women, especially older ones, wear no tops at all around the house compound, but one seldom sees them this way on the streets. Most men in our village wear Western-style clothes during the day and when at work. When they return home from work they change to shorts and a sleeveless shirt or to a traditional *sarung*. This is a 2.5-meter length of *batik* or *endek* with the short ends sewn together.

Many villagers in Jimbaran keep cows and pigs. Pigs are usually husbanded by the women. They are simply leashed when small, and penned when they get too big for the rope. Pigs are fed a mixture of rice hulls and water. The rice hulls, particularly the nutritious *oot alus*, are purchased at the market. Despite the fiber and vitamin content of whole grain rice, the Balinese consider only refined white rice, *baas*, to be worth eating. The pig's diet of rice hulls may be supplemented with sliced up sections of banana plant stem. Cows are led out to a grassy, shaded pasture beneath the coconut trees near the beach, tethered, and left on their own to graze. The men generally tend to the cows. Toward evening, the animals must be rounded up and brought home. If there is not enough pasture land, the cows are grazed along the streets. Toward the end of the dry season, when grass is scarce, both men and women cut leaves or banana stems for the animals. Few people in our area keep ducks because there are no wet rice fields nearby.

Children are home from school by noon, unless they are on the afternoon session. The husband returns from his job or from the fields by early afternoon. The humid afternoon heat makes it easy to take a nap in the shade. About 4 P.M., when things start to cool off a bit, life returns to the house compound. This is everyone's favorite part of the day. Boys go to the beach for the daily soccer game. Guests come, and everyone sits down to gossip over a cigarette and a cup of coffee. One absolutely must serve refreshments of some sort to any sort of guest. Repairs to the house are made. It is amazing how ingenious and inventive the Balinese are in using local materials to effect minor repairs. Armed with only a knife there is almost no end of things that can be made or fixed, using a bit of wire, string made from bamboo, and odds and ends of castoff materials.

I hired a carpenter to make some furniture for my room. It was fascinating to watch him work. Finished lumber is not available on the island, so he had to cut all of his boards to size out of rough pieces and smooth them with a crude plane. He had no plans, and I am sure he had never made a cabinet for a computer before. But after I explained what I wanted, he never hesitated. The entire framework was held together without nails by mortise and tenon joints, all made by using only a hammer and chisel. It took a week to complete, because everyone in the neighborhood would come in to watch and chat and make suggestions. And there had to be coffee and cakes and cigarettes provided for one and all.

Late afternoon is the best time for the older men to exercise their fighting cocks. Mock battles without steel spurs are staged in the *bale banjar*—the pavilion of the local social organization—or on shady streets, while everyone gathers around to discuss the merits or demerits of the fowls. Cockfighting (and all forms of gambling) is illegal in Indonesia now. But one can almost always find one in progress somewhere in the neighborhood, out of sight of the authorities. From April to November late afternoon sees the beaches crowded with fishermen preparing their nets and boats to embark on the all-night fishing trip into the straits between Java and Bali. During the rainy season, onshore winds make the waves so high that boats cannot be safely launched. In late afternoon the *warungs* spring to life again after a lazy and nap-filled interlude. Young men come to talk to the young lady who is in charge or to each other and to watch the cars go by. Others sit in front of their gates and watch village life unfold. The street is the Balinese living room. Some people spend hours doing absolutely nothing, just sitting and watching. Reading is not a popular activity. Almost nobody owns any books. Even students have little homework.

The only television station in Indonesia is operated by the government. Excepting Sundays, when it broadcasts all day, the station begins at 5 P.M. And from then until bedtime TV sets are never off, volume turned up full blast. There is local, regional, national, and international news, but not much of the latter. The news programs show mostly meetings. There are cultural and entertainment programs, religious programs for Hindus,

Christians, and Muslims, sporting events, of which soccer is the most popular, and cartoons and sitcoms—these last usually in English. The audience, which cannot understand a word of the dialog, seems to be just as fascinated with the English programs. Programming ends at 11 P.M., usually finishing up with a late movie of Indonesian origin. The most popular programs by far are Balinese dramatic and musical presentations. Most *bale banjars* have TV sets, and those who live nearby drop around to see the programs and chat. And there is almost always a Ping-pong game in progress. Many villagers flock to our lovely west side beach at sundown to see the magnificent sunsets over the Indian ocean.

Everyone takes a second bath at sunset and then helps himself to whatever is available for dinner. The push carts have been in action all during the late afternoon, and many people have a big bowl of *kacang ijo,* a delicious mixture of boiled green beans, sugar, and coconut milk, or a plate of *rujak,* slices of unripe fruit in a very hot sauce. Local warungs usually sell *es buah,* slices of fruit served on a bed of shaved ice with bright red syrup and condensed milk poured over the top. These treats dim appetites for dinner, which may consist of the morning's leftovers, with perhaps a new batch of rice. As before, there is no formal get together for dinner. Everyone just eats alone, outside somewhere, when the spirit moves.

In early evening the clubs and organization meet. Many villages have a *tuak*—palm beer—drinking club that meets every evening and where men discuss the events of the day and get mildly smashed on the frothy palm beer. This is for men only. This is also the time for musical and dance groups to practice. One of our *gongs* has hired a teacher to come down from Denpasar twice a week, and they often practice until late at night. People do not stay up very late. Almost everyone is in bed by 9 P.M., and the streets are deserted. *Bemos* stop running at dark. The market is closed up tight. House gates are locked. Nighttime is also time for various spirits to be wandering around, and it is best to be safely home and in bed.

THIS DAILY ROUTINE IS FREQUENTLY INTERRUPTED. Friday is officially a half-day for government offices throughout Indonesia, because of the predominance of Islam as a religion. Saturday is a regular business day for everyone, including school children. Sundays are usually spent visiting, playing with the children, repairing the motorcycle, watching TV, or indulging in the national pastime: watching the street from the vantage point of the front gate. In addition to Hindu holy days, most Muslim, Christian, and Buddhist religious holidays are cheerfully observed by one and all, even though there is seldom any understanding of their significance. For example, Christmas is widely known as a holiday, but few people know why. It is officially called Hari Raya Natal, but almost nobody, except the few Christian Balinese, knows whose *natal* it was.

But most interruptions of the daily routine are activities that have to do with Hindu-Balinese religious ceremonies or with *banjar* activities. The important coincidence days of the Balinese Pawukon calendar cycle occur irregularly, but on average about once a seven-day week. (See "Balinese Calendars," *BS&N Vol. I.*) Kajeng Keliwon, one of the most important of these, occurs every 15 days. Some coincidences occur just once a month, but there are enough of them to constantly disrupt the routine. Special offerings are required for these days, and it is job of the wife to make them. Offerings for ordinary coincidence days are usually just placed in the *sanggah* and the various shrines around the house compounds, or, in the case of Kajeng Keliwon, out on the street in front of the gate.

Each of the three important village temples has an anniversary celebration, an *odalan*, every 210 days—one Pawukon cycle. The *banjar* temple has a twice-a-year *odalan*, too. The *sanggah* of the husband and that of the wife have *odalans*. Many families have relationship ties with other temples in Bali, such as the *kawitan* temple—that from which the male or female line of the family originated. There may be an *ibu* temple, at which various related families worship, and its *odalan* must be observed. There are many fishermen in our village, and important ceremonies for them are conducted at our Pura Segara, the sea temple. There is a temple that holds an annual ceremony to mark the transition between the dry and rainy season. Our largest temple, Pura Ulunsiwi, is involved with rice and rice crop diseases—it has an *odalan* and is the site of various other ceremonies. We have a very sacred *barong* and dance troupe, and its temple and its performances are the site of a long series of ceremonies. And, scattered around the village, are other, less important temples. The families in my house compound are fairly typical—they participate, to a greater or lesser degree, in the *odalans* of some fifteen temples, in addition to that of their own *sanggah*.

Attending an *odalan* means that the wife must prepare a series of offerings, the size and complexity and cost of which depend upon the elaborateness of the odalan and upon the feeling of the family toward the temple. Most temples have ordinary *odalans,* interspersed every two or three 210-day years with a *odalan nadi*—one that is bigger than normal. These require more elaborate preparations. Under normal circumstances the ordinary small *canang* will do as offerings. But is is not unusual for a family to promise to prepare a larger offering if the god of a particular temple will grant a special wish. This wish more often than not is a request that a sick person regain his health. If the wish is granted, the wife has to prepare a high offering and carry it to the temple as a *masaudan,* the fulfillment of the promise. And the lay priest, the *pemangku,* performs a special little ceremony in which this offering is made to the god in question. In our area, most people wait to go to *odalans* until about 4:00 in the afternoon, after it has cooled down a bit. The wife may have to work many hours in the preparation of especially fancy high offerings and may have to spend tens of thousands of rupiah on the cakes, fruit, rice, chicken, and other items that are part of the offering. The children must be bathed and dressed. And everyone has to put on his very best traditional clothes for the trip to the *odalan*. If the temple is far away, the family has to start out quite early and working parents will have to miss their jobs.

Other types of ceremonies and events require offerings. Most families erect *penjors*—tall, bamboo-pole offerings—in front of their houses at Galungan time, and at this time, and at Kuningan, offerings are made for ancestral deities. The women in our family sometimes spend a week or more making offerings for the Galungan–Kuningan period, as there are several other events when offerings are called for. If the family owns a kris, an automobile or motorcycle, even a bicycle, special offerings must be made to these devices on Tumpek Landep. Cows and pigs receive special offerings at Tumpek Andang; coconut trees at Tumpek Uduh. Each person has a birthday anniversary every 210 days, and, particularly in the case of younger children, these *otons* can be quite elaborate. In some families offerings are made for every *oton* all throughout the person's life.

Rites of passage ceremonies require special preparations. (See "Rites of Passage," *BS&N Vol. I.*) The special 42-day, three-month and six-month celebrations for a child, a young woman's first menstruation, tooth filing, and marriage all require elaborate ceremonies. And, of course, there are the many ceremonies concerning death, burial, cremation, and sending the spirit to heaven. Each member of the family has a job to do during these rituals. The women of the family contribute their time and skills not only to rites performed for their own children, but also to all of these ceremonies held for families of close relatives, friends and neighbors, which may be many. The husband is obligated to help with the heavier work that is always involved with a major ceremony. There are poles to erect for holding shades for the work area and coconut leaf mats to weave for the roof. A special temporary structure must be built if a Brahmana priest, *pedanda,* will lead a ceremony. Bamboo poles are required for *penjors* and for the construction of temporary shrines. All sorts of equipment, food, spices, articles of clothing, chairs for guests, kitchen utensils, public address system, and so forth must be obtained or contracted. Transportation must be arranged for a *pemangku* or *pedanda* if a religious man is needed, and they must be provided with refreshments. And all of those who work at a ceremony must be fed meals and more or less continuously provided with a supply coffee, tea, cakes, and cigarettes.

Large ceremonies mean that feasts must be prepared, and in our area that means the preparation of *ebat,* a complex dish of spiced turtle meat. The *banjar* members spend the evening before the feast cutting spices. After a few hours' sleep, the men report for work at about 1:00 in the morning to cook, chop, slice, squeeze, stir, make *saté*—and eat—until well past dawn. Events requiring this *mebat* occur at irregular intervals, but seldom a week goes by that there is not one of them at which the men in our house compound must help.

Each of the very largest ceremonies in our village requires what is locally called a *mapinton,* kind of a ritual pilgrimage. The word is used differently in different areas of Bali, but in Jimbaran it refers to a trip to some rather distant temples to obtain holy water. Sometimes this is preceded by a similar, but less elaborate, trip that announces the forthcoming ceremonies. The major *mapintons* of our village may involve several hundred people, all of whom pile into buses or trucks rented for the occasion, on expeditions to such far off temples as Besakih, Pura Lempuyang near Karangasem, and Pura Perancak near Negara. Lunches are packed, and a picnic atmosphere combines with the religious purposes of the trip. Villagers are expected to go along if this is possible, and many do.

The death of any member of a *banjar* makes it obligatory for all male members of the *banjar* to show up immediately, spend every night at the house of the deceased, prepare various temporary structures for the death ceremonies and burial, wash the body, carry it to the cemetery, and help with the burial. The wife is expected to visit the family, bring them gifts and, in some cases, help with the preparation of offerings. *Banjars* often have *gotong royong,* or work gangs. These might be called to repair the *bale banjar,* clean the streets, build a road, or plant trees. Usually one *banjar* is assigned to each temple at each *odalan,* and the entire *banjar* must turn out to help prepare all of the details of the ceremony.

THE LIFE OF THE FAMILY IS ABSOLUTELY INTERTWINED with the life of the village. There is almost no "typical" day, as described earlier. Surely more than a quarter of a man or a woman's waking hours are involved with preparation for a ceremony of one sort or another or in fulfilling *banjar* obligations. Regular employment—particularly by a man—can cause real problems for this societal web. These kinds of obligations are generally unscheduled. And a man who cannot participate, even because of a formal job, faces serious consequences. The social structures of Balinese families and villages are rigid. It is absolutely essential that obligations are reciprocated; it doesn't matter if there are ten times as many workers to do a job of this sort as are actually needed. It is not really a practical matter, it is a symbolic demonstration of community. To violate this unwritten law is to open up oneself to harsh criticism, divine wrath, and being cut off from the village society. Thus the hotel employee who has to be on the job from 8:00 A.M. to 4:00 P.M.—or be fired—is in a real bind. Balinese culture is not adapted to this aspect of the industrial world.

The family is, in a sense, the smallest unit in Balinese society. Thus the social failures of one family member reflect on the rest of the family. If a daughter or son violates an important obligation, the father and mother and brother and brother's wife and children are equally guilty. No wonder the pattern of who invites whom to what takes on such a marvellous complexity. Budi sometimes gets an invitation to a wedding reception in one or another village quite distant from Jimbaran. When I ask why, he says that this particular person was invited to his own wedding, and, therefore, is obligated to invite Budi to his wedding. There were several hundred guests at Budi's wedding. And I have no idea how he or anyone else can remember who was invited. But remember they do, even though it is not computerized. Why should Budi have to *mebat* for family *x* and not for family *y*? Well, family *x* is "part of our family," and family *y* is not. But family *x* is not really part of the family, there are not even any remote cousins in it. Perhaps there is some legend that connects the two, but nobody can remember it. All they remember is the obligation, and it is honored.

Every family usually has some sort of relationship with a family of higher caste, usually Brahmanas. Most families have a special *pedanda* whom they call for the most important ceremonies. These relationships usually extend back quite far in both the villager's, and the Brahmana's, lineages. In our area, these *pedandas* were assigned decades ago by the raja of Pemecutan, in Denpasar. These higher caste people are called upon to help with the most important offerings for really big ceremonies, such as cremations or the dedication of temples. They may be asked to officiate at cremations, or to make special offerings that are buried below a new shrine or building when it is dedicated. The higher caste family is said to be the *surya,* literally "sun," and the dependent, low caste family is the *sisya,* or "pupil." When a village family requires the services of its *surya,* the family sends a group to request the favor. Gifts and offerings are brought, holy water is obtained at the *merajan,* or family temple, of the higher caste family, everyone prays, and a formal request is made. After the help has been rendered, the *sisya* family makes another obligatory trip back to the high caste family to thank them for the work and to deliver still more presents and offerings.

Conversations with higher caste people always involve the use of as high a level of Balinese as can be managed. (See CHAPTER 10.) Since this is a level of speech that is seldom used, there are generally just a few in the family who are fluent enough for the job. Thus, although several carloads of family members may go to the *surya,* the actual conversation is usually limited to two or three. The others sit, smile, and listen. Sudras must be very deferential to Brahmanas. They must sit at a lower level, and never, ever do such a thing as bend over a person of higher caste. In addition to using Medium or High Balinese, the low caste speaker traditionally grasps his right fist, thumb extended, in the cup of his left hand and rocks back and forth as he speaks. Any gesture must be made by extending the right arm, thumb extended and fingers curled over, while, at the same time holding the right elbow in the left hand.

Within the family, one does not observe the same sort of extreme deference that is paid to those of higher castes, but strict rules govern patterns of behavior and language. Mother and father must always be called Meme and Bapa by their children. Their real names must never be mentioned by younger people, who probably do not know their names anyway because they have never heard them. Outsiders must refer to adults within the family by use of such words as Pan *x*, Men *y*, Kak *z*, meaning "father of *x*," "mother of *y*," "grandfather of *z*." The family with which I live uses the word Guru instead of Pan. Uncles and Aunts are generally called Wa, and aunts are sometimes called Wa Luh, *luh* meaning "female." Use of the actual names of any of these people is considered not only rude, but *pramada*, insubordinate. Adults call other adults by their birth order names: Wayan, Made, Nyoman, and Ketut; respectively, first-, second-, third-, and fourth-born. Adults of approximately equal status within the family often do use their peer's real names or, preferably, abbreviations of them. When the Balinese abbreviate a word they drop the first, rather than the last part. For example, the birth order names Wayan, Made, Nyoman, and Ketut become "Yan," "De," "Man," and "Tut." And although I call Budiasa "Budi," according to the Western custom, everyone else calls him "Asa" or "Yasa." His son Aris is always called "Is."

Within the house compound family members speak only Balinese, never Indonesian. And usually it is a very low form of the language, with the same abbreviations, slang, combinations and omissions that people who know each other well use everywhere. This speech bears the same relationship to textbook Balinese as a New York taxi driver's talk does to textbook English. Conversations with close friends and other villagers who are less well known but still familiar are conducted at the same level. Strangers are automatically addressed in Medium Balinese. Government officials often use Indonesian. Indonesian is the language of the schools and most public meetings. It is learned by the Balinese, and generally rather well. But one never hears it spoken among Balinese in an informal situation.

Fine distinctions must be made in the choice of the correct words for "you" and "I" within the family. Mother and father almost always use the third person singular Meme or Bapa, or Me and Pak, in referring to themselves when speaking with their children. Young people refer to themselves as Tiang, I, when addressing their elders. Younger people refer to older brothers and sisters as, respectively, Beli and Mbok. These same words are often used by outsiders when referring to an older person, even if the two are not related. And older siblings refer to younger siblings as Adi. Husband and wife almost never use the word "I" when speaking in private. It is extremely difficult for Balinese to pick the correct word for "you." There are plenty of words to chose from, covering a whole range of statuses, from dog to *pedanda*. The fear is that the speaker will pick one that is too low, and insult the subject, or too high, and flatter the subject excessively. The usual choice is simply to use his name or title. Thus, "I will give you a book" becomes "I will give Nyoman a book." Or, if I am your father, I might say "Pak will give Nyoman a book."

Conversations with friends and guests are quite interesting. There is always a kind of game that is initiated by the host. He deprecates the refreshments that he serves and apologizes for his poor and shoddy home and his inability to entertain his guest in the proper manner. The guest, on the other hand, praises the food and the house extravagantly, exaggerating its virtues and denying the apologies of the host. Everyone knows that it is a game and that nobody means what he says. But the charade is always played out to its well-known end. There is a kind of standard repertoire of cliches that guest and host use and little jokes that each uses to parry the thrusts of the other.

ALTHOUGH FAMILY PLANNING IS ACTIVELY PROMOTED by the Indonesian government, it is difficult to curb the general Balinese appetite for children and the joy that they bring to parents. A childless family is a disaster. Sometimes children from other families are adopted. If a woman cannot bear children, a man may take another wife who can. Babies are terribly spoiled. They are almost never out of contact with adults, since playpens are not in common use. If the mother cannot carry her baby for a moment, an older sibling does. Babies are vulnerable to a great many magical influences. Their weak defenses are bolstered by protective offerings and by their wearing around the neck a small metal box containing the remnants of the umbilical cord. In spite of the hot, humid climate, babies are wrapped up from head to toe in coverings and kept that way for quite a considerable time after birth. The idea is to prevent the malady universally known by its Indonesian name *masuk angin*, meaning "wind enters," a chill and fever. Old fashioned mothers feed their children by chewing up some of the food that the adults eat and then giving it to the baby. Modern parents use baby food purchased in the store. Babies are always breast fed, as long as that is possible.

The government birth control program is generally referred to as KB, standing for *Keluarga Berencana*, "Family Planning." The central government office for this organization is Badan Koordinasi Keluarga Berencana Nasional or BKKBN. Government employees are encouraged to limit family size because, although the monthly rice ration for female employees is increased for each additional child that she bears, this increase ceases after the third child. Family planning is encouraged through the village clinics and through the *banjars*. In some area KB meetings are held weekly, and the *banjar* keeps a list of all families within the jurisdiction of the *banjar*, with an indication of what sort of birth control measures the family employs.

Babies are never allowed to crawl around on the ground "like animals." At the first *oton* of the baby, when it is 210 days old, the child is allowed to touch the ground for the first time. In some villages this is done at a later date. From then on, the child is encouraged to walk. And, as soon as it can, it has pretty much the free run of the house compound, under the guidance of its older siblings. I can't think of a better place for a child to grow up. From walking age to the beginning of school, the child is under few restrictions. There are no schedules. Children eat when they are hungry and run around naked practically all the time. There is always a sibling or a playmate to play with or fight, and the house compound is full of aunts, uncles, cousins, and grandparents, who are always on hand to act as substitute parents if needed.

Some parents shave the head of the child, except for a long forelock, thinking that this will make the hair more beautiful when it grows out. In a tropical climate a baby's skin is a target for insects of every variety as well as a fungus growth that results in white splotches. Most children have legs and arms that are covered with bumps and scars from inflamed mosquito bites. Heat rash and irritation from clothes is a constant threat. There are a great many traditional medicines for preventing and curing these problems, and one often sees a child smeared from heat to toe with some sort of lotion made by boiling various leaves or bark or roots.

There are very few kindergartens in Bali. Almost all children are sent to elementary school, called *sekolah dasar,* or simply "SD." There is an SD within walking distance of most homes. In most of them children are required to wear uniforms—often with white shirts or blouses. Instruction necessarily begins in Balinese, since these children have never spoken Indonesian. But the study of Indonesian is begun at once and, as soon as practicable, Balinese is no longer used. The usual subjects are taught in SD—a rather broader range of them than in comparable schools in the West, with more emphasis upon segmentation of the curriculum than integration. In SD students are introduced to traditional Balinese script, Tulisan Bali. The next level, junior high school, is *sekolah menengah pertama,* or "SMP." Then high school, *sekolah menengah atas,* "SMA." Here sports are encouraged, as are arts and crafts. Children are compelled to study English in school, but few can speak it when they graduate because the emphasis is almost entirely on grammar. A child commonly has ten or more different subjects in high school. Classes are short, and the school day is over in four hours or less. Instruction at all levels emphasizes memorization by rote. Multiple choice tests are still very common in spite of attempts by the Department of Education and Culture to discontinue their use.

BEHAVIOR BETWEEN THE SEXES is very strongly controlled by the force of public opinion. Children grow up in a closely packed environment where it is impossible to conceal the facts of sex and the Balinese are certainly not prudes. Bawdy jokes are enthusiastically told by young and old. Sexual conduct is a favorite topic of *warung* conversations. Women in some villages go around without blouses much of the time when they are at home. Yet adults always conceal their sexual organs with the left hand when bathing in public places, as for example on the beach. Clothes that have come into contact with sexual organs are impure. Menstrual blood renders a woman ceremonially unclean for a period of time. And any sort of physical contact between teenage boys and girls is strictly taboo. One never sees boys and girls holding hands or embracing in public.

Families often place marriageable daughters in *warungs* where they can observe the field and be observed by others as they wait on customers. And *warungs* are popular gathering places for teenagers, because members of the opposite sex can exchange banter under a controlled environment and not be subject to criticism. The Saturday night movie is attended by large crowds of adolescents. But most of them stand in the street in front of the movie theater and chat, without going inside. And there are always clumps of boys and separate clumps of girls. No mixing. I have not snooped around to see what happens after the movie when the street lights go out.

There are three ways in which a young couple can get married. The most common is called *mamaling* or *nyogotin*, "eloping." The boy and girl are in love with each other, supposedly without the family of the girl knowing about it, and decide to get married. At an appointed time they go off together to spend the night at some friend's house. After this the girl cannot retreat. Once she is known publicly to have spent the night with a man (although this is normally not the first time), she cannot return to her own home and take up her old ways—marriage is mandatory. There is a small ceremony conducted by a local *pemangku* and then a traditional wedding ceremony sponsored by the boy's family. The girl's family is not invited, since they are supposed to be mad at the boy and his family for stealing their daughter. In most cases they know full well what was up, but they pretend not to. A few days later the boy's family visits that of the girl, and placates them with presents and offerings, in a ceremony called *ketipat bantal*. After this, everyone lives in harmony again.

The alternative to this is *mamadik,* a marriage in which the boy's and girl's families are notified in advance of the intentions of the couple and to which each agrees. The reason that this sort of marriage is not as popular as *nyogotin* is that it is quite expensive. There are usually elaborate ceremonies first in the girl's family house and then in that of the boy. Many offerings have to be purchased and made; many guests have to be transported and fed; decorations have to be put up. And all this is required if the announcement is made ahead of time. So eloping, although it may be well known to both sides, is much simpler—and cheaper. Actual kidnap-ing, *malegandang*, is against the law and quite uncommon. Outsiders sometimes refer to elopement as kidnaping, but it is not. It is really more or less of a charade, the purpose of which is to save money and effort for both sides.

The wedding ceremony itself is a traditional and formal affair, the elab-orateness of which depends upon the financial resources of the family. At its most complex, it is long and full of the symbolism of purification and sexual union. There is so much variation from place to place that it would be useless to offer a description here. In my village there is always a recep-tion held after the actual wedding. In contrast to the wedding itself, guests at the reception wear "western" clothes, and there are no religious ceremonies involved. I have been to a great many of these. They are held in the evening, the house compound is nicely decorated, and there is either a live *gong* or a cassette player furnishing Balinese music. One must always bring a present. But the code is such that the recipients must not ever open the present in front of the donor. This is because it might be publicly embarrassing to the donor for the recipient to see what a cheap or humble gift he has been given. A set of drinking glasses or coffee cups or a cheap *kamben* are standard gifts. The guest signs a book at the door and is given a white cardboard box that contains *jaja*, a little bag of peanuts, and a banana. He is handed a bottle of warm *teh botol* (bottled tea) and ushered to his seat on a rented chair. The seats are usually tightly packed in rows, preventing anyone except those on the outside from mov-ing around. Often the unmarried men sit on one side and the women on the other. The father of the groom then gives a long speech, welcoming the guests and honoring the married couple. It is always given in Indonesian and may be followed by similar speeches by uncles or other interested family members. Then a buffet dinner of Indonesian-Chinese food is served. This is eaten at one's previous seat. Then everybody goes home. There is very little chance for conversation with others because the chairs are packed so tightly.

When the woman comes to live with the man she gives up her union with her own family temple and deified ancestors and assumes those of the man. She may return to her own house compound for the *odalan* of her father's *sanggah*, but her primary job now is to look after the temple of her husband. Married couples frequently visit the parents of the wife, who take just as much pleasure with their grandchildren as do the pater-nal grandparents. If the woman is from a different *banjar* than her hus-band, she now identifies with the new one. The husband now joins his father's *banjar* as a full fledged *adat* member. The wife is invited to join the PKK, the women's auxiliary of the *banjar*.

Divorce is not common. Childless wives or those with whom a man cannot get along are sometimes simply abandoned, and in that case they may either move back to their parents' house compound or continue to live as before, while the husband goes off to live with another wife. It is very rare for a man to live in the house compound of his wife. But it does happen in a few cases. This is often a result of his own house compound being so crowded that there is no room for a new residence to be built.

BALINESE FAMILIES ALSO FACE some of the same difficulties as families everywhere. Finances are a perpetual problem. Sellers need capital to buy stocks of goods. Farmers must buy seed and fertilizer. Fishermen must buy boats and nets and paint. Many villages have small banks that lend money. But the paper work involved is often so complex and time-consuming that villagers may prefer to borrow from unofficial money lenders in the village. These people will lend small amounts of money to those whom they know to be reliable, without any formal contracts or paper work. Interest rates are high, however. In a typical situation someone might borrow Rp 25,000. He must give the lender collateral, such as a ring or other piece of jewelry. In other words, it is like a pawn shop. The borrower must then pay Rp 500 every day for 60 days. And the lender must go around to the homes of all of his customers every day to collect the money due. At the end of the 60 days he will have been paid back Rp 30,000, the principal plus Rp 5,000 interest. This interest rate is equivalent to a usurious 120 percent a year.

Illness also strikes. Almost every village has a clinic, *puskesmas,* staffed by a kind of nurse who has had some practical training in every aspect of medicine from midwifery to first aid. But many people prefer to go to a doctor for treatment. Doctors' offices usually open at about 4:00 or 5:00 P.M. Most people from our village go to doctors in Denpasar, a half hour's drive by car—longer by *bemo.* Upon arrival at the doctor's office there are usually a dozen to several dozen people ahead of you, waiting patiently in the small room. There is no such thing as an appointment. The patient is issued a number by the single attendant, and simply waits his turn. The actual contact between doctor and patient takes no more than a few minutes. The fee is Rp 6,000, and the result, more often than not, is a series of at least two, and perhaps quite a few more, prescriptions. These must be taken to a pharmacy that is full of others who have just come from their doctors. The experience is a lot like clinics in the West.

Balians, traditional healers, are also a familiar part of family life. In our village *balians* are consulted for a variety of purposes, not the least of which is to determine auspicious days for various activities and to officiate at the various rites of passage, for children as well as adults. They are also healers, prescribing various pharmacologically and superstitiously potent herbal remedies, as well as a strong dose of common sense and human psychology. Such a visit is a family affair, and takes place in more familiar and comforting surroundings than the Denpasar clinic or doctor's office.

THE WESTERNER IS SOON IMPRESSED with the fact that life in a Balinese family is controlled by an unwritten law that involves severe constraints upon behavior. Modern Westerners like to think of themselves as "liberated"—free from the traditional limitations of age and sex. It is not that way in a Balinese family. People cannot behave as rugged individualists if they live in closely packed family groups where everybody is within earshot of everyone else all day long—and all night. People cannot think independently if they are almost totally dependent upon the support of others for most of their activities. Men in Balinese villages do not work for large, faceless corporations in tall office buildings where the job and the family are two totally unrelated occupations. Everything everyone does is seen and noticed by everyone else. And if what one does is not acceptable, people will talk. And that starts the erosion of reputation. Reputation is of inestimable value to a Balinese, and he will go to great extremes to protect and enlarge it. He must hide his feelings and not indulge in outbursts of temper. He must show up to help those whom he detests if the code dictates that he should. He must stop whatever he is doing and assist where his presence is required, no matter how busy he is, no matter how much he would prefer not to do so, and in spite of the fact that he knows that there will be several times as many people such as he available to do whatever work is required. He must show his family's flag—always protecting his own position for the day when he and his family need the help that only his fellow villagers can provide.

CHAPTER 6

The Banjar

SOCIAL HUB OF VILLAGE LIFE

THE SOCIAL GEOGRAPHY OF BALI is tightly knit, and highly collectivized. The island's long dry season has brought about a very elaborate system of collective harvests and shared irrigation systems. The demands of Balinese Hinduism force the staging of large celebrations and ceremonies lasting days, and requiring the participation of hundreds, maybe thousands of people. Bali is not a place where each seeks his own—it is a place that requires collective participation in almost every aspect of political, social, economic, and religious life.

The extended family itself acts like a social organization, but beyond that the most immediate and intimate organization for every Balinese is the *banjar*. The *banjar* is a neighborhood organization, an aggregate of member families that plans, organizes, and executes the great majority of activities that make up Balinese life. The family has particular responsibilities, the *subak* rice collective takes care of most irrigation and farming tasks, and the regional Indonesian government provides the usual services. But the *banjar* looks after everything else.

The function and structure of the *banjar* has few analogs in the West, although the Balinese *banjar* is similar to the volunteer social organizations that flourished in the United States up until about a century ago, the vestiges of which can be seen in organizations like the Elk's Club or the Kiwanis Club. *Banjars* have the equivalent of women's auxiliaries, youth groups, and meeting halls. But they are infinitely more important, and more deeply integrated into Balinese life than, for example, The Odd Fellows are into life in the United States today.

Even the word "*banjar*" has a long history in Bali, the oldest extant record of its use dating from A.D. 914. There is abundant information about the functions of *banjars* from the period of the rajas in Bali. Until rather recently, inter-village communication was difficult, and primitive. To cross the steep mountains and deep gorges to the next village was a major undertaking. Communities were isolated, and a large majority of the social contacts of the people were with those who lived close by. Even today, Balinese villages, especially rural ones, are quite self-contained, and villagers often have minimal contact with outsiders. The village, until perhaps even this century, was the world—and although the raja was the ceremonial head of government, the *banjar* was what we today might call the infrastructure.

So *banjars* developed as organizations of neighbors who engaged in group projects for the welfare of the community, worshipped in the same temples, and sought social contacts in each other's company. Even today, among families who have spent several generations in an urban setting away from the rice fields, the *banjar* still plays an important role.

In most Balinese villages all married males are required to join a *banjar*. The wives and children of these members are considered to belong to the *banjar* too, but only the male heads of families go to regular meetings, and it is they who make the decisions. Sizes of *banjars* vary considerably. Some urban *banjars* in Denpasar have 400 to 500 heads of families, called *kepala keluarga*, often abbreviated KK. Rural *banjars* have as few as 50. One hundred is about average. Considering an average family of a husband, wife, and three or four children, the typical *banjar* has about 500–600 people in it. Theoretically, if the membership gets too large, the group should split in two, creating a new *banjar*. In practice, since this involves considerable expense and the breakup of long established customs—family membership in a particular *banjar* often goes back many generations—this does not often happen. In some villages the membership of some *banjars* has grown so large that they no longer accept new members. They fill their waiting list only when members die.

The *banjar* has religious and cultural functions, but it is also the most accessible government unit. The leaders of the *banjar* are in communication with the civil head of government, the local village head, *kepala desa*, or *lurah*, a kind of mayor. (See CHAPTER 7.)

But there is another kind of "government" in Bali, the *desa adat*. *Adat* means "customary" or "traditional," and it is usually associated with the practice of Balinese Hinduism. Each *desa adat* has a set of traditional or customary laws, the *awig awig*, that dictate the religious operation of the village. *Adat* law deals with matters with which *dinas* law is not concerned, and vice versa. Members of a *desa adat* are usually bound together by the fact that all worship at the same group of village temples. The appointed head of the *desa adat* is known as the *kelian* (or *klian*) *adat*, or, in some villages, *bendesa*. The geographic boundaries of the *desa adat* may or may not coincide exactly with the *desa dinas*, although they always overlap to some extent. A *kelurahan* may include one or more *banjars*. But the *banjar* is more than just a secular organization, because it reflects the *desa adat* as well.

The elected administrative or secular head of a *banjar* is most commonly known as the *kelian dinas*, often simply the *kelian* (or *klian*). Some *banjars* reserve a special term for their *kelian adat* entity, calling him the *kelian suka duka*—*suka* means "happiness," and *duka* means "grief." This is a shorthand to describe the customary and religious duties of the *banjar suka duka*, including weddings and other rites of passage, and deaths. In many areas he is simply called the *kelian adat* of the *banjar* (which should not be confused with the *kelian adat* of the entire local desa or *kelurahan*, who oversees the religious or customary activities of all the *banjars* in his district.)

I live in the *desa dinas* of Jimbaran. The *desa adat* of Jimbaran coincides exactly with the *desa dinas* because everyone in the area worships at the same group of temples. Jimbaran, with a population of about 11,000, is also a *kelurahan* and is under the jurisdiction of a *lurah*. There are 10 *banjars* in Jimbaran, the smallest of which has a membership of 86 KK, and the largest of which has 269 KK. The *kelurahan* of Kuta has three *desa adat*, Kuta, Seminyak, and Legian, each having, respectively, 12, 2, and 3 *banjars*. Sanur includes 3 *kelurahan*, with a total of 24 *banjars*.

Every *banjar* has, or should have, an *awig awig* of its own, a set of customary laws that operate under, but that may differ slightly from, the general terms of the *awig awig* of the village *desa adat*. Since these laws are formulated largely within the constraints of Balinese Hinduism, it would be impossible for one who is not a Hindu to follow them. That being the case, non-Hindu members of regular *banjars* are registered as *dinas* members, whereas those who practice Hinduism are *adat* members.

Many villages require one who comes to settle, even temporarily, to register very soon with the *kelian dinas* of the area *banjar*. This enables his presence to be made known to the local government, because the *kelian dinas* transmits the information to the *lurah* or *kepala desa*. It also gives the *dinas* member access to the office of the local government head, which is usually necessary to make applications for work, government benefits, voter registration, and the like. A *dinas* member is expected to pay a monthly fee to his *kelian*, on the theory that his village government benefits him, but he is not required to attend regular *banjar* meetings or to participate in group work projects. The monthly fee varies from place to place but is commonly about Rp 2,500 per month. Although he must set up such local *dinas* ties, it is not unusual for a man who has permanently moved to another part of Bali to maintain close *adat* ties with his home *banjar* and to remain a member of it, returning as often as he can to participate in *banjar* activities.

As soon as a man marries he is expected to make formal application to join his *banjar*—almost always that of his father—as an *adat* member. Depending upon local rules, the applicant may or may not have to pay a fee to join. In some areas only the eldest son joins the *banjar*. If this is the case, the new member, in effect, replaces his father as the family member primarily responsible for *banjar* work. In most places all married males join. The prospective member makes his application at the regular monthly *banjar* meeting. If he is of good character—he is almost always quite well known to all the members—he is accepted, after treating the membership to rice cakes, cigarettes, and a bit of *arak* rice brandy, all accompanied by an offering especially made for the occasion. Thereafter his life is not the same, because he has now gained a set of duties and responsibilities that will occupy a great deal of his adult life.

The fee for becoming a member varies considerably from *banjar* to *banjar*. In some areas there is no fee at all for the eldest son, whether or not he replaces his father. In *banjars* that have accumulated considerable debt as a result of ambitious building programs, the fee may be as high as Rp 150,000. In most *banjars* it is somewhere around Rp 10,000.

The *kelian banjar* meets regularly with the *lurah* or *kepala desa*, sometimes daily. He must be available at all times, since the members of his *banjar* need his signature on almost all documents of an official nature. He is often active in the transfer of the land of his members, who depend upon his experience (and pay for it) when they buy or sell land in the area. In this case he acts as an agent for his members. It is hard work, and the pay is minimal—about Rp 30,000 per month in the Jimbaran area—and it is difficult to convince a qualified person to take the job.

The *kelian suka duka* generally receives no pay from the village, but he too has to be available to those who need advice and help on *adat* matters. His most common area of service is in helping settle domestic problems. People come to him at all hours of day and night to intervene in various family crises.

IN THE JIMBARAN AREA, the *banjars* meet once every 35 days—one Pawukon calendar "month." Members are obligated to attend, and some *banjars* levy fines for those who do not. Meetings usually begin early in the morning, and dress is always *adat*, never Western. Discussions are held in the polite level of the Balinese language rather than in Indonesian, the usual medium of communication in *dinas* matters. Members sit on the floor of the *bale banjar*, the pavilion that serves as the organization's meeting hall, facing the *kelians* and the other elected officials.

There are not many of the latter. But each *banjar* has several, often many, *kasinoman*, messengers who remind the members of regular meetings and inform them of forthcoming work parties and of deaths among the membership, which require immediate attendance. A *kasinoman* goes door to door, letting the members know what's up. In the more spread out *banjars* there is normally one *kasinoman* for every 10 KK. A *banjar* may or may not have a secretary and a treasurer, *sekretaris* and *bendahara*. There is often a man called a *juru baos*, or *penyarikan*, who gives individual advice and attention to members with particular projects or problems. If the *banjar* covers a large geographical area there may be assistant *kelians* in charge of the several divisions.

The *kelians* of the *banjars* within a *kelurahan* or *desa* meet regularly with the *lurah* or *perbekel*. The government official relays to them information from the central or provincial or district government and, at the next meeting, the *kelians dinas* pass the matter on to their memberships. Sometimes this information covers matters of government policy such as birth control. Some *banjars* have regular monthly meetings at which birth control (called KB, or *keluarga berencana*) is the only topic of discussion. Some *banjars* even keep track of what birth control measures their members employ. Financial matters are other central issues. Meeting pavilions have to be built or repaired, and debts paid off. Some *banjars* require their members to contribute considerable sums of money to defray the costs of new buildings. New members who join must pay their share of recently completed projects. Ad hoc committees may be set up for such things as buildings, forthcoming ceremonies, or village problems.

Money is often a problem for *banjars* that have no income other than membership dues. But others are flush with money from such activities as owning a *barong* or a group of musical instruments and dance costumes that bring in money from tourist performances. Some *banjars* that have large *bales* rent parts of their buildings to shopkeepers and other tenants. Still others own land and generate income from their harvests, often by sharecropping.

Banjar members are often called upon to perform manual labor for the village in a cooperative work project, or *gotong royong*. This may be cleaning up a street, planting trees, building a road, decorating a temple for a forthcoming festival, or building a school. *Gotong royong* does not usually involve farming. The control of irrigated rice fields is handled by the *subak* irrigation collectives. In some areas, however, the *banjar* may oversee the harvest. Attendance at *gotong royong* is usually obligatory, and some *banjars* fine members for not coming, unless a suitable excuse can be provided. In many areas it is proper for someone pay another person to do his work, if he cannot go himself. Or, in some instances, *banjars* allow a member to send a younger brother who is not yet an *adat* member.

Members do not usually have to be coerced into these activities. Balinese villages are very tight organizations. People depend upon each other a great deal for help. In a small town, one's absence is quickly noted. And next time you require help from others, it may not be forthcoming if you have not been generous with your own time. There are usually two or three times as many people in a work group as are required

BALE BANJAR

for the work to be done. One is not really needed. No matter. One must
be seen participating. Good reputations are important when people live
shoulder to shoulder.

All *banjars* have a meeting hall, the *bale banjar,* almost always a large,
open structure with a raised concrete floor, and a roof supported by
pillars. Some are large and fancy, decorated with carved stone, and with a
stage for performances. Others are modest, but functional. *Bale banjars*
are social centers for Ping-pong, TV-watching, playing with fighting cocks,
or just chatting and resting. A *bale banjar* is like a clubhouse, and people
can be seen loitering in the shade there at almost any time of the day.

Some *banjars* use their *bale* to conduct regular classes in reading and
writing. Some have credit unions, whereby members may borrow small
sums of money quickly, without the complex formalities of applying for a
bank loan. The *bale* normally has a kitchen, where the food is cooked for
large feasts. There may be a storage room for dance costumes or musical
instruments.

In a tower on the *bale,* or in a separate *bale,* is the *kulkul,* the signal
drum used to summon members. Various cadences and rhythms, called
tabuh, are beaten out on the drum to notify members of a variety of
events—a regular monthly meeting, an emergency summons in case of the
death of a *banjar* member, a panic signal for help in case of a robbery,
fire, or the like, and a summons to a work party. Since a village may have
many *banjars,* and hence many *kulkuls,* members soon learn to distinguish
the special sound of their own from that of the others. A *kulkul* carries
over a surprisingly large distance. The *banjar* always has a temple,
although usually it is small. It nevertheless has an *odalan,* an anniversary

celebration, just as do all other temples in Bali, and *banjar* members are expected to both help with and enjoy the ceremony.

All *banjars* have a women's group, called *pembinaan kesajahteraan keluarga*—"creation of family prosperity"—abbreviated PKK. The head of the village PKK is often the wife of the *lurah* or *kepala desa*, and the activities of the group usually depend upon her education and interests. Usually they involve family health and hygiene, birth control, raising children, making offerings, planting gardens, and adult education. Most PKK groups meet weekly. There may be one PKK for the whole village, but it is more common for there to be a separate organization for each *banjar*.

Every *banjar* also has an associated *sekehe teruna teruni* (STT) sometimes abbreviated to *sekehe teruna*, meaning "youth club." Both boys and girls belong to this group from about age 16 until they get married and become regular *adat* members themselves. The STT is often involved in raising money for the *banjar*. A popular way of doing this is to convert the *bale banjar* into a temporary restaurant, called an *amahl*, which is run and managed by the STT members. Money raised goes into the *banjar's* coffers. Most villages have at least one *amahl* going during the important Galungan holidays. The STT members decorate the pavilion, serve as cooks, waiters, waitresses, and cashiers and, in some villages, provide entertainment in the form of music and dance programs. The anniversary of each STT is often celebrated with an elaborate program featuring speeches by the village leaders and leaders of the STT, and an entertainment program of music, dance, and sometimes traditional readings from the sacred Balinese texts.

Although these civic functions of the *banjar* are considered worthwhile, to many members the *adat* functions of the organization are the most important. When a man becomes an *adat* member of a *banjar* he assumes a considerable burden of responsibilities toward his fellow members. At the same time, as a member he is entitled to rights of at least equal proportions, since his fellow members are now obligated to help him in time of need. The *banjar* organization assumes great responsibility and support for its members, looking out for them through all life's crises—to the day they are buried and their spirits consigned to heaven.

Such help may take the form of assisting the family of a *banjar* member when it undertakes a large and important religious ceremony. In some *banjars* members must be on call to help others thatch the roof of a building or move a house, or harvest a rice crop. But the function of *adat* members that is most emphatically stressed is to provide help and companionship to a member's family in which death has occurred.

A DEATH REQUIRES A GREAT DEAL OF CONSOLATION, a great deal of special knowledge, a great deal of time, and a great deal of physical work—far beyond the capacities of even the largest family group. This is when the *banjar* provides its greatest service. When a death is reported to the *kelian dinas* he beats out a special rhythm on the *kulkul,* and all members within audible range stop whatever they are doing and come to the house compound of the deceased. The *kasinomans* quickly spread the word, and it is not long before practically the entire male membership of the *banjar* is on hand. This duty is one of the most widely observed among *banjar* members. Few let any personal activities interfere.

There is a lot of work to be done. In our *banjar* every member must contribute Rp 100 on the spot, called *patus,* from the word for 100. This money is used to purchase the burial cloth and other necessary objects. Offerings must be prepared—often a great many costly ones. Many villages have teams of offering specialists who do nothing but prepare sets of offerings for various occasions, from house dedications to cremations. Likely as not such a team will be called upon to provide the proper offerings for the death ceremonies, called *kematian.* The body must be properly washed and dressed for burial, a grave must be dug and fenced in a special enclosure called a *balibit.* A casket must be built. Only the highest castes cremate their deceased members without burial. The practice among most Balinese families is to inter the body until a day when the family accumulates enough money to provide a properly grand cremation.

An auspicious day is picked for the burial, and in the interim *banjar* members spend the night at the house compound of the deceased, comforting family members and seeing to it that the work is properly done. This vigil is called *ngebag.* In our area upon such occasions it is traditional for the men to spend the small hours of the morning gambling. Wives of *banjar* members usually visit and bring a present of cooked rice or cloth. This visitation is called *madelokan.* They must be served coffee and rice cakes, and that requires a group of women to do the cooking.

On the day of the burial the body is taken from the coffin where it has been preserved with ice and is laid out on a bamboo platform. *Banjar* members present offerings and thoroughly wash the body with soap and water. There is usually a great crowding around the body, as each member tries to do his share of work for his former fellow member. This ritual is called *nusiang.* If there are wounds or sores, they are covered with tamarind paste so they will be healed when the person is reincarnated. Small pieces of steel are put over the teeth; a crescent-shaped leaf from the *intaran* tree is placed over each eyebrow; and a little mirror is placed over each eye so that the deceased will be strong, attractive, and have clear sight in the next life. A flower is placed in each ear to make sure that the sounds next heard will be beautiful. And the list of rites goes on.

Finally the body is dressed in new, traditional clothes, splashed with holy water, anointed with flowers, and carried to the cemetery by members of the *banjar.* The grave has already been dug. The body is placed within and covered up, and a large number of offerings are placed near the grave, where prayers are led by one of the older members of the family. Only after all of this has been completed are the *banjar* members free to go home. In our village this ceremony usually ends just before dark.

People have been working all day long, and, more often than not, for two or three days, 24-hours-a-day. Why such a compulsion to help at the time of death? Simply because a *banjar* member knows that, some day, his turn and that of his family members will come. And he wants to make sure that when that day arrives, his own spirit will have the proper send-off. He knows his own family will have to depend upon the help of others. Those he joins today to wash and decorate the corpse of a *banjar* member and to help dispatch its spirit to heaven will one day wash his own corpse and those of his wife and children and send them on their ways. Under these circumstances, one is likely to spare nothing to cooperate to the fullest extent with *adat* law.

The time of a death is not, by any means, the only period during which *banjar* members contribute their time and effort to their fellow members. Every Balinese must undergo a series of rites-of-passage ceremonies celebrating the various steps along the road to birth, infancy, adolescence, maturity, and marriage. These are not just celebrations, in the sense of commemorations. They are also preparations for the next stage of life, and require the purifications, prayers, offerings, and lots of work. One who has not been behind the scenes for even a rather modest ceremony cannot appreciate the enormous amount of detailed work and planning. Most extended family groups can handle these chores by themselves. But if not, *banjar* members are quick to respond to a call for help, knowing full well that, when their own ceremonies are underway, they can benefit from the help of those whom they help now.

Ceremonies always involve feasts. And feasts in Jimbaran mean *ebat*, a complicated dish that requires a day's work by dozens of people just to prepare. The minimum number of individual servings is usually around 100, and there may be three or four times as many required, depending upon the occasion. Obviously such an undertaking requires the work of a large group. And this is not a rare event. In a *banjar* of 100 KK there is quite likely to be some occasion when help is required almost every week. As indicated previously, the obligations of *banjar* membership are time-consuming and tiring. But they are also fun for the members, offering plenty of time for gossip and plenty of food, cigarettes, and *arak* brandy. Now that's the kind of obligation nobody in his right mind would refuse.

CHAPTER 7

Political Organization

STATE, PROPINSI, AND VILLAGE

BALI IS A PROVINCE OF THE REPUBLIC OF INDONESIA, something like a state of the United States. But unlike a U.S. state, Bali—and Indonesia's other *propinsi*—has no laws, courts, and political jurisdiction independent of the central government in Jakarta. Indonesia has a strong central government, and provincial laws, organizations, and structures are both derived from their national counterparts, and uniform throughout the republic.

The sovereignty of the government of Indonesia is formally vested in the people and exercised by the elected People's Consultative Assembly, the Majelis Permusyawaratan Rakyat. The MPR is the highest political institution in the country and every five years elects a president, who acts under a mandate from, and is answerable to the MPR. The assembly has 1,000 members, half of whom are, concurrently, members of the House of Representatives, the Dewan Perwakilan Rakyat. The other half are appointed in proportion to the results of the general election for the DPR.

The DPR is the republic's lawmaking body and meets regularly. Of the 500 seated representatives, 100 are appointed military officers and 400 are elected in a general election that takes place every five years.

The President of Indonesia appoints a cabinet of 21 ministers, each of whom heads a department, as well as coordinating ministers, ministers of state, junior ministers; and high state functionaries. On a level of organization roughly equal to that of the President are the Supreme Court, the Supreme Advisory Council, the State Audit Board, and the above-mentioned DPR.

BALI IS JUST ONE OF 27 *propinsi* in the Republic of Indonesia, three of which are termed special territories: Greater Jakarta, Yogyakarta in

Central Java, and Aceh, in North Sumatra. Each province is headed by a governor. The larger islands consist of several provinces. In the case of the less populated islands, such as those in the Moluccas, a single province encompasses a number of islands.

The governor of a province has a dual role. He is both a representative of the central government (a responsibility delegated to him by the home affairs minister) and the chief executive of a *propinsi*. Provincial offices are called Tingkat I, or Level I offices. The governor of Bali's formal title is Gubernur Kepala Daerah Tingkat I Bali, meaning "governor and head of the Level I region of Bali." The expression Daerah Tingkat I is used so often that it is commonly abbreviated to DATI I. governors are appointed by the president for a five-year term at the home affairs minister's recommendations from a group of two or three candidates nominated by a Level I Regional Representative Council.

Each of the republic's executive departments, such as social affairs, education and culture, religion, etc., maintains a provincial department office, called a *kantor wilayah,* commonly shortened to KANWIL. The head of such an office, the *kepala* KANWIL, is normally referred to as KAPKANWIL. Most of the KANWIL offices in Bali are in the Renon-Niti Mandala area of Denpasar.

In addition to these branches of central government offices, a province has its own set of related offices called *dinas.* These offices are in a sense autonomous, and are, in fact, sometimes called *otonom* offices. A Level I *dinas* office is administered by the governor, whereas a Level I KANWIL office is directly under the control of the KAPKANWIL, who gets his orders from Jakarta.

Each province also has an analog of the republic's DPR House of Representatives, called the DPRD, Dewan Perwakilan Rakyat Daerah. The provincial houses of representatives vary in size from province to province. Bali's DPRD is the maximum allowable size, with 50 members elected every five years in the general election.

ONE LEVEL BENEATH THE PROVINCIAL GOVERNMENT lies Tingkat II. These are the *kabupaten,* or districts, something like counties in the United States. There are 246 *kabupaten* in Indonesia, each headed by an officer called a *bupati.* In Bali there are eight *kabupaten.* Table 1 on the following page shows their sizes:

At the same level as *kabupaten* are 54 *kotamadya* in Indonesia, "medium cities" or municipalities. Each is headed by a *wali kota madya* who has the same status as a *bupati.* There is no *kotamadya* in the province of Bali. District offices, in the *kabupaten* or *kota madya,* are said to be at the Tingkat II. Offices of the central government at Level II are called *kantor departemen,* each headed by a *kepala kantor departemen,* or KAPKANDEP.

Just as the governor of a province has a dual role as representative of

Table 1. *KABUPATEN* OF BALI

Kabupaten	AREA	PERCENT
1. Buleleng	1,320.80 sq. km.	23.45%
2. Tabanan	863.06	15.32
3. Karangasem	861.70	15.30
4. Jembrana	841.80	14.94
5. Badung	542.50	9.63
6. Bangli	520.00	9.23
7. Gianyar	368.00	6.54
8. Klungkung	315.00	5.59
TOTAL AREA	5,632.86	(100.00)

Table 2. *KECAMATAN* IN BADUNG *KABUPATEN*

Kecamatan	AREA
1. Denpasar Barat	50.06 sq. km.
2. Denpasar Timur	27.73
3. Denpasar Selatan	46.19
4. Kuta	152.51
5. Mengwi	82.00
6. Abiansemal (*north of Denpasar*)	69.01
7. Petang (*north of Abiasemal*)	115.00
TOTAL AREA	542.50 sq. km.

the central government and head of his own area, so do the *bupati* and *wali kota madya*. Each is a representative of the central government at Level II, Kepala Daerah Tingkat II (Kepala DATI II). And each is the head of his own district. Each has a set of *dinas* offices at level II. *Bupati* and *wali kota madya* are appointed by the minister of home affairs at the recommendation of the governor from among the candidates nominated by the local house of representatives.

The house of representatives at Level II is known as the DPRD Tingkat II. Since there are eight districts in Bali, there are eight of these legislative groups. The one in the Badung District, which covers Sanur, Denpasar, Kuta, and Nusa Dua, among other areas, consists of 45 members. This is the largest allowable. DPRD Level II assemblies can contain as few as 25 members, depending upon the district.

Lying somewhat below the level of *kota madya*, but higher than the next lower division of government are certain cities, Denpasar among them, designated as *kota administrasi*. There is no DPRD Tingkat II connected with such an administrative city. The head of the unit is called a *wali kota*, lower in status than a *bupati* or a *wali kota madya*.

EACH *kabupaten* (AND *kota madya*) is divided into sub-districts, called *kecamatans*—roughly the same as a township or a municipality in the United States—each headed by an official called a *camat*. There are 3,517 *kecamatans* in Indonesia. The *kabupaten* of Badung in Bali has seven *kecamatans*, the areas of which are listed in Table 2 on the previous page. The office of *camat* is not autonomous and has no representative council. It is just an administrative sub-division of a *kabupaten* or *kota madya*. But the *kecamatan* has considerable direct influence on village life.

Under the *camat* is a secretary who oversees the four major sections of activity of this office. Each section is called an *urusan*, and the head of each section is a *kepala urusan*, or KAUR. The four sections are:

1) Government, Urusan Pemerintahan. Sees to minor appointments, moniters the transfer of power during elections, issues identification cards, *kartu penduduk*, to all married citizens and citizens age 17 or older, records population and other vital statistics, coordinates birth control efforts, and sets the value of property needed for government projects.

2) People's welfare, Urusan Pemasyarakatan. Coordinates government-sponsored school activities, administers youth and sports activities such as Boy Scouts, coordinates religious activities, in charge of public health efforts, including the Red Cross, the tuberculosis organization, and birth control, oversees art and culture in the area, and leads a number of women's organizations.

3) Economic development, Urusan Pembangunan. Administers government money and plans physical, spiritual, and economic development projects, including encouraging small industry and setting up environmental protection programs.

4) Administration, Urusan Administrasi. Department includes the treasurer, who collects taxes and supervises the government's equipment, and the supervisory staff, which sees to promotions, vacations, and in kind payments to civil servants in the area.

Because it is often difficult for villagers to travel all the way to a distant *kantor kabupaten* in order to contact officials of the national government, the more important central government branches maintain small offices in the *kantor camat*. These usually include the Departments of Education and Culture, Social Affairs, Religion, Information, as well as representatives of the police and military. These offices are usually called *instansi otonom*.

The office of the head of the village security forces is in the *kantor camat*. This organization is popularly known as HANSIP, standing for *pertahanan sipil*, which translates as "civil defense." This is not a very apt translation, since the duty of the HANSIP is mainly to preserve law and order and keep the peace, rather than defend anything or anybody. Every village has a local HANSIP head. Members of the organization usually work as volunteers without pay. Service in HANSIP is not a full-time job for anyone. Theoretically, every citizen, ages 15 to 55 should be a member of HANSIP. And all government employees should be issued HANSIP uniforms. Actually, the organization is not very visible or strong in some villages, other than a small headquarters building, a *pos* HANSIP, which may be staffed during events that are likely to require crowd control. Some villages, Kuta and Ubud among them, have very active HANSIP groups that patrol the area 24-hours-a-day and guard shops and other places of business. Merchants gladly pay them for their services. HANSIP works with the police at all times. Its members are likely to be the first on hand in case of emergencies and notify higher authorities if help is needed. There are three branches of HANSIP at the *kecamatan* level: first aid for accidents, help in case of emergencies such as fires, and aid for natural disasters.

Another section in the *kantor camat* is headed by the *mantri polisi pamong praja*. *Pamong praja* are regional administrators appointed by the Indonesian Minister of Internal Affairs—the core of the civil service. *Mantri* is a term of rank, indicating that the person is between *camat* and clerk in rank. The *pamong praja* maintains a not very visible police force, the duty of which is to enforce the protection of the natural areas and to help the *camat* keep things under control.

EACH *kecamatan* consists of a number of even smaller administrative units—*desas* and *kelurahans*. A *desa* is a village; *kelurahan* has no good English equivalent. There is a sharp distinction between a *desa* and a *kelurahan*. The head of a *kelurahan* is called a *lurah*. Like the *camat* (the head of a *kecamatan*) the *lurah* is a civil servant, appointed according to merit from the ranks of local government employees. A *desa*, on the other hand, is governed by a *kepala desa*, who is elected by the people of the village. A *desa* usually has a smaller population than a *kelurahan*. Being a smaller administrative unit, it has considerably more autonomy than a *kelurahan*, and its governmental structure differs accordingly.

The heads of these smaller administrative units of the *kecamatan* are under the jurisdiction of the *camat* and meet with him regularly. The *lurahs* and *kepala desas* of the *kecamatan* are at the lowest rank in the organizational levels of the *kecamatan*. Unlike a *kantor camat*, a *kantor lurah* has no offices of the Indonesian government. Otherwise, the organization is similar to, though smaller than, that of a *kantor camat*. The organization of a *desa* is quite different. It would be instructive to compare the two.

A *desa* has a more or less autonomous administration. It is not an organization of the central government. Its head, the *kepala desa*, is not a civil servant. (The old term for the *kepala desa* was *perbekel*, or *prebekel*, which has now been abandoned.) The *kepala desa* is elected for an eight-year term, rather than appointed. He receives a stipend from the provincial government, doled out by the office of the *bupati*. The *desa* can, within limits, decide upon local policy, without having constantly to refer to a higher office or officer for orders and approval. A *desa* can even have organizations that produce income for itself—which would be quite impossible in a *kelurahan*. Of course, the *desa* must follow the general guidelines of government rule and policy. And the heads of all the *desas* and *kelurahans* meet once a month with the *camat* to give and received information.

Lacking a formal House of Representatives (such as the DPRD found at the Tingkat I and Tingkat II levels) a *desa* has an organization called *lembaga musyawarah desa*, or LMD for short. The LMD is a village council, a deliberative body, composed of 9–15 prominent leaders of the *desa*, that makes decisions in concurrence with the head of the village. This is the grassroots administration in the village, with its indigenous system of democracy and reciprocal cooperation. Membership is voluntary and unpaid. The LMD is headed by the *kepala desa*, and is composed of the heads of all the area *banjar* community groups, the oldest and most experienced people of the village, representatives of religious groups, the professions, and those who are concerned with politics. By law, the *banjars* of a *desa* are supposed to be called *dusuns*, but most people still refer to them as *banjars*. Each *dusun* has an elected head, the *kelian dusun*. The *kepala desa* meets with these leaders routinely once a month if there is important business. Another important person in the *desa* is the *kelian adat*, the religious head of the village. He also meets with the *kepala desa* when necessary.

Every *desa* has a secretary. There are usually only two branches on the government organization chart. There should be five, but in practice there are normally just two: government and development. The LMD takes the place of the three empty offices: KESRA (from *kesejahteraan*, "prosperity") which sees to the upkeep of religious buildings, health, and welfare; *keuangan*, chiefly concerned with raising money for the village; and *umum*, which tends to the paperwork needed by the villagers to get jobs. If, as is usually the case, these last three branches are lacking, the two branches that do always exist handle the work with the LMD's assistance.

City planning is an important function of the LMD. It decides where buildings will be built, how much money will be needed, where it will be obtained, and where the building materials will be secured. When this information is reported to the *kepala desa*, the work can proceed.

In a *kelurahan*, a project such as the above could never be executed at the local level. Planning takes place through the chain of authority beginning at the *kabupaten* then to the *camat*, and only then to the *lurah*. But the higher offices cannot be bothered with details in the smaller *desas*, and thus the local planning is left up to the LMD.

THERE IS NO LMD in the organizational structure of a *kelurahan*. As a complete unit of the central bureaucracy, the kelurahan has no elected policy-making body, but does offer the sevices of five departmental branches. The government branch looks after the local residents, keeping track of where they stay, when they leave and arrive, die, are born, and so on and is in charge of the local census and elections. The branch called *pembangunan*, best translated as "development," manages and promotes local economies, issuing building permits, and running or overseeing the market, banks, and movies. The third branch, KESRA, offers social welfare programs—old age assistance, anti-poverty programs, and help for the sick and handicapped. This branch is also the channel that leads from the sub-district head, the *camat*, to the local religious leader, the *kelian adat*. KESRA oversees school activities outside of the classroom, such as art education and local dances. And it is a conduit between the national education department and the local schools. The fourth branch of the *kelurahan* government is an accounting office, and the fifth branch, *umum*, collects, files, and delivers government records.

The *lurah* is considered to have the same organizational status as the *kepala desa*, although they operate under rather different circumstances. Both meet monthly with the *camat*. In a *kelurahan*, *banjars* are officially supposed to be called *lingkungan*, which means "area" or "environment." However, just as in the case of the word "*dusun*" in a *desa*, most people still use the traditional "*banjar.*"

One of the most important bodies in a *kelurahan* is the LKMD, *lembaga ketahanan masyarakat daerah*, the village development council. A body of the same name is also found in the organization of the *desa*, but its importance there is usually overshadowed by that of the LMD. An LKMD has three chairmen. The general chairman is the *lurah*. His responsibilities with the LKMD center around the study and implementation of the Pancasila—the Indonesian "Five Principles" of national conduct—as well as matters of religion, security, and education and information.

Under the general chairman is a secretary, usually the secretary of the *kelurahan*, a treasurer, and a first chair. This chair is chosen by the *lurah*, but his choice must be approved by the *kelian adat* and other important community members. The first chair has responsibility for infrastructure and the environment, economic development and cooperatives, youth, sports, the arts, and social welfare. Because of his far-reaching responsibilities, this man is often second only to the *lurah* in political importance on the local level.

The wife of the *lurah* is usually the second chair of the LKMD. Her responsibility is the operation in the *kelurahan* of the PKK, the *pembina kesejahteraan keluarga*, or family welfare promotion movement. This organization has a branch in every *banjar* of the villages. The PKK has a number of functions: implementation of the Pancasila, organizing cooper-

A GOTONG ROYONG COLLECTIVE WORK GROUP

ative work groups (*gotong royong*), education, teaching skills, encouraging the development of a broad range of cooperative efforts in the village, health and health plans for the family, and management and conservation of the environment.

Just how effective a given PKK is depends to a large extent on the education and interests of the wife of the *lurah*. Considering the above list of goals and purposes, the PKK could be a real driving force in the village, if its goals were pursued with vigor. I know of some *kelurahans* in Denpasar where there is not a single illiterate *banjar* member. The wives of the *lurahs*, well-educated and conscientious, organize special literacy classes. In some villages the PKK sponsors weekly exercise classes for women—attendance is compulsory. In many villages there are active classes on such subjects as cooking, home-making, child care, and the like. On the other hand, in my village there is almost no effort made along any of these lines, and the PKK has had very little influence upon the women in the area.

In the Badung province n 1986, the latest records at my disposal, there were 23 *kelurahans* and 53 *desas*. There were 152 *desa adat*, 618 *banjar dinas*, and 873 *banjar adat*. (For an explanation of *desa adat* and *banjar* organizations, see CHAPTER 6.) In the same year, in all of Bali, there were 50 *kecamatans*, 79 *kelurahans*, 1,456 *desas adat*, and 564 *desas dinas*.

COOPERATIVES OF MANY KINDS play an important part in the lives of many Balinese. In our general area, the most important is the fisherman's cooperative at Kedonganan, just north of Jimbaran. Nearby on the Bukit there is a small co-op at Pecatu, handling mostly locally grown dry farm crops. Many villages have what amount to village credit unions, in the form of financial cooperatives. Bakor Motor, the alliance of motorcycle and automobile renters that caters mostly to foreigners, is a cooperative.

Cooperatives in Indonesia are all under the control of the Departemen Koperasi, one of the central government departments in Jakarta, under the minister of cooperatives. This branch of the government has a KANWIL office in Denpasar. And each *kabupaten* has its Tingkat II cooperatives department. The organization of the various government levels of cooperative control is rather complex and need not concern us here.

Basically there are two branches of co-op administration in Bali—*pusat koperasi unit desa* (PUSKUD) *gajah minah,* which administers the fishing co-ops in the Kedonganan area, and PUSKUD *Bali dwipa,* which oversees all the other co-ops. Both branches have offices at both Tingkat I and Tingkat II. Under the PUSKUDs are the various village cooperatives, called *koperasi unit desa,* KUD, or *primer.* There are 9 *primer* in PUSKUD *gajah mina* and 80 KUD in PUSKUD *Bali dwipa. Bali dwipa* handles food, sugar, wheat flour, salt, fertilizer, insecticide, limestone, vanilla, seaweed, credit unions, stores, and transportation co-ops like BAKOR motors. And there are about a dozen other type of coops that are not part of either of the two PUSKUDs. These include pension plans for the armed forces, banks, and insurance companies, and the well known Sanggraha Kriya Asta, the government handicrafts cooperative at Tohpati.

The structure and organization of a co-op depends to a large degree upon the nature of the work of the institution. A fisherman's co-op is bound to be different from that of a motor bike renting co-op. The advantages are that the work can be managed, a fair price obtained, and standards of quality upheld.

A SHORT DESCRIPTION OF THE COOPERATIVE with which I am most familiar, in Kedonganan—next to Jimbaran—gives some idea of how one of these operates. There are 23 members of the KUD Mina Segara at Kedonganan. A member of the KUD must be a member of a *banjar* in that area. No itinerants may belong. But members may employ itinerants to staff their boats. The members meet yearly and give and receive advice from various concerned government departments. There is a local manager under whom are various duties and responsibilities, such as providing ice, salt, cold boxes, repair, oil, money, and so on.

Members of the KUD must show loyalty and follow the rules. They must pay a fee called *simpanan pokok,* an entrance fee, upon joining. This can be paid on credit. They must pay a compulsory deposit, *simpanan sukarela,* each month for the KUD. This is rather like putting deposits into a credit union. And each member has to pay the KUD 5 percent of the value of his daily catch. The privileges are that every year a member receives a share of the profits. This is especially important during the so-called *paceklik,* January through April, when there is no fishing in the Jimbaran Bay area because of high winds and waves. During this period, a co-op member receives a monthly stipend called *dana paceklik.* Part of the 5 percent payment goes to this off-season income fee, the result is used to support the KUD organization.

MARKETS ARE AN IMPORTANT PART OF LIFE IN BALI. There are two kinds, those run by the village and those run by the regional government—usually by the *kantor kabupaten.* The Jimbaran market is a typical village market. It is run by the *kelurahan,* which also owns the property. Anyone may sell his or her wares there, but three types of fees are collected. A charge of Rp 100 is made for each basket (*keranjang,* a very large woven bamboo basket) of merchandise brought into the market. This is collected by employees who are stationed at the entrances. A charge of Rp 50 to Rp 200 is made per space per day, the exact price varying according to the desirability of the space, and a charge of Rp 100 per square meter per month is levied to those with permanent shops or stalls. Gross income from the market is about Rp 700,000 per month. The profit is about Rp 150,000 per month for Jimbaran. Of this, the regional government collects 20 percent.

The Sukawati market is run by the *kabupaten* of Gianyar. And the rules are somewhat different. Here the sellers are divided into those who have regular stores (*toko*) and those who operate from open booths (*los*). The charge for bringing one container (called *bakul* in Sukawati) into the market is Rp 50. Owners of *toko* pay Rp 50 per square meter per month. *Los* owners pay Rp 40 per square meter. A third category, *di bawah,* which pays only Rp 30 per square meter per month, occupies lower and less desirable places. Sellers who use sidewalk or street space do not have to pay rent, but they must pay for each container of merchandise. The Sukawati Pasar Seni Art Market next door is a separate entity from the market, and is run by the *kecamatan.*

In 1984, ten *desa* markets in the Denpasar area, each of which had been separately administered under the *kantor kabupaten* of Badung, were combined into one huge market. A big new building, the Pasar Taman Ria IWAPI (IWAPI is the name of a nationwide union of female restaurant and hotel owners), was constructed in downtown Denpasar at a cost of Rp 2.4 billion. The building was paid for by IMPRES—a nationwide development fund—and is being repaid by income from the market.

Anyone may sell in any of these Denpasar markets, provided he or she pays the necessary fees. Each day a seller must pay a fee of Rp 50-100 called *cukai harian* that is used for expenses, investment, and development. There is a *uang sampah* fee for garbage collection, Rp 25-100 per day. Guards costs each seller about Rp 50 per day. Electricity is charged for at the rate of Rp 50 per 40 watts per day. *Sewa tempat* is rental for space, which ranges from Rp 2,500 per square meter per month for permanent sellers, to Rp 400 for *los,* to Rp 100-200 for open ground. There is a *barang masuk* charge for bringing in merchandise. This is charged either per *peti* (box), or per *karung* (sack). This fee varies from Rp 20 to Rp 200. All ten markets together collect about Rp 1.5 billion per year, out of which comes payroll expenses, repayment of the loan, and development. Figures from 1986 show that about 3,800 people sold at all 10 markets. At Pasar Badung there were about 1,350 sellers.

THERE IS NO SINGLE ORGANIZATION devoted to welfare in the villages. Rather, family welfare is an activity of many of the branches of government. Bali's families are cohesive, group-conscious, supportive, closely knit organizations, and abandoned or destitute people are uncommon. Welfare is also a major function of *banjars,* of the PKK, and, indeed, of almost all government agencies. The Departments of Manpower, Transmigration, Cooperatives, Health, and Education and Culture are among those with major welfare responsibilities. But the Department of Social Affairs is the most important arm of government in this area, acting as a coordinator for the efforts of other departments.

There is no social insurance in Bali. Only retired government employees have regular pensions. There is no national pension law. Insurance is just starting to become available to the average person, but policies are normally far outside the reach of the average person. Life insurance is available and is sometimes purchased by middle class people. Property and vehicle insurance is almost never purchased.

There is a family health clinic, *pusat kesehetan masyarakat* (PUSKESMAS), in just about every small village, run by the central government's health department. The village normally has nothing to do with this operation. There is seldom a doctor at the PUSKESMAS, but the person in charge usually has a fair stock of medicines and is able to treat minor afflictions. Various PUSKESMAS have various reputations. Those who get sick in Jimbaran often make the trip of 5 or so kilometers to the PUSKESMAS in Tuban, to the north, even though we have one right in the middle of town. It is unlikely that one would find a doctor's office in a small town. There are plenty in Sanur and Kuta, and sick people from Jimbaran usually go there, or to Denpasar. We have two doctors in town, but their office hours are not convenient, and the common wisdom is that it is better to go to a doctor in the city.

The village cemetery is generally run by the *kelian desa adat,* the religious head of the village. There is not much to "run." Each large family has an extended area where its dead are buried until it is time for cremation. Those who have been excommunicated or who are not Hindus have to pay for burial space in our cemetery. Otherwise there are no particular restrictions.

The larger cities have fire departments. But the small villages have only cooperative work groups to help. Fires are reported to *banjar* heads and they do what they can to prevent damage and theft. Of course, the local HANSIP is notified, and then the police. But fire trucks and pumpers are generally not available. Emergency help is no problem. There are any number of eager and able hands to fight natural disasters. But the chief weapon is almost always the hoe.

The Department of Education and Culture, commonly called "P&K" (pronounced *pay dan kah*) has an elementary school in most villages. The only thing that the village has to do is maintain the school building. The village has nothing to do with what goes on inside the school. Some villages have elementary and high schools, but these are usually found only in the larger cities. Lacking a government school, Jimbaran created a private foundation, or *yayasan* that operates our kindergarten, elementary school, and high school. The results are—well—better than nothing. In a village where education is not considered a worthwhile goal, money is not forthcoming, and the schools just squeak by. School fees are about Rp 5,000 per month for high school, Rp 4,000 per month for elementary school, and even less for primary school. Students in private schools are asked to contribute to a development fund, if they can.

Other private groups run school systems. The Catholic Archdiocese has some excellent schools. Several Chinese-run school systems provide an alternative to the public school system. Before the educational system really develops, it will have to be shown that a better job and a better life can result from a good education. Such is not now the case.

VILLAGES AND REGIONAL GOVERNMENT BRANCHES find several ways of financing their activities. There are, of course, budget allocations from the central government to local governments. There are grants from central government to local governments. One important grant is a fund called Instruksi Presiden Bantuan Desa (INPRES BANDES) which is used for building roads, bridges, schools, health facilities, and green strips. These grants are generally obtainable without too much red tape. It is not unusual to hear a villager calling a particular building, for example a school, an "INPRES." The INPRES BANDES awards about Rp 1.25 million each year every *desa* and *kelurahan* for development.

Certain taxes may be collected by local governments. Up until recently Indonesia has lacked effective ways of identifying those who should pay taxes of various kinds and of collecting these taxes. At the moment, an individual in the villages pays no income tax at all. Of course businesses, both domestic and foreign, are closely and carefully regulated. But at the village level, taxes are not a major concern. The village level name for tax is *pajak bumi dan bangunan,* PBB, meaning "tax on land and buildings."

The tax on buildings is collected only in the larger villages. In the villages, only the *bumi* (land) tax is collected. The procedure varies from place to place. In our village land is classified as either *abian*, (dry, unirrigated) or *yeh*, (wet, irrigated). Taxes are referred to as *sedahan agung*. This may be a *sedahan abian*, or a *sedahan yeh*, depending upon the nature of the land. Notice of tax due is given to villagers by the head of each *banjar*, and the tax is paid to the *kantor camat*.

Funding for government may be obtained by profits earned by state companies owned by local governments. For example, some of the revenue from the large limestone quarry south of Jimbaran goes to run the village of Jimbaran.

Responsibility for road building and maintenance varies. Main roads, called *jalan besar*, are under the jurisdiction of the *kantor kabupaten* and the Departeman Pekerjaan Umum (Department of Public Works), usually called PU. If main roads need repair, PU handles the problem, and the local government has nothing to do with it. Local minor roads within the village are considered to be under the jurisdiction of the individual *banjars* through whose areas they pass. These roads are maintained by work gangs from the individual *banjars*.

Garbage disposal is the job of the village. Some municipalities have no regular garbage disposal facilities at all. On the other hand, Sanur, Kuta, and Denpasar run garbage collection routes with household pickup. Some of the smaller villages have this service too. Jimbaran, for example, has its own garbage pickup, for which each person served pays a small fee.

Electricity is generated by the Pusat Listrik Negara (PLN) power plant near Benoa harbor. Villages have nothing to do with this matter, except each area has a meter reader, a local resident, who usually adds a small fee, perhaps Rp 250 per month, to the bill of each consumer for his services. High voltage transmission lines to bring hydroelectric power from the Malang area of East Java are in place and have just begun to function. These lines run under the Bali Strait.

Telephones are under the jurisdiction of the Department of Tourism, Post, and Telecommunications, through an agency known as Perusahaan Umum Telekomunikasi (PERUMTEL). Village organization has nothing to do with this. Indeed, except for the major population centers, there are few telephones. Other than at the Nusa Dua tourist area, for example, there are no telephones south of Kuta. Some hotels have their own radio telephones, however.

Water supply is a variable matter. One branch of the provincial government is concerned with making available drinking water to the villages. The larger cities have water pipes and taps. But the water is usually not safe to drink without treatment. Large water tanks have been installed in remote villages, filled by pumps and providing faucets from which local people can fill their buckets. Many villages have no permanent source of drinking water at all and rely upon wells or springs. This is not a problem with which most smaller villages have occupied themselves. I know of no effort in Jimbaran, for example, to provide a source of drinking water.

Banks are rather recent arrivals at many villages. Five years ago there were none in our village. Now there are two small branches of larger, private banks and one credit union that is run by a government bank. Most people still go to Kuta or Denpasar to do their serious banking, however. At the Lembaga Perkreditan Desa in Jimbaran one can borrow money at an interest rate of 2.5 percent per month. One needs a citizenship card and the signature of the *lurah*. The maximum amount loaned is Rp 500,000. The organization normally only lends to local people whom the office of *lurah* takes to be good credit risks.

The private banks usually charge 3.5 percent interest per month. But the signature of the *lurah* is not necessary to borrow from them. These banks also have savings accounts of two types. In a *tabangun nasional*, offered only by some banks, one can deposit savings and withdraw whatever is desired whenever one wishes. The savings account called *deposito* involves a higher interest rate, but limits the number and frequency of withdrawals.

Most villages have private money lenders who lend money to friends and neighbors for rather high rates of interest, taking as security personal possessions of the borrowers. Typical private lending rates are 10 percent per month, with payments made daily. For example, if one wants to borrow Rp 25,000, he must pay Rp 500 each day for 60 days. That is about 120 percent per year. But credit is still difficult to obtain for many people, and this sort of arrangement is better than nothing.

THE ORGANIZATION OF THE POLICE in Indonesia was always a puzzle to me because I kept trying to fit it into the mold of city, county, state, and federal police in the United States. It is much simpler than that. Stated briefly, there are no local police in Indonesia. All police in the country rank with the three military services as one of four services comprising the armed forces of the Republic of Indonesia, ABRI, Angkatan Bersenjata Republik Indonesia, which is under the jurisdiction of the Department of Defense—Departemen Pertahanan dan Keamanan (HANKAM).

The general name of the police force is Polisi Republik Indonesia, or POLRI. POLRI has eight Directorates:

1. INTEL   Intelligence
2. SAMAPTA   Includes the Brigade Mobil, an elite group that controls demonstrations and helps in emergencies, and the SABHARA, which offers crowd control services, tourist police, protection for VIPs, and patrols the larger roads

3. BIMMAS   Short for Bimbingan Masyarakat, the duties of which
            include crime prevention and education, and special
            police, civil service police, forest police, and SATPAM,
            the usual guards one sees at hotels and tourist places.
4. RESERSE Detectives
5. DIKLAT   Education, training, practical work
6. PERSONIL Records, statistics, pay, employees
7. LOGISTIK Equipment, cars, uniforms.
8. DITLANTAS Traffic police, *polisi lalulintas.*

These eight directorates are under Polisi Daerah (POLDA) at the *propin-si* level. Successively lower, in the chain of command, are the Polisi Resort (POLRES) at the *kabupaten* level, Polisi Sektor (POLSEK) at the *kecamatan* level, and the Pos Polisi (POLPOS) at the local or village level.

THERE IS AN INTERESTING ORGANIZATION that one sometimes hears about in the rural villages of Bali called Kelompen Capir, or KP4. Its official name is: Kelompok Pendengar, Pembaca, Pemirsa, Penulis. This literally means: "Group that Listens, Reads, Watches, and Writes." This is a kind of ad hoc group to study a particular subject, say the management of a certain kind of crop. After finding out all it can from the four *P*'s it enters into competition with other similar groups throughout Bali. Like the 4H clubs—Head, Heart, Hands, Health—in the United States, the goal of this group is to encourage education and production, but unlike the U.S. group, the KP4 is government-run.

The transfer of land from seller to buyer is now usually effected through the *agraria* function of the Government section of the *kantor camat*. There is a space for a separate Urusan Agraria, but this idea has been abandoned. One problem with land transfer in Bali is that deeds are not at all clear. A lot of the land has been sold to others in recent years, and disputes over what part of which family owns what part of which land are quite common. There are no clear boundary markers. Papers are often quite vague and open to considerable dispute. Quite commonly one person will hold land for the benefit of an entire family. And when the land is sold, division among the various beneficiaries is difficult.

If one wishes to open a place of business in a village, one should theoretically go to the *kepala desa* or *lurah* and get a permit. This is seldom done. *Warungs*—roadside stands—and little shops open and close more or less at random. Theoretically a permit is required in order to display a sign for a place of business. This is the business of the commerce department. Larger businesses observe the rules, but village sellers do not bother, and they are usually not bothered.

INDONESIA IS THE UNDISPUTED ACRONYM CAPITAL of the world.

Names of organizations tend to be so long and convoluted that abbreviations are often the only way out. If one is on the inside, this is no problem. As a foreigner in Indonesia, trying to thread one's way around, it is sometimes very difficult to associate functions and responsibilities to an organization that is represented by a name that is meaningless unless you have the key. We in the West use acronyms a little. Acronyms such as laser and radar and scuba are so commonly used in English that probably not one in a hundred could tell you what the letters stand for. In Indonesia this situation is a thousand times worse. People, particularly in government offices, use acronyms so often that they tend to forget the origins of the abbreviations. As a service to my fellow foreigners, therefore, I offer the following list of acronyms that I have trimmed from hundreds down to essentials.

ABRI. Angkatan Bersenjata Republik Indonesia; Indonesian Armed Forces

APBD. Anggaran Pendapatan dan Belanja Daerah; Regional Income and Expenses Budget

APBN. Anggaran Pendapatan dan Belanja Negara; Government Budget

APPKD. Anggaran Penerimaan dan Pengeluaran Keuangan Desa; Village Receipts and Expenses Budget

AS. Amerika Serikat; United States.

ASEAN. Association of the South East Asian Nations

ASITA. Association of the Indonesian Tours and Travel Agencies

BAKN. Badan Administrasi Kepegawaian Negara; Civil Service Administration Agency

BANDES. Bantuan Desa; Village Assistance(grants)

BAPPARDA. Badan Pengembangan Pariwisata Daerah; Regional Tourist Promotion Board

BAPPARNAS. Badan Pengembangan Pariwisata Nasional; National Tourist Promotion Board

BAPPEDA. Badan Perancang Pembangunan Daerah; Regional Development Planning Board

BAPPENAS. Badan Perencanaan Pembangunan Nasional; National Development Planning Board

BATAN. Badan Tenaga Atom Nasional; National Atomic Energy Agency

BINMAS. Pembinaan Masyarakat; Social Development

BKKBN. Badan Koordinasi Keluarga Berencana Nasional; National Coordinating Agency for Family Planning

BKLH. Bina Kependudukan Lingkungan Hidup; Environmental Protection Board

BKPM. Badan Koordinasi Penanaman Modal; Investment Coordination Agency

BPD. Bank Pembangunan Daerah; Regional Development Bank

BPLP. Balai Pendidikan dan Latihan Pariwisata; Center for Tourism

Education and Training

Bps. Biro Pusat Statistik; Central Bureau of Statistics

Bpu. Biro Perjalanan Umum; Travel Agency

Bsdsb. (Sometimes sdsb) Bukti Sumbangan Dermawan Sosial Berhadiah; Evidence of Contribution to the Gift-giving Social Welfare Fund (the national lottery)

Btdc. Bali Tourism Development Corporation

Bulog. Badan Urusan Logistik; National Logistics Agency

Dati. Daerah Tingkat (I, II); area level (provincial, district)

Dinas. District office, Tingkat I and II, *otonom*

Diparda. Dinas Pariwisata Daerah; Provincial Tourist Promotion Board

Dirjen. Direktur-Jendral; Director-General

Ditjen. Direktorat Jendral; Directorate General

Dpr. Dewan Perwakilan Rakyat; Peoples' Representative Council (parliament)

Dprd. Dewan Perwakilan Rakyat (Daerah); Provincial Assembly, Tingkat I and II

Golkar. Golongan Karya; Functional Groups (political party)

Hansip. Pertahanan Sipil; Village Police

Humas. Hubungan Masyarakat; Public Relations

Inkud. Induk Koperasi Perikanan Indonesia; Chief Fishery Cooperative of Indonsia

Inpres. Instruksi Presiden; Presidential Decree

Irjen. Inspektur-Jendral; Inspector-General

Itjen. Inspektorat Jendral; Inspectorate General

Kamtibmas. Keamanan Ketertiban Masyarakat; Security and Correct Conduct of the People

Kandep. Kantor Departemen; District (*kabupaten*) Office, Tingkat II

Kanwil. Kantor Wilayah; provincial office, Tingkat I

Kapkandep. Kepala Kantor Departemen; Head of Tingkat II Office

Kapkanwil. Kepala Kantor Wilayah; Head of Tingkat I Office

Kaur. Kepala Urusan; Head of a Division (as in a government office)

Kb. Keluarga Berencana; Family Planning

Kelompen capir. Kelompok Pendengar Pembaca Pemirsa Penulis; Farmer's Study Group

Kesra. Kesejahteraan Rakyat; Prosperity of the People

Kk. Kepala Keluarga; Head of the Household

Kodam. Komando Daerah Militer; Provincial Military Command

Kokar. Sekolah Menengah Karawitan Indonesia; Indonesian Middle School for the Performing Arts

Koramil. Komando Rayon Militer; Military Area Command

Korpri. Korps Pegawai Republik Indonesia; Government Employees' Corps

Kosek. Komando Sektor; Sector Command

KTP. Kartu Tanda Penduduk; Identity Card

KUD. Koperasi Unit Desa; Village Cooperative

LAN. Lembaga Administrasi Negara; National Administration Institute

LIPI. Lembaga Ilmu Pengetahuan Indonesia; Indonesian Institute of Science

LKMD. Lembaga Ketahanan Masyarakat Desa; Organization for Village Defense

LMD. Lembaga Musyawarah Desa; Village Council

LPD. Lembaga Perkreditan Desa; Village Credit Union

MAWIL. Markas Wilayah; Regional Headquarters

MENDAGRI. Menteri Dalam Negeri; Ministry of the Interior

MENDIKBUD. Menteri Pendidikan dan Kebudayaan; Minister of Education and Culture

MENHANKAM. Menteri Pertahanan dan Keamanan; Ministry of Defense and Security

MENHUB. Menteri Perhubungan; Minister of Transportation

MENLU. Menteri Luar Negri; Minister of Foreign Affairs

MENPARPOSTEL. Menteri Pariwisata, Pos, dan Telekomunikasi; Minister of Tourism, Post, and Telecommunications

MENPEN. Menteri Penerangan; Minister of Information

MENPORA. Menteri Pemuda dan Olahraga; Minister of Youth and Sports

MPR. Majelis Permusyawaratan Rakyat; People's Deliberative Council

NIP. Nomor Induk Pegawai; Government Employee Number

NUSRA. Nusa Tenggara; Southeastern Indonesia

NV. Naamloze Vennootschap; Inc., or Ltd.

P&K. Pendidikan dan Kebudayaan; Education and Culture

P3I. Pusat Promosi Pariwisata Indonesia; Center for the Promotion of Tourism in Indonesia

P3K. Pertolongan Pertama Pada Kecelakaan; First Aid For Accidents

P4. Pedoman Pengamalan dan Penghayatan Pancasila; Guide to the Five Principles of the Indonesian People

PATA. Pacific Area Travel Association

PBB. Pajak Bumi dan Bangunan; Property Tax

PDI. Partai Demokrasi Indonesia; Indonesian DemocracyPparty (political party)

PEMDA. Pemerinta Daerah; Provincial Government

PERTAMINA. Perusahaan Pertambangan Minyak dan Gas Bumi Negara; National Enterprise for the Mining of Oil and Natural Gas

PERUM. Perusahaan Umum; Public Enterprise

PERUMNAS. Perumahan Nasional; National Housing Development

PERUMTEL. Perusahaan Umum Telekomunikasi; Public Telecommunications Company

PGRI. Persatuan Guru Republik Indonesia; Indonesian School Teachers Association

PKGB. Padat Karya Gaya Baru; New Style Labor Intensive Projects
PKK. Pembinaan Kesejahteraan Keluarga; Family Welfare Organization
PLKB. Petugas Lapangan Keluarga Berencana; Family Planning Field Office
PLN. Perusahaan Listerik Negara; State Electric Company
PMI. Palang Merah Indonesia; Indonesian Red Cross
POKGAS. Kelompok Tugas; Organizing Group
POKJA. Kelompok Kerja; Working Group
POLDA. Polisi Daerah; Provincial Police
POLRES. Polisi Resort; District Police
POLRI. Polisi Republik Indonesia; National Police
POLSEK. Polisi Sektor; Sub-district Police
POM. Polisi Milter; Military Police
POSYANDU. Pos Pelayanan Terpandu; Village Health and Nutrition Center
PPLD. Pemugaran Perumahan dan Lingkungan Desa; Housing and Village Environment Restoration
PPP. Partai Persatuan Pembangunan; United Development Party (political party)
PPP. Polisi Pamong Praja; Civil Service Police
PPPK. Pertolongan Pertama Pada Kecelakaan; first aid
PPTI. Pemberantasan Penyakit Tuberkulosis Indonesia; Tuberculosis Eradication Association of Indonesia
PPWKS. Peningkatan Peranan Wanita Keluarga Sehat; Increased Women's Role in Family Health
PRAMUKA. Praja Muda Karana; Boy Scouts
PRIMKOPAD. Primer Koperasi Angkatan Darat; Primary Cooperative of Ground Forces
P. T. Perseroan Terbatus; Inc., or Ltd. company
PUSKESMAS. Pusat Kesehatan Masyarakat; Village Health Center
PUSKUD. Pusat Koperasi Unit Desa; Village Cooperative Center
PWI. Persatuan Wartawan Indonesia; Indonesian Journalists Association
RAKORBANG. Rapat Kordinasi Pembangunan; Development Coordination Meeting, Tingkat II
RAKORNAS. Rapat Kordinasi Nasional; National Coordinating Meeting
REPELITA. Rencana Pembangunan Lima Tahun; Five-Year Development Plan
RI. Republik Indonesia; Republic of Indonesia
RSUP. Rumah Sakit Umum Pusat; Central Public Hospital
SAMSAT. Sistim Administrasi Manunggal Di Bawah Satu Atap; Centralized Administrative System
SATGAS. Satuan Tugas; Work Group
SATPAM. Satuan Pengaman; Defense Control Guard
SD. Sekolah Dasar; Elementary School
SEKJEN. Sekretaris Jendral; Secretary General

SEKNEG. Sekretaris Negara; Secretary of State

SGO. Sekolah Guru Olah Raga; School for Sports Instructors

SIE. Seksi; Section

SIM. Surat Izin Mengemudi; Driver's License

SISKAMLING. Sistim Keamanan Lingkungan Masyarakat; System for the Security of the Community

SMA. Sekolah Menengah Atas; High School

SMP. Sekolah Menengah Pertama; Junior High School

SPG. Sekolah Pendidikan Guru; Teachers Training School

SPSK. Serikat Penerbit Surat Kabar; Newspaper Publishers Association

STM. Sekolah Tehnik Menengah; Vocational-technical High School

STSI. Sekolah Tinggi Seni Indonesia—Indonesian Academy of Art

STT. Sekehe Teruna Teruni; Village Youth Organization

TIBUM. Ketertiban Umum; Public Order

TKK. Taman Kanak-kanak; Kindergarten

TPI. Tempat Pelelangan Ikan; Fish Auction Place

UDKP. Unit Daerah Kerja Pembangunan; Regional Development Agency

UNUD. Universitas Udayana; Udayana University

VOC. Vereenigde Oostindische Compagnie; Dutch East India Company

WAPRES. Wakil Presiden; Vice President

WIB. Waktu Indonesia Barat; Western Indonesian Time

WITA. Waktu Indonesia Tengah; Central Indonesian Time

WK. Wakil Ketua; Vice Head

CHAPTER 8

Pan Balang Tamak

A CURIOUS FOLK HERO AND DEITY

WHEN I FIRST CAME TO LIVE IN JIMBARAN many years ago, Budi undertook to show me around some of the main temples. I marveled at the beauty of the 11-tiered *meru* in Pura Ulunsiwi, the largest temple in the village, important to all of Bali as the home of the god who protects wet rice fields from disease. As we walked around I noticed a very dilapidated little shrine of the sort that is known as *gedong*, a kind of rectangular box with a door, built upon a decaying brick platform. Next to it was an equally beat-up *piasan*, a small, covered area for preparing offerings. I asked Budi what this shrine was all about.

"That is the shrine and *piasan* for Pan Balang Tamak, who was a kind of joker. He played many tricks on people. *Balang* means 'grasshopper.' I don't know what *tamak* means."

"But why should there be a shrine in a temple to a joker?"

"I don't know."

"The Pan Balang Tamak shrines faces west, but all of the other shrines in Pura Ulunsiwi face east. Why is that?"

"I don't know," Budi said. "We should find out."

And this is where the matter stood for many years. But every time I went to pray at Pura Ulunsiwi I passed by the Pan Balang Tamak shrine that stands near the northeast corner of the *jeroan*, the inner courtyard, next to the wall that separates this area from the outer courtyard, and each time it struck me as odd that a joker should have a shrine like a god. Then, as luck would have it, I read an article by C. J. Grader, written in 1963 in Dutch and published in English under the title "Balang Tamak" in the collection *Bali: Further Studies in Life, Thought, and Ritual*. Grader mentions a temple with a shrine dedicated to Pan Balang Tamak in the village of Nongan, not far from Rendang, on the road between Klungkung and Besakih. In fact, Budi had once said that he accidentally stumbled upon a ceremony at that temple. Most of the people of Nongan raise dry field crops, such as coconuts and fruit, and Grader states that Pan Balang Tamak's shrine there is the focus of attention should there be any sort of disease or pestilence that affects these crops. Holy water from the temple is sprinkled on the crops to protect them. In other words, Pan Balang Tamak is something like an agricultural deity in this area.

Pura Ulunsiwi is a very important agricultural temple for all of Bali. If Pan Balang Tamak is considered a protector of crops in Nongan, I reasoned, perhaps that is also why he has a shrine in Jimbaran. As Budi said, *balang* means grasshopper—an enemy of crops. I determined to find out more about Pan Balang Tamak and about any possible relationship between this personage, or deity, and Pura Ulunsiwi in my own village. After visiting the Nongan temple—and 12 others with Pan Balang Tamak shrines—and after devoting two years on and off to the study of this problem, I conclude that there is no demonstrable relationship at all between the presence of this Pan Balang Tamak shrine at Pura Ulunsiwi and the temple's function as a protector of crops.

Investigations in Bali often lead to these sorts of dead ends, but the time spent was by no means a failure because in the process I have come upon the fascinating story of a folk hero and how he was deified. To see what I mean, let me share some Pan Balang Tamak stories with you. The ones presented here have been translated by Budi and me from "Pan Balang Tamak dan Kawan-kawannya Yang Cerdik" ("Pan Balang Tamak and his Clever Friends") which is included in *Cerita Rakyat Klasik* (Classic Folk Tales), Universitas Udayana, 1973.

PAN BALANG TAMAK

THE AGE OF 50 IS MUCH LESS than that of an average old man in the village. But look at that man over there. His forehead is wrinkled, and that makes people think he is 12 years older than he really is. Many people in this village say that he became old-looking so fast because he is eaten by his thoughts, and his thoughts make his face look old. That man sitting over there is Pan Balang Tamak. His body is very small.

Pan Balang Tamak is very rich, but many people in his village dislike him. If he ever were to do something nice, everyone in the village would like him. But because he is always thinking up new ways of cheating, his fellow *banjar* members do not like him at all. He is always cheating someone. He is sly, and clever at answering questions. He has an answer for everything. Nobody can beat him when it comes to talking and he is always right. This is why people keep their distance from him—if they can.

Yesterday the village leader called a meeting of the villagers to find a way to trap Pan Balang Tamak and exact revenge upon him for all his bad deeds. His behavior is often bad, and he cheats others all of the time. So the villagers decided to find a way to make Pan Balang Tamak pay a big fine. Finally the people at the meeting worked out a plan. This time, they knew, Pan Balang Tamak would not escape punishment.

That same day all the *banjar* messengers went to the members' houses to make an important announcement. Pan Balang Tamak's *kesinoman* came to his house late that afternoon.

"Eh, Pan Balang Tamak, tomorrow morning when the chickens come down from their roosts in the trees, all the villagers must go to the forest and collect wood to repair the Pura Bale Agung," said the messenger. "Nobody can be late. Whoever is late must pay a big fine."

"I understand," said Pan Balang Tamak. "I won't be one second late."

The next morning Pan Balang Tamak waited for his chicken to come down from her "roost." He waited until nine o'clock in the morning, but still the chicken remained in the tree by his house. Finally, when the sun was almost overhead, the chicken left her nest—you see, she was sitting on her eggs. This is why Pan Balang Tamak was late getting to the forest to collect wood.

When Pan Balang Tamak arrived at his *banjar,* the *banjar* members were already coming back from the forest, each bringing a load of wood, as the village leader had directed. Pan Balang Tamak met some of the villagers not very far from his house. But he did not look sad or ashamed about what he had done. He looked happy and he felt happy. He was not embarrassed either. If he had been a different person his face would have been red with embarrassment.

When Pan Balang Tamak met the villagers nobody spoke to him, and Pan Balang Tamak did not open his mouth. Maybe he felt sorry because the people had to work so hard in the forest and carry such heavy loads of wood.

On his way to the forest he was thinking about what answer to give to explain his tardiness. The villagers would want to know why he came late, and he must have an answer. All of the villagers had already come from the forest, so Pan Balang Tamak returned from the forest without carrying anything on his shoulders. But his face looked like that of a person who was carrying something heavy—he was thinking about the questions he would have to answer.

The villagers all arrived and a meeting was held to determine the punishment for Pan Balang Tamak. They asked each other and the village head what they should do. It was important for them to prepare this way because everybody knew that Pan Balang Tamak would have a great many answers for any questions that they asked him. They concluded that he would have to pay a big fine because of his bad deeds. Maybe that would pay for all of his bad behavior in the past.

After the villagers had decided upon the amount of the fine, Pan Balang Tamak was invited to join them. Many people thought that he would finally not be able to answer their questions because he had obviously not done what he had been told to do. The *kelian* of the *banjar* said to Pan Balang Tamak:

"All of the members of your *banjar* have said that you broke the law of the *kerama desa*, and that you should pay a compulsory fine. The amount of the fine will be..."

Pan Balang Tamak cut the leader's sentence short: "Eh, what is this fine for?"

The villagers were startled, and murmured like honey bees scared by a bat.

"You have to pay a fine because you have not followed the rules that we made about collecting wood in the forest." The leader said, in a high, nervous voice. The people sitting near Pan Balang Tamak stirred uneasily.

"Wait a minute, and be patient," said Pan Balang Tamak calmly. "Don't get excited." The villagers quieted down. Some of them held their breaths. "Who said that I have not followed the rules? Who? Who! Who said that I was lazy and did not follow the rules?" He had small, but bright eyes. He stood in front of the villagers, who looked on quietly. Pan Balang Tamak's small dog wagged its tail as if he knew that his owner had done nothing wrong. Nobody answered. So he continued.

"I obeyed the *kasinoman's* message. It was this: 'Tomorrow morning when the chickens go down from their roosts in the trees, all of the *kerama desa* must go out to collect wood in the forest for repairing the Pura Bale Agung.' All of you know that I have only one chicken. And she has been sitting on her eggs. I was waiting for her to come down from her nest. I was in a hurry to take my equipment for collecting wood, but I waited, according to the instructions. I obeyed the message. I was exactly on time. The sun was overhead when I left home. In this case, who was wrong? Was it I or all of you?"

This was the last of his speech, and nobody could answer his questions. One of the villagers went out and rubbed his face in despair, leaving the meeting because he knew the instructions given to Pan Balang Tamak were wrong. But many people thought that Pan Balang Tamak was just being sly, and that he had deceived them. But what should they do? "He knows better than we how to switch his tongue," said the village head.

Next day, the village called a work gang, a *gotong royong*, to repair the Bale Agung. The villagers were asked to bring *senggauk*, dry cooked rice, to eat while working. Pan Balang Tamak came, but he did not bring *senggauk*. Rather, he brought a *sanggah uwug*, a broken shrine. (*Senggauk* sounds like *sanggah uwug* if spoken rapidly.)

"This is the *sanggah uwug* that I have brought so that it can be repaired by the villagers," he said. All the people wondered what he was doing and why he brought the broken shrine. But nobody could blame Pan Balang Tamak. Nobody was willing to accuse him and face his sly tongue. They were reluctant to say anything. *Gotong royong* is an activity for the public welfare. And nobody is allowed to work for his own private good, such as to fix one's own shrine. So, to avoid another trick, the villagers all repaired Pan Balang Tamak's broken shrine.

The repair of the Bale Agung took many months. The *kesinoman* said that all villagers must go to hunt together in the forest. Each person would have to bring a fierce dog—one that can bark loudly and is strong and clever. Most important of all, the dog must be able to climb a tree. This is the message that Pan Balang Tamak received from the messenger, who was told by the *kelian* that, this time, he should be absolutely clear in his instructions to Pan Balang Tamak, and he should be on the lookout for tricks.

The *kesinoman* gave this information to Pan Balang Tamak while he was working in his field. And it looked as if Pan Balang Tamak didn't hear the message. It looked as if he would not be able to do as he was told. This made the *kesinoman* very happy because he did not like Pan Balang Tamak and knew if he failed he would have to pay a fine. Pan Balang Tamak knew that the *kesinoman* did not like him. These were directions that he could not follow, he thought. He knew that the other villagers were deliberately trying to trap him and he had to figure out a way to avoid the trap.

The *kesinoman* and the villagers knew that Pan Balang Tamak would not be able to do the required things because he had only one dog. Now he would have to pay the fine. His dog is very small and thin. No dog can get fat with Pan Balang Tamak, because this man is cunning and a chiseler. He was always skinny and never had a fat dog. Pan Balang Tamak is rich, but he is stingy. His dog never gets enough to eat. Pan Balang Tamak feeds the dog very little, and offers even less to his neighbors. But even though the dog was very thin, it liked his master very much. Wherever Pan Balang Tamak went, the dog followed.

All the villagers knew about Pan Balang Tamak's dog. You could count its ribs. All of the people knew that he would be trapped. Many of the villagers did not have their own dogs, but they could borrow them from their neighbors. But Pan Balang Tamak had only this one dog and, since nobody liked him, he could not borrow one.

Pan Balang Tamak is rich. He is also stingy, sly, and deceiving. But he is always lucky. Most of the villagers have handsome, fat, and fierce dogs. Many people thought their dogs would easily catch a squirrel or an old monkey, or a wild rooster or a wild hen or some other animal. The better dogs might catch a deer. Pan Balang Tamak didn't expect his dog to catch anything, not even an old blind turtle, because his dog was old and skinny and could not catch anything. His dog could not even bark, but it could say: "Kaing, kaing, kaing."

Next morning they were ready to go to the forest to hunt with the dogs. Early, before the chickens had left their roost, the big dogs in the villages began barking very loudly, and the village was noisy. Pan Balang Tamak, although slow and lazy, was now certain about what he would do. His dog was very dirty and mangy, but Pan Balang Tamak took it to the forest.

This dog was different from the dogs the others brought. The other big dogs jumped around very energetically. Pan Balang Tamak's dog was not strong. It was cold and slept by his master's side or in his lap. Pan Balang Tamak carried his dog in his arms and, on this chilly morning, the dog felt comfortable and warm.

Pan Balang Tamak walked very slowly in the rear of the crowd of men who were going to the forest. He did not want to be in front of the others. When they arrived at the edge of a river, Pan Balang Tamak could not go across. He thought about this as all of the others crossed ahead of him. Then he shouted loudly: "Bangkung sing magigi! Bangkung sing magigi! Bangkung sing magigi!"

When the people in front heard the shout they didn't know it was Pan Balang Tamak, and they thought that one of their friends behind had caught a wild pig without any teeth—*bangkung sing magigi*. Some of the villagers dashed back to help their friend. But when they arrived they saw it was Pan Balang Tamak. One of the men muttered to himself: "Asia!" (unlucky).

"What is wrong with you?" one of them asked. "Why are you making noise?" Pan Balang Tamak held a stick in his hand.

"Where is the pig that you yelled about?" asked some others.

"I didn't say 'Bangkung sing magigi,'" said Pan Balang Tamak. "I said 'Pangkung sing matiti'" (the river has no bridge).

The villagers thought about Pan Balang Tamak's tricks and added this new one to the old ones. They helped him cross the river by building a small bridge.They thought that maybe he would not have to pay a fine this time because, so far, he had not broken the rules.

The forest was very noisy because of the hunting activities. Some people were trying to catch deer, both large and small. Dogs were jumping here and there. Some were trying to catch monkeys. Some barked at squirrels. Some fought with snakes. Some people were shooting wild pigs. And most of the dogs got very tired and cried "kaing, kaing" as dogs do, because they were bitten by wild pigs or gored by deer. Some dogs waited for the monkeys that were still in the trees.

Pan Balang Tamak found a spot where there were some good bushes and vines. His little dog, which Pan Balang Tamak still held in his arms, was very afraid of the barks of the other dogs and held his tail between his legs. Then—all of a sudden—Pan Balang Tamak threw the dog into a tall *ketket* vine with vicious thorns. The dog howled with pain. The other dogs were tired, and Pan Balang Tamak's dog was the only one making any noise. The other dogs were only saying, "Kaing, kaing."

Because of the fierce thorns, Pan Balang Tamak's dog couldn't go up or down from the *ketket* vine. Pan Balang Tamak clapped his hands, as if his dog were catching an animal. The villagers came running.

Pan Balang Tamak said: "Eh, you villagers, look at my dog. He climbed the *ketket* vine. Who else has a dog that can climb a dangerous vine like that?" Nobody could answer his questions and the people all thought that his dog was fierce and strong.

"Now all of you should pay a fine to me because none of your dogs is fierce and strong like mine and can climb a tree," Pan Balang Tamak added. And while he was talking he looked at each villager, his eyes emphasizing that he was right and they were wrong.

The villagers promised to pay a fine to him. They wanted to trap him and were trapped themselves. Nobody could say why he shouldn't pay Pan Balang Tamak a fine. In the late afternoon the villagers went home. They were not happy about what had happened in the forest that day.

Next day the *kerama adat* called another meeting and Pan Balang Tamak was invited. He thought about the meeting and devised a plan. He told his wife to make some *jaja uli injin*, a kind of soft rice cake made out of sticky black rice. When the time came Pan Balang Tamak went to the meeting with his *jaja uli*.

The *kerama adat* saw that there were a lot of dog droppings and urine on the floor of the meeting place. When all of the people had arrived and had taken their seats on the floor, Pan Balang Tamak stood up and told the people that he would make a bet with them.

"Eh, all of you, who dares to eat dog shit?"

The people muttered. Many people turned aside and talked to each other. Some closed their noses with their hands. Some spat in front of others, as if to clear their mouths. No one answered. They all felt insulted. Pan Balang Tamak continued his questions:

"If someone will accept my challenge, I will give him a prize of Rp 1,000. Who wants to do that?"

The *kelian desa* answered his question with a look of anger: "Eh, your mouth is rotten.Your voice is like that dog shit—disgusting. Do you like to eat dog shit? If you can eat it I will pay you Rp 1,000. Can you?"

Pan Balang Tamak didn't answer the questions. He pretended that he would push himself and force himself to eat the dog droppings. And then he said:

"Yes, I'm going to try."

The Kelian said: "Go ahead. I'll pay you Rp 1,000."

Pan Balang Tamak ate some of the dog droppings, and all of the *kera-*

ma desa felt very disgusted. Some of the onlookers closed their eyes. Some vomited when they saw Pan Balang Tamak eating the droppings. But Pan Balang Tamak smiled in his heart. Now he would get some money. The *kerama* would be obliged to pay. He made it seem as if it were difficult to swallow the droppings.

The dog droppings were made of the *jaja uli injin* that his wife had cooked. Pan Balang Tamak had shaped the doughy cakes into the form of dog droppings. He had gone to the meeting place before anyone had arrived and put the rice cakes around on the floor of the hall. Around the cakes he spilled some water which looked like puddles of urine.

The next day Pan Balang Tamak again received an order. All of the people in the village were prohibited from entering and walking through someone else's land. If someone did so he would have to pay a fine. In addition, nobody would be allowed to take someone else's property without the owner's permission. If someone so much as entered a field that was not his own, he would have to pay a large fine. As usual, the purpose of this law was to trap Pan Balang Tamak.

But Pan Balang Tamak was happy to hear about this new law. He planted a new garden right next to the village market. He didn't put any valuable crops in it—no cucumbers, *nangka*, or *rambutan*. This garden was fenced only by *lidi*, the thin central spines of a coconut leaf. Unlike the other villagers, he deliberately didn't build a strong fence. He let the grass grow on his land, and he planted a lot of *pulet* bushes. This is a small bush with red fruit. Its leaves, flowers, and fruit are very sticky and attach themselves easily to anyone who brushes against them.

Nobody was interested in having a garden like this one. And nobody wanted to steal anything from the garden because there wasn't anything in it worth stealing. So what was the purpose of Pan Balang Tamak's having it?

On market day many people went to his garden because it was right next to the market. But they were not interested in seeing the garden. They just needed to urinate. Nobody intended to steal anything. While the people were in the garden relieving themselves Pan Balang Tamak was watching. He was walking though the market. Looking at his garden he saw what the people were doing there. He shouted: "Eh, everyone, I caught those people over there entering my garden without my permission. They are trying to steal things and must pay the fine according to the law."

Many people who went to the garden were startled to hear what Pan Balang Tamak had just said. Some people were about to leave to go to the toilet in the garden, and they were so startled they stopped in their tracks.

Caught in the garden, one person said: "Ah, what was my mistake in being here? You said I was doing something wrong. What am I doing wrong? You said I should pay a fine. That is a very strange law, isn't it?"

"You broke the law because you entered my fields without my permission," said Pan Balang Tamak. "And also you stole things from my garden. Look at this! What do you have on your clothing?"

He pointed at the *pulet* flowers that had stuck to the clothing of the people who had been in the garden. There was nothing the people could say. *Pulet* flowers stick very easily to clothes. They couldn't answer Pan Balang Tamak because the *pulet* flowers were, indeed, on their clothing. And so the intruders had to pay the fine. People were very annoyed at Pan Balang Tamak's trick.

The villagers were now at their wits' end to know how to face Pan Balang Tamak. Tactics and tricks and cunning were always what he used. He always wanted to trap others. Someone who wanted to catch Pan Balang Tamak was always, himself, caught by Pan Balang Tamak. The villagers had run out of ideas.

Finally they decided to kill Pan Balang Tamak. They were very mad at him because he constantly made them unhappy. So they reported their decision to the king. When he heard their report he agreed. He gave the villagers a very strong poison to kill Pan Balang Tamak.

Pan Balang Tamak heard that he would be killed. He thought the matter over very carefully, and then he gave very long and detailed instructions to his wife to follow when he died. His wife listened very attentively and said that she understood.

Pan Balang Tamak sat down to his last meal, knowing that his food had been poisoned. Even before he had finished, he toppled over dead. The servants of the king, who had been sent to see to it that Pan Balang Tamak died, rushed back with the partly eaten food to show the king that the enemy had perished. They spread the good news.

Then his wife began her work, according to his instructions. She dressed the corpse all in white and propped it up against one of the pillars of the open *bale* where he had died. She untied his hair and spread it out over his shoulders as a man does when he prays. She set out a tray containing holy water and a bell, a lamp, flowers—in short, all of the things that a priest must have when praying. She spread a cloth woven with gold and silver threads on the lap of her husband's corpse and put his kris in the band at the back. And then, above his head, way at the top of the *bale* near the ceiling, she hung the cage of a fighting cock filled with a large swarm of bees. Incense from the fire below drifted upwards and aroused the bees to a great humming noise.

Many people in the village heard the news, but they wanted to see for themselves whether or not Pan Balang Tamak had really died. Some of them crept up to the house compound and peeked inside. Nobody was crying, as is usually the case when there is a death. Instead they heard someone chanting mantras in a low voice. They crept in a little further, and, much to their surprise, there sat Pan Balang Tamak, leaning against a pillar in his *bale,* all of his sacred equipment in front of him, unmindful of intruders while he was reciting holy mantras. The muttering sound, of course, was the angry bees.

The people who saw this rushed to tell others, and a group went to the king to report that the poison was no good. The king was outraged. He thought that the poison was very strong. And so, to test it, he ate a little of the leftover food himself. Of course, he toppled over dead.

Now the village had to mourn the passing of their king, and everyone was very sad. Meanwhile, Pan Balang Tamak's wife had another job to do. Most Balinese people keep their valuable possessions in a large wooden chest. Pan Balang Tamak's wife removed all of these valuables from the chest and put them in a large coffin that she had made. She then put the body of her husband in the treasure chest. She put the treasure chest in its usual location in the bedroom of the house, and went outside to cry by the coffin.

As darkness fell, thieves came to the house. They knew Pan Balang Tamak was a very rich man. They saw his wife weeping in front of the coffin in the *bale.* So they sneaked into the house, found the heavy treasure chest in the bedroom, and quietly stole it. The thieves were very happy because they had stolen a treasure that was undoubtedly of great value.

In a quiet place that was hidden by bushes, one of them said: "Why don't we open the box here?"

Another said, "Oh no, it smells like a corpse in these bushes. Let's move on to another place." Once they had moved the box to a better place, one of the thieves said, "Let's open the box here. Why should we carry it farther?"

But another said, "Ah, there is a bad corpse smell here, too. Let's move it again."

None of the thieves knew where the smell was coming from. One of them said: "Let's take the box to the *pura desa* (village temple). Nobody would dare bury a corpse in a holy place like that. So if we go there we won't smell anything." And the rest agreed.

The thieves struggled and strained and sweated carrying the box to the *pura desa,* where they set it down on the ground next to the *bale agung* in the outer courtyard. Then they pried the lid open. The awful smell of the corpse and the sight of a body wrapped entirely in a white cloth so frightened the thieves that they dropped the lid of the box and fled.

Next day, early in the morning, the *pemangku* of the *pura desa* went to the temple, as usual, to pray. As he passed in through the *candi bentar* he was frightened because in the yard he saw a box. After gathering his composure, he sat down in front of the box, crossed his legs, and prayed, giving homage to god:

"Oh, god, thank you for your blessing. You are very nice to us; you are generous to your people. Thanks you for this great gift."

PAN BALANG TAMAK'S FINAL TRICK

Meanwhile, others had heard the news and came to the temple where the *pemangku* was praying. Surely a god had given this box as a sign that he had specially chosen the *pura desa* as a new home. A *balian* mystic was consulted, and he went into trance. The god spoke through him and commanded that an elaborate purification ceremony be held and that a new shrine erected to the god. This was done. There were great feasts. All of the villagers joined in the preparations. The new shrine was hung with cloths and banners. And *penjors* were set up everywhere.

On the big day all of the villagers came to the *pura desa* and sat on the ground in front of the new shrine next to the *bale agung*. Everyone prayed to the god, thanking him for his gift and his favor. The shrine was dedicated with all due ceremony and solemnity. Then the box was opened.

It was as if everyone's throat had been stabbed with a dagger, the smell was so bad. And, to a man, anger arose in the hearts of the villagers as they realized that their village trickster, Pan Balang Tamak, had had the last laugh.

But this feeling faded as the *pemangku* pointed out to them that obviously the corpse could only have been placed in the temple courtyard by divine intervention. And, after all, they had already dedicated the shrine and gone through all of the proper ceremonies. They couldn't very well undo what had been done. And besides, why bear a grudge against a dead man? The body was buried with all due ceremony. The *pura desa* was ritually purified. And people have continued to pray at the shrine of Pan Balang Tamak ever since.

THIS IS ONE OF THE BEST-KNOWN of all Balinese folk stories, and people never tire of hearing it. Why? Maybe it is because we see a little of ourselves in the hero. He is not a stock good guy or bad guy. He may not be extremely intelligent. But he is cunning. He "gets back" at society. He defies the establishment and turns the tables upon them. His crudity in the *jaja uli* incident and his cruelty to his little dog may offend us. But we cannot refrain from uttering a silent cheer when, at the end, his life-long enemies find out that they have actually deified the person whom they most wanted to vilify. One cannot really love Pan Balang Tamak. He takes advantage of people. He turns the weaknesses of others into his own strengths. But one cannot really hate him either. He uses his wits, not his hands. If he takes advantage of others, perhaps they deserve it. How nice it would be to do a few things like that to those scheming rascals down at City Hall. Isn't there some of that in everyone of us, unless he is a saint or a liar?

Much of the humor comes in the form of that favorite Balinese device, the pun. Such was the case with the broken shrine and the toothless boar. Note the deliberate literal interpretation of the common idiomatic expression "when the chickens come down from the trees." Note the liberal use of what one could best be called earthy humor—the dog droppings, the people urinating in his garden. The Balinese sensibility is not a delicate one.

The relationship of this folk tale to the various Pan Balang Tamak shrines is far from clear. The shrines are likely, but not always, to be found near the *bale agung* where, according to the tale, Pan Balang Tamak's body was left. About half of the Pan Balang Tamak shrines that I visited are associated with curing or preventing plant diseases or blessing crops, which seems to have little to do with the story. Almost all of the shrines face in a direction opposite to that of the other shrines of the temple. Grader, and other sources, suggests that Pan Balang Tamak is a kind of secretary for the gods, taking "notes" on their proceedings. Grader suggests that the shrine has something to do with divorce, but I found that not to be the case anywhere, even at the Nongan temple.

In most of the villages, my informants were reluctant to discuss Pan Balang Tamak as a person and as a god simultaneously. They would admit the name of the shrine as being associated with a deity named Pan Balang Tamak, but they would quickly point out that, although they knew that Pan Balang Tamak was involved with various stories, this was not really the same person. This may be due to the principle of *pramada*, insubordination, that is responsible for so many euphemistic expressions in Bali.

Several people to whom I spoke stoutly denied that the Pan Balang Tamak legend had anything whatever to do with the shrines that one sees near the *bale agung*s of villages. They say the name for the shrines comes from *pawalang tamak—pawalang* from *alang*, "block" or "obstruct";

tamak, from *tamas*, "greed." They say the shrine is a reminder for wor-shipers to "obstruct greed" when they enter the temple to pray. The shrine, they say, was not dedicated to any prankster, but is a reminder to rid oneself of bad thoughts before praying.

There is one contribution that is universally credited to the prankster Pan Balang Tamak—the invention of the *erang-erang*. The *erang-erang* is an architectural feature of traditional Balinese thatched roofs. It is said that one day Pan Balang Tamak was late (as usual) for a *subak* meeting at the *bale agung* in his village. The purpose of the meeting was to repair the roof of the *bale agung*. Each person was to bring strip of *lalang* thatch or else pay a fine. When the villagers tried to make Pan Balang Tamak pay because he was late, he offered instead to fix the roof of the *bale agung* so that it would be less unsightly. Thatched roofs in the traditional style have a peaked roof along one dimension, with smaller, triangular sections of thatch inserted at either end. The geometry of the roof leaves a gap, how-ever, between these end sections and the roof proper. Pan Balang Tamak's innovation was to tie a *lalang* strip over the gap—the *erang-erang*.

So, like so many stories and customs in Bali, the role and importance of Pan Balang Tamak is ambiguous. He is at least a popular folk hero. He is at most a kind of deity. People know the folktale and they visit the shrines, but are reluctant to relate the two. Perhaps they are unrelated. My original quest was to find out why the shrine was in Pura Ulunsiwi in Jimbaran. I still don't really know. But who does?

CHAPTER 9

Chinese in Bali

FOLKLORE, CONFUCIOUS, AND COINS

THE CHINESE were some of the first immigrants to Southeast Asia, and their arrival in Bali predates the oldest recorded documents on the island. Nationalism and political discrimination have in recent years pressured the Indonesian Chinese community to integrate, and adopt the language and customs of Indonesia. But the Chinese influence on Balinese culture remains profound. There are, of course, Chinese restaurants and food, and several active Chinese temples. Chinese coins, though not legal tender, are used everywhere in offerings. Chinese porcelain decorates the walls of temples. But the most interesting legacy is less tangible: folklore, dances, and mythology.

It is almost futile to speculate about the circumstances attending the arrival of Chinese culture in Bali. It was certainly earlier than the date of the first written records, the 9th century A.D., because these contain references to Chinese coins. Chinese communities were flourishing along the northwest coast of Borneo at about this time, and a large porcelain industry existed in Borneo during the Sung Dynasty in China, A.D. 960–1280. Historians from the Bali Museum hypothesize that Chinese coins were in circulation in Bali in the 7th and 8th centuries. The oldest ones that have been found were cast during the Tang Dynasty—A.D. 618-907. But even as far back as the Tang Dynasty, commercial contact between China and Bali had likely been going on for centuries, perhaps even a millennium.

Throughout Southeast Asia, Chinese communities have faced resentment and, particularly in the 20th century, political discrimination. The overseas Chinese were traders, and the communities they established were invariably seats of relative wealth. Compounding this economic division, the Chinese were quite insular, and kept to homogeneous groups—which spoke Chinese, were educated in Chinese schools, and which, at least in appearance, disdained the local society. In the newly formed Republic of Indonesia, the Chinese became identified with the Communist Party of Indonesia which, after leading an abortive coup against the Indonesian government in 1965, was systematically stamped out. Although the Chinese of Indonesia are now granted all the rights of citizenship, they still keep a low profile. Most have adopted Indonesian names. Signs using Chinese characters are no longer used. Chinese calendars are not for sale. There is only one newspaper (published by the government in Jakarta) using Chinese ideographs.

CHINESE COINS ARE THE MOST IMMEDIATELY VISIBLE SIGN of Chinese influence in Bali. They have not been used as money for decades, but every market sells them, and every household has a quantity of them because they are essential for many kinds of offerings. They are so essential that some of the most important counting words in the Balinese language originally applied to strings containing various numbers of the coins (See CHAPTER 12). The distinctive coins, which are holed in the center like flat washers, are called *pis bolong. Pis,* an abbreviation of *pipis,* is Low Balinese for "money." *Bolong* means "to possess a hole." The Indonesian word is *képéng.* Some of the oldest inscriptions found in Bali refer to "*ku,*" which experts believe is a shortened form of *kupang,* the same word, it is said, as *képéng.*

Typical Chinese coins that are used in Bali today are about 2.5 centimeters across and a millimeter thick. The hole in the center is 5 millimeters across and square. There is an undecorated band around the outside edge, and both sides are adorned with inscriptions. The "front" of the coin has four Chinese characters; the two inscriptions on the back vary, and some people say the unidentified ideographs are Old Javanese. They do not appear to be ordinary Chinese ideographs. Most of the coins are badly corroded. There are no denominations. The coins are sold in bundles of 200 at most village markets and, as of this writing, one string of coins, depending on the quality, sells for Rp 7,000 to Rp 9,000. They are strung in circles and one string of 200 is about 12 centimeters across.

All "Chinese" coins did not necessarily originate in China. Round metal coins with square, hexagonal, or round holes in the center—copies of Chinese coins—were minted all over the Indies. One important source was the Daha area of East Java. Many of the coins, which were legal tender until fairly recently, were imported directly from China. Mads Lange, a Danish trader who, between 1839 and 1856, operated a large mercantile establishment headquartered in Kuta, is said to have made most of his profits from the import of coins from China. Lange paid for the coins—along with such things as textiles, opium, steel utensils, and luxury items—with rice from Bali. He employed Balinese women at his establishment to string the coins together in bundles of 200, making up a bundle known as an *atak*. One *atak*, or *satak* (the prefix *sa-*, or *se-*, designates one of something) was the basic unit of accounting for larger amounts of money. Today, *satak* has come to mean 200 of anything.

Lange could sell the coins in Bali for twice what he paid for them. There was a need for a unit of money that was widely recognized and would be accepted by traders, merchants, sailors, and the Balinese people—the *pis bolong* became the standard. In Bali, even goods that were bartered were assigned value in terms of *pis bolong*. Lange so aggressively pushed the *pis bolong* standard that, it is believed, he imported too many of them, producing inflation. But since he had a monopoly on the import of *pis bolong* he could control prices and insure exclusive access to the various goods he sought to buy in Bali, particularly rice.

Pis bolong represented conveniently small units of value with which ordinary commercial transactions could be carried out. Since they had holes in them, they could be easily strung together to form larger bundles for major financial transactions. They were made of bronze, and to the Balinese people all metals have mystical power. The *pis bolong*, as an alloy, has come to be associated with the *panca datu*, an important offering of iron, silver, copper, and gold, which is used to bless the foundation of an important building. Thus, even today, *pis bolong* are associated with wealth. A single *pis bolong* was never really valuable—but it is a charged metal object that is associated with, and a vehicle of, wealth. And so when gifts are made to the gods in the form of offerings such as flowers, fruits, cakes, and meat, *pis bolong* are offered also. *Pis bolong* are included as the "base" of certain kinds of offerings. The exact number of coins is almost always specified, although the significance of the numbers is not known.

Pis bolong are used as what is called *urip*, a ritual "giving life" to an object. For example, when an important building is constructed, offerings called *pedagingan* must be placed below the foundations. The presence of coins in the *pedagingan* provides what is called *pengurip-urip* for the building, a prayer for its integrity and safety and well being. One of the common small offerings that is used by individuals for praying in certain kinds of ceremonies is called a *kwangen*. It is in the shape of a small triangular or conical folded pocket, containing flowers and other ingredients and is held between the fingers as is a flower when one prays. Each *kwangen* must contain a *urip* of one *pis bolong*.

Pis bolong are commonly used as *sesari*, a kind of gift to a priest or offering maker. It is common to put a small amount of money on top of an offering when bringing it to the temple to pray or when dedicating it under other circumstances. After the prayers, the money is left there with the understanding that the person who officiates should keep the money. In the case of *sesari* made at temples, the money is supposed to be used for temple activities. It is a kind of contribution on the part of the wor-

A BARIS CINA DANCER AND A SRI SEDANA NGADEG

shiper, since those who conduct ceremonies are not often paid otherwise. *Pis bolong* are also used as decorations, most particularly around shrines and pavilions when a ceremony is taking place. The common *lamak*, long banners of cut-up coconut leaves, are often studded with coins. The *tamyiang*, a kind of round decoration hung from the roof of a shrine or pavilion, is made with *pis bolong*.

The coins are important to burial and cremation rites. Before a corpse is interred it is common to sprinkle it with *pis bolong*, yellow rice, and flowers. And just before a body is cremated, a life-sized flat figurine, called an *ukur*, is constructed of attached Chinese coins and placed on a white sheet. The *ukur* represents the corpse, so that the actual body can be left in the cemetery where it will not contaminate the living space. The last act of gratitude that a family member can show toward its deceased relative is ritually enacted by each family member sticking a pin into one of the coins adorning the *ukur*. This represents "dressing"—by this pinning act, the figurine is fastened to the white cloth. Once the ritual is finished, the *ukur* is wrapped in a white sheet and carried to the cemetery on the cremation tower. There the cloth is removed from the tower, the *wadah*, and laid on the disinterred bones before the burning.

Chinese coins are used to make the figurine known as Sri Sedana. *Sedana* means "livelihood," and *sri*, in this usage, refers to something like "essence." Many families have a figurine in human form that they call Sri Sedana and is a kind of token of good luck or wealth. Most people think of Sri Sedana as the god of wealth, and there is a special day in the Pawukon anniversary cycle when offerings are made to him. The day is Buda Cemeng, (Wednesday) of the 28th week, Kelawu, of the recurring 30-week cycle. There are two kinds of Sri Sedana figures. Each is made of five *satak*s of *pis bolong*, a total of 1,000 coins. The Sri Sedana Ngadeg is an actual standing human figure about 25 centimeters high (see illustration on page 117); Sri Sedana Ngerem consists of the coins in a bag, not formed into a figure. *Ngerem* is High Balinese for "resting"; *ngadeg* means "stand."

A *pis bolong satakan*, a large bundle of coins, is usually carried in the *melis* procession—this is the ceremony, just before the new year, in which village gods are taken to the sea for ritual cleansing. In the ceremony called *magunting bok*, or *mapepetik*, commonly performed upon such occasions as the *oton* (birthday), weddings, and other Hindu rite of passage ceremonies, the priest cuts the hair of the person for whom the ceremony is being given as a symbol of purification. It is common for the subject of the ceremony to hold on his lap a bundle of *pis bolong* called *jinah sandangan*, which contains 1,100 coins. This is a symbolic "payment" for the right to cut the honoree's hair. Holy water, when collected from a far-away temple, is often carried in a *bungbung*, a hollow length of bamboo. It is usual to tie a *pis bolong* on the *bungbung*, since the container carries such a sacred substance.

Although not nearly as important or as common as the coins, Chinese plates—from as early as the 9th century Sung Dynasty—have been found all over Bali, along with porcelain from Korea, Japan, Europe, and the Tonkin area. At first these plates and bowls were used for ceremonial purposes, such as containers for holy water. They were not sacred in themselves, but they were used for sacred purposes, much as Chinese coins are today. The use of these porcelains did not begin until the coming of the Dutch to Bali in the mid-19th century. The idea seems to have been that porcelain has a higher status and is more *alus*, or refined, than the usual terra cotta of Bali, making it suitable for decorating holy places. Most of the chinaware that is seen on temple gates and walls is Dutch. But there are outstanding examples of Chinese porcelain plates in the temple *gong* pavilions in Kerambitan, in Geriya Tegal near the Tegal Bus Station in Denpasar, and on the signal drum tower, *bale kulkul*, of Puri Pemecutan in Denpasar.

ALTHOUGH THE "RELIGION" OF MOST CHINESE IN BALI had been the philosophy of Confucianism, since the first principle of the Indonesian government's Panca Sila is the belief in a supreme deity, many of the island's Chinese, already facing considerable political estrangement after the abortive coup, converted to Theravada Buddhism. Theravada is the most personal and philosophical of the two major forms of Buddhist thought. Mahayana Buddhism, with a fairly elaborate pantheon and much ceremony, is a strain rather like Hinduism. (See "Bali's Other Faiths," *BS&N Vol. I.*)

Bali's only Buddhist monk is Biku Giri Rahito, who lives in Banjar, just west of Singaraja, and presides over a Buddhist temple, a *wihara*, there. Biku Giri has supervised the conversion of some of the traditional Chinese temples in Bali from their original entities to *wiharas*. The changes have been effected completely, as far as he is concerned, at the temples in Kuta and Tabanan. And in the Kuta and Tabanan areas there are many Chinese-Balinese who worship at these temples and call themselves Theravada Buddhists.

There are "Chinese" temples in Blahbatuh, Denpasar, Gianyar, Mumbul, two in Singaraja, and another at Tanjung Benoa. Most Balinese call these places *klenteng*, a word that has no religious or philosophical meaning but is probably onomatopoeically derived from the sound of the temple bell. Sometimes the word *kongco* is used to refer to Chinese temples. However, the proper use of the word is with reference to a holy person or a manifestation of God. Worshipers commonly come to pray at new and full moon, as well as on the dates of special Chinese and Buddhist holy days. There is no traditional religious dress. People wear their best Western style clothes, take their shoes off before entering the

main building, and pray in a kneeling position in front of the shrines.
Many bring simple offerings of fruit and flowers and cakes.

THE LEGEND OF TAN HU CIN JIN is closely connected with the Kuta
and Tabanan *wiharas* and some of the other *bios,* and is an important factor in the beliefs of many Chinese-Balinese. Many Chinese in Bali know
various versions of the story. But it is not well known by practically anyone else in Bali. For that reason I would like to repeat the tale briefly. It is
history, legend, folklore, and religion, and there are many versions of this
tale. The entire story is quite long, so I have shortened it here.

Tan Hu Cin Jin came from China to Bali some time during the 17th
century. His name was Tan Bun Chiong, although others give it as Tan
Bun Tiang and Babah Made. The name by which he is best known, Tan
Hu Cin Jin, is a title meaning "Great teacher from the Tan family," and it
was given to him only after his death. He settled in the Kuta area, and was
employed as a tax collector for the raja of Mengwi. Tan Hu Cin Jin was
also a well-known architect, and it is around these talents of his that the
story revolves.

The raja was in the process of consolidating his grip upon as much of
South Bali as possible. As part of this larger plan, he decided to move his
palace—*puri*—from Bekak to the present village of Mengwi. The raja
wanted to build a large park next to his new *puri* and chose Tan Hu Cin
Jin for the job. The king stipulated that the job had to be completed
within three months from the date he commissioned Tan Hu Cin
Jin—this was a command, not an offer. Tan Hu Cin Jin could not refuse
an order from his raja, even though he knew that this was an impossibly
short period of time in which to complete such a large project.

The weeks dragged on, and work continued daily on the *puri.* But Tan
Hu Cin Jin did nothing about the park. He went home to Kuta and meditated at the site where the present *wihara* is located, seeking divine help
with his problem. When he returned to Mengwi the king kept asking him
when he would start work on the park. And Tan Hu Cin Jin told the king
that it would be completed as ordered. Meanwhile, Tan Hu Cin Jin began
communicating through meditation with the spirits that lived in the
forests around Mengwi. The king developed an antagonism against what
he felt was a lazy foreigner. And these negative feelings were encouraged
by the king's followers, since they did not like the Chinese man and felt
threatened by him. When only three days were left before the deadline,
the king ordered his followers to guard Tan Hu Cin Jin in the *puri* to
make sure he would not run away.

The night before the park was to be completed Tan Hu Cin Jin took a
long piece of red cloth to the hill where the park was to be created. He
arranged the strip of cloth in a kind of circle, lit some candles and put
them around the edge, and then went inside the enclosure to meditate

and pray. Having finished imploring the spirits, Tan Hu Cin Jin went back to the *puri*, told his friends that his job had been completed, and said that he knew that he would be killed. He said he had left a message for his followers and for the king carved into a piece of *paras* stone at the spot where he had meditated. (The message foretold of the collapse of the kingdom of Mengwi.)

That night all the villagers heard mysterious sounds of hammering, building, hauling things, and general construction at the site of the park. And when the first light came, the park had been completed. It was a lovely place. There was an area where the king could sit and observe the beauty of the natural scene from an eight-sided pavilion next to the pretty lake or moat that surrounded the park. This is the park of Tamun Ayun.

The king saw this and, instead of being happy, was incensed, because he now realized that he was dealing with a very powerful man. So the king ordered his ministers to take Tan Hu Cin Jin to Kuta and kill him. Tan Hu Cin Jin had built the park so that, from above, it looked like a duck or goose. The hill that extended northward from the main body of the duck where the park was located, stretched off to the north and was the neck and head of the duck. A sweet, fresh stream ran down a valley on each side of this "neck" and into the large moat that surrounded the park. Now Tan Hu Cin Jin cut a deep trench between the two streams, connecting them. With its head severed from its body, the magical duck died. The water of the moat turned yellow and sour. And a spring on the east side of the moat suddenly changed from running fresh, clean water to discharging foul smelling liquids—the body fluids of the dead duck. This spring is called Pancoran Bengu; literally, a "shower of stench."

[The spring is still there today. There is a trail to it leading from the parking strip in front of Pura Tamun Ayun south and part way down the embankment upon which the road is located. There is a small temple just west of the spring. The deep trench where the neck of the duck was cut is visible by walking along the shore of the moat toward the west. It is quite a deep and narrow gorge cut into a hill. It is hard to make any connection between the topography and a duck or goose. Informants have told me that the imagery is *niskala*, not *sekala*.]

The King had told two of his followers, Ida Bagus Den Kayu and I Gusti Ngurah Subuk to kill Tan Hu Cin Jin. Although they liked their prisoner, they had to follow their ruler's instructions or be killed themselves. After changing clothes at his home, Tan Hu Cin Jin went down to the beach, where the two men assigned to the job tried to kill him with their kris. But his power was so great that they could not harm him. They realized that they could now not return to Mengwi, and so they decided to join Tan Hu Cin Jin and flee.

When the King heard of the failure of his plan he sent a group to chase the three offenders. They fled to the northwest along the sea to a point near Seseh. When the pursuers were almost upon them, Tan Hu Cin Jin meditated, and two new followers appeared. With a powerful mantra Tan Hu Cin Jin changed these two into a tiger and a crocodile and told them to guard the group. Then Tan Hu Cin Jin summoned a huge white crab from the sea, and he and the other two mounted its back, and were transported across the sea to a place on the coast of East Java near Banyuwangi. But the group from Mengwi followed in hot pursuit. Tan Hu Cin Jin succeeded in holding them off for a while, and then escaped northward to a strip of coast north of Banyuwangi called Basuki. The King's men followed. Once again he fled to Probolinggo. And he changed himself into a great *naga*—a dragon snake—that spat such great plumes of water upon their boat that the raja's men had to retreat to Mengwi. And here, in Probolinggo, Tan Hu Cin Jin ended his days.

Some say he attained Hindu oneness, *moksa,* here. Others deny this. Some say that the group flew from the Seseh area in Bali on Tan Hu Cin Jin's magic robe and landed on a rock beach near Banyuwangi named Watu Dodol. Others say that they did not actually land here, but, rather, just flew off to *moksa,* and that somehow this rocky beach became associated with the three. At any rate, a temple has been built near here, but not on the beach. And there is another temple at Basuki. It is said that fishermen still pray to Tan Hu Cin Jin at Watu Dodol for good luck in their profession. And soil from that sacred spot has been taken to the temples at Banyuwangi, Kuta, to the Leeng Gwon Kiong Bio at Singaraja, and to Tabanan. And in East Java soil was taken to a very sacred temple at Probolinggo, called Pancoran Naga or Leong Chang Bio. Some also went to temples at Rogojampi in East Java and to Lombok.

The Tabanan *wihara* has three shrines, *kongco,* which represent the three protagonists of this story—Tan Hu Cin Jin and his two companions. You will recall that *kongco* is the name of a holy person or manifestation of God. The interior of the Tabanan *wihara* has, on the right wall, a *paras* carving of a man meditating in a cave above a spring; on the left wall is a carving of an octagonal pavilion. The pavilion is almost photographically identical to the one at Pura Taman Ayun. And the spring is a depiction of Pancoran Bengu just across the road from Taman Ayun.

THE FAMOUS MAYADENAWA TALE, which centers around a village called Balingkang, north of Kintamani, has elements that relate to Chinese culture on the island. Balinkang is part way down into the huge caldera at Batur, and can be reached only by a very rough road that leads down and to the southeast from Penulisan, which is at the crater's rim. The road leading northwest from Penulisan to the north gradually twists its way downhill to the coast at Kubutambahan.

It is said that some time in the 6th century there was a just and benevolent king, Sri Jaya Kesunu (sometimes Ki Detya Sri Jaya Pangus) who ruled this area. His government followed Mahayana Buddhism. He had a beautiful wife, who bore only one male child, Mayadenawa. The government of Sri Jaya Kesunu ran smoothly and the ruler was just and wise. He always paid attention to the welfare of his subjects.

One day a Chinese man from the family of a famous sage arrived at Sri Jaya Kesunu's kingdom. The old stranger, Empu Liem, and his companion, a young Chinese woman, were received with good will and friendship by the king. The *empu* soon became indispensable to the king because of his great knowledge. As the King's advisor he taught Sri Jaya Kesunu many things about government, economics, commerce, agriculture, and military affairs. It is said that Empu Liem taught the local people the original *baris dapdap* and *baris tumbak* dances, which are still performed today, especially at the temple of Pura Dalem Balingkang. And the *empu*'s companion was always present, helping with great industry and efficiency.

The result was that the kingdom prospered greatly. The crops were abundant. People flocked to hear the *empu* and asked to be led by the king. There was peace, quiet, prosperity, and good feeling everywhere as the kingdom spread. Meanwhile, Mayadenawa was growing up. Realizing that he would one day become king, Sri Jaya Kesunu made him crown prince and gave him some power. But he soon realized his mistake. Mayadenawa usurped the power from his aging father. The first thing that he did was change the religion to Theravada Buddhism, the main point of which, the story goes, is a disbelief in God. So Mayadenawa ordered the temples shut and all worship stopped. Mayadenawa became such a tyrant that he was expelled from Balingkang.

Mayadenawa fled to southern Bali where he began to build a small kingdom. With this area as a base, he set out on a program of systematic destruction of all rivals and the imposition of his godless tyranny. War and harshness were the only certainties. Mayadenawa announced himself as a god and forced the people to pray to him. He was hated by everyone, but he was so powerful that the people could not resist him and lived in an atmosphere of fear.

Mayadenawa's mother, the wife of Sri Jaya Kesunu, suffered greatly from the news about her wicked son. After a long illness, she died on an unlucky day. This made Sri Jaya Kesunu heartbroken, for he adored his wife. Seeking to fill this great gap in his life, the Chinese *empu* offered his female helper to the king. The king accepted, knowing of her great industry and intelligence. The girl grew so dear to the king that he asked the *empu* if he might marry the girl. The *empu* replied that the wedding could take place if the king would agree to stop eating all sorts of raw meat, have his teeth filed, and promise to keep Mahayana Buddhism as the religion of the land. The king agreed to all three, and the two were married.

However, after the king had lived for a long time with his new wife, whose name was Kang Tjin Hwe (or Kang Chi We), no children were born of the marriage. His wife now came to be called Dewi Mandul. *Mandul* means "barren." The king was very sad over the failure to be able to have children and meditated on the problem for many years. Finally Empu Liem suggested to the king that he should make a pair of tall figures that looked like himself and his wife. The king was old and had long teeth; his wife was young and had a pale complexion. These two figures, the *empu* continued, should perform a dance that told the story of the old king and his young Chinese wife. The wife should have a face that reflects an aspect of motherhood and an expression that is wise, merciful, and affectionate.

This advice was followed. The two figures created are the two well-known *barong landung* figures that one sees all over South Bali. The faces are exactly as described as above. The male figure with the black face is called Jero Gede. And the female figure with the Chinese face is Jero Luh. The dance is sacred and has never been commercialized. Many temples and family groups own *barong landung* and perform the dance, especially on Kajeng Keliwon

Meanwhile, Mayadenawa's disastrous government had produced fear, disease, crop failure, and general chaos. The gods cursed him and acted to destroy him. Betara Indra was sent to earth with a large army to smash Mayadenawa. Mayadenawa's magical powers allowed him to be forewarned of Indra's attack, and he prepared accordingly. He was strong, but the gods were stronger. After a particularly fierce battle, close to defeat, Mayadenawa was saved by nightfall. That night, while Indra's army slept, Mayadenawa crept into their camp and conjured up a poison spring. So that he would not be detected he walked on the sides of his feet. The next morning the gods awoke, drank of the spring water, and became very sick. Betara Indra realized what had happened and created a new spring—this gushed forth pure holy water and quickly cured his followers. He called the spring Tirtha Empul. The place where this occurred is called Tampaksiring, because the word *tampak* means "the sole of a foot," and *siring* means "edge."

Indra's army continued to attack Mayadenawa, who now fled. He tried changing himself into various shapes: a *manuk* (chicken), a *timbul* (vegetable), a *busung* (young palm leaf), a *susuh* (kind of snail), and a *bidadari* (angel). The places where each of these transformations took place are now supposedly named after the event: Desa Manukaya, Desa Timbul, Desa Blusung, Desa Penyusuhan, and Desa Kedawatan. Finally he changed himself into a *paras* stone. Indra knew about all of these disguises and was not fooled. When he saw the stone, he shot it with a magic arrow and killed Mayadenawa. Mayadenawa's blood flowed out of the rock and down the hill, where it became the River Pekerisan. And Indra cursed the river for 1,000 years, saying that if someone used it for irrigating a rice field, the crops would be bountiful and large. But if the rice were ever harvested it would turn bloody and smell like a corpse. And when the waters of the Pekerisan are viewed by the light of the full moon one can see the red color of this blood. For a long time the Balinese did not, in fact, use the Pekerisan for anything at all. But now, it appears, the curse has expired.

Mayadenawa's wicked rule is attributed in the legend to the evils of atheism, of adharma. And the defeat of Mayadenawa is the symbol of the conquest of dharma over adharma; religious duty over atheism. The famous Galungan days celebration is considered by many to be a celebration of the defeat of Mayadenawa and the return of Bali to a religious, peaceful existence. (Others deny this connection between the two stories and give as evidence the pre-Mayadenawa existence of the word and the celebration of Galungan in East Java.) It is also said that the predecessors of Raja Sri Jaya Kesunu all had short lives. In a revelation, God told Jaya Kesunu that he and his followers must erect *penjors*—offerings suspended from tall, curved bamboo poles—in the celebration of Galungan. Sri Jaya Kesunu took up this practice, and the Balinese continue it to this day.

Evaluating the Jaya Kesunu–Ratu Mandul–Mayadenawa story is difficult. Some take the marriage between the king and his Chinese servant to be symbolic of the fusion of Balinese and Chinese cultures. Others believe the story to have considerable historical basis in fact. There is still a very large temple at Balingkang, and it is certainly closely connected to the Jaya Kesunu–Mayadenawa story. But the connections are ambiguous. Some authorities attempt to derive the name "Mayadenawa" from the word *maya*, "illusion," and *danu*, "lake"—referring to nearby lake Batur. The name of the area and the temple may have been derived from the name of Sri Jaya Kesunu's Chinese wife, Kang Chi We. According to some informants the wife of Sri Jaya Kesunu is also known as Ratu Subandar. And therein lies another story.

WHETHER SUBANDAR IS OR IS NOT ANOTHER NAME for Jaya Kesunu's wife is highly debatable. The fact that Subandar is an important figure in Bali is beyond question. There is a large shrine dedicated to Ida Ratu Ayu Subandar located in the extreme northeast corner of the outer courtyard of Pura Dalem Balingkang. Inside of it is a long megalith that is considered to be very sacred and in the shape of a *barong landung*. At any rate, there seems to be some connection between Subandar and the Balingkang stories. With this in mind, let us examine the other Subandar phenomena in Bali.

The word *bandar* means "harbor" or "port" in Indonesian. Subandar then refers to a harbor master, or one who supervises the trade of a port. In its most simple aspect, the deity called Subandar may be a deification of the historical importance to Chinese people of trade. At least this is the thought of some authorities. The Chinese, who have been trading for more than a millennia, had various gods of trade. There are shrines to Subandar not only at Balingkang, but also at Besakih, Pura Ulun Danu Batur, and Pura Silayukti at Padang Bai. The names are interesting. At Balingkang, the "Ida Ayu" prefixed to the name indicates a female. At Batur temple the name of the shrine is Jero Gede Subandar, implying male. The name of the shrine at Besakih is female and identical to the one at Balingkang.

The Subandar shrine at Pura Ulun Danu Batur is by far the most interesting of these and the only one that displays any obvious external Chinese influence. Here is, to all intents and purposes, a Chinese temple right in the inner courtyard of one of the most important Hindu temples in Bali. It is located in the northeast, or far left hand corner of the sacred inner courtyard of the temple. The Chinese temple is not large—about five meters wide and long—and is built upon a white platform. The shrine itself is in a traditional Balinese *bale* with four pillars on the open porch and a thatch roof. But the pillars, and indeed, the whole interior of the open porch, are painted bright Chinese red. Two red sitting lions with their paws and claws facing outward guard the steps up to the entrance, which is enclosed by a low carved stone wall. The bright red door to the room inside is covered with gold decoration and is guarded by two large green snakes with bared teeth. On each side of the snakes is a mustachioed Chinese figure in a bright green robe. The wall facing the temple courtyard is decorated with two carvings in deep relief. The one on the left is of a typical heroic figure from one of the Hindu epics; the one on the right is a *pedanda*, a Brahmana priest. The carvings are painted gold, with green and red borders.

The story is that Batur temple was originally located at a site down in the caldera, next to the lake. And the holy soul of Jero Gede Subandar was worshipped at a shrine there, along with Ida Betara Sri Jaya Kesunu (he had apparently also become a god) and his Chinese wife. In 1926 Mount Batur erupted with violence. At the moment of eruption, the story goes, the temple priests arrived on the scene and became possessed by a spirit. The spirit said the Subandar shrine would not be harmed, but they must evacuate everyone to the west side of the lake where there would be no damage. They did so. Upon returning, the *pemangkus* (lay priests in charge of the temple) found that none of the Subandar relics had been harmed by lava, but everything else in the temple was destroyed.

The temple was rebuilt up on the crater rim in its present location. The Subandar shrine was inside the *jaba*, the outermost courtyard, with all of the other shrines. Then, in 1952, the government decided to move it completely outside the temple because the Chinese who came to worship there went in and out of Pura Batur without wearing the required traditional clothing. Shortly after the shrine was moved, it is said, disasters appeared in the Kintamani area. The water dikes broke without apparent cause. Plant diseases ruined the crops. People became seriously ill. One day, at a ceremony in the temple, several *pemangkus* went into trance. The spirit that possessed them was that of Subandar, called in this story Chong Poo Kong, who said that because the shrine was moved outside of the temple, he could no longer guard the gate if an accident or disaster appeared. He said the people should move his shrine back to its original place in the temple. The *pemangkus* asked where the shrine should be placed. The reply was that it should be placed where a stone appears from inside the earth. The stone, visible only at night, did appear, it is said, and got larger every night. The present shrine of Jero Gede Subandar was built here and has protected the temple ever since.

AN INTERESTING AND LITTLE KNOWN RELIC of Chinese culture in Bali is the *baris cina* dance. There are dozens of varieties of *baris* dances performed as parts of religious ceremonies in Balinese-Hindu temples. To my knowledge, however, there are only two *baris cina* groups, one in Banjar Semawang in the south part of Sanur, the other given by a group from Banjar Renon Kelod, just west of Sanur. These dances have no connection with any of the Chinese-oriented religions or temples. They are performed by Balinese Hindus in the context of Balinese Hindu ceremonies.

The story goes that a Chinese ship was beached along the Sanur coast many years ago. While the ship was being repaired the Chinese crew camped on the beach and, during their spare time, went through group exercises something like a manual of arms with their swords. The Chinese were the only people in Bali who wore long pants in those days. The Balinese had never seen anything like this, and so, when the ship had been repaired and gone on its way, they imitated the actions of the sailors and the instruments that were used to accompany the military exercise. This story is, obviously, open to dispute. Some claim that the dance comes from the Majapahit empire in Java. At any rate, the whole thing is quite interesting.

The orchestra that accompanies the dance is known as the *gong beri*. The largest instrument is a barrel-shaped drum called *bedug*. It rests on a platform on the ground and the player beats both ends with long sticks. There are six gongs, called *bende*, that have no central boss and look something like rice winnowing trays. There is a large rack of cymbals, *ceng-ceng*, two *kompli* (a small bronze pot-like percussion instrument) and a conch shell that is blown near the end of the dance. The group has no melody instruments.

At the beginning of the dance a group of nine men dressed in black pants and black jackets files into the arena. Each wears a loop of white cloth draped like a sash. Each wears a black *koboi*—"cowboy"—hat and carries a long, black Western-style sabre. The leader is similarly dressed, except that his sash is checkered *poleng* cloth and he wears a pith helmet and red pants. The eight men line up in two rows with the leader facing them, and, while he watches, they go through a very slow motion series of brandishings of the sabers, all the while crouching, rising, and lifting alternate feet. It does look like a manual of arms. The *ceng-ceng* player then goes into a frenzy, and the leader does the same sort of dance only about three times as fast. When it has been completed the eight men repeat their performance, and then all sit down next to the *gong*.

A second group of nine men enters. They are clad all in white, including the hats, and their sashes are plain black. Their leader also wears a pith helmet. Sometimes he and the leader of the "blacks" wear huge fake beards. The white group does the same dance as the blacks. When they have finished, a group of followers quickly forms a large circle around the dancers as the black dressed dancers get up to face the whites. Suddenly the whites attack the blacks, and everyone goes into trance, swords waving in the air, the followers restraining the dancers from violent acts. The entranced dancers are led to a nearby shrine, where *pemangkus* administer holy water and remove the dangerous sabers as the dancers come out of trance. Two Balinese kris are now brought out and are used by a few of the dancers and group members in much the same self-stabbing routine as one sees at a *barong* dance. All the while the *gong* is playing and the conch shell sounding. It is quite a wild scene.

The Banjar Semawang group performs this dance at Pura Kesuma Jati, just east of the crossroads in Sanur where the road to the south leads to the Sanur Beach Hotel and the road to Kuta leads to the west. The dance is not scheduled, but is commissioned irregularly by families seeking to fulfill an agreement made to a local deity, or by the village to cleanse the area of such disasters such as crop failure. The Banjar Renon Kelod group performs regularly upon several occasions. The most interesting of these is at the anniversary of Pura Peti Tenget, just north of the Oberoi Hotel, north of Kuta. This is the performance described above. The other group's performance differs only in minor details. The *odalan* date of the temple is Buda Cemeng Merakih. The dance is also performed at a few other *odalan*s and at other irregular times.

PART III

Language

The Balinese Language
LEVELS, INFLECTION, AND CULTURE

ONE ESSAY, OF COURSE, IS NOT ENOUGH to "Speak Balinese Like a Native." My intention, in addition to offering some basic linguistic rules and pronunciation hints, is to look at some of the aspects of the language that offer clues to Balinese culture and society—the distinctive "High" and "Low" modes of address, the words for time, direction, and measurement, and the characteristically Balinese use of euphemism.

Austronesian, sometimes known as Malayo-Polynesian, is the linguistic family from which Balinese derives. Today, this family extends from Madagascar in the east to southern Vietnam, the Malay Peninsula, Indonesia, the Philippines, Taiwan, New Guinea, the Melanesian, Micronesian and Polynesian islands, and New Zealand. However, large areas within this zone are at least partly occupied by people who do not speak an Austronesian language—New Guinea, for example. The official languages of four large countries are Austronesian: Indonesian, Malay, Tagalog in the Philippines, and Magalasy in Madagascar. Thai is not an Austronesian language, but it is related.

Balinese is not the same language as Indonesian. Before they were united into one nation after World War II, each of the many cultures within the archipelago had its own language. Most were varieties of Austronesian, but the languages were, and still are, quite distinct. Since Malay had for centuries been the trading language of the Indies, when Indonesia achieved its independence the language was adopted, in a rather piecemeal fashion, as Bahasa Indonesia. It is spoken everywhere in Indonesia, but in most places it must be learned in the state-run schools. A Balinese child hears nothing but Balinese in his home. He first comes into contact with Indonesian when he goes to primary school.

As with most languages, Balinese as it is spoken today is a great mixture. It contains many Sanskrit words, which is not surprising considering the strong Hindu influence upon both Bali and neighboring Java. Strong elements of Old Javanese or Kawi can also be found in modern Balinese. There are Arabic words, Chinese words, Parsi words, and Tamil words. And, because of colonial and commercial activities, many words from the Dutch, Portuguese, and English. For example, such words as *sekolah, dokter,* and *buku* have Dutch origins. Portuguese influence has produced such words as *kemeja, bola,* and *jendela.* English expressions such as "stop," *botol,* and *tiket* are heard everywhere.

Balinese is primarily a spoken language. The Balinese, as a rule, are not great readers. Few families own any books at all and, if they do, they are likely to be written in Indonesian. Balinese literature is confined mostly to sacred religious works, which are generally not available to ordinary people. Some effort has been made to stimulate the writing of Balinese. Balinese is a required language for school children, and the first books that a student uses in school are written in his native tongue. A few books of stories written in Balinese have been published. There is a Balinese column in the Sunday edition of the *Bali Post,* the rest of which is printed in Indonesian. But that is about the extent of it. Balinese may be, and usually is, written using the ordinary Roman alphabet. The sacred books, however, are always written using the script alphabet known as Tulisan Bali. Tulisan Bali is a required subject in primary school, but most students forget it quickly.

A visitor is likely to make the assumption that, since Bali is such a small island, the language is homogeneous. This is far from the case. There are distinct regional differences, not only in pronunciation, but also in vocabulary. Budi's wife, Wati, is from Denpasar. And she had to learn a great many new ways of expressing herself when she moved to Jimbaran, a mere 20 kilometers from her home town.

AN ATTEMPT HAS BEEN MADE by some authorities to standardize Balinese spelling, which varies quite a bit. But, since there is so little literature in this medium, the effects are scarcely noticeable. Balinese lacks the letters *f, q, v, x,* and *z.* Most dictionaries have almost no words with the initial *h.* The *h* sound is silent in Balinese except at the end of a syllable, such as the word *belah,* "break." It was formerly pronounced at the beginning of such suffixes as *-a, -an, -ang, -é,* and *-in,* as well as in other circumstances, but the loss of the pronunciation of the initial *h* has led some writers to include it in the spelling. The *h* (and *a* and *e*) problem leads to such strange situations as the following equivalent spellings of the word for "group": *seka, sekehe, sekaa, sakahe,* and *sekaha.* The authoritative *Dictionary of Balinese-English,* by C. Clyde Barber, lists under initial *h* almost all words that begin with a vowel. Most other dictionaries and word lists do not follow this practice. Pronunciation presents no difficulty to the speaker of a Romance language and is largely phonetic. The few simple rules are summarized below:

PRONUNCIATION

Pepet   the *a* sound as in "sof*a*"
Taleng   the *a* sound as in "d*a*te"
Suku   the *ou* sound as in "y*ou*"
Ulu   the *ee* sound as in "w*ee*p"

Note: An "open" syllable ends in a vowel; a "closed" syllable ends in a consonant.

SOME BASIC RULES

1. *A* is pepet if it is in a prefix, such as *pa-*, *ma-*, *ka-*, *sa-*, or *nga-*, or if it is the last letter in a word. Note: some preliminary syllables of this variety, such as the *sa-* in saput, are not prefixes. Examples: palinggih, mapajar, babuten, lima, buta, niskal*a*.

   A is pronounced as the *a* in "father" elsewhere, never like the *a* in "cat." Examples: Bali (it upsets me to hear people make this word rhyme with "alley"), dalem, nisk*a*la.

2. *E* is taleng if it is the last letter of a word. Examples: bale, rame.

   E is pronounced like the *a* in "bad," or *e* in "get" if in a closed syllable. Examples: kenken, daken. Note: the *e* in bale is taleng. It changes to pepet when suffix *-ne* is added; *e* of *-ne* is taleng. Example: balen*e*.

3. *I* is ulu in an open syllable. Examples: Bali, milu, k*i*kir.

   An *i* is pronounced like the *i* in "did" in closed syllable. Examples: sugih, pelih, kik*i*r.

4. *U* is suku in open syllable. Examples: malu, ujan, ulu, t*u*tup.

   A *u* is pronounced as *u* in "pull" in a closed syllable. Examples: mayus, saput, tut*u*p.

   It is never pronounced as *eau* in "beautiful."

5. *Ng-* and *-ng-* are pronounced as the *ng* in "singer." Example: ngurah.

6. The combination *-ngg-* is pronounced like the *ng* in "single." Example: palinggih.

7. Final *-d*, *-t*, and *-k* represent a glottal stop—as between the two parts of

"Oh, oh"— and are symbolized by an apostrophe (') and not pronounced. Example: tida' = tidak.

8. The final -h is pronounced as a gentle puff of air. Example: kasih.

9. Bh-, ph-, dh-, etc. appear in Sanskrit-derived words (the h is often omitted). If present, pronounce h separately. Examples: phala (pronounced like shepherd, never as f sound) Bhatara, Dharsana.

10. C is always pronounced as ch- in "church"; never as c in "cow."

Spelling problems usually arise only with respect to the a and e sounds. School children used to learn to put a circumflex accent over the pepet a, as, for example, mâpajar, and to leave the long a without an accent. This is no longer done, and students are left merely to follow the rules given above. Many do not, and one commonly sees the letter e written in place of a pepet, as in mepajar. By the same token, it was standard to use an acute accent over the e for the taleng pronunciation, as for example, balé, and to leave the pepet pronunciation unaccented. This practice is seldom followed anymore. There is considerable variation in practice when writing the letter e in such words as keliwon and ngerauhang. The e is not strongly pronounced and is often simply omitted in the spelling, giving kliwon and ngrauhang. There is also variation in the case of a double u, as in tuun. The spelling tuwun is regularly used.

Balinese and Indonesians alike tend to de-emphasize such final consonants as -d, -k, and -t to the point where they are almost inaudible. Since these high frequency sounds are frequently emphasized quite strongly by a Westerner, this practice may lead to an initial lack of comprehension.

The practice of using the Sanskrit consonants bh-, dh-, and ph- is variable. Even when they occur in their proper places Balinese do not pronounce these sounds any differently than they do the ordinary b-, d-, and p- sounds. And so their use is of questionable value except to show their Sanskrit origins.

Although everyday household, family, and village conversation is relaxed, informal, and inevitably full of slang and abbreviations, a great change is effected when the slightest excuse presents itself for formality. Such would occur when speaking to an audience, such as at a village banjar meeting, or when speaking to a stranger, an acquaintance of higher caste, a person of high status and importance, or a pedanda priest. This is also the case upon those few occasions when Balinese people have to write documents using the Balinese language, such as in formal announcements like invitations. In these cases the speaker or writer adopts a very artificial, formal style, full of flourishes and decoration. Very often the form is much more evident than the substance. Balinese are generally very conscious of the symbolism of sound. Formal speeches are delivered with an inscrutable, mask-like smile. Sentences are intoned rather than spoken, and it is obligatory to end each one with a rising inflection. In the old days the lower people would have to sit on the floor when speaking to those of higher status, using stylized hand gestures. This is still done to a reduced extent when speaking to a *pedanda*. In the extreme case, as for example when reading sacred texts or performing *wayang kulit* shadow puppet plays or drama of some sort, the speaker uses a peculiar whining voice, a sign that he is declaiming lines spoken by gods or other refined people, as compared with the harsh, guttural exclamations of the coarse characters.

There is no gender in Balinese. In fact, even when gender is inherent in the subject of conversation, it may not be expressed. For example, the third person pronoun *ia* or *ipun* can mean either "she" or "he," and there may not even be a referent as to which it does mean. Verbs are conjugated, but not in a complex fashion. The conjugation has nothing to do with tense, but rather, indicates whether the verb is transitive or intransitive, active or passive, and if the verb is active, the ending may indicate the location of the action. Two common examples will suffice, but it must not be assumed that this same pattern is observed elsewhere:

GAE = MAKE (WORK, DO)

gae	imperative	Fred, make a toy
gaena	passive	The toy was made by Fred
ngae	active	He makes a toy
magae	intransitive	I am working
ngaenang	dative*	I make a toy for my son

SALUK = PUT ON

saluk	imperative	Fred, put on that sandal
saluka	passive	That sandal was put on by someone
nyaluk	active	Fred puts on his sandals
masaluk	intransitive	This sandal has already been put on
nyalukin	dative	I put on this sandal for Fred

*The term dative is used here in the sense of a noun case in Latin—the noun that receives indirect action is dative. In English we use the prepositions "to" or "for." In Balinese there is no declension of nouns, rather the verb is inflected— either *-ang* or *-in*.

Of course, these are simple cases. And there are other verb forms. But, this should convey the general idea. The prefix *ng-* that is used on many verb stems to make them active looks odd, but it is pronounced with a soft *g* exactly as the *ng* in the English word "singer." As indicated in the pronunciation guide, a hard *g* sound, as in the English "single," is always indicated by a double *g*, as in *palinggih*. Note that the prefix *ny-* is used to make active verbs from those stems that begin with the letter *s*. Incidentally this has resulted in the word *nyetop*, the transitive form of "stop."

Time is usually indicated by verb tense and a variety of adverbs. The Balinese language is more capable of expressing these relative times than English. For example, in the Low form of the language:

	FUTURE
Sanjane	in the late afternoon
Nyanan	later today
Bin akejep	in a few minutes
Bin jahan	just a little bit later

	PRESENT
Jani	now

	PAST
Mara	just now
Mara tunyan	a very short time ago
Tunyan	earlier today, about 1 hour ago
Tuni	earlier today, a couple hours or more

The Balinese equivalents of "not yet" and "already" are often used to indicate action that is incomplete or that has been completed. The words are:

ALREADY	NOT YET
sampun (Medium)	durung (Medium)
suba (Low)	tonden (Low)

Sometimes these words alone are used to indicate the English expressions "Yes" or "No." For example, if you ask a friend if he is married, instead of replying in the affirmative or negative he will say "Bâ," meaning *suba*, that he is "already" married, or "'Nden," for *tonden*, meaning that he is "not yet" married, and implying that it is more or less inevitable that he will marry.

Household and village Balinese is full of the same sort of slang that afflicts informal conversations everywhere. Particularly noticeable is the repeated use of the word *malu*. The word means "first" as in "first in order," but it has fallen into the class of the English "You know..." and seems to have lost any sort of significance. The Balinese use various other emphatic expressions more commonly that one hears similar sounds in English. "Ja," meaning roughly something like the "do" in "Do come here...," is so commonly used that it means nothing at all. Balinese use something equivalent to "Yes" quite often. In the High language the word is *inggih*, in the Low language *ao*, pronounced something like the American "Ow" that is used when one is hurt. The "hurt" expression in Balinese and Indonesian is "Aduh!" or "Duh!" often said very explosively. This also serves as the equivalent of "Alas!" or "Woe!" *Nah* also means "yes," but it is used in the sense of agreeing with an idea, or sometimes as a kind of emphatic particle when giving directions, rather than as a simple affirmative.

The Balinese use the "this" and "that" adjectives much more than is common in Western languages. The words are:

THIS	THAT
puniki (Medium)	punika (Medium)
ene (Low)	ento (Low)

In some conversations practically every noun is followed by a "this" or a "that," sometimes even when the article is used. There is no indefinite article. The definite article takes the form of a suffix -*né* attached to the noun. Another common suffix is -*n*, which signifies that that noun is intimately connected with the pronoun or noun that follows. For example *guru* means "teacher" or, in Jimbaran, "father of." Gurun Aris, the polite form of Budi's name, means "Father of Aris." *Seka* is group. *sekan barong* is the *barong*'s group.

ONE OF THE MOST OBVIOUS DIFFERENCES between Balinese and English is that Balinese has "levels," a fact which has been pointed out repeatedly in these volumes. And it is frequently mentioned in guidebooks and in the literature in general. Although the not always accurate representations in the literature may make this seem quite complicated, from the point of view of the average Balinese householder, the level rules are quite straightforward. He uses variations of one kind of speech to talk to his wife, family and friends. We can call this "Low Balinese." He uses another variety to talk to people of higher caste, strangers or people of status and importance. This is Medium Balinese. He uses yet a third style, High Balinese, to speak to *pedandas*. Few Balinese know much High Balinese, for the simple reason that they seldom have any occasion to speak to a *pedanda*. If this occasion arises, as for example if the family wishes to ask the *pedanda* for holy water or to participate in a ceremony, the group simply takes along one of the few people in the village who is fluent in High Balinese.

The vast majority of common, everyday words in the Balinese language remain the same regardless of level. Only those words that involve reference to the body, to bodily motions and actions, and to religious matters are what I shall call "level sensitive," meaning that they vary according to the status of the speaker and his or her listener. One who knew Low Balinese well would probably need to pick up no more than about 1,000 of these level sensitive words to converse reasonably well in Medium or High Balinese.

The difference in these levels is quite marked, however. It is not a matter of changing the pronunciation of a few words, the substitution of a few polite personal pronouns, or the change of an accent here and there. In many cases the Low, Medium, and High words are etymologically distinct. For example, the words for "he" or "she" in the three levels are, from Low to High, *ia, ipun,* and *ida.* The three words for "water" are *yeh, toya,* and *tirtha.*

On the other hand, such words as feather, fly, weave, compare, branch, goose, room, sand, and so on are the same in all three levels. This large group of insensitive words consists mostly of innocuous, non-controversial words that have nothing to do with ceremonial activities or body functions. A great many words exhibit a large difference between the Low and Medium levels, but none at all between the Medium and High levels. For example, blood is *getih* in Low Balinese; it is *rah* in both Medium and High Balinese. Thus learning High Balinese, in the sense of being able to speak with a *pedanda,* is not all that difficult if one can speak acceptable Medium Balinese. Many Balinese can speak acceptable Medium Balinese, since this is the only way that they can communicate with total strangers. But again, acceptable is used here in the sense of not offending the listener. It does not mean pure Medium Balinese. The focus of a conversation with a *pedanda* is necessarily rather narrow, being limited to religious matters. And thus the breadth of vocabulary required to speak High Balinese is not exceptionally large, especially since there is little or no difference between Medium and High words that do not refer to the body or bodily actions.

Caste and its accompanying system of deference and respect is something that Westerners almost instinctively recoil from, but it is imbedded in Balinese society in deep, complicated, and not necessarily "bad" ways. (See "Caste and Clan," *BS&N Vol. I.*) For our purposes here, it is enough to know that it exists. Interesting things happen when people of different status engage in a conversation. High caste people talk to low caste people in Low Balinese. And low caste people talk to high caste people in Medium or High Balinese. (This is somewhat ironic, since the high caste person needs to use only one level; the low caste needs to be able to use all three.) Let us suppose that there are three people, a *pedanda,* an Anak Agung (a ksatriya, a caste almost as prestigious as a brahmana) and a sudra (a commoner), having a conversation.

1. Sudra speaking to Ksatriya:
   "Ambilang Ida lanjaran."
   Take the cigarettes for the *pedanda.*

The sudra is using Medium Balinese, since he is speaking to a person of caste—*lanjaran* is the Medium and High word for "cigarette"; *ambil* is a High form of "take."

2. Sudra says to *pedanda:*
   "Titiang jagi ngaturan lanjaran puniki ring Ida."
   I will give these cigarettes to you

The sudra is using High Balinese, since he is speaking to a *pedanda*—*ngaturan* is the high form of the verb "give"; *puniki* means "these" in High or Medium Balinese.

3. Ksatirya says to sudra:
   "Aturin Ida lanjaran puniki."
   Give the cigarettes to the *pedanda.*

The ksatriya uses Medium Balinese, even though he is speaking to a sudra, because he is talking about the *pedanda.*

4. Ksatriya says to sudra:
   "Jemakang beli rokone ento."
   Give me those cigarettes.

The ksatriya uses low language because he is talking to a sudra about himself—*roko* is the low word for "cigarette"; *beli* refers to the Ksatriya man, who is older than the sudra; *ento* means "those."

Had another sudra been present, he and the first sudra would have conversed in Low Balinese, if they were friends or family members. However, if they had talked about doing something to or for the *pedanda* or Anak Agung, they would have to switch to Medium or High Balinese. There is also an extremely low form of Balinese, which we can call *kasar,* or coarse, which would only be used when referring to animals. It is considered a terrible insult to use *kasar* words when referring to people.

I have a list of nine different words for the verb "eat." This is one of the most sensitive of all words, in the sense that it is extremely offensive to use a low "eat" when referring to a person of caste or status. Perhaps the most interesting word for "eat" is *nunas,* from the stem *tunas,* meaning "beg." The idea is that a person of low caste possesses something—even food—only by favor of the higher castes. One does not ask for food from someone of higher status, one "begs" for it. Often the word *kaicen* is used together with *nunas.* The base of this word is *icen,* meaning "give," "allow," or "grant." The prefix *ka-* makes the word passive. Thus "Titiang kaicen nunas" is a common way of saying "I eat," but it is more or less untranslatable literally. About as close as one can come is "I am given eat." The *kaicen* emphasizes the fact that the speaker is lowering himself before the higher status person; it suggests the food is being given as a favor. This is almost never the case, of course. But it has to be expressed and one's behavior is impolite unless the idea of subservience is expressed.

Whenever one of low status asks for something from a superior person he is obligated to use the expression "Icen tiang nunas" meaning, roughly, "I ask beg." Having obtained what he wants, the recipient replies "Tunas titiang..." meaning "I have received...." This is only used in cases where the object or service is free, as when someone gives a present or a free meal. It would not be used for commercial transactions.

Ngunggahang is a suitable "eat" word for a *pedanda*, being very High. It means, literally, "lift up food so that it may be eaten." *Ngajeng*, from the root *ajeng*, meaning "to set before," is suitable for high caste people who are not *pedandas*. *Nglungsur*, from the base *lungsur*, "ask," is suitable for ordinary people when speaking to others. *Naar* is suitable for family use. *Neda* is suitable only for animals. *Ngamah* is almost too low even for animals. If you really want to get into a fight with someone, use this last word with reference to his eating.

There are similar sensitive words for such things as speaking, holding, sleeping, washing, and other bodily functions. But eating is by far the most sensitive and presents the most opportunities for pitfalls. Elaborate

A PERSON ASKS "WILL YOU TAKE A BATH?" OF HIS WIFE, A STRANGER, AND A PEDANDA.

formalities are involved in eating. It is obligatory to offer guests refreshments, no matter how casual the visit. People helping with preparations
for religious festivals are fed more or less continually all day and night.
One must never push a guest to eat. And a guest must never refuse food.

IN THE UNITED STATES, when my wife tells me to go down to the
supermarket and buy some coconut for her cake, there is no question in
my mind what she is saying. She wants sweetened, shredded coconut that
comes in a small transparent packet. I will find it in the baking goods
department, next to the cake mixes. There is no problem because that is
the only part of the coconut that ever makes it to Scottsdale, Arizona.

But suppose we had been in Bali when she said this. I have a list if 45
different words, each of which refers to the coconut or coconut culture in
Bali. (See CHAPTER 27.) It would be meaningless for my wife to ask me
simply to get "coconut." There are so many choices that she would have
to specify which variety she wants. An English speaking person, faced with
coconut culture, is forced to use "coconut" as an adjective and apply it to
generic tree parts. A Balinese speaker, however, has a distinct and unique
word for each:

coconut leaf, mature	*selepan*
coconut leaf, immature	*busung*
coconut charcoal	*adeng kau*
coconut husk	*sambuk*
coconut wood, cut	*seseh*
coconut leaf mat	*kalangsah*
coconut leaf spine	*lidi*

If describing various stages of the growth of a coconut or its color, the
English speaker must use the word coconut as a noun and add adjectives.
But again, the Balinese has a unique word for each stage of development:

very young coconut	*bungsil*
young coconut with a little meat	*bungkak*
young coconut with soft meat	*kuwud*
mature coconut	*nyuh*
sprouted coconut	*pujer*

Since coconuts, bananas, bamboo, and rice play such important parts
in the culture of the Balinese, the vocabulary connected with the planting,
growing, harvesting, preparing, cooking, eating, and other use of these
plants is enormous. Fine distinctions are made between ever so slight
slight variations in quality, color, taste. Just as the English vocabulary is
impoverished in rice, coconut, and bamboo words, so is the Balinese

vocabulary impoverished in those areas where Westerners place importance: electronics, economics, corporate management, banking, commu-
nications, travel, and so on.

But many are surprised to learn that Balinese descriptive terms lag
those of Western languages in referring to the beauties of nature and art.
One would think that, living on such a lovely island, literally immersed in
natural beauty all their lives, the Balinese would have evolved a rich
vocabulary to describe their environment. That is not the case. About the
best they can come up with is *luwung*—"good." This applies to scenery,
statues, sunsets, TV shows, paintings, and meals. There is no Balinese
word for "art" or "artist." The word *seni* is used, for example, with
respect to the annual Art Festival in Denpasar. But *seni* is Indonesian, not
Balinese. Art, as an expression of individual creativity, is not native to
Balinese thought. The Balinese refer to an artist or craftsman as a *tukang*,
roughly translated as "workman." A painter is a "picture workman." A
stone carver is a "stone workman." A woodcarver is a "wood workman."

Although the concept of musical key is crucial to the performance and
understanding of music in the West, Balinese musicians have no understanding of this idea and no word that expresses it. The principal instruments that are used in Balinese musical groups have only five notes per
octave, and so they cannot be played in any key except the one dictated
by their construction. My wife, in the course of her study of Balinese
music, soon learned that the terms "high pitch" and "low pitch," referring to the frequencies of notes of the scale, were not understood at all.
She learned that the closest words the Balinese had were *cenik* and *gede*,
"small" and "large." This comes from the size of the keys on the *gangsas*,
the smaller ones producing a higher pitch than the larger ones.

Or consider this. I once asked Budi about the older members of his
family. He told me about his grandfather and mentioned that the grandfather had only one child, whom I knew. Some weeks later the grandfather
showed up at our house, accompanied by several women, whom he introduced to me as his daughters. After he had left I quizzed Budi on the
matter of how many children this man had. "Well," said Budi, "we don't
really count the women." This is perhaps not as bad as it sounds. Women
join their husbands' families for religious and ceremonial purposes, and
Budi's aunts live in separate house compounds and attend different temples—thus they are not in his "family" any more.

DIFFERENCES IN LANGUAGE CAN RESULT from different attitudes, different standards of behavior, different customs. Central to Balinese cultural practice are the concepts of *pramada*, "insubordination," and *tulah*,
"divine revenge." It is insubordinate, *pramada*, for anyone to say or do
anything that puts him in a higher or more prestigious position than is his
rightful due, and it risks *tulah* to question matters involving mystical

forces. This concept has had a great influence upon Balinese vocabulary. The habit of addressing individuals of higher status indirectly, not using their real names, is a result of the doctrine of *pramada*. As is the large number of euphemisms—innocent and non-controversial terms used to refer to sacred or powerful people, objects, and gods. For example, people in Jimbaran refer to our Barong, a powerful character in the famous dance, as Pelawatan—"a dance costume animated by people."

The Balinese have a terrible time deciding what word to use for "you." If too high or too low a word is used, this is *pramada*. More often than not, particularly when dealing with foreigners, Balinese simply avoid the second person: "Would Fred like some more coffee?" Budi asks me. The *pramada* principle affects the way in which one must talk to others about himself. Self-deprecation is common in everyday conversation. When entertaining a guest, the host must apologize for the low quality of food he serves and the inadequacy of his home. He should mention that he is poor and cannot afford anything better, and he regrets that the guest has to accept what little there is. For his part, the guest constantly praises the same objects for which his host apologizes and indicates how much better they are than those that he himself can afford. It is a game both have played many times. And there is a standard language that is involved. Nobody takes it seriously, but everybody plays it.

Excusing oneself from the presence of another, or explaining why one has not visited in so long involves other *pramada* principle techniques. One must never say that he has to leave now because he has some other important things to do. That would imply that speaking to one's host is not important. One must not say that he hasn't stopped by for a long time because he was very busy, because that means that the host must rank low in the order of important things that this man has on his mind. Elaborate fictions must be invented. Or else one just says that he is going and asks to be excused, without mentioning where or why. It is especially rude to ask to leave a group because one has to get something to eat. This implies that the group one is leaving failed in its hospitality to provide the food. If asked when he will return for another visit the person who leaves his host must never use the word for "later," because this word, *benjang-benjang*, although it does, in fact, mean "later," implies "never."

This same "later" word, *benjang-benjang*, is the proper way to refuse an offer. Saying "No" to an offer involves another kind of game. One must never say to a seller, not even to a peddler, "I don't want anything, please go away and don't bother me." This would be very impolite. It would mean you have elevated yourself—inappropriately—into a position of importance greater than the seller. This is rude. You must say: "I don't have any money right now, and I will consider the matter *benjang-benjang*." Of course, the seller knows exactly what you mean.

There simply are no words in Balinese for "please" and "thanks" and

"Have a nice day." Guides and hotel people are trained to say those things, but it is a strain. I still am a little upset when I give someone a nice gift and get not a word of appreciation—ever. It is simply not a part of Balinese thinking. Moreover, when you give a gift to someone, or receive a gift from someone, he or you must never open it in front of the giver. This avoids the problems that result from the gift being rather modest, which embarrasses the giver. When giving a present to a person, one must be very careful lest it arouse the envy of those nearby or cause people to think you are wealthy. Instead, you tell the intended recipient of the gift that it is for his children, not for him.

Not only must one deprecate himself constantly, but he must almost always use Low Balinese when speaking about himself or his wife to someone else. For example, suppose that two friends go into a store to buy a shirt. In the first sentence below, one of the men tells the clerk that he himself wants to buy a shirt, and so speaks in Low Balinese. In the second sentence, the same man tells the clerk that his friend wants to buy the shirt, and so he speaks in Medium Balinese.

1. "Tiang jagi meli baju abesik."—I will buy one shirt.
2. "Ipun lakar numbas wastra asiki."—He will buy one shirt.

Every word is different, even the work for "one." One must refer to one's wife as *kurenan,* the Low word. But, someone else's wife is *rabin,* the Medium word. Unfortunately for the non-Balinese student who is trying to learn the language, there are numerous exceptions to the "rule" that one must use low Balinese for oneself. For example, if you want to say "I don't know," it is impolite to use the Low expression "Sing nawang," although many people do use it. It is better to say "Tan uning," in Medium Balinese. If you want to express the fact that you are going to do something for somebody of higher caste or status, you must use the Medium language, even though you are the one who is going to perform the action. The action is directed toward and refers to a higher person.

All of this necessitates a constant awareness of who deserves what. And the foreigner trying to get the hang of it must have great flexibility of vocabulary. But even little Balinese children learn quickly, and I have seen them shifting back and forth from level to level and to Indonesian with no hesitation at all. It sounds silly for a speaker to use higher language than the recipient deserves; it is downright rude to use lower language. I have found it safest to use Medium Balinese on anyone about whom I am doubtful. Still, occasionally one slips up. I remember being criticized, albeit in a friendly way, by a man I met at a temple ceremony. He seemed of high status, so I used Medium Balinese. All went well until I inadvertently slipped in the Low word *sakewala,* meaning "but." He immediately corrected me by indicating that I should have said *sakewanten.*

One must be very careful to keep the *pramada* principle in mind all the time. Budi once returned home from a ceremony of some sort. I asked him if the ceremony was good or bad, in much the same tone and diction that we would use to ask someone how a movie went. Budi immediately pointed out to me that ceremonies are never "bad." Ceremonies are ceremonies and involve powerful forces. One should never even think of them as "bad," let alone say that. My phrasing should have been: "How did the ceremony go?"

The Balinese concept of "family" can lead to all sorts of difficulties in interpretation. Budi is forever going off to *mebat*—a ritual preparation of food—when some "family" member has a wedding or a tooth filing. When I ask him just what the relationship between him and this person is, about all he can come up with is that their families are the same. This person is not a distant cousin, or even an in-law. Sometimes the "family" is such because one of Budi's remote ancestors belonged to that village organization, *banjar*, before marrying into Budi's family. Nobody has any idea whether there is any blood relationship or not. It doesn't matter. The tie is quite strong, and the extended family, if it may be called that, even has a name. And all members of this family easily distinguish themselves from other similar extended families in the village. And all have a common temple at the *odalan* of which they—and only they—worship.

Sometimes terms of relationship are confusing because of different conceptualizations. The word *kumpi* means both "great grandparent" and "great grandchild." The name refers to the religious status the two share—a great grandchild is something like a god, since it has just recently arrived from heaven; a great grandparent is something like a god, since he or she will shortly go back to heaven.

THE ENGLISH "IT," USED AS AN UNREFERENTIAL PRONOUN, is a source of endless confusion to the Balinese who are trying to learn English:

> What time is it?
> It is four A.M.
> It is hot.
> It is red.
> It is raining
> It is humid and sticky

English is a language that privileges syntax; it is linear and forward-directed. We have trouble with conditions—like time, weather, etc.—because we need a subject and a predicate, a thing and an action, before we can call a construction a "sentence." But who or what is time? "It." The Balinese are quite comfortable with conditions, and feel no need to invent a pronoun to serve, for example, as a temporary personification of clock time. The Balinese equivalents of the above are:

Jam kuda?	Clock (hour) how much?
Jam pat	Clock four
Panes	Hot
Punika barak	That red
Ujan	Rain
Ungkeb	Humid and sticky

There is no subject-predicate structure. The condition is merely stated as if it were something that is in the process of going on rather than that it is the property of some mysterious "it." If one is visiting and wishes to excuse himself to go home, he would not say that "It is late." He would say "I am late." The English sentence "Summer is hot" would have to be translated to "Masan ujan panes" meaning "Heat occurs during the rainy season." (There is no equivalent of "summer" in our sense.) Of course, "summer" isn't hot. "Summer is hot" is a way of avoiding the clumsy "It is hot in the summer." This is exactly what the Balinese sentence says, without the strange "it." Similarly, we might say "A light flashed." But the light didn't flash; the flash *is* the light. The Balinese equivalent is "Byar," meaning "a flash occurs." Balinese simply states the fact that there exists or existed a flash.

Although watches are common these days, the Balinese concept of time does not center around a series of incidents, it is a more general "flow" of events. Traditionally, the Balinese day was divided up according to two systems. In one system the period of activity of the day, from dawn to dusk, approximately 12 hours, was divided into eight periods called *dauh*. Each of these one and one-half hour periods was simply named according to its order. Thus *dauh pisan*, the first period, extended from about 6:00 to 7:30 A.M. (See CHAPTER 12).The other system, commonly used today, is a much less precise one.

Semengan	Early morning; sunrise to about 7:00.
Tengai	Morning; 7:00 to noon. From *tengah* (middle) and *matan ai* (sun).
Tengah tepet	Noon.
Ngelingsiran	Afternoon; literally, "getting older."
Sandikala	Dusk; the time (*kala*) of joining *sandi* (the day) and night.
Sandikala Saru Mua	Early evening; the time of indistinct (*saru*) faces (*mua*).
Peteng	Night; beginning about 7:00 P.M.
Tengahlemeng	Midnight.

THERE ARE SO MANY COMMON ENGLISH EXPRESSIONS that are meaningless to the Balinese, and vice versa, that to attempt a complete list would be folly. I can only list a few that interest me.

In Bali, one cannot "have a good time," for example at a party. One can translate these four words literally, but nobody will understand. One must have "good *feelings*" about the party or anything else.

The Balinese use exactly the same word for "teach" and "learn," and the same word for "search" and "find."

In my notes I have listed 17 different Balinese words for "carry," depending upon how the object is carried—on the back, on a stick slung over both shoulders, on a stick slung between two men, dangling from one hand, held by the top, as a child with a leg on each side of the neck, and so on. Each is a separate verb.

One cannot say that a book is "about" something, for example a "book about drawing," or "a drawing book." One must say that a book "is in the style of a person who draws."

One must get used to the idea that everything has a "back" and a "stomach," which is something like our concepts of upside down/rightside up and inside out. An orange peel has its "stomach" on the inside. The door of a cabinet has its "stomach" on the inside, but the door of a room has no "stomach."

Humor is one of the most difficult aspects of a culture for an outsider to appreciate. Much Balinese humor is rather direct and unsubtle. Bawdy jokes and allusions are parts of daily conversations. But one must be an insider to appreciate such humor as is involved with my baldness. It is not unusual for a Balinese, upon seeing my shining pate, to say: "Buung ujan"—"The rain has been canceled." Or he might say "Sing meli TV"—"I don't want to buy a TV." The first of these gems compares a bald head to the clear sky; the second refers to the smooth face of a TV tube.

The passive voice is found more frequently in Balinese than in English. We would say "I bought a book and gave it to my wife"; A Balinese would say "I bought a book and it was given to my wife." The passive is used after negative commands, such as those beginning with "Don't." The Balinese are quite content to accept the obvious conclusion of an action. Budi's wife Wati brought some mangos home from the market, and I asked her why she had bought them. She thought that this was hilarious and just about collapsed in laughter. When she recovered, she explained that this was a stupid question. What could one possibly do with mangoes other than eat them? I ventured that one could take a picture of them, make a painting of them, give them to someone else, make offerings of them, use them to hold down paper, and so on. But I was unconvincing. I should have phrased the questions differently to ask *what* the mangos were going to be used for, rather than *why* she had purchased them.

CHAPTER 11

Onomatopoeia

A PENCHANT IN BALINESE SPEECH

THE ENGLISH LANGUAGE is said to be one of the best with which to describe complex abstract notions and nuances of meaning. The Balinese language, though rich in simile and metaphor, is at a loss when faced with a notions like "beauty" or "quality." To a Balinese, a beautiful painting and a tasty dinner are both *luwung*—which means, simply, "good." But the English language is poverty stricken compared to Balinese when it comes to onomatopoeia—words that sound their meaning. We have a few—Bang, Buzz, Crash, Pow, Smack, Thud, Zap—but these are limited to comic books and children.

In Bali, however, everyone—rich and poor, *pedanda* and peasant—peppers his speech with onomatopoeic expressions. Suppose you were up last night and saw the wind blow a coconut off a tree, narrowly missing the house. How would you tell the story over the next morning's coffee?

English speaker: The wind blew hard last night, gusting from all
        directions.
Balinese (Low form) speaker: The wind *kesir-kesir* last night.

E: I heard it blow through the trees, rustling the coconut leaves.
B: The wind *krasak-krosok*.

E: A big coconut fell and hit the ground hard.
B: A coconut *gelebug*.

E: My heart quickened because I was afraid.
B: My heart *ketug-ketug*.

Nothing need be added to the onomatopoeia. The listener knows exactly what the speaker is talking about. A coconut does not make the sound "gelebug" when it hits, for example, a roof. That requires the use of a different word.

The identification of a sound as being one word or another is not done by definition, as for example, "small wooden object dropped on hard floor." Rather, one must hear the sound and then assign one of the well-known words to it, based upon experience. It is as if the sound were talking to the listener and telling him through his ears the proper word to use. The sound itself is usually something like:

beg	deg	tak	tog	tong	dug	tung	cang	sok	neng
bug	plug	teg	tok	pung	teng	pet	cing	pik	yap
buk	pung	tek	tug	biang	byag	yuk	ceng	dug	yad
dag	prit	ting	rug	tung	blag	yet	wak	kang	yud

A Balinese immediately recognizes, for example, a door slam as *byag* or *blag*, and a pen rapping on a wooden table as *tak* or *tek*. Usually the vowel sound in the word is *a* or *e* for higher pitched sounds and *o* or *u* for lower pitches. Ringing sounds have *ing* in them. Thumps have *pung* or *plug* or *pug*. The actual sound is often preceded by two weak syllables as a kind of prefix to the syllable, which is the sound itself, producing a di-di-DAH sound, like ke-le-TEK, or ke-len-TONG. The vast majority of these words begin with *k*, and *g* is a distant second.

It is hard for a Balinese to define the sound abstractly, such as "noise of long pieces of wood rattling or bumping on a concrete floor." Rather, he thinks immediately of ger-a-DAG, ger-a-DEG. The sounds actually name themselves and Budi, for example, is capable of distinguishing easily between a *kletak* and a *kletek,* or between repeated *kletaks* and repeated *kleteks,* or alternate *kletaks* and *kleteks* or continuous *kletaks* or *kleteks.* It kind of amazes him that I cannot. He keeps saying: "Don't you HEAR the word? How can I define it for you? I just hear it." Perhaps I fail because of the paucity of the English vocabulary in onomatopoeic words. Our "bangs" and "crashes" are rather gross compared to the fine distinction between a *pug* and a *plug,* or a *dag* and a *deg.*

Some of these sound words come directly from the thing that is hit to make the sound. For example, a *gentong* is a very large wooden vat, made from a coconut stump, used in Jimbaran to store salt water prior to evaporating by heat. If you hit a *gentong,* you get the sound ke-len-TONG. I asked Budi if a *gentong* could make a ke-len-TUNG sound instead. "Oh, no," he said, "That's the sound of a *kulkul* (a signal drum)."

Of course, one is free to create one's own onomatopoeia, even in English. There are no rules except communication with others, and meanings have to be clear. The interesting thing about Balinese onomatopoeia is not just that it is there and plentiful, but that it is rather standardized. There are very particular words for very particular sounds. The sound of wind rustling through green coconut leaves is different from that of wind rustling through dry coconut leaves. And everybody automatically knows what the words are. When a group of us from Jimbaran went to see the *pedanda* who usually officiates at ceremonies in our area, he described to us a big storm that had occurred a few days ago. And when he used a long, powerful string of onomatopoeia to describe a

hard rain, he didn't have to say, "The rain went like this: chukachuka-chukachukachuk." He just said "Chukachukachukachukachuka" without bothering to tell anyone what it was the sound of, because he knew everyone there would recognize it as a hard rain sound.

I sometimes sit in on practice sessions of one or another of the percussion orchestras, *gongs*, in our village. A couple of years ago a musician from Denpasar was hired to teach the *gong* a new composition. It was fascinating to hear this man communicate with the musicians. He would never say "You have to play that section a little more slowly," or "More staccato." He would simply say "You have to play it da-da-dit-dada-DIT." The melody, he would say, goes "neng nong neng nung nung nang." He made active verbs out of the names of the five notes of the *pelog* scale: *ding, dong, deng, dung,* and *dang.*

Budi's little boy Aris often rides in my car. When we come to a dip in the road where the car swoops down and then up quickly, he excitedly repeats: "Ciung, ciung!" because that is the sound that cars make when they dip into and come out of dips. No other sound will do or is used. There is no use in belaboring the point. All you have to do is listen to two or more people talking and you hear this sort of thing constantly. For the record, I have made a collection of more than 100 different onomatopoeic words that are in common use in Bali. These were collected from various sources—dictionaries, ordinary conversations, and, of course, from Budi. There are probably ten or more times as many as I have listed. But I have never seen them listed anywhere else, so I will mention at least these here. Those marked with an asterisk are unknown to people in Jimbaran, but are apparently common elsewhere. There are, obviously, many variations both in spelling and pronunciation.

BERUWAG-BERUWAG. Cracking sound of breaking wood.
BRAKBAK-BROKOK. Flow repeatedly from ducts or tubes.
BRAKBAK-BRUKBUK. Bubbling water.
BRUAK-BRUAK. Snapping of thin pieces of wood.
BRUAK-BRUAK. Talking noisily and coarsely, bragging.
BRUT, PRUT. Pass gas, fart.
CAH-CAH, CACAH. Chop up. Also refers to something chopped up when noun is not specified, such as sweet potatoes. These may be called *cahcahan.*
CECEK, CECAK, CEKCEK. Sound of small gecko lizard.
CEGUR. One stroke of a big gong. *aceguran.*
CEMPLUNG. Something falling into water
CIUNG. Sound of car passing a dip in the road. A favorite of kids.
CLAGCAG-CLIGCIG, CAGCAG-CIGCIG, CLACAG-CLICIG. Walk to and fro.
CRACAK-CREKCEK, CRATCAT-CRETCET. Drip here and there.
DAAH-DUUH. Groan, moan.

DAG-DUG, GELEDAG-GELEDUG. Sound of hitting a drum

EBÉT-ÉBET. Sound made when one fans a fire.

GAOK-GAOK. Sound of a crow.

GEBIUG, GEREBIUG. Sound of a wall falling.

GEDABYAG, GEDABLAG. Door slam.

GELEBUG, GEDEBUG, GELEBEG. Thud, as a coconut falling. One would say that the coconut *magelebug*, or *magelebeg*.

GERADAG-GEREDEG. Noise of long, heavy sticks of wood rattling together or bumping on a concrete floor.

GERADAG-GEREDEG. Sound of heart beating.

GERADAG-GERUDUG. Run back and forth in great fear.

GERASAK-GERASOK. Move restlessly like someone who cannot sleep. toss and turn. move about.

GERUDUG, MAGERUDUG. Sound of thunder. *magerudug*. (Thunder = *kerug*.)

GRODOG-GRODOG, GRODOG-GRADOG. Sound of loud, slow, repeated hitting.

GURASAK-GURISIK. Move restlessly like someone who cannot sleep. toss and turn. move about.

GUWAK. Sound of a crow.

JANGIH. Loud, clear, piercing sound.

KABANG-KABENG. Open and close repeatedly, like fish gills.

KACAR-KICIR, ICIR-ICIR. Child, person, or dog always following someone around.

KAING-KAING. Sound of dog whimpering.

KOK-KÉ. Sound of the large tokay gecko, called a *tuké*.

KALINCAK-LINCAK, KALINCAK-KELINCOK. Move about aimlessly (refers only to animals and people).

KASAD-KISID. Move something repeatedly from one place to another, such as a statue, or chairs.

KASAR-KESIR. Wind blowing first one way, then another.

KATAR-KITIR. Wag tail. move to and fro.

KAYAD-KIYUD. Stretch body.

KEBET-KEBET. Fluttering of wings of bird or butterfly.

KEBIYAR-KEBIYAR. Light and flitting. flame flickering. smell spreading out. light going on and off.

KEBIYUS-KEBIYUS. Smell spreading out.

KEBIYUR-KEBIYUR. Flame flickering. smell spreading out (must add what kind of smell).

KEBYAR. Burst open.

KECRIT-KECRIT. Sound of gushing liquid.

KECUH-KECUH, KECAH-KECUH. Spit continually.

KEDEP-KEDEP. Sleepy eyes.

KEJAT-KEJIT. Go into convulsions.

KEJAT-KEJIT, KEJIT-KEJIT. Wiggle eyebrows at someone.

KEJET-KEJET. Go into convulsions. tick of eye. twitch of muscle.

KEJIT-KEJIT, KEJUT-KEJUT, KEJET-KEJET. Twitch of muscle.

KEKEPLUGAN. Three culms of green bamboo tied together and put over fire to make explosion at many ceremonies

KEKEPUAKAN. Bamboo crow-scarer. culm is partially split, so when shaken it makes a clapping sound.

KELAP-KELEP. Flicker, like a lamp.

KELAP-KELIP. Fluttering of falling paper.

KELEMPUNG. Sound of *kajar* in a *gong*. sound of something falling, as in water. The *pung* sound.

KELENTING. Tinkling sound of keys hitting a hard floor or jingling together.

KELENTONG. Sound of hitting the side of a *gentong*—a large container of water, often made of coconut stumps and used to store leached salt water in Jimbaran.

KELETOK. Knock on door. *ngetok pintu.*

KELIK-KELIK. Rolling the eyes.

KELIK-KELIK. Flicker like a lamp.

KENYIT-KENYIT. Twinkling of star.

KEPLUG-KEPLUG. Crackling sound of burning bamboo.

KEPRIT-KEPRIT. Come out in spurts. sound of mouth whistle with ball in it. Whistle itself is *lepri.*

KERASAK-KEROSOK. Move restlessly. hen scratches with feet on garbage, roof, etc.

KEREPET-KEREPET. Crackling of burning charcoal, embers, or *kretek* (clove) cigarette. The *e* in the words can be either *taleng* or *pepet.*

KERET. Sound made when a bamboo string, *tiing tali,* is pulled tight around a bundle of rice. So the verb *ngeretang* is used to refer to tightening any sort of string.

KERET-KERET. Tightening up a string or rope wound around a round object.

KEROSOK-KEROSOK. Sound of rustling paper, leaves, etc.

KERUG. Sound of thunder.

KERUPUK-KERUPUK. Sound of a *krupuk* cracker being crunched.

KESIYAH-KESIYUH. Continually pass by the nose, as smells or drafts.

KESIYAR-KESIYUR. Different smells repeatedly passing by the nose.

KESYAH-KESYUH. Alternately feeling good and bad.

KETAK-KETAK. Snap fingers.

KETUG-KETUG. Heart beating. The part of the chest over the heart is *ulun hati.*

KIAK-KIAK. Cry of a chick that has lost its mother

KIJAP-KIJAP. Flutter eye lids. blink.

KIJAP-KIJEP. Blink the eyes. in the twinkling of an eye.

KILENG-KELENG. Looking around, moving head sideways, as a chicken searching for food. or a person that is confused and doesn't know where to go or what to do.

KILUNG-KILUNG. Wag tail.

KIYAD-KIYUD. Stretch body.

KIYAP. Sleepy eyes.

KIYAP-KIYAP. Sleepy eyes.

KLADKAD-KLIDKID, KLIYAD-KLIUD, KLIYANG-KLIYENG. Squirm.

KLATAK-KLATAK. Clicking of tongue.

KLEBET-KLEBET, KLIBIT-KLIBIT, KETUG-KETUG. Heart beat.

KLENANG-KLENENG. Sound of bell in the hands of a *pedanda* during a ceremony.

KLENENG. Bell sound.

KLENTENG. Ringing sound produced, for example, by hitting a glass ashtray with a piece of wood.

KLÉPAT. Twist and turn, as a fan in the hand.

KLÉPAT-KLÉPAT. Move about like a kite out of control. wobble

KLETAK-KLETAK. Snap fingers. click tongue.

KLETAK-KLETEK. Hitting the wooden part of a drum with a drum stick. hitting a larger or smaller piece of wood with a stick. *Kletak* is the sound of a small piece of wood. *kletek* is for a larger piece.

KLÉTAK-KLÉTÉK. Knock. rap. drum.

KLÉTÉK-KLÉTÉK. Click with tongue, as in annoyance.

KLIKIH-KELIKIH. Creep stealthily on hands and knees.

KLIYANG-KELIYENG. Lead a wandering life. change one's opinions often. argue in a circle.

KRABAK-KRUBUK. Walking in water. squishing sound. sound of bubbling water

KRABUK-KRUBUK. Sound of air bubbles coming up from a coconut shell container that has been immersed in water.

KRADAK-KRUDUK, KRADAK-KRODOK, GRUDUG. Rumble in stomach.

KRANCANG-KRINCING, KRINCING-KRINCING. Jingle, as with money or keys. sound of a *gentorag.*

KRASAK-KROSOK. Green coconut leaves or banana leaves rustling.

KRASAK-KROSOK, KRAPAT-KREPEK, KRATAK-KRETEK. Dry coconut leaves rustling.

KREPET-KREPET. Crackling sound of burning wood.

KREPET-KREPET. Sound of soft, fast, repeated hitting.

KREPIK. Sound of a crispy chip, such as *krupuk*, breaking.

KRIYET-KRIYET. Sound of a wood drill or an insect or mouse chewing on wood.

KRIET-KRIET. Sound of grinding teeth.

KRUPUK-KRUPUK. Sound of eating crisp cracker.

KRUWAK. Crackle like skin of *be guling*—crisp roasted pork.

KRUWAK-KRUWAK. Snapping of thin pieces of wood.

KUKURUYUK. Crow, like a cock.

KULUK-KULUK. Call to a puppy (puppy = *kuluk*).

KUMANGKANG-KUMING-KING. Dust lice.

KUNANG-KUNANG. Firefly.

LABLAB. Sound of boiling water.

MAGREMBIANG, MAGADAMBYANG. Sound of dropping a glass on the floor, so that it breaks. same for a metal tray.

MAKELENTUNG. Hit a *kulkul*. the sound is *tung*.

MAKELETOK. Hit something repeatedly.

MAKEPLUG. Explosion.

MENGEWING. Siren sound.

MENGUWING. High pitched, ringing sound.

MEONG, NGEONG. Cat sound.

NEK-TEK. Fast chopping, as at a *mebat* spice chopping session.

NEPAK. Sound of hitting drum, etc. with flat of hand.

NGAPLUK. Hit, as hitting a dog.

NGARÉNYEH. The sizzling sound made when a piece of *gedebong* is put on a fire, as when one covers a piece of meat that he is grilling with the *gedebong*.

NGELULUK. Sound of something rolling.

NGENONGIN. Make a *nong* or *mong* sound, as with a *gong*.

NGEREBET. Sound of malfunctioning gasoline engine.

NGERÉPET. Crackling sound of *kretek* cigarette.

NGERODOK. Sound of boiling water.

NGESKES. Scratching sound.

NGROCOK. Sound of boiling water.

NONGKANG-NONGKANG. Jump and skip back and forth.

NYEET-NYEET. Kind of insect that makes this noise.

SELAP-SELAP, KELAP-KELAP. Appearing and disappearing repeatedly, as airplane in clouds or a person in a crowd.

SLIYAR-SLIYUR. Back and forth.

CHAPTER 12

Counting and Numbers

SA, DUA, TELU, EMPAT, LIMA...

AS HAS BEEN MENTIONED EARLIER in this series, the Indonesian language is foreign to the Balinese. Most people speak it, of course, but they learn it in school, not at home. Balinese people do count using the Indonesian language, but at home, and at the public markets, counting in Balinese is the rule. This chapter is an investigation of the linguistic use of numbers, and a look at the historical basis for some of the number words, particularly those that are irregular. One matter that will not be treated here is the magical symbolism and power connected with numbers, and the way in which many Balinese people think about counting and grouping things. To Westerners numbers are merely convenient symbols used for enumeration of objects, having no significance in and of themselves. To Balinese people, numbers are often closely associated with magical power and may not be merely the abstractions that are assigned to nouns in order to handle these ideas efficiently. Numerology, and the religious significance of numbers, is mentioned in several chapters appearing in the first volume of this series.

THE WORDS FOR THE NUMBERS ONE, TWO, AND THREE have two forms, the High and the Low. The forms *sa, dua,* and *telu* are Low Balinese, used only when speaking with family or close friends. The forms *siki, kalih,* and *tiga* are High Balinese and are used when talking with those of higher caste or strangers or priests.The numbers, as given in the list on the following page, are in the "independent" form. They may be used in this form for counting and calculation. They are used in forming compound number words of more than 30. And they are used as the numerative modifiers of two special words: *wai,* Low Balinese for "day,"

INDEPENDENT FORM OF NUMBERS

ENGLISH	BALINESE	INDONESIAN
one	sa (Low), siki (High)	satu
two	dua (*l*), kalih (*h*)	dua
three	telu (*l*), tiga (*h*)	tiga
four	empat, pat	empat
five	lima	lima
six	(e)nam	enam
seven	pitu	tujuh
eight	kutus	delapan
nine	sia	sembilan
ten	dasa	sepuluh

and *bulan,* "month" (except as it is used for a lunar calendar month). Thus, one can say *dua wai,* or *kutus wai,* in Low Balinese, meaning "two days," or "eight days." One says *pitu bulan,* or *sia bulan* to mean "seven months" or "nine months," if talking about months in general, as on the Gregorian calendar. But the independent form of the number cannot be used with the High Balinese word "day," *rahina.* Here, and with all other nouns, one must use the "dependent" form of the number.

DEPENDENT FORM OF NUMBERS

1	*a*-; prefix to head word
2	duang (*l*); kalih (*h*)
3	telung (*l*); tigang (*h*)
4	petang
5	limang
6	nem
7	pitung
8	kutus (ulung)
9	sia (sangang)
10	dasa

One cannot say *dua meter* for "two meters," but rather, *duang meter.* "Three kilograms" is *telung kilo,* and so on. One of something is expressed by prefixing *a* to the word, as *ameter,* "one meter"; *akilo,* "one kilogram." Note that the dependent forms have High and Low words for the numbers 2 and 3 and that some of the dependent forms are the same as the independent forms. With 8 and 9 there are two ways in which the dependent form may be expressed. Usually the first form is used for the number shown in the table only. "Eight meters" would be *kutus meter.* The form shown within parentheses is used for multiples—thus 80 is

ulung dasa and 9,000 is *sangang tali.*
There is yet another form of the numbers. The "reduplicative" form is used when the number follows the noun that it modifies

REDUPLICATIVE FORM OF NUMBERS

1	abesik
2	dadua (*l*), kakalih (*h*)
3	tetelu (*l*), tetiga (*h*)
4	patpat
5	lalima, lelima
6	nemnem
7	pepitu, papitu
8	akutus
9	asia
10	adasa

In answer to the question "How many children do you have?" the answer might be "Lalima." The forms for 5 and 7 are pronounced the same way but spelled interchangeably. "Two cakes" would be *jaja dadua.*

Western languages have certain "counter" nouns, or classifiers that are used to indicate what kind of an object one is talking about. Such nouns are generally used with number words. For example, in English we speak of 25 "head" of cattle, six "sheets" of paper, three "pieces" of fruit, nine "sticks" of wood, and so on. The Balinese language contains many more such classifiers than does English, and the use of them is more obligatory than it is in English. Nobody would get upset if someone said "six bananas." In fact, that is the usual way of referring to such items. In Balinese, however, one would have to use a classifier. In this case it would be the word *bulih,* meaning "stalk," or "fruit," and one would have to say "biu telung bulih"—literally, "bananas three fruits."

COMMON CLASSIFIERS

aneh	divisions of a pair
besik	thing
bidang	something flat or thin, leaves
bulih	stalk, fruit
bungkul	something big and round, also buildings
diri	individual, person
katih	something long and thin, e.g., a coconut tree or bamboo
kuren	couple, family
lembar	flat sheet, as of cloth

lempir	sheet of paper
paon	family
papah	leaves on the same stalk
puun	tree
sibak	something broad and flat
sikut	rice field
tebih	something broad and flat, divisions of rice field
tugel	something round and long
tuluk	rice field
ukud	animal

ORDINAL NUMBERS ARE EXPRESSED in several ways in Balinese. Usually the auxiliary word *kaping* is used to make an ordinal number out of a cardial number.

kaping kalih (*h*)	second
kaping telu (*l*), kaping tiga (*h*)	third
kaping pitu	seventh

These expressions are often prefixed by the words *ane* (*l*) or *sane* (*h*), meaning "that which is."

ane kaping telu	that which is third (*l*)
ane kaping pitu	that which is seventh (*l*)

There are several special words that are used for expressions that mean "first," and "second." *Cepok* (*l*), or *pisan* (*h*) used by themselves, mean "once." *Pindo* is Low Balinese for "second" or "twice." They can be combined with the above auxiliary words as follows:

ane kaping cepok (*l*)	first
sane kaping pisan (*h*)	first
ane kaping pindo (*l*)	second
sane kaping kalih (*h*)	second

There is another expression for "first," *kaping ngarep*, in which the latter word means "put in front." Sometimes the expression *sane dumunan* is used to mean "first in time." *Dumunan* means "earlier." Sometimes the cardinal number expressions take the form of, for example, "that which is number six": *sane nomor nem*.

Pisan, used in High Balinese to express the idea of "first," can be used as an adjective to mean "all" or "whole," or as an adverb to mean "very." The traditional system of expressing time in Balinese divided the day into eight *dauh*, or periods of time, each about an hour and a half long. They were named by appending the number word to the word *dauh*.

TIME (OBSOLETE)

Dauh pisan	6:00 A.M.	—	7:30 A.M.
Dauh ro	7:30 A.M.	—	9:00 A.M.
Dauh tiga	9:00 A.M.	—	10:30 A.M.
Dauh pat	10:30 A.M.	—	12:00 M.
Dauh lima	12:00 M.	—	1:30 P.M.
Dauh nem	1:30 P.M.	—	3:00 P.M.
Dauh pitu	3:00 P.M.	—	4:30 P.M.
Dauh kutus	4:30 P.M.	—	6:00 P.M.

After *duah kutus* it was time to go to bed and one did not bother measuring the time.

In Indonesian, the ordinal number words are formed by adding the prefix *ke-* to the independent form of the number. Thus *tiga* is "three" in Indonesian, and *ketiga* is "third." The *ke-* forms in Balinese are generally limited only to the words for the 12 months of the Balinese lunar calendar, or, as it is usually called, the Saka calendar, in which the months are called *sasih*.

MONTHS OF THE SAKA

1	Sasih Kasa
2	Sasih Karo
3	Sasih Ketiga
4	Sasih Kapat
5	Sasih Kalima
6	Sasih Kenem
7	Sasih Kepitu
8	Sasih Kaulu
9	Sasih Kesanga
10	Sasih Kedasa
11	Sasih Jiyestha, or Desta
12	Sasih Sadha

These names are taken more or less directly from the Sanskrit. (For more information on the Saka, see "Balinese Calendars," *BS&N Vol. I.*) *Sasih Kedasa* is the first month of the Saka year and almost always begins the day after new moon in March.

THE EXPRESSION OF HOW MANY TIMES SOMETHING IS DONE, "once," "twice," and so on, is expressed by combining the ordinal numbers with *pang* in Low Balinese and *ping* in High Balinese.

pang cepok (*l*)	once
ping pisan (*h*)	once
ping kalih (*h*)	twice
ping lima	five times

Pang cepok is also expressed as *acepok*, and *ping pisan* as *apisan*. There are other expressions, referring to how many times bigger or further away etc. something is, in which the words *pang* or *ping* are omitted entirely. For example, if the question "How far is Batuan from here" were asked, the answer might be:

Ada telung ka Sanur johne.
—It is three (times) to Sanur the distance.

The following words are used for the mathematical operations:

plus	ken, teken, jangin
minus	kuangin, juang
times	pang
divided by	dum, palih, pah
equals	patuh teken, pada teken

Thus we have the following:

Telu pang telu pada teken asia.
—Three times three equals nine.
Limolas kuangin pat pada teken solas.
—Fifteen minus four equals eleven.
Kutus teken sia pada teken pitulas.
—Eight plus nine equals seventeen.
Selae dum lima pada teken lima.
—Twenty-five divided by five equals five.

Fractions with one in the numerator are expressed with the word *apah*:

apah telu	one-third
apah dasa	one-tenth

There are special words for the common fractions:

tengah	one-half
pahpat	one-fourth

Using the Balinese division system, in which "two units "and" one-half" means "one of the two units is halved":

tengah dua	one and one-half
tengah pat	three and one-half

Fractions that have a number other than one in the numerator use the word *pah*:

dua pah pitu	two-sevenths
tiga pah pat	three-fourths

The word *saka*, used as a prefix, is used to express the idea of doing a certain number of things at one time:

sakabesik	one at a time
sakadasa	ten at a time

WITH THE ABOVE INFORMATION IN MIND, you can do quite well at bargaining in the market. Bear in mind that the Balinese method of expressing the cost of something requires you to say the equivalent of "pay the cost 500 rupiah," where the word for cost, *aji*, or *ji*, may not be omitted. Similarly, when one talks about monetary transactions, the word "money" must be included. This leads to such literal translations as "I would like to borrow money 10,000 rupiah." Below is an imaginary scene in a store in which you, the reader, *r*, ask the store owner, *so*, the price of a wood carving and then bargain. Translations are given literally so that you can see what each word means. The conversation takes place in Medium Balinese.

R: Aji kuda togog kayu puniki?
   (Price how much statue wood this?)
SO: Puniki ajinne aji dasa tali rupiah.
   (This its price costs ten thousand rupiah.)
R: Nika bes mael. Sapunapi yening titiang naur ji pitung tali rupiah?
   (That too expensive. What about if I pay price seven
   thousand rupiah?)
SO: Inggih. Taur sampun aji kutus tali rupiah.
   (OK. Pay already price eight thousand rupiah.)
R: Inggih. Bungkus ajebos.
   (OK. Wrap it up now.)

It is interesting to note how numbers are used to express events on a time line, from several days previous to the present to several days past the present date. Note that there are special words for one, two, and three days into the past or future, but, thereafter, the regular numbers are used with suitable auxiliary words:

Low	High	
Four days ago	ipetang dina	sampun petang rahina mangkin
Three days ago	itelun	sampun tigang rahina mangkin
Two days ago	ipuan	sampun kalih rahina mangkin
Yesterday	ibi	dibi
Tomorrow	bin mani*	benjang
Day after tomorrow	bin puan	malih kalih rahina
Three days from now	bin telun	malih tigang rahina
Four days from now	bin petang dina	malih petang rahina

*In Low Balinese the word *bin* is a contracted form of *buin*, and both are commonly used.

The basis of the Balinese number system is a decimal technology derived from Sanskrit. But since Bali got this system from Old Javanese, which had introduced some irregularities of its own, many of the numbers have been changed. The numbers from 2 through 8 retain their Sanskrit origin. As do the following decimal numbers:

1	ekan
10	dasan
100	tus
1,000	sian
10,000	keti
100,000	laksa
1,000,000	ayuta

Most, but not all Balinese numbers are formed just as they are in Western systems by specifying multiples of the basic decimal numbers and adding them together. For example, 723 is the Balinese equivalent of 7 times 100, plus 2 times 10, plus 3. On the opposite page is a list of the Balinese cardinal numbers:

The numbers that are printed with an asterisk are those of particular interest because, as you can see, they do not follow the usual decimal notation that, in its own way, Balinese counting shares with other Western systems. Omission of numbers in the list merely implies that the counting system is regular.

The first example is the number 18. Note that the numbers from 11 through 19 all have the suffix *-las*—the equivalent of the English suffix "-teen." This is expressed in various Sanskrit-derived languages as *-ras* or *-das* or *-welas* or *-belas*. In the Austronesian language group the letters *r*, *l*,

THE BALINESE CARDINAL NUMBERS

1	Sa, Siki, Besik	51	Seket Besik
2	Dua, Kalih	52	Seket Dua
3	Telu, Tiga	60	Nem Dasa
4	Empat, Pat	70	Pitung Dasa
5	Lima	74	Pitung Dasa Pat
6	(E)nam	75	Telung Benang*
7	Pitu	76	Pitung Dasa Nem
8	Kutus	80	Ulung Dasa
9	Sia	81	Ulung Dasa Besik
10	Dasa	90	Sangang (Sia) Dasa
11	Solas	100	Satus
12	Roras	125	Satus Selae
13	Telulas	150	Karobelah*
14	Patbelas	175	Lebak*
15	Limolas	200	Satak*
16	Nembelas	300	Telung Atus
17	Pitulas	400	Samas*
18	Pelekutus*	500	Limang Atus
19	Siangolas	600	Telung Atak*
20	Duang Dasa	700	Pitung Atus
21	Selikur*	800	Domas*
22	Dualikur	900	Sanga
23	Telulikur	1,000	Siu
24	Patlikur	1,100	Siu Satus
25	Selae*	1,200	Nem Bangsit*, Siu
26	Nemlikur	1,300	Nem Bangsit Satus,
27	Pitulikur		Siu Telung Atus
28	Ululikur	1,400	Pitung Bangsit, Siu
29	Sangalikur, Sialikur	1,500	Siu Limang Atus
30	Telung Dasa	1,600	Sepe, Sapaha*,
31	Telung Dasa Besik		Siu Telung Atak
32	Telung Dasa Dua	1,800	Siu Domas
33	Telung Dasa Telu	2,000	Duang Tali*
34	Telung Dasa Pat	3,000	Telung Tali
35	Pasasur, Pesasur*	10,000	Alaksa*, Dasa Tali
36	Telung Dasa Nem	15,000	Lebak Sapaha*,
40	Petang Dasa		Molas Tali
41	Petang Dasa Besik	100,000	Aketi*, Satus Tali
45	Setiman*	1 M	Ayuta
46	Petang Dasa Nem		
50	Seket*		

and *d* are more or less interchangeable, as are *b* and *w*. For example, the tree that the Balinese call the *lontar* palm is called *rontal* in Javanese. The Balinese word for 18, *pelekutus*, is the only irregularity in this series. *Pele-* comes from the Indonesian word *puluh*, meaning "ten." In the South Sulawesi system of numbering, *puluh* is used for all the number words from 11 through 19. For example:

Sampuluh satu   11
Sampuluh dua   12

The original word for 18 was *sampuluh* (or *sepuluh*) *kutus*—"ten plus eight." The prefix has been dropped, and the abbreviated version is *puluh kutus*, or *pelekutus*.

The next irregularity is encountered at the word for 21. The word for 20 is perfectly regular, "two times ten," *duang dasa*. But we are suddenly confronted with *selikur* for 21. And all the rest of the "20s"—except 25—are formed by adding the appropriate unit name to the suffix *-likur*. In Kawi, a Sanskrit-derived language closely related to Old Balinese and Old Javanese, the word *likur* means "in the back of." Thus *selikur* means "one in the back of two," *dualikur* means "two in the back of two," and so on.

The next irregularity is *selae*, "twenty-five." This is the first of what I refer to as the *pis bolong* numbers. *Pis bolong* is the Low Balinese word for the common Chinese coins, which look like flat washers, that are used throughout the island in offerings. (See CHAPTER 9.) *Pipis*, abbreviated to *pis*, means "money"; *bolong* is the Balinese word for "hole" (the coins have holes in their centers). Such Chinese coins, also called by their Indonesian name, *kepeng*, have been important in Balinese culture throughout, and probably long before, the historic period. The earliest dated coins that been found in Bali were minted during the Tang Dynasty, approximately the 6th century A.D. Historians guess that these coins were first used in Bali in the 7th or 8th centuries. Although they are no longer used in monetary transactions, *pis bolong* have lost little of their importance in Balinese Hindu religion. Up until fairly recent times, even during the Dutch occupation of Bali, *pis bolong* were regularly used for everyday monetary transactions.

Individual bronze or copper Chinese coins do not, and never had, great value. Even at today's inflated prices, one can buy them for about Rp 35 to Rp 45 each, depending upon quality, or approximately U.S. 2.5¢. Because of their small value, large numbers of them had to be used even for ordinary purchases. And the fact that the coins had holes in them made it very convenient to string them on a thread or piece of string in standard size bundles. One Dutch *sen* was equivalent to 25 *pis bolong*, and the smallest denomination of *pis bolong* in common use was 25 of the coins strung together. The Old Javanese word for "thread" is *lawe*. And the prefix *sa-* or *se-* means "one." Thus the word for 25, *selae*, is an ab-

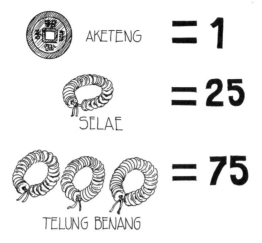

AKETENG $= 1$

SELAE $= 25$

TELUNG BENANG $= 75$

SOME IRREGULAR NUMBERS FORMED FROM PIS BOLONG

breviated form of the word *selawe* that means "one thread" of Chinese coins. The word is universally used in the Balinese language. As we shall see, other number words are derived from bundles of Chinese coins.

The number 30 in Balinese poses no irregularity, nor do 31 through 34, but then comes the odd word *pesasur* for 35. *Sasur* is Old Javanese for "half of ten." In Old Javanese there are three ways of dividing numbers: *tengah*, *sasur*, and *belah*. The word *tengah* means "half." In the archaic form of the Indonesian language *dua tengah* is not "two and one-half," but, rather, "one and one-half." You have two (*dua*) things. You divide one in half (*tengah*) and throw one of these halves away, leaving a remainder of one and one-half. Similarly *tiga tengah* is two and one-half. Using the *sasur* system, the word "thirty-five," *pesasur* is derived from *kapat sasur*, meaning "four *sasur*." The prefix *ka-* is frequently dropped from the number four, which is almost always expressed as *pat*. If you have 40 objects, you cut ten of them off, and, following the terminology, throw half of them away. This leaves 35 objects—and *kalima sasur* would be 45, *kenem sasur* would be 55, and so on. But only the word *kapat sasur*, shortened to *pat sasur*, and finally to *pasasur* is used nowadays. The third way of dividing, *belah*, will come up when we discuss 150.

The rest of the "thirty" words are perfectly regular, as is 40 and the "forty" words up through 44. Then we encounter the irregular word *setiman* for 45. There are at least two versions of the origin of this word. Up until fairly recently, even in Dutch times, opium was widely sold and used in Bali. The word is *madat* in Low Balinese, *candu* in Indonesian. Opium was imported from China wrapped in small packets covered with metal foil, probably lead foil. Each packet sold for 45 *pis bolong* (or possibly 45

Dutch *sen*, it is not clear which). The Balinese word "metal" is *timah*. So, one package of "metal" was called *se-* (one) *timahan* (package of metal)—abbreviated *setiman*. And so the common word for 45 became the word for the package of opium wrapped in metal foil that cost 45 *pis bolong* or *sen*.

The other version of the origin of this word is as follows. Balinese fishermen use a round throwing net, called *jala*. In use, the bundled net is held folded in the left hand and arm. Grasping an edge of the net with the right hand, the net is flung away from the body in a horizontal plane. It falls into the water, and lead weights on the periphery of the net cause this part to drop quickly, thus trapping within any objects upon which the net falls. The net is retrieved by pulling on a string attached to the center, and the contents dumped out for sorting. Traditionally there were 45 metal (*timah*) weights along the edge of the net. So, one set of fish net weights was called *se–timah–an*. As in the other version of the story, the word for 45 originally referred to the set of lead weights.

The very common word for fifty, *seket*, comes from *se-* (one) and *ikat* (to tie something up). This is another *pis bolong* word, referring to a bundle of two *selae* (25 coins each) tied together.

The numbers from 50 through 74 are all regular; then we arrive at the interesting word for 75, *telung benang*. This is another *pis bolong* word. *Benang* means "thread" or "string" and *telung* is the adjectival form of "three"—thus *telung benang* means "three threads," three strings of *selae*, or 75 Chinese coins in three bundles tied together.

The numbers stay regular, except that past 100, the irregulariites already mentioned are kept with the addition of *satus* (100)—*satus pelekutus* (118), *satus selae* (125), etc. For 150, many people use the word *satus seket*, following this pattern. But usually the Balinese use the word *karobelah*, pronounced as if the first *a* and the *e* were not there, as "kroblah." Here we encounter the third Old Javanese method for dividing numbers—using *belah*, which means "split" in both Old Javanese and Balinese. In this case it is 100 split in two. The word *karo* is the same as *dua*. It appears, for example, in the word for the second Balinese lùnar month, *sasih karo*, and we have already seen it in the form *roras*, meaning 12—*ro* (2), and *ras*, a form of *las*, or *belas*, the "-teen" word. So you take two bundles of 100 objects each—presumably bundles of *pis bolong*. You split one of them in half and throw one of the halves away. You then have 150 left. *Dua belah* would be the same thing. *Telu belah* would be 250, and so on. But the number for 150 is the only *belah* word that commonly appears in Balinese. It is never used in any other context.

The series continues regularly until 175, *lebak*. The origin of this word is a bit murky. It is said to be derived from the word *lembah*, which, in a language unknown to me, is said to mean "less" or "minus." From this word is derived the word *labak*, which means "lower" or "less" in

Balinese. *Labakan,* meaning "make lower," or "make less," leads to *lebak.* The word *lebak* is known to almost all Balinese, but most prefer to use *satus telung benang,* which expresses the same number.

We progress regularly from 176 through 199 and then encounter the word for 200, *satak.* This is another "bundle of coins" word. An *atak* is a quantity of 200 of something in Balinese, including *kepeng.* The most common way in which *pis bolong* are sold in the village markets are in strings of 200, one *atak,* or, *satak* (the prefix *se-* or *sa-*, remember, means "one"). The word *atak* is probably Old Javanese and it is the same as *ikat,* "tie." This, of course, refers to 200 *pis bolong* being tied in a bundle on a string. One *atak* of *kepeng* is thus a bundle of eight *lawe.* We can see that many of these irregular numeral words represent successively larger bundles of bundles.

The numbers progress regularly from 201 to 399, using some of the combinations of irregular number words previously described. For example, the number 250 is always expressed as *satak seket.* Three hundred is *telung atus,* a normal combination of decimal notation. But the word for 400 is *samas,* which is a bit unexpected. And the origin of this word is not completely clear. It seems obvious that the word means *sa-* (one) *mas*—with *mas* being the the Balinese word for "gold." The hypothesis is that there was a gold coin in common use that was worth 400 *pis bolong.*

The series continues regularly up to 600, which, instead of being the expected *nem atus* turns out to be *telung atak,* using the idea of three *atak,* three bundles of 200 *pis bolong.* And the next irregular number word is that for *800, domas.* The meaning is quite clear here. Since the letters *d*, *l*, and *r* are interchangeable, the prefix *do-* here is equivalent to *ro-,* meaning "two." The word *domas* simply means "two *mas,*" or 800.

There is now a long series of regular numbers, using the normal Sanskrit-Kawi decimal bases. One thousand is *siu.* And past 1,000 the usual method of naming the number is to add the words previously discussed to the word for 1,000. For example, 1,100—*siu satus.* But the word for 1,200 is another irregular one and another "bundle of coins" word, *nem bangsit.* The word *bangsit* has the same meaning as *atak,* a bundle of 200 something—for example *pis bolong. Atak* is used for numbers less than 1,200—but normally only with the word for 600. *Bangsit* is used for numbers equal to or greater than 1,200, but normally only with the words for 1,200 and 1,400. *Nem bangsit* means six *bangsit,* six strings of 200 *pis bolong* each. Six is a common number of divisions in Bali, and sellers will often group their wares in sixes. In Dutch days the important Dutch coin, the *ringgit* was worth 1,200 *pis bolong.* Not all Balinese use the word. In fact, I have used it on some of the younger sellers in village markets, and they have not understood. When told that *nem bangsit* is the same as *siu satak,* they express surprise and interest. But the older ladies know and always laugh at the inexperience of youth.

After 1,200 the series progresses normally, using the previously defined irregularities. For example, 1,300 is often named *nem bangsit satus.* The word for 1,400 is normally the only other case in which one hears the word *bangsit* used. Fourteen hundred is seven *bangsit,* or *pitung bangsit.* Most people say *siu samas,* however. Theoretically one could call 1,600 *ulung bangsit,* but this is never done. Instead this number has its own rather odd and special name, *sepe,* or, as it probably should be written, *sapaha.* The origin of *sapaha* is not definite. One explanation is that it comes from *paha* (sometimes *pehe*), the Balinese word for "thigh." Lengths and widths of various parts of the body, from the width of an index finger to the span of outstretched arms, are very commonly used in Bali as standards of measurement. It is not clear whether the word *paha* means the width or the length of the thigh. At any rate, a bundle of eight *atak,* 1,600 *pis bolong,* would be about the thickness of a thigh. Or, if laid side by side, the length would approximate that of a thigh. Only a very few Balinese, usually older women who have put in many a year in the village market, are familiar with the word *sapaha.* The younger people have never heard of it.

Everything proceeds uniformly and regularly now up to the word for 2,000. *Siu domas* is the usual way of saying 1,800, although *sia bangsit,* nine *bangsit,* is theoretically proper. The word for 2,000 utilizes the last of the "bundle of coins" words. *Tali* is the Balinese word for "string," or "cord," and one *tali* is a string with 1,000 *pis bolong* tied on it. One never hears the word used in the singular to mean 1,000. *Siu* is always used in that case. But, *duang tali,* is always used to mean two *tali,* or 2,000, and on up the line. "Thousands" are always counted in *tali*s, never in *siu*s. For example, 3,000 is *telung tali.*

Laksa is the Balinese word for 10,000. This is very curious, because in Sanskrit the word *laksah,* or *laksha* means 100,000—and is the basis of the common word *lakh,* used in many countries to mean 100,000. But in both Kawi and in Balinese, as well as in Indonesian, *laksa* means 10,000. I have no idea why there is this discrepancy. The Balinese and Indonesian word for 100,000 is *keti,* derived from the Sanskirt *koti,* which means 10 million. The word is sometimes spelled the same way in Balinese as in Sanskrit. *Keti* is often used simply to refer to an unimaginably large number of things, with no specific number in mind.

The largest common number word in Balinese is that for 1 million, *ayuta.* The general word is *yuta,* the *a-* prefix meaning "one." The word is directly derived from the Sanskrit word *niyuta.* The Balinese word *bengong* is sometimes used to mean 100 million—It also means "amaze," "make speechless," "astonish," and so on. Like the word *keti,* it does not seem to have a definite number meaning. Rather, it simply refers to such a great many objects or such a large number that one cannot imagine the idea and is amazed by the thought.

CHAPTER 13

Proverbs and Puns

BALI-ISMS AND WISECRACKS

COLLOQUIAL EXPRESSION IN BALI, be in it the street, market, or home, is seasoned with a great many aphorisms, epigrams, maxims, axioms, and just plain wisecracks. Perhaps they should just be called "Bali-isms." There are so many of these, and they cover such a wide variety of subjects, that one well versed in them could almost carry on an entire conversation using nothing but these well-known and almost always earthy expressions. In my notes, I have accumulated a collection of some 300 sayings, most of them told to me at one time or another, and others gleaned from books long out of print. I can't reproduce all of them here, of course, but I have excerpted some to give the reader a sense of the range of the Balinese verbal imagination.

The Balinese delight in puns and double meanings. A fair number of the expressions deal with personal relationships and interactions. Most of these are descriptions of how an individual relates to society or to his family. Some of them are purely sexual references, although surprisingly few contain really crude language. Some of the sayings express the same ideas as familiar sayings of our own in the West using different means of expressing them. A few are identical to our own. There are relatively fewer references to abstract concepts such as anger, love, beauty, and so on, as compared to tangible things. Some of them are puzzles. And the puzzles are linked to puns in such a way that one has to know Balinese thoroughly in order to come up with the correct answer. Some of the sayings are standard similes that are used to describe an ideal person—usually, of course, a pretty girl.

The vast majority of these sayings are turned as similes—a person or action is like a particular kind of fish, fruit, or flower with certain attributes. The object to which the action or person or thing is compared is usually an integral part of the Balinese scene, but so unfamiliar to non-Balinese that the simile is incomprehensible. Even if the listener knows the name of the comparison word, he may fail to appreciate the relationship and thus may miss the point completely.

Relatively few of the expressions in my lists are metaphorical, which is an interesting difference between Balinese colloquialisms and, for example, American ones. We use, and sometimes over-use, such metaphors as "a torrent of words," or a "storm of protest"—in these figures of speech the "words" and "protest" are implicitly compared to, respectively, a river and bad weather. We are accustomed to such poetry as "take arms against a sea of troubles," or "Put a tiger in your tank!"

Some metaphors are so common that speakers often fail to recognize them as metaphors. But the Balinese seldom use such expressions. Generally they use similes. Or the speaker will simply state the proverb, relying upon the context to make it clear that his use is metaphorical. As an example, let us use the common English proverb "A rolling stone gathers no moss." Let us suppose that two people are speaking about the recent upsurge in popularity of a political candidate.

English speakers would use the metaphor like this:

> "Senator Sneed is certainly making news lately."
> "Yes, you won't catch him gathering moss."
> —*The proverb is contracted, and used metaphorically.*

In Bali, the conversation would probably go like this:

> "Senator Sneed is certainly making news lately."
> "A rolling stone gathers no moss."
> —*The proverb itself is left unchanged, and the connection between it and Mr. Sneed is completely implicit.*

Both English speakers and Balinese might use it this way:

> "Senator Sneed is certainly making news lately."
> "Yes, Senator Sneed is like a rolling stone. He gathers no moss."
> —*The proverb has been introduced into the narrative as a simile. In English this might be considered a little graceless or pedantic, but in Balinese simile, and repetition of the entire proverb, is the rule.*

Let us now take a look at some examples from each of the groups that were outlined above. I have tried to pick those that are easily understood by a foreigner, yet typical. I have divided the sayings up into shorter groupings to give a general sense of what a Westerner might hear and be able to interpret.

GROUP I

Sayings built around uniquely Balinese items or cultural habits—without explanation, these would be nearly impossible for a foreigner to fathom.

1. Ngalih balang, ngaba alutan
   Get grasshoppers, bring fire

Some Balinese collect grasshoppers, bringing them home, cook them over a fire and eat them. The proverb here refers to one who would bring the fire along while collecting the grasshoppers, thus being able to eat them immediately upon their capture. Figuratively, this is a person who spends money as quickly as he earns it.

2. Cotek sambungin layur
   A *cotek* fish is joined to a *layur* fish

This would probably not be known to non-fishermen. A *cotek* is a very common short fish. A *layur* is another common fish, but much longer. The meaning here is something short becomes something much longer. This refers to gossip—as it spreads the story gets longer and more impressive, exaggerated out of all original proportion.

3. Nyangut
   Refers to Sangut, one of the *penasars* in the *wayang kulit* plays

Balinese shadow puppet plays are moral tales in addition to religious parables and just plain entertainment. Sangut is one of the *penasars*, figures who are both servants to the warriers, and the source of much of the play's comedy. Sangut's trademark is that he always tries to align himself with the side that looks like it will win, giving up old friends and former close acquaintances when they are on the way down, and favoring the apparent winner. The word is used in Bali to describe a person that always wants to be on the winning side for selfish reasons and always helps the person that can help him the most.

4. Angkabin barong somi
   Be frightened by a *barong* in the straw

A *barong*—a mythical lion-like beast that features in the popular dance of the same name—looks rather fierce, but it is a goodnatured and harmless, a pussycat at heart. But it is likely to scare someone who is not familiar with its gentle nature. The expression is used to mean that one should not be afraid of something that is not dangerous.

5. Cara idup padine. Di punyunge jegjeg. Dimisinne nguntul.
   Like the life of rice. When empty it stands up. When full it looks down.

This refers to a "know-it-all" type. He has an empty head (like a young rice stalk), but he stands up and talks a great deal. A wise person, on the other hand, looks down at his feet all of the time. His head is full (like mature rice), but it bends over. He may know a lot, but he says little.

6. Payuk perumpung misi brem.
   A cracked clay pot is full of *brem*.

Brem is rice wine that is thought to be delicious by many Balinese. It is very desirable, but it may be inside a container that looks bad on the outside. The meaning is that something may look bad on the outside, or at first glance, but it may be very good on the inside, or after closer investigation. Something like "don't judge a book by its cover."

'*LIKE THE LIFE OF RICE...*'

7. Buka nglawar capune gedenan beya.
Making *lawar* out of dragon flies is bigger than it is worth.

Lawar is a collection of dishes made of finely chopped meat, spices, coconut meat, and other ingredients. The food is usually prepared as a feast for many people who are celebrating some major ceremony or event. Dozens of men may have to chop for several hours to prepare all the ingredients. The meat used is usually turtle or pig. If one were to try to make *lawar* out of dragonflies one would have to go to so much trouble and expense to get enough of them to feed the hundred or more people who will get the food that it would not be worth the effort. Hence the expression is used to refer to something that is more trouble than it is worth.

8. Selem-seleman jukut undise rasane bangkit.
A black *undis* has an attractive taste.

Undis is a bean that has a black color and a somewhat bitter flavor. However, the Balinese find it to be a delicious vegetable. The Balinese consider black to be an undesirable color, but although *undis* has this "bad" color, it is quite desirable as a vegetable. Hence the expression means that one should not be deceived by external appearances because something that looks bad on the outside may be good inside. Virtually the same expression is used to refer to black coffee beans, which are considered to produce the most tasty coffee.

9. Putih-putihan pamore apepel aji keteng.
The whitest lime costs only one *kepeng* per *pepel*.

A *pepel* is a measure for selling lime, being a small, round blob, normally sold in the markets to be used as an ingredient of the betel chew. One *kepeng* is a very small amount of money. White, as opposed to black, is the most desirable color for anything. The meaning is that, although the lime is white, it is very cheap. This is used figuratively to mean something that looks good on the outside but may be of no value.

10. Cara lalah tabiane.
Like the spicy taste of a *tabia*.

A *tabia* is a very small green chili that is extremely spicy. Its spicy tang is evident as soon as the *tabia* is eaten. This expression is used with reference to a person who does something bad and, for the moment, gets away with it without punishment. But, sooner or later, his bad deeds will be discovered, and he will be punished.

11. Buka naar krupuke; gedenan munyi.
    Like eating *krupuk;* a lot of noise.

Krupuk is a large, crispy cracker made out of manioc dough and other ingredients. It makes a lot of noise as it is eaten, but it is rather spongy and is mostly air. The expression is used to refer to a person who is a loud mouth. He makes a lot of noise, but he says nothing at all.

12. Buka ngejuk be di pasone.
    Like catching fish in a *paso.*

A *paso* is a small water jar. If the fish is in a jar, of course it is easy to catch. This is said about a man who marries a girl who is within his extended family. He will find the girl without having to look very long or far away.

13. Sekadi mesemu baas dolog.
    Like rice stored in a *dolog.*

A *dolog* is a government storage warehouse where large quantities of dried rice are stockpiled. Rice kept there may look normal, but it is often bad because it has been kept too long. This is another expression that is used to refer to a person or object or event that looks satisfactory at first glance, but which may be bad on the inside.

14. Buka becicane ujanan.
    Like a *becica* bird in the rain.

Becica is a bird a lot like a magpie. It makes a great deal of noise, especially when rained upon. The expression is used to refer to a person who talks too much or too fast.

15. Kayang puuhe maikuh.
    When the *puuh* has a tail.

Puuh is a type of quail. It seldom flies, being somewhat like a chicken. It does not have a tail. So whatever is referred to by this expression will never happen.

16. Cara dadalune kampid baan nyilih.
    Like the *dadalu* borrowing wings.

A *dadalu* is a kind of ant-like insect that swarms on a few nights of the year at the beginning of the rainy season. As the swarming occurs, each insect drops its wings on the ground, and there are great piles of them about. It is said that the *dadalu* borrows its wings for a short time and them leaves them behind. This expression is used to refer to a person who borrows something and then acts like it is his own. The expression is also used in the opposite sense to refer to someone who really does own something nice but wants to conceal this fact and so pretends that he has borrowed it.

17. Alah jangkrik ketebin.
Like when you stamp on the ground next to a cricket.

If one is out collecting crickets (for cricket fights), one must be very quiet and tread carefully. Crickets are located by hunters by the distinctive sounds they make. But they can sense vibrations in the ground, and they will stop sounding if they detect unusual noises. If one stamps on the ground next to a cricket, the noise will stop. This is used to refer to a person who is very quiet and never says anything. It is often used to refer to someone who is very talkative at home or in a familiar environment, but who says nothing in a strange environment.

18. Pengit-pengitan sere, gede gunane.
Sere has a bad burned fish smell, but it has lots of uses.

Sere is a fermented fish paste (*trassi* in Indonesian) that is widely used in Balinese cooking. It smells bad, but, when used properly, lends a delicious flavor to dishes. The expression is used to refer to a person may be undesirable looking in a village (for example, very dirty), but who is very useful and important to the life of the community.

19. Buka dewane ungkulin emper-emper.
Like a god that has dirty cloth hanging over him.

Emper-emper are strips of dirty cloth that are used to fence in an area from which people are to be excluded. Balinese will never walk under clothes hanging on a line, because clothing is impure. So these strips of cloth act as a barrier. If you hang *emper-emper* over a god, he will never come close to you. Thus the reference is to someone who is always distant and never friendly. The saying is also used as a moral for children: never put *emper-emper* over a shrine.

20. Buka sesabete; dadi jang di luwanan, di tebenan.
Like a small broom; it can be put at the *luwan* side or the *teben* side.

A Balinese must orient everything in his house compound toward *luwan*, the "pure" or "good" direction, either *kaja* or *kangin*, toward the mountains or toward the east. His bed must be lined up so that his head faces toward *luwan*, never toward *kelod* or *kauh*, away from the mountains or toward the west, which are called *teben*. A *sesabet* is a small broom that, in the old days, everyone used to keep next to his bed. Before he would go to bed he would sweep the bed with the *sesabet*. A *sesabet* can be put anywhere next to the bed, *luwan* or *teben*. A pillow, on the other hand, would have to be *luwan*, as would the small bedroom shrine. The simile refers to a person who can do all kinds of jobs, likes all sorts of entertainment, food, and so on. He can be counted upon to perform all sorts of tasks, attractive or not.

GROUP II

These sayings use comparisons with items that are not necessarily unfamiliar (although they may be), but are introduced in unusual or interesting ways:

1. Anake ene cara kepundunge etuh.
   That person is like a dry *kepundung*.

A *kepundung* is a small fruit that does not look very attractive, but which has a delicious taste. This said of a person that may be externally unattractive, but who is actually very good, interesting, and worthwhile.

2. Ngawaluh mabunga di jit.
   A drinking gourd that has flowers on its bottom.

A gourd does grow flowers. But if it is used for drinking, flowers are of secondary importance. If a gourd grows flowers on the bottom, which would then be displayed clearly when the gourd is tilted up so that its contents may be drained, then this is an excessive and unnecessary display. This saying is used to refer to someone who brags a great deal.

3. Sayang-sayang kendang pamuputne masih gupeka.
   Loving a drum, but at the end it is still hit.

A drum hangs around your neck. Even though you like it, you hit it. This is said of a woman who loves a man who is always hanging around her neck. Even though she may love him, she bosses him around a great deal and may hit him.

4. Buka batun buluane.
   Like a *rambutan* seed.

The *rambutan* (usually called *buluan* in Bali) is a hairy fruit that has one large seed. This expression refers to a man who has only one wife and stays with her, ignoring all other women.

5. Buka goake ngadanin ibane.
   Like a crow naming himself.

The word for crow in Balinese is *gowak*, an onomatopoeic word taken from the bird's cawing. When a crow makes its characteristic sound it is calling itself by its own name. This is said of a person who tells a lot of interesting stories, but mostly about himself. Most of his stories are probably lies, but his audience does not know whether they are true or false.

6. Cara canting campluge.
   Like a dipper made of *camplug* fruit.

Camplug is a large tree that produces a spherical fruit. A shell is left when the fruit dries up, but it is only a few centimeters in diameter. A dipper made of such a small shell would not hold much. This expression is used as an excuse for not lending someone money. Or it can be used to deny the fact that one has much money.

7. Cara botor, tusing bakat baan nyeet.
   Like a *botor*, he cannot be tied up.

A *botor* is a common black bean. One cannot tie up unwrapped bean seeds with string in a bundle. This is said of a person who is very smart and cannot be fooled. He always gets the best of bargaining.

8. Makemuh marep menek, iraga lakar tapena.
   If you rinse out your mouth and spit upwards, the spit will fall on you.

This is said of a person who talks about his own problems to others. People criticize him for bothering them with matters that are his own, not theirs. He should keep his misfortunes to himself.

9. Buka siape sambehin injin.
   Like throwing black rice to chickens.

If you throw ordinary white rice to chickens they will peck at it and eat it up. Then, if you throw black rice, *injin*, they will not know what it is, and they will move their necks and heads and bodies back and forth in confusion. This is said of a person who is not sure what he is going to do.

10. Sekadi bebeke sambehin padi.
    Like throwing rice to the ducks.

When you throw rice to ducks, they make a lot of noise. This is said about a person who talks too much when he is eating.

11. Buka bikule pisuhin.
    Like scolding a mouse.

The Balinese believe that if someone gets mad at a mouse because it is damaging the house it will understand this anger, and because this person is mad, the mouse will steal more things and do more damage. This expression is used to refer to parents who scold a disobedient child excessively. The child will react to the continued abuse and deliberately do even worse things than those for which he is being criticized.

12. Buka nyampat di beten punyan biingine; saisai ada luu.
    Like sweeping underneath a banyan tree; every day there is garbage.

The leaves of a banyan tree drop off so frequently that it is rather useless to keep trying to sweep up beneath the tree because there will soon be another pile of leaves. The expression is used to indicate a situation in which someone tries to do something to change a bad situation, but his intervention makes the problem even worse than it was previously.

13. Buka dalang nyiatang wayang.
    Like a *dalang* making his puppets fight.

A puppeteer in a *wayang kulit* performance, the *dalang*, can make whichever side he wishes win the fight, since he is manipulating the puppets. The expression is used to refer to a person who asks a question and then answers it himself. Or it may be used when someone says one thing to one person and a different thing to someone else, changing his story to meet the situation.

14. Buka negakin gedebonge; tau teken jit belus.
    Like sitting on a *gedebong*; he knows that his rear end will get wet.

A *gedebong* is the stem of a banana plant. Such a seat is usually damp, and everyone knows that. This is said of a person who acknowledges that he has made a mistake. It also applies to someone who got himself into trouble but should have known better.

15. Buka nulis di yehe; tusing matampak agisgis.

. Like writing on the water; there is not even a small print.

This is said of a person who tries to influence someone else without results, for example a parent who tries to teach his child proper behavior, but is ignored.

16. Buka linuhe, ngidupang ibane.
    Like an earthquake, it starts itself.

This is said about a person who acquires knowledge or skill by himself, without having been taught. The person is inspired toward learning by internal motivation.

17. Beruk takil.
    A *beruk* that is *takil*.

A *beruk* is an empty coconut shell container. *Takil* means wrapped up in the leaf sheath of an *areca* palm. There is no point in wrapping up an empty container. This is said about making a big fuss over a little matter.

18. Kadirase tikeh uek tusing ada.
    Moreover he doesn't have a broken mat.

A torn or broken mat is worthless. If you don't even have that, you have very little. A broken mat is the cheapest thing imaginable. This is said about someone who brags a great deal about his possessions and money.

19. Buka cicinge singal.
    Like carrying a dog on your hip.

Babies are usually carried on the hip before they can walk. Carrying a dog that way is very bad because it is an animal and should not be carried so high (using the Balinese idea of elevation being proportional to status). The dog will get used to being higher than it should be. It will want to get even higher and lick your face. You are spoiling it. This is said of a person who spoils someone to the point that the recipient wants more and more.

20. Sing nawang empugan.
    He doesn't know where the waves break.

Empugan is the word for the place where the waves break on the shore. It is rather obvious to anyone who looks at the beach where this place is. If someone doesn't know where the waves break, he is particularly stupid.

GROUP III

These are just a few of the enormous number of puns that are such favorites of the Balinese. They love the sound of words and the double meanings that can result from even the slightest similarity between words.

> 1. Ia madon jaka.
>   He has *jaka* leaves.

Jaka is the sugar palm. *Jaka* leaves are called *ron*. The Balinese verb *makaronan* means "to confirm a date." This has no relation to the *ron* of the *jaka* tree. *Makaronan* is the verb usually used when one wishes to set the time and place for some event, such as a wedding. So, if one wishes to set such a date he would say that he has *jaka* leaves (*madon jaka*), which his listeners will know is the same thing as saying *makaronan*. Far fetched? To our way of thinking. But this is a standard Balinese pun.

> 2. Ia maboreh kayu.
>   He makes *boreh* for wood.

Boreh is a lotion made of plant parts that is applied to the skin. The Balinese noun for paint is *cat*. Painting wood is sort of like putting a lotion on it. The word for being fired from a job is *mapecat*. This word is similar to the word that means "having paint." So, if someone is fired from his job, people say that he is making a *boreh* for wood, or putting *cat* on wood, or *mapecat*.

> 3. Titiang cicing cenikanga teken ia.
>   I am thought of by him as a small dog.

A small dog is a puppy. The word for puppy is *kuluk*. The word *uluk-uluk* means "to lie." So if someone thinks of you as a puppy, *kuluk*, he "uluk-uluks" to you, or lies to you.

> 4. Kacang suba wayah.
>   Peanuts that are already old.

Kacang are peanuts. *Wayah* means "old." This sentence has the same sound as "Basang suba layah" which, in Balinese, means "Stomach is already hungry." If you are hungry, then you say "Kacang suba wayah" and people will know what you mean.

5. Ia majukut dinatah.
   He is growing vegetables in the yard.

It is common to grow vegetables in one's yard. One popular thing to raise is the *kelor* tree, because its leaves can be cooked as a vegetable, and its beans, *kelentang*, are very good as a vegetable. The word for "weak" is *elor* or *lelor*. If someone wants to say "He is weak," he says "He is growing vegetables in his yard."

6. Ia ngorta makatak wayah.
   He talks like an old toad.

Wayah here means "old," "hard," or "rough-skinned." The word for toad is *dongkang*. A word that rhymes with *dongkang* is *nongkang-nòngkang*, which means "jump and skip." Thus a person said to talk *nongkang-nongkang* talks in a disconnected way so that one cannot follow what he is saying.

7. Ia masatak kuang selae.
   He is 200 minus 25.

Two hundred minus twenty-five is 175. The word for 175 is *lebak*. *Nyebak* is the transitive form of the verb *sebak*, which means "wide open." The word is commonly used to refer to the mouth. So, that if a baby's mouth is open he may be crying. Thus if a person is 200 minus 25 he is crying.

8. Angkihan tiange matelung dasa lima.
   My breath is 35.

The word for 35 is *pesasur*. The verb *ngangsur*, from the root *angsur*, means "pant" as if out of breath. Hence, if one's breath "is 35," he is winded.

9. Makunyit de alase.
   Turmeric growing in the forest.

Temu is an Indonesian word referring to a general class of rhizomes that are used for spices, such as ginger, *kunyit* (turmeric), and others. But in Balinese, the word *temu* refers to a particular rhizome that is used in mixed spices. It has a strong taste, much stronger than the common turmeric. The Balinese believe that this plant is a special kind of *kunyit* that is wild and growing in the forest. The word for "meet someone" is *matemu*. So, if you want to meet someone somewhere, you say that you are growing turmeric in the forest.

10. Ia cara jagung.
He is like corn.

Jagung means "corn kernels." They surround the cob, which is called *atin jagung* in Balinese. Thus the corn, *jagung*, is bigger than the cob, which is on the inside. But, *ati* is a word that means not only "liver," but also "mind," "will," or "soul." *Gedenan ati* means a conceited person who is indifferent to others. So the corn bigger than the cob is a person who is conceited and indifferent.

GROUP IV

Some expressions in Balinese are analogous to ones we use in the West.

1. Dija kaden langite endep?
Where is the low sky?

There is no "low sky." This functions just like our Western "pot of gold at the end of the rainbow."

2. Genite bakat gasgas.
If you have an itch, scratch it.

Similar to the Western expression that means one should take advantage of an opportunity.

3. Nuturang tuak labuh.
Talking about spilled *tuak*.

Tuak is palm beer. This expression functions exactly like "There's no point in crying over spilt milk."

4. Kuluk ngongkong, tuara ngutgut.
A puppy barks, but it never bites.

This is almost exactly the same as "his bark is worse than his bite," meaning that he threatens a lot but never carries his threats out.

5. Be apaso aduk sere aji keteng.
A water pot full of fish is ruined by cheap *sere*.

This is similar to the Western expression "one bad apple spoils the whole barrel"meaning that one bad person can influence an entire crowd of people. *Sere* is fermented fish paste that smells bad, but which is widely used in cooking. Cheap *sere* smells especially bad, and, if mixed with a large quantity of fish, can spoil the taste of the entire lot. The expression is also used to refer to a person who has only one small, bad trait that ruins his otherwise good character.

6. Buka bukit johin; luwung pengenahne.
   Like a hill seen from afar; nice looking.

This is like the Western expression "The grass is always greener on the other side of the fence."

7. Ngajahin bebek ngelangi.
   Train a duck to swim.

Obviously ducks don't need to be taught how to swim. We have a similar genre of expressions about putting fish in water, hauling coals to Newcastle, or selling refrigerators to Eskimos.

GROUP V

Expressions that are similar to those used in the West, but use a different comparison object:

1. Ngelidin sema, tepuk setra.
   Avoid the cemetery, find the cemetery.

Sema and *setra* both mean "cemetery," the first in Low, the second in High Balinese. The expression refers to a choosy person trying to avoid something, but ending up with the same situation as was originally present. It is much like "Out of the frying pan, and into the fire."

2. Anggon pengentug isin paon.
   Add smoke from the kitchen.

This refers to getting extra money from another job, in addition to your regular job. We would call it "moonlighting."

3. Dandan anak buta; kayang iraga labuh.
   Led by a blind person, at the end I fall down.

This is the same as "The blind leading the blind"—one who does not know something has no business teaching the subject to another.

4. Guak kingsanin taluh.
   Leave an egg in the safekeeping of a crow.

This is the same as our expression about leaving a fox to guard the hen-house, meaning that such a guard is not likely to guarantee the safety of potential food. The same idea is the subject of another expression about leaving *be guling*, rotisseried pig, with a cat. In this case it can also refer to the dangers involved with leaving a pretty girl in the guardianship of a man.

5. Inane nyalian; panakne nyalian.
   Nyalian mother; *nyalian* child.

A *nyalian* is a kind of small fish that is very good at diving. As soon as a baby *nyalian* is born it dives very well. This is the same as the Western saying "Like father, like son."

6. Ririh-ririhan semale macecog diacepoke masih taen magelebug.
   The cleverest squirrels fall out of trees once in a while.

This is identical to the Western expression except that we usually use the monkey as the animal. Anyone, no matter how good, will always make a mistake once in a while.

GROUP VI

Sayings that are involved with sex:

1. Buka cicing mademin jalikan paone; kudu-kudu anget bulunne lilig.
   Like a dog sleeping in a stove, his body is warm but his fur falls out.

Jalikan is the word for the inside of an old-fashioned clay stove that stays warm long after the fire has gone out. This is said about a man who likes to go out with a woman and make love to her. He will be happy (warm). But by the time he gets married he will not have any money left because he spent it all on his sweetheart.

2. Nasak duren; nasak manggis.
   Ripe durian, ripe mangosteen.

When a durian fruit is ripe you can smell it from far away. A boy knows that a pretty girl is somewhere nearby and will go to her. A ripe mangosteen has no odor until you open it. A woman does not run after a man.

3. Buka tekor biune, suwud anggo entungan.
   Like a banana leaf plate; when you are finished using it you throw it
   away.

This is said of a man who takes sexual pleasure from a woman and does
not marry her.

4. Mamukal; petengne luas, lemahne pules.
   Like a bat; goes out at night, sleeps during the day.

Bukal is a kind of big bat. This is said of a prostitute.

5. Abut keladiange; panakne katut ina barengane.
   Pull a *keladi* from the ground; children are attached to the mother.

Keladi is taro, which has a big, starchy underground root. There are usually smaller rootlets attached to the main root that come out along with
the main root. This is said about a man who marries a woman who
already has a pretty daughter so that he can make love to the daughter.

6. Ngakawa; naglih amah ngandelang jit.
   A spider; it depends upon its rear end for food.

Kekawa spins its web from its rear end. This is said about a prostitute.

7. Buka petapan alune; ngandelang ikuh.
   Like a lizard meditating; it depends upon its tail.

The Balinese believe that a lizard that stands perfectly still waiting for prey
kills the prey by hitting with its tail. This is said about a prostitute.

8. Buka kebone ningeh munyin gong.
   Like a water buffalo hearing a gong.

A water buffalo, upon hearing a strange sound, stands and stares. This is
said of a man who sees a pretty girl.

9. Sayang sayang ketimun.
   Take pity upon a cucumber.

Nobody would ever pity a cucumber. If one is thirsty, one would eat it
immediately. This is said about a man who takes pity upon a pretty girl for
a while. He might do some favors for her in good faith. But, eventually,
he will make love to her. No man would keep his hands off a pretty girl.

10. Makedengan ngaad.
    Pull sharp edge of bamboo.

Ngaad is the sharp edge of cut bamboo that is on the outside of the culm. Pulling it can cause a bad cut. This is said about a situation in which someone in the family of a younger brother marries someone in the family of the older brother. It is strictly against custom, for example, for the child of an older brother to marry the child of a younger brother. If this happens, Balinese believe that it is *pramada*, religiously and socially insubordinate, and all sorts of terrible things will result. It is even worse if there is this sort of intermarriage in the third generation, which is called "Kebo mulih kandang"—water buffalo comes home to the barn.

GROUP VII

Balinese riddles are interesting, not only because of the ingenuity of the trick question, but also because there is only one answer. Children are taught these puzzles in school or by their parents.

1. Apa yen usud ngoyong, yen tolih ngejohang?
   What is it that, if you touch it, it stands still, but if you turn your head, it goes away?

Answer: *Cunguh*; your nose

2. Apa panakne jekjek enjekin, memenne slelegang?
   What is it that a child steps on, but its mother leans against?

Answer: *Jan*; a ladder. The steps of a ladder are called *panak jan*, "children" of the ladder. Thus the ladder itself can be considered to be the mother of the steps.

3. Apake anak ulung nyaup luu?
   What is it that, when it falls down, grabs garbage?

Answer: *Nangka*; jackfruit. The outer part of this large fruit is covered with sticky protrusions upon which debris catches.

4. Apa magelebug ngejengit?
   What is it that, when it has fallen down, bares its teeth?

Answer: *Nyuh pongpongan*; a coconut into which a squirrel has gnawed a hole. The coconut then is said to look as if it were smiling (sort of).

5. Apa pageh anake tepuk, pageh iragane tuara tepuk?
   What is a fence that, if it is your own, cannot be seen, but if belongs to someone else, can be seen?

Answer: *Gigi*, teeth.

GROUP VIII

Related to these riddles is a collection of very well known similes that are related to the ideal appearance of a girl. Note again that there is no room for variability or invention. For example, the very first one in the list below was posed to me as a question by a friend. He asked me what beautiful teeth were white as. And I replied that they were white as pearls. That was quite wrong. Yes, he said, it is true that beautiful teeth are white as pearls, but that was not the correct answer. Beautiful teeth are as white as ivory —nothing else. The same is true of all of the rest of these.

Giginne putih kadi danta
   —Teeth white as ivory

Sledetne kadi tatit
   —A glance like lightning

Jrijinne buka gancane
   —Fingers straight as a *gancan* (a stick for winding thread)

Isitne ngembang rijasa
   —Gums like a (bright red) *rijasa* flower

Bangkiangne acekel gonda layu
   —Waist like a handful of limp *gonda* (a kind of long, thin vegetable)

Betekan batisne mapah biu
   —Calf like a *papah biu* (tapering banana stem)

Pamulunne langsing lanjar
   —Body thin as a cigarette

Bokne demdem samah
   —Hair that is all black

Munyinne jangih buka sunarine ampehang angin
   —Voice like a *sunari* (a bamboo wind chime) blown by the wind.

PART IV

Craft

CHAPTER 14

Architecture

BUILDINGS AS EXTENSIONS OF MAN

IN THE WEST, the world of architecture reflects the changing whims of a polyglot culture, from Los Angeles hot dog and taco stands that are shaped like the products they sell to the gleaming towers of glass, steel, and plastic that seem too often to be mere advertisements for the companies they house. Tom Wolfe once wrote: "Has there ever been another place on earth where so many people of wealth and power have paid for and put up with so much architecture they detested?" Where people feel no attachment to their physical surroundings, these surroundings will be allowed to go their own way.

Balinese architecture does not simply consist of taking natural materials—wood, grass, and stone—and shaping them to fit human needs. Instead, it seeks balance and propriety, in a Hindu sense, between occupant and building, and building and cosmos. Using an ancient doctrine of architectural principles, the Asta Kosala Kosali, a Balinese architect seeks to design a building that is in physical, environmental, philosophical, and organizational harmony with the human body, which itself is nothing but a scaled down version of the Balinese cosmos.

Man's body is considered in Hindu thought to be a microcosm of the universe at large, which has three parts: *bhur*, the underworld and abode of evil, *buwah*, the world of man, and *swah*, the world of heaven. The island of Bali has three parts, the highest, and therefore the most sacred, being Gunung Agung, Bali's tallest mountain. Mountainward, called *kaja* in Balinese, is the most sacred direction. (See "Kaja and Kelod," *BS&N Vol. I.*) Since Mount Agung is roughly in the center of the most populated part of the island, *kaja* is toward the north in South Bali and toward the south in North Bali. Antipodal to *kaja* is the seaward direction, *kelod*, which is is profane. Between lies the world of man, the fertile fields where most Balinese live and work. Like the world of gods and the island itself, the human body also has three parts—low, middle, and high. The feet are profane and unclean, being in contact with the earth; the torso is the middle region of the microcosm; the head is holy.

The tripartite organization of the Hindu cosmos and microcosmos is reflected in the constructions of man. Each Balinese village is divided into three—the *kaja*-oriented "head" contains the temple called *pura puseh*, dedicated to Wisnu, the controller of the mountain streams. The impure, *kelod*, end of the village contains the cemetery and the *pura dalem*, a temple dedicated to Siwa, the dissolver and recycler of life. In the middle of the village is the *pura desa*, the village temple, dedicated to Brahma, creator of life. The plan of each of these three temples, and indeed, of most Balinese temples, reflects the same organization. There is a sacred, *kaja*-oriented, inner sanctum, where only the most important ceremonies occur, and where only special kinds of dances and music may be performed. The *kelod*-oriented outer courtyard is for more secular entertainment and everyday activities. The middle area is the space where preparations are made for inner temple activities, and where ceremonies and entertainment of intermediate religious importance are held.

It is only natural, therefore, that the Balinese should regard their house compounds as extensions of the same concept of environmental and organizational balance. Traditional Balinese homes consist of a house compound, with a cluster of small buildings, called *bales,* organized around a central courtyard, called a *natah*. Within the compound live several families, the heads of each of which are brothers. Each family occupies a separate sleeping quarters, but the other structures are usually shared. In the *kaja–kangin* (*kangin* is east, the second-most sacred direction) corner is the family temple, the most sacred part of the house compound. In the *kelod* direction, and usually also to the west, *kauh*, is the animal pen or barn and the garbage pit. In the middle, surrounding the central courtyard, is a group of sleeping *bales*.

The most senior head of a family generally lives in the most *kaja* of these bales, called the *bale daja* (from the word *kaja*), or sometimes *meten*, which is walled in and secure. To the east and west, respectively, are the *bale dangin* and the *bale dauh*, their names deriving from their directions, *kangin* and *kauh*. There may also be a *bale delod*, from *kelod*. The kitchen, *paon*, and the rice barn, *lumbung* or *jineng*, are also located in the *kelod* end of the compound.

This concept of balance extends further than just the arrangement of *bales* within the compound. The very proportions used in the construction of these buildings—which are considered extensions of their occupants—must be balanced, harmonized, and properly configured for their specific owner.

To insure that a traditional Balinese house compound—or even just a single *bale* within the compound—is in balance and harmony with the macrocosm and with its owner, the basic measurements for the layout are taken from the head of the household's body. Instead of a tape measure, the architect transfers special measurements from the owner's body and uses them as units of measure for laying out the posts and walls. The laws that govern these dimensions come from the Asta Kosala Kosali, sacred palm leaf texts—*lontars*—written in the ancient Javanese language called Kawi. The study, interpretation, and execution of Asta Kosala Kosali is performed by a specially trained group of traditional architects, *undagi*, who are treated with the same combination of respect and awe that is accorded any scholar in Bali. The School of Architecture in Bali's largest university has 18 different Asta Kosala Kosali *lontars* in its library, each differing in significant points from the others. And *undagis* from different areas vary in their interpretations. But the similarities are fundamental enough for us to offer a description here.

Suppose you are the oldest brother in a family and that you and your other brothers want to buy some land and build a house compound. First you have to pick an auspicious day. The Balinese calendar specifies appropriate and inappropriate days for almost every conceivable activity, from killing a pig to getting married, and you must first pick an appropriate day to visit the *undagi* and begin planning your home. You will probably have to consult a specialist in such calendrical matters.

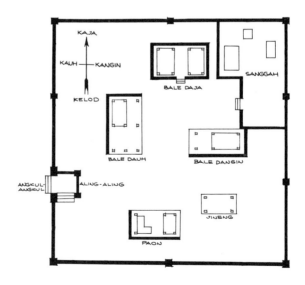

A TYPICAL BALINESE HOUSE COMPOUND

As the head of the household, you would go to the *undagi* on the proper day and state your wishes. He will immediately ask you some questions. What is your caste? Asta Kosala Kosali specifies different rules for different castes. Where is the land on which you wish to build? For what purpose was it previously used? One cannot build a house compound on land that was used for impure purposes unless a very expensive and involved purification ritual is performed. How elaborate do you want the family temple and the *bales*? As with almost anything in Bali, you have a choice of three levels appropriate to your caste: *utama*, *madia*, and *nista*, i.e. elaborate, usual, or modest. How about the decorations of the *bales* and the shrines? Do you want to use precast concrete for gates and shrines or hand-carved stone?

Although there are many options in building a compound, the most important decisions involve the *bales* for sleeping. The traditional house compound may have as many as four of these surrounding a central yard, one in each of the four directions. The framework of each *bale* consists of stout wooden posts (*sasaka*) which are set in a stone or concrete foundation. The posts support a bamboo and coconut wood frame, to which a hip-style roof of grass thatch (*lalang*) is tied. Sleeping places are formed within the *bale* by making rectangular frameworks for beds and incorporating them into the pillar structure, so that the pillars not only support the roof, but also serve as bed posts.

Balinese weather being mild and equable, protection from rain is really all that is necessary, and most *bales* are at least partially open. They will typically have one or two walls, but the *bale daja* (from *kaja*), the residence of the head of the household, will usually be completely walled-in. This is where the family heirlooms are stored and the front porch of the *bale daja* serves as the focus of household group activities.

You will have to tell the *undagi* what kinds of *bales* you want and how many. Architecturally, a *bale* is named for the number of *sasakas* that it contains—for example, a six-pillar *bale* is called *bale sakenam*, from *enam*, "six." The largest pavilion found in an ordinary house compound is the *bale gede* with 12 *sasaka*.

Having arranged the details, the *undagi* will then take measurements from your body. These will determine the dimensions of the entire compound and the lengths of the *sasakas*. The lengths of the *sasakas*, in turn, determine the size of each *bale*. The measurements for the layout of the buildings within the compound is done later, using a different technique, as we will see.

After first making an offering to insure that everything is in balance and harmony, the *undagi* prepares his measuring stick. This is a long strip of bamboo, about two or three centimeters wide, onto which he will transfer your measurements. The first of these is the *depa*, the distance separating the tips of your middle fingers when your arms are stretched out to each side as far as they will reach. (The *depa*, by the way, is a measurement that has many other uses in Bali). To the *depa*, the *undagi* adds the distance from your elbow to the tip of your outstretched middle finger, a measurement called *hasta*. One *depa* plus one *hasta* is the basic wall length measurement, and the *undagi* pencils in these measurements on his bamboo stick.

But Asta Kosala Kosali also specifies that to each basic measurement a small adjustment, called a *urip*, must be added to help bring the building to life later on. The *urip* for the *depa* is the width of the fist. Place your fist (little finger side down) on a flat surface and extend your thumb—the distance from the surface to the tip of the thumb is the *urip*, in this case called *musti*.

The *undagi* now has three measurements on his stick and their combined length—*depa asta musti*—is notched into the stick and becomes the basic unit for laying out the walls of the house compound. At this point, the architect consults the *lontars*, which specify how many *depa asta musti* lengths are appropriate for various castes and in various locations. (There is, by the way, local variation in the interpretation of the *hasta* measurement. Some *undagis* insist that an *hasta* is as indicated above—equivalent to the ancient Western measurement called the cubit. Others say the *hasta* is measured only from the elbow to the wrist, not out to the middle finger.)

Using the *depa asta musti* measuring stick, the *undagi* now stakes out the corners of the house compound, following the rules specified for your caste and the amount of land you wish to build upon. One important decision is the location of the entrance gate, usually near the *kauh–kelod* corner. The wall where the gate is to be is first marked into nine equal divisions. According to Asti Kosala Kosali the gate can be centered on any one of these eight section divisions, but the choice is not strictly aesthetic. Chose one and the *lontars* say you will be wealthy, but be blessed with few children. Another choice will result in people liking you, but sickness plaguing your family. There is usually one choice that will result in a fortune that is all good.

With the walls laid out, the *undagi* takes measurements for the construction of the *sasaka*. The posts are very important, because they, in turn, determine the dimensions of the *bales*. The *undagi* starts with the length of your index finger, a measurement called the *rahi*. For ordinary *bales*, one *rahi* spans the first three joints of the finger. For larger structures, such as rice barns, the *rahi* extends from the tip of the index finger to a point on the edge of your hand where a line from your palm terminates. There are many different lengths of *rahis*, and considerable variation among *undagis*. The next measurement is the *guli madu*, the narrow space between the second and third joints of your index finger, the exact points of measurement indicated by skin wrinkles. Finally, the *urip* for the *sasaka* measurements is the *anyari kacing*, the width of your little finger.

The *undagi* first records these measurements on a strip of young coconut leaf and then transfers them, in various combinations, to another long bamboo stick, the *gagulak sasaka*. The combinations of measurements and how and in what order they are used, repeated, and modified are fascinating, but to describe these would occupy a chapter in itself.

A typical *sasaka* is tenoned at the bottom to fit into a socket in the cast foundation or into a precast foundation block. If the post is also to support a bed, mortises are cut at an appropriate height to receive the beams that will hold up the bed platform. These beds are often used much as we would use chairs during the daytime, and a mat is rolled out at night for sleeping. Halfway up the post's height it is decorated with a traditional carved design, the *paduraksa*. Until this point, the post is square in cross-section, but from just above the *paduraksa* to the point at which the rafters begin, the corners are planed off producing an octagonal cross-section. Here the traditional *uler* is carved.

Almost all *sasakas* are one *rahi* by one *rahi* square—something like a common "four-by-four" post in the West. But the length varies from about 19 to 25 *rahi* (perhaps 2-2.5 meters). The *lontars* indicate what sort of fortune you can expect from various combinations of lengths, each of which has a different *urip* added to it. The length and width of the *bale* itself is a function of the number of pillars and the spacing between them. The latter is, again, a matter of choice, with various choices indicating various fortunes and each requiring a different *urip*.

When the *undagi* has completed the *gagulak sasaka* stick, a matter of an hour or two, it is full of notches and protrusions. For the carpenter, often the *undagi* himself, the stick serves as a blueprint of the *sasaka*, based upon the measurements of the owner's body. Two other *gagulaks*, much simpler, are prepared which will be used to ensure that the frames for the beds are properly notched and shaped. One stick is for the lengthwise sides of the platform, the other for the shorter, crosswise sides. The three *gagulaks* are then bound together, an offering is made for them, and they are delivered to the carpenter or are kept until needed at the *undagi*'s house.

THE *lontars* SPECIFY just what kinds of wood should be used for a given kind of structure. Most *sasakas* for household *bales* are made of teak, and many stores sell teak beams, one average *rahi* in width and thickness, ready to be trimmed to *sasaka* size by a carpenter. There are some small teak trees in Bali, but teak imported from Java and Kalimantan is considered to be of superior quality. Theoretically, wood for buildings must be sought from a living tree. Offerings are then made to the tree and only then can it be "sacrificed" for lumber. This practice is always followed when wood is sought for sacred buildings, such as temples and shrines, or for particularly sacred dance masks, but today wood for ordinary uses is usually purchased ready-cut in a store, and the offerings preparatory to killing the tree are dispensed with.

Before a carpenter can make a *sasaka* he must determine which was the root end of the timber. It would be unthinkable to create a *sasaka* and mount it upside down from its original growing position. The root end of a length of store-bought wood can be determined by balancing the planed timber at its exact midpoint—the heavier end will be the root end. Alternatively, the wood can be floated in a tank of water where the heavier end will sink slightly relative to the lighter end.

After the wall and gate locations are established the compound is ready to be laid out. The system used involves a basic length measurement called the *tampak,* which corresponds to the length of the owner's foot. The first *bale* to be located is always the *bale daja,* the sleeping quarters of the head of the household. Beginning at the *kaja* wall, the *undagi* guides the owner inward as, barefoot, he paces off a specified number of *tampak.* The *undagi* finishes the measurement with the *urip,* in this case the width of the foot, called *tampak ngandang.*

The system dictating the number of *tampaks* separating the various parts of the compound is based on the Balinese eight-day week, the Astawara. The 210-day Balinese ceremonial cycle or calendar, the Pawukon, has ten different week systems, each with a different number of days and all running concurrently. (See "Balinese Calendars," *BS&N Vol. I.*) The three-, five-, and seven-day weeks are the most important for religious celebrations, but the eight-day week is significant to the architect.

DAYS OF THE ASTAWARA

1. Sri	5. Rudra
2. Indra	6. Brahma
3. Guru	7. Kala
4. Yama	8. Uma

All of these day names are names for various Hindu deities, which is not the case for the other weeks. Eight is an important number to the Hindu-Balinese, representing the four cardinal directions and the four intercardinal directions. One god is assigned to each of these eight, plus Siwa in the center, completing the so-called *nawa sanga,* the compass rose of Balinese Hinduism that is so important in religious and ceremonial symbolism. Each god, or manifestation, has an associated color, characteristic, and a whole host of other attributes in addition to direction.

In the *nawa sanga,* Dewi Sri is *kaja–kangin* (northeast in South Bali), and the directions proceed clockwise around the circle, Indra being *kangin,* and so on back to Uma, which is *kaja.* Dewi Sri is god of rice, the source of life to the Balinese. Brahma is associated with fire, and the other

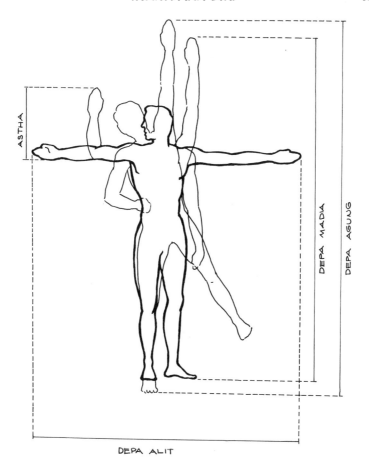

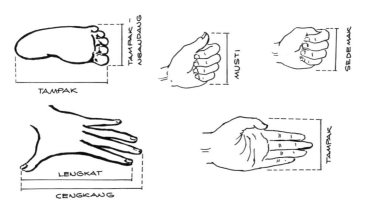

SOME ASTA KOSALA KOSALI MEASUREMENTS

names all have specific associations. When pacing off distances in the construction of the house compound, one *tampak* length is called "Sri," two *tampak*s "Indra," and so on up to eight, which is "Uma."

Since the home of the head of the household is the *kaja*-most *bale*, the *lontar*s specify that it be a distance equal to "Uma" from the *kaja*-most wall that encloses the house compound. Uma is eight *tampak*s. If that is too crowded and does not leave enough space between the wall and the *bale* the *undagi* adds eight more *tampak*s to the measurement, or any multiple of eight, all of which are called "Uma." No matter how many multiples of the basic measurement are used, only one *urip* is added.

The distance from the *bale daja* to the kitchen should be "Brahma," six *tampak*s or some multiple thereof, plus one *urip*. Brahma is specified here because he is associated with fire, in this case the cooking fire of the kitchen. From the *bale daja* to the rice barn must be "Sri," one *tampak* or some multiple thereof, plus one *urip,* since Dewi Sri is the rice mother. Without going into further, almost endless, detail, all of the other buildings of the house compound, including the family temple, are laid out and staked, following the specifications of the Asta Kosala Kosali *lontar* that the *undagi* uses.

Once the *bale*s and shrines are laid out, the job of the *undagi* is now largely over. If he is also a builder, he may help with the construction, but his role is basically just that of architect. He does not "design" or "plan" buildings in the sense that an architect in a Western country does. He does not innovate according to the tastes of the owner. He merely makes choices from the strict rules and regulations of Asta Kosala Kosali. He is more an interpreter of law than an artist. A team of carpenters, some of them possibly *undagi*s in their own right, make the *sasaka*s and wooden framing of the *bale*s. The grass thatching is usually accomplished by a team of roofers, and masons will be hired to do the foundation work and the stone or concrete work for the shrines.

BEFORE ANY CONSTRUCTION BEGINS OFFERINGS must be made and a special ceremony held. The *lontar*s specify that an offering called *panca datu* be placed in the foundation of each building. This consists of five (*panca*) metals of five different colors: iron, silver, gold, bronze, and copper, plus a yellow coconut wrapped with five different colors of thread. Today these offerings are seldom made except for very sacred buildings, such as in temples.

But a short ceremony and a more modest offering called the *banten nasarin* is always made to ensure that the work will proceed in harmony while the building is being constructed. *Nasarin* comes from *dasar,* meaning foundation. This ceremony often involves a *pemangku*, a lay priest, who wraps some of the bricks in white cloth, sprinkles them with holy water, and places them in holes that have been dug for the founda-

tion. Naturally this ceremony and the day of commencement of construction have to be done on properly auspicious days as determined from the
calendar.

When the materials are actually about to be joined together another
ceremony takes place, and finally, when the work is complete, a rather
elaborate series of ceremonies takes place before the compound can be
occupied. The *undagi* may conduct this if he knows the proper procedures, and if no, a *pemangku* is called in. In special situations, or for
important buildings like temples, a high caste priest (*pedanda*), may have
to officiate.

The final ceremony for a newly constructed building is called *melaspas,*
a purification rite that "brings the building to life." The construction
materials were "killed" so as to be used to construct the buildings. They
have, up until now, been referred to as stone, wood, and grass. The final
series of ceremonies results in their reincarnation. Once brought to life,
the house becomes a living thing. It is no longer made of stone, wood,
and grass. It now possesses feet, the foundation, a body, the *sasaka,* and a
head, the roof. *Wayang kulit* shadow puppets, sacred masks, and other
important cultural or religious items, even *lontar*s, are brought to life in a
similar ritual.

On special occasions, such as ceremonies in the house compound, the
bales are even dressed up like people. A Balinese man usually wears a special cloth, called an *udeng,* around his head when he goes to the temple to
pray and both men and women wrap a piece of cloth around their waists,
like a skirt, upon such occasions. During ceremonies, the family dresses
the *bale* in analogous "clothes"—strips of colored cloth attached to the
base of the roof, the *ider-ider,* function like the *udeng;* and the *pangaput
sasaka* is like a waistcloth for the *sasakas..*

THE RULES OF ASTA KOSALA KOSALI are very extensive, covering houses, meeting halls, shrines, temples, and all other buildings, public and private. The formulas are so complex that the above can be considered only
a tiny taste.

But what happens when you try to apply these same rules to modern,
multi-storied hotels, banks, and office buildings, none of which was ever
conceived of centuries ago when the rules of Asta Kosala Kosali were formulated? The answers to this question can be readily seen in and around
Denpasar, Bali's capitol city. Some are without taste, some are downright
grotesque, and a few are actually quite successful.

A modern architect cannot simply lay out a single-room Balinese *bale*
and then make it 500 times bigger to turn it into a 500 room hotel. All
sense of proportion would be lost, and the building would probably collapse under its own weight. Asta Kosala Kosali rules, strictly interpreted,
are utterly inappropriate for anything except small, open buildings, the

very largest being the big *wantilans,* or cockfight arenas.

Builders have taken different tacks in approached the problem of trying to suit modern architecture to Balinese tradition. Many of the government buildings in the Denpasar area are not Balinese at all and don't pretend to be. In other cases, architects from Java have laid out some rather drab attempts at traditional Balinese structures. All too often these consist of a standard office building usually multi-storied, decorated with a tile roof done in something of a Balinese style. But there is no sense of texture of materials, no openness, no grace.

Hotel builders have chosen different routes. First they build rather conventional and efficient blocks of rooms for their guests. Then they add on as many Balinese, or pseudo-Balinese appendages as space permits—here a temple gate, there a *bale kulkul,* over there a bathing place with water spouts and fountains, and everywhere lots and lots of elaborate stone carving. Some bungalow-style hotels have their guests living in oversize rice barns, which have a Balinese look to them, but amuse the locals, because no Balinese would ever live in a rice barn. At least one famous large hotel has made no concessions to its location and could be uprooted and plopped down right in the middle of Chicago, Sydney, or Paris, and nobody would even notice it.

The more efforts have been by Balinese architects who have tried to preserve the feeling of Asta Kosala Kosali without necessarily adhering to the letter. The Governor's office in Denpasar, though not yet complete, is an interesting experiment. The office consists of three multi-storied structures arranged around a central open area, representing three-quarters of the central part of a traditional house compound. Exact concrete replicas of *sasakas* are visible in front. There is even an attempt to capture the feeling of a *lalang* roof with modern materials. The scale is a bit overwhelming, but one cannot mistake this for anything else but a modern variation on an ancient theme.

Two other government office complexes in the Denpasar area that are even more effective, because they are built on a smaller scale. One is the office complex of the Kantor Bupati of Badung, the district head of the South Bali area, which is located north of the main part of Denpasar on the extension of Jalan Achmad Yani, on the road to Sangeh. The other is the office complex of the Indonesian government's Dharma Wanita branch, in the Niti Mandala area north of the Central Post Office (the post office, by the way, is an architectural horror).

In both cases the architect has settled on several small buildings surrounding a central court. Each building, though modern in design, materials, and function, maintains the feeling of traditional style in texture, proportion, and arrangement. Perhaps this is the best solution to the problem.

CHAPTER 15

Stone Carving

HEROES, GARGOYLES AND RIBALDRY

THE STONE WALLS OF MANY OF BALI'S TEMPLES are a riot of decoration. A bewildering variety of toothy stone faces with bulging eyes and long fangs peer, leer, grimace, and smirk from a veritable stone jungle of vegetation. Some walls show battle scenes, with refined men in elegant costume. Some murals are downright dreadful, with grotesque and gory scenes of torture. Still others are plain, everyday events—men drinking *tuak,* children riding bicycles. Statues, large and small, guard every gate and shrine. The profusion is such it would seem that Balinese stone carvers can't abide a blank space.

Museums and the popularity of painting are 20th century phenomena in Bali. Before these came along, the principal space available for the portrayal of gods, demons, and the Balinese universe were the walls and gates of temples and the palaces, *puri,* of kings and princes. Private homes were never much more than plain dwellings of wood, stone, and thatch. The notion of *pramada,* a kind of religious insubordination, maintains that a private space should not be as highly decorated as the place of kings and gods. Sculpture was, and is, for public buildings. Anthropologists estimate that there are some 20,000 temples in Bali—my guess is that this is probably an order of magnitude too low. Today, with additional spaces to be decorated on hotels, and government and office buildings, the art of the stone carver is more popular than ever.

Stone carving, like any of the activities in Bali that Westerners call "artistic," is not a secular, or individual, undertaking. Music, carving, and the construction of offerings are all a form of celebration of the Hindu-Balinese faith. While an individual carver may have a reputation for producing quality work, and his services in particular may be sought out by a village to carve its temple walls, he is not considered to be "great" in the same way as a Western artist. His work—and the Balinese word for all craftsmen is the generic "worker"—is just part of the many necessary and continual preparations and celebrations that make up the religious and cultural life of Bali.

The stone used for carvings is known mineralogically as "tuff," called *paras* in Bali. It is a kind of volcanic sandstone, a compacted combination of ash and dust that contains some sand and clay. Bali's several volcanoes have, through the millennia, regularly spewed ash which has accumulated on the flanks and alluvial slopes of the peaks. Full of essential mineral matter, this ash is responsible for the island's lush vegetation and rice fields. In places, the ash has been compacted into a soft stone, and these beds of *paras* are revealed where the streams cut their gorges down the volcanic slopes. Tuff is almost as soft as wood, although it hardens somewhat with age, and it can be carved very easily into the ornate designs that the Balinese love. But rain, the mosses and lichens that seem to thrive upon it, and abrasion quickly erode the stone. An ancient-appearing statue, features barely discernible and entangled in vines, may be no more than a decade or so old.

BALINESE TEMPLES ARE NEVER FINISHED. It is not unusual to find uncarved stones in place for years before the sculptor attends to them. Often as not this is because insufficient funds were available to complete the structure at the time it was built. Rather than leave the spaces empty, the raw stone, roughly shaped, is put in place, and time passes until funds are available for hiring a carver. By the time the money is raised, still another part of the temple needs renovating because age has reduced other carvings to dust. The Balinese generally feel uncomfortable when everything is finished and there is nothing more to do. This seldom occurs. Carvings have a short lifespan, and there are an incredible number of them to maintain, replace, and refurbish.

Various anthropologists, Margaret Mead among them, have observed that the Balinese are always happier when they are preparing for something—a musical performance, a ceremony, or building a structure of some sort—than when they have completed it. Reaching the goal is kind of an anticlimax.

Thus the stone carver is a busy man. He works together with the *undagi*, the traditional architect, who lays out the temple walls and structures according to the established principles of the ancient Asta Kosala Kosali building codes (See CHAPTER 14). A team of carpenters handles the wooden structures. The stone carver is usually just that—he takes no part in the building design or carpentry.

Crafts in Bali tend to be quite regionally specialized. The center for stone carving is Batubulan, a small village on the main road northeast from Denpasar. Batubulan is perhaps best known for the popular tourist *barong* dance shows performed there. If a village needs some stone carving to be done, more likely than not those in charge will go to the Batubulan area to hire a master carver and his team of assistants. The carvers will then travel to the village where the work is to be done and stay there until it is completed. They receive no special pay for their talents—any more than would a maker of offerings, a musician, or a dancer.

A Balinese temple is quite unlike a Hindu temple in India, being much more closely related in appearance, if not in lineal descent, to the megalithic Polynesian temples. In Bali temples have no roofs. God must descend into them when invited. The sacred parts are the shrines within. The gates and walls serve only to keep impure and evil influences away. Most temples are divided into three parts, consistent with the Balinese concept of the tripartite division of the universe. The holiest part, called the *jeroan*, is usually located in the direction of Bali's holy mountain, Gunung Agung. The middle part of the temple, the *jaba tengah*, is for less sacred uses, such as preparation of food for workers, making and arranging offerings, and performing ceremonies that are not quite as sacred as those for which the inner sanctum is reserved. The third division, the *jaba*, is for more or less purely secular activities. Some temples do not have a clearly defined *jaba*, but instead have just an open area in front of the gate leading to the middle courtyard.

The three courtyards of a temple are separated from each other by walls and by gates. The outer gate, the *candi bentar*, looks as if someone built a gate, decorated it, and then split it in half from top to bottom and separated the halves. The outside surfaces of this split gate are usually lavishly carved, but the inside is almost always plain. It is said that, if an evil spirit intrudes, the two halves will come together to crush him. The entrance to the sacred *jeroan* from the middle temple courtyard is through a massive *kori agung*, the division between the world of god and that of man. This gate is usually elaborately carved and above the lintel is a huge carving of the head of Bhoma, child of the earth. Bhoma's bulging eyes, fangs, and threatening grimace scare off any evil spirits that might enter and contaminate the inner sanctum. The *aling-aling*, a freestanding wall directly inside the *kori agung*, thwarts demons who might make it past Bhoma. (Demons can travel only in straight lines, it is believed.)

Several of the temple's associated buildings, *bales*, and shrines are also highly carved. The *bale kulkul*, the tower for the *kulkul* log drum, usually features stone carving. And within the inner courtyard there are numerous carved stone shrines. One of the most important of these is the *padmasana*, a symbolic representation of the tripartite Balinese universe. At the bottom is the world turtle, Bedawang Nala, entwined by two dragon-snakes, Naga Basuki and Naga Anantaboga, who represent man's earthly desires and needs. In the middle is the world of man, with leafy

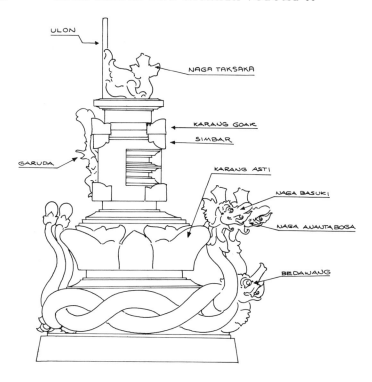

ULON

NAGA TAKSAKA

KARANG GOAK

SIMBAR

GARUDA

KARANG ASTI

NAGA BASUKI

NAGA ANANTA BOGA

BEDAWANG

THE VARIOUS PARTS OF A PADMASANA *SHRINE*

forests and mountains. And on top is the world of God, often surmount-
ed by an empty chair. Only the bases of the shrines within the *jeroan* are
made of *paras*—the upper parts are usually wood, with thatched roofs.

IN NORTH BALI THE RIOT OF STONE CARVING is carried to its ultimate— the temples are constructed entirely of *paras* and carvings are
everywhere. The temples in South Bali are often made of red brick, with
blocks of carved *paras* inset here and there. The temples in the Singaraja
area, far to the north, have every square centimeter covered with elaborate decoration. In many cases the carvings are outlined with white paint
or even colored with wild, bright hues. The *subak* temple in Sangsit, Pura
Beji, is a classic example of decoration gone wild.

Balinese stone carving is not religious carving in the sense that what
are produced are icons. Stone carvings are frequently portrayals of religious figures, perhaps even deities. But they are really just pictures in
stone, nothing more. One almost never finds a portrayal of, for example,
Siwa. The favorite subjects are the demons, giants, monsters, and evil spirits that populate so many Balinese tales.

Another popular stone carving theme is in the portrayal of the great Hindu epic poems, especially the *Ramayana* and the *Mahabharata*. Every Balinese child knows the highlights of these long and complex stories, as they are the subject of countless songs, dramas, operas, shadow puppet plays, and dances. But the most popular figures in the epics are not the heroes, who tend to be rather unworldly and remote to the average person, but rather the underdogs, the down-to-earth characters. In the case of the *Ramayana* the favorite, without a doubt, is Anoman, the general of the army of monkeys who help Rama save Sita from her evil and monstrous captor, Rawana. In the case of the *Mahabharata,* the favorite is Bima, Arjuna's brother, who is much more human than Arjuna—hot-headed at times, a huge, terrible fighter, a stubborn man of action.

It is always easy to distinguish between the heroes and the villains in Balinese art. In general, heroes and gods have what the Balinese called "refined" (*alus*) features. These are delicate, what a Westerner might call effeminate. The faces are serene, eyes delicately lidded, and the bodies thin and poised. Villains, on the other hand, are invariably "coarse" or "rough"— *kasar*. They are stout and hairy, and have bulging eyes and fang-like canines. It is almost impossible for a foreigner to distinguish between different refined characters unless he is an expert, because they tend to look very much alike except for the characteristic clothing and headdress. Much the same is true for the rough characters.

There are certain standard motifs. Over the Kori Agung, as previously mentioned, one almost always finds the head of Bhoma, very definitely a coarse character. At centers of less artistic focus is found the *karang bintulu* design, with a single eye over a row of upper teeth and a symbolic mountain on top. At corners are found the *karang curing*. Each of these is the upper part of a bird's beak with pointed teeth. And over everything there is a profusion of carved leaves, vines, and tendrils.

The Balinese are a fun-loving, and often ribald people. Among the carved monsters and giants there is very often explicit pornography. The Balinese take their religion very seriously, but temple walls are not "holy" the way, for example, a cathedral is in the West. The favorite spot for sexual carvings is the *pura dalem,* the village temple dedicated to Siwa—the dissolver—or his wife Durga. It is sometimes said that depicting sexual acts on the temple walls keeps out demons. Demons are known to enter human bodies through any and all orifices, so provide lots of carved orifices and the evil spirits will enter them—and not the temple itself.

Some of the rather gruesome scenes on temple walls show what will happen to the offender if customs are not observed or taboos broken. They usually leave little to the imagination. And some of the temple sculptures are pure whimsy. Here is a simple scene of a group of men drinking palm beer (*tuak*) out of bamboo containers, just as is done in every village today. There a leering stone cat pokes its head above a wall.

On a temple wall near Singaraja, at Kubutambahan, a man is depicted riding a bicycle with huge flower blossoms for wheels. Near Jagaraga, again in the Singaraja area, there are scenes as from a comic strip: an airplane crashing into the sea; a car being held up by thieves; a ship being pulled down by a sea monster.

A VISIT TO THE STONE CARVING CENTER of Batubulan makes a worthwhile excursion for the visitor. Here, there are vast assemblages of statues awaiting customers. Most of the customers are Balinese, for a one-ton *paras* likeness of a god or demon is hardly the sort of souvenir a tourist would pocket and take home. There you will see the carvers, many of them mere children learning the trade, busily at work in a shady spot. And you will see piles of carved stones ready to be installed in the temples. Even a visit to one of the *paras* quarries is possible. There is one between Ubud and the Goa Gajah ("Elephant Cave") that is easy to find. Just after you descend the long hill from Ubud you will see stacks of *paras* blocks along the road. Climb down the hill on the north side and you can see the stones being cut from the cliff.

Today, precast concrete carvings are beginning to make a dent in the traditional stone carver's market. Sometimes fine sand or powdered *paras* is added to the mix to give the surface some texture, but the effect is nothing like the real material.

CHAPTER 16

Mask Making

MAGIC AND CRAFTSMANSHIP

WHEN A WESTERNER PUTS ON A MASK he pretends that he is someone else. When a Balinese dancer puts on a mask he *becomes* someone else. A traditional performing mask in Bali is not just a piece of costuming; it is, in a very real sense, alive. The Balinese do not draw a line between natural and supernatural, secular and religious. Objects, particularly objects used in the performance of sacred dance and theater, such as masks and *wayang kulit* shadow puppets, are sometimes charged with a kind of spiritual magic—*kesaktian*—and are said to be *tenget*.

Thus, the traditional mask maker is not just a sort of carpenter, hacking away at a piece of wood with mallet, chisel, and knife. He is not creating decoration. He is crafting an object that will, at the very least, be handled and treated with great respect, and at the most, venerated in the most sacred and formal manner of which the Balinese are capable. The status of the mask maker derives not so much for his ability as a craftsman, but from his knowledge of the power of masks. A similar form of respect is accorded the makers of *wayang kulit* puppets, and *undagi*, the traditional architects of Balinese buildings. All of these activities involve powerful supernatural forces, and it takes a strong man to insure that these forces do not inadvertently get out of hand and create imbalance.

Most Balinese dramatic performances are enactments of ancient Hindu epics and, as such, are inherently sacred. The hero of the *Ramayana* is an incarnation of Wisnu, one of the so-called Hindu Trinity. Twalen, the wise servant who allies himself with the forces of the good, is a brother of Siwa, another member of the Trinity. Even performances of historical dramas involve kings and heroes who claim divine origin. No traditional Balinese dance, drama, shadow play, or music is unaccompanied by deep religious feeling, from the audience as well as the players. There are hilarious, even bawdy comic episodes, usually audience favorites, but the theme and feeling are no less sacred because of this.

Since the actor in a religious drama may portray a sacred character, the paraphernalia that transforms him into his role becomes sacred. Because the head is considered the most pure and important part of the body, and the masks actors wear in certain of the dance-dramas are especially important. The most important masks are sacred and *tenget,* and when not in use are kept out of sight in a temple or shrine. Every full moon, new moon, Kajeng Keliwon (a special day of the Balinese ceremonial cycle that comes every 15 days), and before a performance, offerings must be presented to the mask. A *tenget* object keeps its power permanently. Some Balinese religious objects, such as the symbolic vessels, the *pratima,* are considered *tenget* only when gods or ancestral spirits occupy them during a ritual. When the special ceremonies are over the spirits depart and the power of the *pratima* disappears (although the objects themselves are still treated respectfully). But masks that are *tenget* are always powerful.

Most masks are not sacred, but even these are handled with great care and respect. They are never stored in low places where someone might step over them. They are never allowed to be handled by just anyone. Instead of being hung on the wall as decoration, as might be done in the West, they are usually kept wrapped inside a box or a cloth bag. And every 210 days, usually on the day called Tumpek Wayang, special offerings are made to all masks that are used in dance dramas. This is the same day that ceremonies are performed for the *wayang kulit* puppets. Traditional masks are treated almost exactly the same as the puppets, since both portray characters who are sacred, or participate in sacred dance dramas. In some parts of Bali the day for making offerings to the masks is Tumpek Krulut instead of Tumpek Wayang, but the principle is the same.

A *tenget* mask is considered to be literally alive, and when the performer puts on such a mask, this power enters his body. The dancer's identity is temporarily suspended, and he assumes the personality and behavior of the mask. Sometimes the power of such a mask is so great that a performer cannot cope with it. He falls into an uncontrollable trance, unable to stand or act, and he has to be revived by a priest with holy water and sacred mantras. Some masks are so powerful that only those performers with great internal power themselves dare use them. Tales are told of high priests, *pedandas,* actually falling dead while bringing an especially important and sacred mask to life. Masks that are not given their proper treatment, respect, and regular offerings are commonly reported to bring their owner imbalance, trouble, sickness, and uneasy feelings. It is not an easy job to own a *tenget* mask.

Theoretically, any mask can be made or can become *tenget.* Most masks are simply kept in special places, treated with respect, and not exposed to improper treatment. The few really sacred ones, which have been brought to life in a special ceremony, usually conducted by a *pedanda*, must be accorded the respect and attention due any holy object—kept secluded, often in a temple, and never, under any circumstances, exposed to impure situations.

Even an ordinary mask can become *tenget* if it has been in the possession of the owner for a long time, and if the owner has made regular offerings to it out of respect. In fact, almost anything in Bali can become sacred, depending upon one's feeling toward it and the way one treats it. Masks are especially prone to this, even without special ceremonies that bring them to life, because they are the physical embodiment of the deity. Each is the dwelling place of its spirit. For example, if a village possesses a *barong* dance troupe, and a great many villages do, it is to the *barong* mask to which prayers are said and offerings made—not to the body of the costume which, if the *barong* is not assembled and in use, may be simply hung up in the temple store room and more or less ignored.

The visitor is likely to ask himself or his guide: "Is this really true? Do masks have this power?" The question misses the point entirely. The way the masks are built, treated, performed, and thought of presumes their great supernatural power. "Is this real?" is a question only a visitor could ask. In the West we have a large investment in such beliefs as, for example, the existence of a small agglomeration of forces called an atom. A visitor could ask "But have you seen one?" Such a question, from our point of view, is irrelevant.

THERE ARE THREE PRINCIPAL GENRES of mask dances: *topeng, wayang wong,* and the Barong-Rangda drama. These involve masks that are, respectively, human-like, animal-like, and demon-like. To be sure, actors in other types of performances may be found wearing masks. But these are either very minor art forms, or else they have been derived from one or more of the above three.

It is really a bit redundant to talk about a "topeng mask," since the word *topeng* in one sense means "mask." But it also refers to a type of dance. In fact, the more common word for "mask" is *tapel*. There are two types of *topeng, topeng pajegan* and *topeng panca*. The former is a very sacred dance-drama performed in the inner and most holy part of a temple, the *jeroan,* on special ceremonial occasions. It is danced by a single male dancer who, by changing masks in full sight of the audience, transforms himself into a variety of characters. Some of the masks are full-face, preventing any sort of speech. But there are also half-masks that allow the performer to tell his story. The story itself, taken from the part historical, part legendary chronicles of Hindu-Balinese kings, is more or less unrelated to the real purpose of *topeng pajegan,* which is concentrated upon the last mask to be performed, Sida Karya. Sida Karya's name means "can do the work." This final dance is performed to insure that the purpose of the ceremony, which the Balinese call "work," has been achieved satisfactorily.

Topeng panca, on the other hand, is really more or less pure entertainment, and is held in a less sacred part of the temple or even outside the temple. But this entertainment is not just for the human audience, it is also for the visiting spirits for whom the ceremony is being held. The word *panca* means "five," and the dance-drama is performed by a group of men (although not necessarily five). The stories are taken from the same historical chronicles as those of *topeng pajegan*, but there is usually no Sida Karya. In both varieties of *topeng* there may be many masks. Although at least 30 different *topeng* masks are recognized, seldom are so many used in a single performance. The mask styles range among refined kings, kings bent upon evil deeds, simple peasants, crafty courtiers, and idiotic clowns. It is not unusual to see one or more masks portraying deformed or physically handicapped people. *Topeng* is usually accompanied by a *gong*, a group of xylophone-like instruments led by a pair of double-ended drums, with large gongs and small cymbal-like instruments providing the rhythm.

Balinese *wayang wong*, like its Javanese cousin of the same name, is a dance-drama depicting parts of the very long, very important, and much-loved *Ramayana* epic, one of the great, ancient Hindu stories that is known all over Asia. The Javanese version is a theater piece, performed without masks. Almost all of the characters in Balinese *wayang wong* wear masks, and it is generally only performed for religious occasions, being considered a sacred drama. There are human characters in *wayang wong*, but most of the masks are of monkey-like animals. The most popular part of this story comes when the monkey army helps Rama, the hero, rescue his sweetheart Sita from the demon Rawana. Some of the *wayang wong* masks are extremely sacred, and great personal power and knowledge is required to use them without suffering harm.

The Barong-Rangda drama, as performed in the villages, involves a variety of demons and monsters. There are two types of *barong*s, the four-legged and the two-legged. The latter, called *barong landung*, literally "tall barong," are giant puppets, each three meters or more high. The most common four-legged *barong* is the *barong ket*, the lion *barong*, but there are several other types in common use today. Such a *barong* is always danced by two men, one in front, furiously clacking the movable jaw, the other supporting the majestic, curving tail. The principal theme is the fight between Barong and the evil witch, Rangda. But there is always a cast of supporting players, those on the side of good, assisting Barong, and those assisting Rangda. The actual showdown between the two main characters is preceded by a confrontation between these two groups of supporters—the white-faced, gentle-looking *sandar*s, on the Barong's side, and the fierce *omang*s on the other. In some villages the two groups

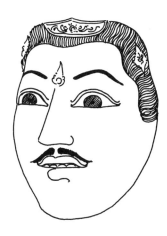

MASKS SHOWING COARSE AND REFINED CHARACTERISTICS

are known, respectively, as *teleks* and *jauks* (See "The Barong," parts one and two, *S&N Vol. I.*)

The particular expression of a mask is very important, particularly in *topeng*, where the character of each role must be immediately distinct. Good people must be pleasant looking. Bad people look evil or cunning, and often have bulging eyes and fang-like teeth. Aggressive people are war-like and strong. Good kings and heroes are serene and regal. The basic personality of the mask is always indicated by its color. Black masks are strong and forceful—they may be wicked and evil, but are not necessarily so. White masks are pure, upright, and refined. *Alus* is the Balinese word for this type. Red masks are brave, courageous, and possibly hot-headed. A purple face indicates that a character is *keras*, hard, strong, and loud.

Except for the few human-like masks involved in *wayang wong* and Barong-Rangda stories, expressions are not very important in monsters and animals. These masks tend to be quite elaborate, with great fangs, bulging eyes, lots of fancy decorations, and sometimes, movable jaws. *Topeng* masks, on the other hand, are more expressive and less ornate, since the dancer is portraying a subtle character rather than a simple animal or a demon.

TRADITIONAL MASK MAKERS always use the wood of the *punyan pule,* a common tropical tree found from Sri Lanka to Australia. The tree grows abundantly in the higher elevations of Bali. In Australia the tree, *Alstonia scholaris,* is called white cheesewood, milky pine, or milkwood. The wood is light-colored, strong, and of low density. It is easily carved, yet resistant to cracking. Ordinarily the mask maker buys the wood already cut. The two centers of mask making on the island, Mas and Singapadu, are not far above sea level and there are few *pule* trees in their vicinity. But for sacred, *tenget* masks, or even for those very important ones, such as Sida Karya, it is best if the mask maker himself cuts the wood. The Balinese regard all living things, trees included, as manifestations of the Hindu unmoved mover, and it is considered wrong to kill any living thing without first making offerings and asking its pardon and permission. This extends even to the cutting of rice. Of course, for a sacred mask, it is especially important that the tree from which the wood is taken is accorded proper respect and feeling.

The ceremony for felling a *punyan pule* for mask wood is called *ngepel,* derived from the Balinese word *pel,* "cut." As with all important ceremonies, an auspicious day has to be chosen from the calendar, often after consulting a priest. On the appointed day, the mask maker goes to the chosen tree and wraps the bottom of the trunk in a white cloth. The offerings for the tree, prepared by the women in the mask maker's family, are spread out on a mat in front of the tree. The mask maker himself or, preferably, a *pemangku,* a lay caste priest, dedicates the offerings with holy water, prayers, and burning incense or sandalwood. The *pemangku* takes the first symbolic stroke with the axe. The whole tree may be felled or, and this is preferred, just enough cut off to make the masks required at the moment. The wood is then wrapped in a white cloth, carried home on the head of the mask maker, and left, along with the offerings, in the family temple. It has to be seasoned for several months before it can be worked because if green *pule* wood is used, the vapor is said to make the mask maker sick. (The bark of the *pule* tree contains a number of alkaloids, some of which are considered to have pharmacological properties.)

Sacred masks, such as for *barong*s, are often taken from *pule* trees growing in temple courtyards. If several such sacred masks are made from a single tree, the *barong*s are considered to be brothers. When the anniversary ceremony, or *odalan,* for the temple in which the tree was located occurs, all the *barong*s whose masks were made from that tree must come to the temple to spend the night. In some parts of Bali it is considered important that when one of the *barong*s has a ceremony in its own village, all of its "brothers" must visit.

Wood intended for very sacred masks must be carried to a temple, offerings must be made to it, and that is where all the carving and painting work must be performed. For non-sacred masks, the mask maker works at home or in his shop. But he must always be careful to orient the wood as it was in the tree. That is, the top of the mask must be the part of the wood that was farthest from the ground.

WHEN I MADE INQUIRIES as to a good mask maker to commission for the purposes of this article, there was surprising unanimity among my sources' recommendations: "Go to see I Wayan Tangguh at Singapadu." I had trouble finding his house. There was then no sign advertising his wares or his trade, and he lives on a back road in the village, seldom traveled by tourists. Tangguh makes only traditional masks for Balinese dancers and for museums and collectors, who already know where he lives. He doesn't need to advertise. He makes no souvenirs. His work, from start to finish, employs only the old-fashioned, traditional methods.

Tangguh, 55, is a shy, balding, muscular man, with angular features and an extremely intense manner. He started carving masks in 1947 as a student of Cokorda Oka Tumbelen. The Cokorda, who died in 1983, was one of a group of five Singapadu men who achieved great fame as mask makers and dancers. Tangguh's retiring manner conceals a person of great warmth and friendliness who obviously lives and breathes his trade. He works surely and quickly, yet with painstaking care and precision. He puts something of himself into each of his masks. The oldest of Tangguh's five children is studying at an art academy in Yogyakarta, Java. The next eldest boy is studying to be a puppeteer at ASTI, the college level music and dance academy in Denpasar. The oldest girl is married, and her husband

and Tangguh's two youngest children, fine carvers on their own, help sand and paint his masks when they have time.

Tangguh's favorite working place is the open area under his rice barn, where he sits cross-legged on a mat, using his feet to hold the wood and leaning occasionally against one of the four posts. The work place is littered with wood chips and the simple tools of his trade—knives and chisels of every size, forged from concrete reinforcing rod or automobile springs, and mallets of hard *celagi* wood. Partly completed masks lie in a jumble in a box or hang from the rafters.

As with most self-employed craftsmen, Tangguh is also a rice farmer. At certain times during the rice season, and at certain times of the day, he walks the several kilometers to his irrigated fields and the visitor must wait patiently or try again another day. But his wife always brings tea and rice cakes, and his helpers and son-in-law are generally mixing paints in a nearby *bale*, unless it is time for lunch or the afternoon nap. Tangguh will not work on masks on the day Pasah, the first day of the Balinese three-day week, which is considered a very unlucky day for almost everything and anything in Bali.

I told Tangguh that I had plenty of time and wanted to follow the progress of a single mask from tree to finished product, and, if possible to its use in a dance. "What mask shall I make for you?" he asked.

"Perhaps you should choose," I replied. I told him I couldn't wait several months for something as elaborate as a *barong* mask, and I couldn't ask him to make a *tenget* mask because I couldn't take care of it properly. (Although I have since bought a *barong* mask from him.) "I want a nice, typical mask that will be kept in a place of honor in my home."

Tangguh suggested Sida Karya, the final mask of *topeng pajegan*, and I eagerly accepted. Although the mask was not to be sacred, it would be purified after completion, and this made it desirable to have offerings made for the tree from which its wood was to be cut. So, on an auspicious day, all of us went to a *punyan pule* several kilometers from Tangguh's home, and the *ngepel* ceremony was performed by a *pemangku*. Tangguh told me to return in two or three months, and he would commence work when the wood had dried.

On the appointed day, Tangguh set to work. He sawed the log into a round slab about 15 centimeters (6 in.) thick and rounded the chin. Then he put an offering for the mask nearby, sprinkled holy water on his tools, and literally attacked the wood with a small adze, chopping a concavity into the back and shaping the sides with quick strokes into the rough outline of a face. Then, switching to a chisel and mallet, he began on the rough details of the face. He had an old Sida Karya mask at hand and used a pencil and a sliver of bamboo to mark the eventual positions of eyes, mouth, and nose.

The chips flew, and in two-and-one-half hours the typical buck-toothed, leering smile, deeply-recessed eye sockets, and bulging cheeks of Sida Karya were beginning to take form. Next day he began to work with the knives. He held the wood sometimes with his feet, sometimes with the fingers of his left hand, and, holding the knife in his right hand, pressed the blade against the wood with his left thumb. He took great pains to make the mask symmetrical. Most difficult were the curls on each side of the mouth and the cheek wrinkles on the smiling face, later to be painted gold. He would measure a distance on the right side of the mask with pencil and a strip of bamboo, then transfer the bamboo over to the left side, make a mark on the mask, and accomplish the small correction with a few deft slices. Knives with bent blades cut the deeply incised, hard to reach areas. When the eyes, nose, and mouth had been roughly shaped, Tangguh scraped out more of the back of the mask and finally punched through and enlarged the eye and mouth holes.

After the carving had gone on for about three working days, three or four hours a day, the mask looked great to me, ready to paint—but not to Tangguh. He spent a full working day holding the mask out in front of himself, correcting an imbalance here, improving a curve there. He was now accomplishing the finishing touches to the all-important facial expression. This is the slowest process of all, but the one that is the most important for a true craftsman. When he was satisfied he very quickly carved out the back of the mask, periodically fitting it to his face to see to it that it was comfortable and that there was enough room for the wearer's own nose and mouth. At this point he had spent a total of about 12 hours carving.

Then came a day of smoothing with sandpaper. First he used a fairly coarse paper, cut into 3-centimeter squares and folded for the flatter parts. To reach into the nooks and crannies he inserted a narrow strip of sandpaper into the split end of a length of bamboo, rolling the sandpaper up into a ball so that he could reach down into the crevices. Every now and then he would scowl, make a minor correction with a knife, and sand the section all over again. This was followed by another sanding with finer grit paper, which left a satin-smooth finish. Total sanding time was about four hours.

Tangguh had left a lump between the eyes that he ignored throughout most of his work. He said that, since Sida Karya was a king, his mask would have a jewel, the *cudamani*, set here. He was having a jeweler friend of his set the stone in a copper fitting that would be attached after painting. Tangguh then punched a hole in each side of the mask near ear level for the head strap, took one last look, and turned the mask over to his son-in-law to take to the painting *bale*.

TANGGUH'S MASKS ARE PAINTED only in the traditional manner. No commercial paints are ever used, although it would cut the painting time and expense enormously. The amount of time spent just preparing the paints was unbelievable. White is the most difficult pigment to make. He buys calcined pig jawbones to make his white paints. Deer bones are better, but Balinese deer are both scarce and protected by law. The bones are broken up and then ground by hand using a smooth pestle in a porcelain plate. It takes about an hour and a half of grinding to yield a sufficiently fine powder. Black pigment is the easiest to make. A clay roof tile is held over a smoky coconut oil flame to catch the soot. The soot is quite fine enough for use and doesn't have to be ground. A very bright vermilion, called *kincu*, is purchased from a Chinese store in Denpasar that imports it from Hong Kong. Yellow comes from a kind of clay that must be ground, but it is softer than the pig bone. Most of the intermediate colors can be obtained by mixing these four. Gold comes from real gold leaf.

All of the ground pigments must be mixed with a binder called *ancur*. *Ancur* is purchased from a source in Surabaya, Java. Tangguh told me that it was made from milk and water buffalo skin. (Others have said that it comes from a kind of fish gelatin.) The product comes in little white rectangles, each very thin and wrapped in a piece of grass to keep them from sticking together. This is the same sort of binder that is used in the ancient Kamasan-style of painting that is still done in the Gelgel–Klungkung area.

Since my Sida Karya mask was that of a king, its basic color was white. So Tangguh's sons-in-law started grinding the pig jawbones. After an hour and a half he measured out the proper quantity to use with the *ancur* by pressing the white powder into a soda bottle cap. Three capfuls were required for the day's work, the proper amount to mix with 15 pieces of *ancur*. Then he added a little water, the *ancur* strips, and continued the monotonous circular grinding. Periodically the sides of the pestle were scraped down with a piece of tortoise shell and a little more water added to keep the mixture the consistency of a thin paste. After another hour he judged the mixture to be sufficiently fine, and he covered it with a leaf to keep out the dirt.

Tangguh himself applied the first coat, using a commercial paint brush. It took only a short time. The paint, however, looked gray and splotchy on the mask. As it dried, however, the color changed to a uniform, chalky white. Only the front of the mask is painted, nothing behind. After the first coat had dried for half an hour, the paint was stirred up and the second coat went on. Seven layers of paint went on the first day. Eight more were added on the second day. That was enough for white paint, which is strong and covers well. "I sometimes use 150 layers of paint for a *barong* mask," Tangguh said, "because the red paint is not very strong."

On the second day, at the same time as the white was being added, the lips and nostrils and two areas above the ear level were painted red. The red pigment had to have lime added to it. Lime is not needed for white, but with red, black, and the other colors, you have to add to every 12 pieces of *ancur* "a ball of lime as big as a *cecak* (gecko lizard) egg." Grinding the *ancur* with the red pigment took "only" an hour and a half. The pink paint for the gums was made by mixing a bit of red with the white. Only enough paint can be made for one day's use, since it spoils if kept even overnight. Thus, the grinding ritual is a daily affair at the paint *bale*. There is obviously a great temptation to yield to commercial paints, and many mask makers do. But Tangguh simply will not have his masks finished in this untraditional material.

The next day was for black and gold. The soot was ground with *ancur* for about one and one-half hours, just as in the case of red. But the gold required a completely different technique. First some *ancur* was soaked in water for an hour or so and then ground very fine for another hour and set aside. The gold leaf, made in Hong Kong, is called *prada*. It comes in small books, about five centimeters (2 in.) square, each book containing 80 leaves of extremely thin real gold, separated by paper. The craftsman, using small scissors, cuts one of the leaves, paper still attached, into strips about two millimeters wide. Then he cuts all of the strips perpendicular to the first cuts, resulting in tiny pieces perhaps a half-centimeter long. As he cuts, the small sections fall into a box.

A small section of an area to be gold leafed is then painted with a plain, watery paste of *ancur*, using a very fine tipped brush. The tip of the brush is then applied to the paper side of one of the tiny gold leaf strips, to which it adheres, since the *ancur* is a glue. The little piece is then lifted to and placed gold side down upon the tacky *ancur*. The brush is then lifted, and the *prada* sticks to the mask. On my Sida Karya mask, all the gold areas except the outline of the lips had grooves or ridges to guide the painter. But on some masks there are no such lines, and the gold areas must be drawn in with pencil or pen. A triangular embellishment above each ear, like a horn, had *prada* applied over red paint to make it a bit darker. The larger gold areas were covered with larger strips of *prada*.

While the ancur glue for the *prada* was drying, fine red lines were drawn in the incisions separating the teeth, and the gums were painted so that each tooth had an arch of red and pink above it. Then a thin layer of red was applied over the pink on the roof of the mouth to make it look realistically splotchy where the hard palate is. The day was finished by brushing down the *prada* with a paint brush, smoothing out its wrinkles and joints. The next two days were spent painting the entire front of the mask with a ground mixture of *ancur* and water only, without any pigment. Ten coats resulted in a bright, glossy, protective varnish that did not alter the colors below.

Only the hairy parts and the *cudamani* remained to be added. Tangguh once again assumed command. It took him about two hours to cut a piece of black goat skin into two pairs of matching strips, one pair for the eyebrows, the other for the mustache. He was extremely particular about obtaining perfectly symmetrical pairs. When he was satisfied he attached them by whittling thin pegs of bamboo, punching a hole through hide and mask with an awl, and inserting the pegs as nails, cutting them off flush with a knife. Finally the *cudamani* was attached using straight pins cut in half and then bent at right angles, hammered in as nails with the flat of a knife. The mask was complete.

During the process of making the mask, it had been held by the feet—considered extremely dirty and unholy—and had been put on the floor, stepped over, and, in short, subjected to a variety of unavoidable treatments that are considered quite inappropriate for an important object. As a result Tangguh decided to hold a ceremony, called *pengambean,* to clean up all the impurities and improper treatment and restore the mask, if not to sacredness, at least to a state of ritual cleanliness, where one could feel good about it.

As usual, an auspicious day had to be chosen. By chance, the day after the completion of the mask was full moon, *purnama,* considered to be an especially good day for purification. Tangguh's wife made the necessary offerings, the principal of these being a *daksina.* This is a cylindrical basket made of coconut leaves, a bit larger in diameter than a coconut, inside of which are placed a coconut scraped of all its hair, many different kinds of leaves, rice, flowers, the three principal ingredients of the betel chew, small pieces of banana, sugar cane and other fruits, and a stick of incense. The *daksina* is considered to be the most important of all the many, many different kinds of offerings. She also made several other offerings of plaited coconut leaf, some with fruits, others containing colored rice cakes.

Tangguh placed the newly completed mask on a table in front of his family temple, amidst the offerings. Nearby he put a clay brazier in which sandalwood chips smoldered over hot coconut charcoal. Dressed in his traditional Balinese clothing, he prayed that the mask be purified and that mistakes and transgressions of etiquette and procedure during its making be forgiven. He sprinkled the mask and the offerings with holy water, and then he placed offerings on the ground for the *butas* and *kala*s, the negative forces of life that constantly attempt to upset the equilibrium between good and bad. Finally he poured an offering of *brem,* rice wine, upon the ground, a common way of appeasing these demons.

The brief but beautiful purification was over. Wrapping the mask in a checkered black and white bag, the magic cloth the Balinese call kamben *poleng,* he handed it to me. And, as I received it from his talented hands, I felt very much as if I were receiving a part of him and his intense feelings and creativity—one of his children, so to speak.

It so happened that, a few days later, Tangguh's son—a student at ASTI— was to give a performance of *topeng pajegan,* wherein the Sida Karya mask is used in the final dance of the series. I persuaded him to use my new mask and was able to photograph the final step in the series that began so many months before with a single tree and that progressed through so many interesting stages until its final use for which it was intended.

My Sida Karya mask is purified, but is not a sacred or *tenget* mask. Belief in *tenget* objects is a common, but not essential part of Balinese Hinduism. Although I adopted the Balinese Hindu religion in 1982, I am not one who is preoccupied with the world of magic and the supernatural. Nevertheless, I make an offering to my Sida Karya every full moon and every new moon and every Kajeng Keliwon. Why? Well, perhaps it's because I feel that Tangguh would want it that way. And, in Bali, it's the feeling that matters most.

Clothing

SARTORIAL TRADITIONS IN BALI

TODAY BALINESE MEN AND WOMEN wear ordinary pants, shirts, and dresses while they work. Traditional clothing is worn only in informal settings around the home and village, and at very formal events—temple ceremonies or important social events. This chapter will focus on traditional clothing in these two settings.

The traditional male waistcloth is called a *sarung,* sometimes *kamben sarung. (Kamben* is the generic Balinese word for any cloth used to wrap the lower body.) *Sarung* means "sheath" or "tube." A *sarung* is a two-meter length of cloth that has its ends sewed together to form a tube. The cloth is about one and a quarter meters wide. Visitors, especially those who remember Dorothy Lamour in *Road to Bali,* will be tempted to call any sort of lower body cloth a "sarong." But the term is generally reserved for this tubular garment worn by men. A man usually pulls the *sarung* on over his head and holds it so that the lower border hangs just above the ground. The top edge comes up to the upper chest. While the cloth is held against the chest by the man's chin, he gathers up the excess cloth on either side and folds it around his body. A man always puts the right hand fold on the outside, pulling it across the front of his body to his left. Then the top of the *sarung* is rolled tightly down to the hips, thereby holding it up. It is seldom that a belt is worn. The roll of cloth produces a considerable bulge that may be taken for a pot belly if concealed by a shirt. Tourists who wear *sarung*s without using a belt are asking for trouble unless they practice.

Most *sarung*s have a panel of a different color or design woven into the center of the cloth which, when the *sarung* is worn, ends up in the back. The Javanese favor *sarung*s made of batik—a type of cloth in which the design is produced by blocking out areas with wax, dyeing the cloth, and then boiling out the wax. But the most popular *sarung*s in Bali are made of the native *endek*. *Endek* is usually rayon, and the design is tie-dyed into the weft strands. Rayon is softer than cotton, and has an attractive sheen. (See CHAPTER 18.) In the early morning chill a man can pull his *sarung* up high and wrap part of it around his head as a sort of shawl. It is usually long enough to cover the necessary parts below. In colder parts of Bali men wear ordinary long pants—*jaler*—and use the *sarung* as a head wrap.

Many men wear no shirt at all around the house. Some wear cotton knit T-shirts, which are called *baju kaos oblong* where I live. *Kaos* means sock or stocking, which refers to the knitted material. The recent fashion is for men of all ages to wear sleeveless undershirts, which are called *baju kaos singlet* (from the British "singlet").

Nobody ever wears any sort of shoes inside the house. The standard Balinese foot apparel are cheap rubber-soled sandals, or "flip-flops." These are called *sandal India* or *sandal jepit*. Some people never wear anything else except maybe to go on a long trip or when at work in an office or store. They are cheap and available everywhere. For more formal occasions, Balinese often switch to a *sandal kendip*, which are more what Westerners would call "slippers" without a counter or heel piece. Almost no Balinese wear sandals with heel straps, because they must be taken off so frequently, for example, when entering a house. Someone like myself, who depends on the heel strap, is forever buckling and unbuckling. When praying in a temple it is standard practice for men to slip their sandals off and sit upon them as a combination cushion and barrier against dirt.

Many modern Balinese men and boys wear regular Western short pants as their everyday dress around the house. Babies and children are usually dressed in the same sorts of clothes as their Western counterparts. In Bali's warm, humid climate it is startling to see young babies swathed from head to foot in heavy knit booties, blankets, gloves, jackets, and hoods. This is to prevent that most prevalent of all Balinese diseases, *masuk angin*, "wind enters," the standard diagnosis for coughs, colds, and other respiratory disorders.

WOMEN DON'T WEAR *SARUNGS*. Many wear ordinary cheap Western-style printed cloth dresses around the house and village. More traditional women wear the most popular of all articles of traditional Balinese dress, the *kamben lembaran*, usually just called *kamben*. *Lembaran* means a "leaf," as of paper, or a "sheet." It refers to the fact that the *kamben* is not sewn into a tube like a *sarung*. There is likely to be confusion about the words *kamben* (and the Indonesian *kain*). Both are perfectly acceptable for referring to any piece of cloth, but it is necessary to add an adjective—for example, the popular black and white checkered cloth that one sees wrapped around the middles of so many stone carvings is properly called *kamben poleng.* But the Balinese usually use *kamben* to refer specifically to this standard lower body wrap.

Both men and women wear *kamben*s, but men usually do so only for religious or important social events. Women may wear the *kamben* all the time, for both house and village activities as well as for temple use. A *kamben* is two-and-one-half meters long (8.2 ft.), but slightly narrower than a *sarung.* Men and women wear them in different ways (see illustration opposite). A woman always wraps the cloth quite tightly, so that it almost forms a tube. This restricts leg and foot motion considerably, but provides a graceful figure. Around the house, a woman is likely to ease up a bit on the tightness. To eliminate unsightly bulges, the *kamben* may be fastened with a safety pin at the waist. Sometimes a belt is worn.

Expensive materials are never worn around the house. *Endek* and batik are equally favored for *kamben,* but today the batik is often machine printed in Jakarta. This is much cheaper than real batik and more practical around the house. Many women even use it for ceremonial occasions. Balinese women wear the same types of sandals as men most of the time. They usually switch to Western style shoes if they have jobs in offices.

Most women wear a *tapih,* a slip, under their *kamben* and they almost always wear brassieres, *buju hutang* or "B.H." Over that may go almost anything: an ordinary store-bought T-shirt, just like that of a man, a cheap cotton print blouse, or a traditional *baju kebaya,* often just called *kebaya.* This last is a kind of long-sleeved jacket that reaches to the hips. It is fastened with buttons or snaps, or commonly with safety pins down the front. The neck is low and V-shaped, and a horizontal rectangular panel covers the breasts. The right edge of this panel is sewed on vertically down the inside of the right half of the opening of the *kebaya.* The panel is then brought over the breasts and attached on the left side with snaps, buttons, or safety pins. Some years ago the fashion was for these shirts to be made of lace, but now they are usually made of ordinary cloth, sometimes with embroidering.

When a woman leaves the house to go to market or to visit she often wears a sash of some sort, a *selempot,* wound around her waist. This does not serve to keep things from falling down like a belt. It is mostly decorative, but it also has two additional functions: the dangling end of the sash may be tied into a *buntil,* a loose knot into which money can be placed for safekeeping; if the *selempot* is terry cloth, the woman can use it as a head pad to ease the load of whatever she carries back from the market.

Some sort of pad that she can put on her head to cushion a load is part of the standard equipment of every Balinese woman. Light objects may be carried directly on the head, but some cushioning is always placed between a heavy, hard object and the hair. This usually takes the form of a long piece of cloth. The general word for the material is *cerik.* It may be a

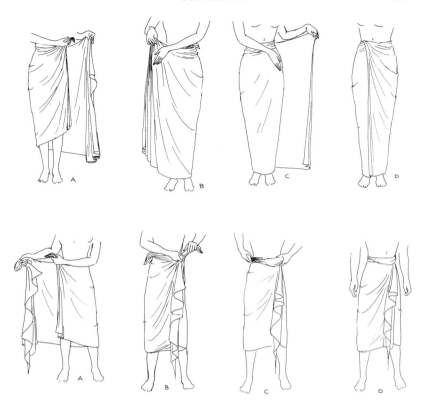

STEPS IN FOLDING A KAMBEN BY WOMEN AND MEN

bath towel made of terry cloth, or it may be almost any sort of material, preferably rather thick. It may be wrapped around the waist when not in use simply to get it out of the way yet have it handy, or it may serve as the sash around the waist that all people are required to wear in a temple.

The *cerik* is used in several ways. Sometimes it is wrapped around the wrist to form it into a coil, and then the coil is placed on the head to cushion the load. This is called a *sesuunan*, a term that can also mean anything that is carried on the head. Alternatively, the *cerik* may actually be wrapped around the head, as one would a turban. If the free end is placed over the top of the head and tucked in one side this is called a *tengkalung*. If the free end does not go over the top of the head, it is called a *tengkuluk*. If the *cerik* is wrapped around the fist in a coil and then placed elsewhere than on the head for supporting small objects it is called *lekeh*.

WHEN A MAN DRESSES FOR A TRADITIONAL, *adat*, occasion, he must wear clothing that is somewhat different than that which he wears around the house. The occasion might be a *banjar* meeting or a *gotong royong* group that is working in a temple or preparing a ceremonial feast. Very informal clothing is not appropriate, nor is Western clothing. He always wears a shirt, no matter how plain, a *sarung* or *kamben,* and some sort of sash around his waist. The general word for any kind of sash worn around the waist is *selempot.* It doesn't much matter what is worn. Many men favor colorful rayon or cotton sashes made just for the purpose, but bath towels or knitted blankets are common. A man should wear his *selempot* over his *kamben,* but under his shirt, but many young men wear the *selempot* on the outside. Women always wear a *kamben* and a *selempot* for such events, which may involve helping family or friends make offerings, working in the kitchen preparing food for a big event, or decorating shrines in a family or public temple. This is ceremonial clothing on a somewhat basic level Although young children are generally exempt from clothing restrictions, most parents provide their children with at least a *selempot* for *adat* affairs. Some go to much greater lengths, and complete sets of traditional clothing are available in children's sizes.

For worshiping in a temple and for large, festive occasions, such as a tooth filing or a wedding, both men and women must dress in their finest traditional clothing. Some people call such clothing *pakaian adat,* but this is an Indonesian term. The Balinese word for clothing in general is *pananggo* in Low Balinese and *pangangge* in High Balinese. When referring to fancy clothing, such as is worn to a temple, the usual words used are *payas* or *payasan.* These terms refer to adornment or decoration of any sort, including jewelry, cosmetics, and shoes. *Mapayas adat* is the usual way of saying that one is wearing traditional Balinese clothing. *Payas adat* is different only in degree of elaboration from that described above as a kind of basic level. In fact, it would not seriously offend custom if one were to wear the same sort of clothing to a temple as one would wear to a village feast. But people would probably talk.

A man must wear a *kamben.* But, he wraps and secures it in a different manner than does a woman. When a man wraps the *kamben* he ends up with a plaited fold that drapes down in front. The material is adjusted so that that the tip of the "tail" is far enough above the ground that it won't be stepped on. This tail is called a *kancut.* Men take great care in arranging the folds of the cloth artistically and are rather vain about the appearance and adjustment of the *kamben.* The *kancut* serves another purpose. If the man must engage in some sort of physical activity while in *adat* dress, he reaches from behind underneath his crotch, pulls the *kancut* between his legs and upward behind his rear end, and tucks it into his belt at the center of his back. This, in effect, provides a pants effect and keeps the lower part of the kamben from interfering with his movement or dragging on the ground or in the puddles. This style, called *mabulet ginting,* is the way male dancers wear their *kamben*s when performing. In our village, the *seke barong,* the village men who tend to the *barong* dance troupe, wear white *kamben*s that have a half-meter length of red cloth sewed to the right side. When properly folded, the *kamben* appears to be all white, with a red *kancut* hanging down in front. If the *kancut* is not tucked in behind, a really low hanging one can get in the way when climbing stairs into a temple. It is usual to see a man hold the *kancut* in his left hand as he ascends or descends, or when crossing a puddle.

For formal dress, most men, particularly older ones, wear a head cloth called an *udeng*. Some men wear *udeng*s for any *adat* occasion, even those that do not necessarily require their use. And some men wear them all the time, just as some men in Western society wear hats. There are almost as many ways to wear an *udeng* as there are Balinese. It really matters not what style is used. There is almost no limit to the ingenuity that one can display in wrapping a piece of cloth around one's head, and some men take great pride in the appearance of their particular favorite technique.

An *udeng* is usually a piece of square batik material that measures about one meter on each side. *Endek* is never used because it is not stiff enough and will not hold pleats. The cloth may have an overall design, but it is usually symmetrical. In some popular *udeng* patterns a large plain white square occupies the center of the cloth. The wearer folds the cloth in a triangle, rolls up the long end, and ties it to his head. The entire *udeng* is tied to the head in such a way that the point of the triangle faces toward the rear and the knot is centered on the forehead. If you really want to have class, you do not tie a complete overhand knot, but, rather make a loop like tying a single shoelace. The tip of the triangle forms a kind of crest, symbolizing the *ongkara,* widely used to represent the Hindu triad: Brahma, Wisnu, and Siwa. (It also looks stylish.)

Some people call this crest *jambul,* after the tuft of feathers found on the heads of some birds. One can tell the personality of a man by his *udeng*. Extroverts leave a big, protruding *jambul* that looks like the comb of a cock. Introverts leave only a tiny tip protruding. The jauntiness of position and tilt of the *udeng* tell a great deal about the wearer. It is usual to stick a flower in the *udeng* so that it extends upwards either in front, in back, or both. Stores that sell *adat* clothing may carry pre-formed *udeng*s, shaped and sewed firmly in place, that fit over the head like a cap. These offer the same kind of convenience as does the clip-on tie in the West.

Prefabricated *udeng*s are often made of *songket,* a cotton cloth brocaded with gold or silver threads. *Songket* is traditionally woven on a small horizontal loom called a *cagcag* and used only in a few places in Bali. Real *songket* is quite expensive. There is now available a gaudy, machine-made substitute that bears little resemblance to the real thing, but which is attractive because of its low price. It is often called *songket Singapur* after its supposed place of manufacture. *Songket* is a popular material for *udeng*s that are used for festive or ceremonial occasions. These are never used for everyday wear, since the material is not long lasting. An *udeng songket* is usually triangular rather than square so that one does not need to fold it into a triangle, as in the first step described above.

The single most important clothing requirement in a temple is a covering over the middle body. For men this is normally a *saput,* a piece of cloth worn over the *kamben.* The High Balinese word is *kampuh. Saput*s vary in size and material. They are not as long or as wide as *kamben*s, generally reaching only a little more than once around the body. Men wear them in the same fashion as a *kamben,* but with no *kancut.* A *saput* may be held up by tucking in the top, or a belt may be worn. The most expensive and elaborate *saput*s are made of *songket.* However, *songket* is very delicate, and cannot be washed because it is not colorfast. The gold or silver threads are not tightly woven into the fabric and catch and break on every available protrusion. Even the best *songket* becomes so shoddy after a year or so that it must be replaced. Some people wear *saput*s that are yellow or an orange-yellow. The *barong* group in my village always wears *saput*s of this color. Some people wear *saput*s of checkered *kamben poleng.* Others prefer an ornate brocaded cloth that is made in the Batuan area. Certain *endek* patterns are also popular.

A man usually wears a Western style shirt to the temple or for festive occasions. The most formal and best dressed men wear long-sleeved batik shirts. But most people simply wear a clean, short-sleeved shirt. White is the preferred color. The temple priests, the *pemangku*s, are always dressed in all-white, including their *udeng*s, which are tied in a special way.

APPROPRIATE TEMPLE WEAR FOR A WOMAN is not much different from that which she would wear all the time anyway, except that the *kamben* is wound extra tight, with a very narrow opening at the bottom. This is responsible for the characteristic mincing steps adopted by women so dressed. Only the finest affordable *kebaya* and *kamben* materials are worn. Some women pleat the free edge of the *kamben* in front and hold the pleats together at the top with special clips that look like flat hair clips. Some women wear a girdle. In our village this has the unique name *sabuk streples,* or *treples,* which I presume comes from "strapless."

Not only do women wear their best *kamben* to a temple, they also hold it up differently. This is not immediately evident from an outside view. Once the *kamben* has been properly adjusted, the woman wraps it firmly in place with a long, wide cloth belt called a *sabuk bulang* or *sabuk satagen.* The word *sabuk* is a generic term for any sort of belt that actually holds up something—not just used for decoration. The word *bulang* means "wrapped" or "tied around." The belt is a strip of woven material about 10-centimeters wide (4 in.) and up to five-meters (16 ft.) long. It may or may not be decorated. Starting low on her waist, a woman winds the strip around and around in an upward spiral. This not only keeps the *kamben* up, it also enhances the figure. The *sabuk* is then pinned in place.

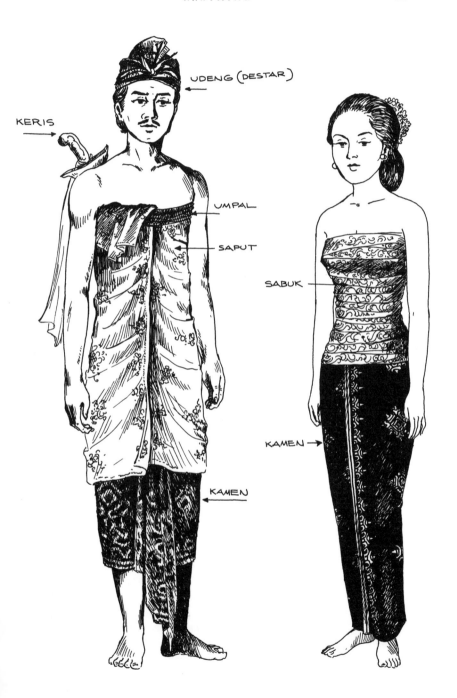

TRADITIONAL DRESS FOR BALINESE MEN AND WOMEN

The *kebaya* jacket is worn over the *sabuk,* and the *selempot,* the cloth belt, is worn over all of that. Women do not wear a *saput.*

For *adat* occasions, a woman should wear her hair in a large bun that hangs down from the back of the head to the shoulders, angled a little to the right. The problem is that modern Balinese women have taken to wearing their hair short. There are two solutions. An *antol* is a long wig that is not formed into the folded bun. It is just a long bunch of black human hair sewed together at the top. Various grades of these can be purchased at many village markets. The *antol* has to be folded into the desired bun and held in place. The other type of wig is called a *sanggul,* which is Indonesian for "wig," or *pusungan tagel,* which means "folded bundle,"—a bun or knot of hair. When a wig is used, the woman uses various pins and a *arnet* (a Balinization of "hair net").

On formal occasions most women wear a *bungan mas,* a gold flower, in their hair. The flower is actually a brass pin constructed of individual leaves and petals that are embossed and mounted on springs. The leaves bob and wiggle as the wearer moves his or her head. Sometimes men will wear these in their *udeng.*

Most women also wear earrings. A *sumpel* is an earring for a pierced ear. *Sumpel ceklek* is an earring with a clamp for a non-pierced ear. *Subeng* is an ear plug. A rather startling sight is an older woman with a roll of paper money thrust into the lobe of her pierced ear. Women also wear a decorative pin, *bros,* a necklace, a bracelet or several, and a ring.

WHEN A MAN PARTICIPATES IN AN IMPORTANT Hindu rite-of-passage (*manusa yadnya*) ceremony, such as a tooth filing or a wedding, he must wear traditional clothing that is even more elaborate than usual. Instead of the ordinary *kamben* of batik or *endek,* he generally wears a *kamben songket.* Since *songket* does not come in pieces wider than about 75 centimeters (30 in.), two of these must be sewed together in parallel. The man ties a belt, called an *umpal,* high on his chest just underneath his arms. This is sometimes attached to one corner of the *kamben songket.* The *umpal* is then wrapped tightly around his body and tied firmly. The *kamben songket* is then brought up under the *umpal* and folded over the top so as to conceal the belt itself. This is really the most traditional man's dress, but it is seldom used except for the special occasions mentioned. If the man's family has a kris, it is inserted into the space between the *umpal* and his back, the handle pointing up and to the right. The word *umpal* is also applied to a belt or sash that is tied to a *saput* and wrapped around the waist as a belt.

Traditional dress for a woman in an important *manusa yadnya* ceremony demands a finer *kamben* than usual. It is often made of *prada,* cotton cloth upon which large designs are painted with gold paint, rather than woven. *Prada* is usually used in Bali for wall decorations, curtains for ceremonies, and draped in bands from the eves of buildings as a decoration called *ider-ider*. It does not wear or wash well. But it is traditionally used for women's wedding *kamben*s and belts as well as for dancers' costumes.

For a wedding, the woman usually does not wear a *kebaya*. Rather, she holds the *kamben* in place using a very fancy *sabuk bulang* made out of bright *prada*, wrapped in a spiral around and around her waist. Her upper body is covered by a wide piece of *prada*. It is wrapped by starting at the left shoulder in such a way that the free end hangs down behind the girl's back. The long end is then brought down from the left shoulder, across her chest to the right, and wrapped around the body clockwise and pinned in place. The effect is that of a sash thrown over the left shoulder, hanging down behind.

The traditional Javanese *selendang* is a separate piece of material worn loose over the shoulder or pinned in place, or held front and back with a belt. This is almost never used in Bali except by Javanese women who attend formal receptions or meetings. But almost all Balinese traditional dances require some sort of sash for both male and female dancers. Which shoulder the *selendang* is worn over depends upon its use. Each type of dance has a prescribed side. Dancers portraying males wear it on the right shoulder and those portraying females wear it over the left shoulder.

THERE ARE VARIOUS TABOOS pertaining to clothes. These are not casual. Not properly observing the customs can result in offending Balinese people greatly. There is a general feeling about the impurity of clothing, particularly that which is in contact with the genital organs, which are considered to be quite impure. This impurity has nothing to do with dirt, but is explainable only in terms of the magical forces associated with procreation, birth, and reproduction, the feeling of the Balinese toward menstrual blood, and anything that is associated with these ideas. Clean underwear, in this sense, is just as "profane" as dirty.

One cannot avoid having clothes or washing clothes. But one must always avoid putting oneself in a position that is underneath clothes. And one must avoid putting clothes in a position that invites people to pass below them or that makes it possible for someone to accidentally pass below them. For example, a clothes line for drying clothes must be in an out-of-the-way corner of the house compound. Some very traditional Balinese refuse to go into a building that has more than one floor because of the presence of people above them. And Balinese farmers will string dirty rags along a line to keep trespassers from their fields.

One must never sit on the corner of a desk, as we in the West are so likely to do, because this puts impure parts of the body too high, where they shouldn't be. One must never lean over or step over a person, for the same reason. One must never drape clothes over a wall, particularly a temple wall. One must never put clothes in a rack overhead. One must never put clothes of any sort in the *luanan*, the sacred or mountainward—part of a room. Not even a closet for clean clothes can be *luanan* of a bed. One must never put clothes higher than or especially on top of an offering of any sort or step over an offering. Conversely, one should never put offerings of any sort on the seat of a car or on a chair, or any place that has been in contact with the impure parts of a person. One must never sit on a pillow that is used for sleeping, because this puts impure parts in a position where the purest part of the body, the head, normally rests. The list is quite long, and there is no point in belaboring the point. The above should give the reader the general idea. Just be careful.

BELOW ARE SOME OF THE TERMS the reader might encounter if going shopping for clothes in Bali. The list is far from complete, but it will serve as a starting point for shopping or bargaining:

Clothing	*panganggo* (*l*), *pangangge* (*h*)
Cloth	*lembaran; lakar*
Weft side	*tundu* (the smooth face, the outer surface)
Warp side	*basang* (the rough back, the inner surface)
Remnants	*wek-wekan* (scraps of cloth)
Kasa	a rough, white cloth (for religious uses)
Blacu	white sackcloth
Endek	Balinese weft ikat
Batik	waxed and dyed fabric (usually from Java)
Payas	traditional Balinese clothing
Laundry	*umbah-umbahan*
Wash clothes	*ngumbah* (*l*), *meresihin* (*h*)
Mend	*menain*
Sew	*nyait*
Spare clothes	*séh*
Try on	*negarang*
Change	*nyalin*
Put on (clothes)	*nyaluk*
Take off (clothes)	*negembus, ngelus*
Wear	*nganggo* (*l*), *ngangge* (*h*)
"Fits"	*nyandang*
"Loose"	*goloh*
"Tight"	*kelet*
"Long"	*dawa* (*l*), *panjang* (*h*)
"Wide"	*linggah* (*l*), *limbak* (*h*)

CHAPTER 18

Endek

BALINESE WEFT IKAT CLOTH

BATIK IS USUALLY CONSIDERED the national fabric of Indonesia. And parts of Indonesia, particularly Java, are justly famous for this unique material which is as sought after by Indonesians as it is by foreign visitors. But batik, a waxed pattern technique that is thought to have come from India, is by no means the only native textile in Indonesia. Very little batik is made in Bali, for instance, although the demand is so great that the visitor to the island will be offered every imaginable variety of batik: from Java, from Singapore, and from Malaysia. There is even a special "Bali-style" batik (made in Jakarta) that has a pattern of tiny Rangda masks.

The only native textile made in quantity in Bali is a woven, tie-dyed weft cloth that the Balinese call, variously, *endek* (pronounced en-DUCK), *ikat* (from the word meaning "to tie") or *kain tenun* ("woven cloth"). This *endek* has the distinction of being one of the few native crafts in Bali that is more popular with the Balinese than it is with visitors, who seem to be more interested in non-Balinese batik.

Endek is produced in dozens of factories, large and small, scattered all around the Denpasar and Gianyar areas in South Bali. There are even a few around Singaraja in the North. Some are family affairs, employing as few as a dozen workers. Others are sizable factories with hundreds of employees. Producing the fabric is highly labor-intensive, with no machinery except for wooden, hand-operated looms.

Endek is tie-dyed, but not in the familiar way. The tie-dyed fabric that became popular in the United States in the '60s was created by knotting and tying fabric or finished articles and then immersing them in a dye bath. The tied areas absorbed little or no dye, and left unpredictable swirls and patterns. Balinese *endek* is tied and dyed *before* the threads are woven into cloth. And the designs are planned, and regular. This is an exceedingly complex operation.

Balinese *endek* is "weft *ikat*," a technique that is not exclusive to the island. Nearby Lombok and Timor, to name just two places, also produce a similar cloth. In preparing *endek*, the weft or cross threads are dyed; the warp, the threads that are initially strung on the loom, are left in a solid color. To prepare the pattern, the weft threads are temporarily strung on a frame and workers use strips of plastic tape to "tie" a pattern into the threads. The threads are taped off in bunches, and then the threads are removed from the frame and soaked in vats of dye. They are dried, the tape removed, and the thread is spun onto a shuttle. When the dyed threads are woven into a loom set up with a solid warp, the design reappears. Because the warp threads are taped off in bunches, and because perfect registration of the design is impossible, the finished *endek* pattern has an attractive, fuzzy-edged look.

THE FIRST STEP IN THE MANUFACTURE of *endek* is to lay out the weft threads on a tying frame. This is an open, rectangular wooden frame the same width as the loom on which the cloth will eventually be woven. Although it varies somewhat from place to place, *endek* is typically woven in sheets that are 110 centimeters wide (43 in.) by a bit over six meters long (20 ft.). Women are generally employed to string the weft threads into the frame. The operator first mounts 20 spools of thread on a rack near the frame. Taking up the end of each of these 20 spools, she draws off a rope, or ribbon of threads, and winds this five times around the base of the frame. This thick ribbon—200 threads—will form a single unit for tying off. She then moves up the frame a small amount and lays down another five wraps. This operation is continued until the entire frame is strung with thread. For a typical six-meter length of fabric, about 80 of these five-wrap sets will have to be laid down.

The weft-wound frame is now taken to the tying room. Men almost always do the tying, although most of the workers in the factory are women. Using centimeter-wide rolls of plastic tape, the men tape a design into the threads. Each wrap encircles only one of the eighty "ropes" and is no wider than the width of the tape. It would seem like tedious work, but the men work with lightning speed, their fingers flying over the frame faster than one can follow. The pattern can be geometric—triangles, zigzags, diamonds, and dots. Or it can consist of crude outlines of animal forms, a face, or one of the grotesque masks of which the Balinese are so fond. The men never work from a sketch and nothing is drawn on the weft threads. The pattern is in the head of the man doing the tying, and yet when finished the pattern is perfectly symmetrical in the frame. A man can tie three frames in about two days by himself, but often two men work together on a single frame.

TYPICAL BALINESE ENDEK DESIGN

When the men tie up the pattern, they must also take into account the distortion it will undergo when the threads are woven into cloth. Eighty thick wraps, enough weft thread for six meters of cloth, is fit onto a tying frame 75 centimeters (30 in.) high. But remember the woman started with 20 threads. Later in the process, these 20 strands are separated, and woven into the cloth one at a time. Thus the finished cloth will have a pattern that repeats 20 times. But considering the thread count, and the length of the final product, the patterns repeat every *32* centimeters, not every *75* centimeters. Thus the mental designs that are being tied up are elongated versions of what will eventually appear on the finished fabric.

When all the threads are taped the frame is knocked apart and the loose bundle of threads is taken to the dye vats. Dyeing is a messy, dirty job, and is assigned to men only. The vats of dye are hot and smelly, and puddles of dye are everywhere underfoot. Everything is done by hand. The bundles of weft are dipped into the vats, wrung out, rinsed, and wrung out again. The men wear long rubber gloves and knee-length boots, but all of their exposed parts tend to assume the color of whatever dye is being used. The skeins of dyed and washed weft, ties still attached, are then hung up to dry in the sun.

If the thread is to be dyed just once, at this stage the plastic ties are cut off. This gives the skeins a dappled look, deeply colored where the dye reached, and the original color where the ties had been. The result looks like a giant striped snake all coiled up. If fabric is be multicolored, only some of the ties are removed. This is yet another variable for the men who tie up the frames. To indicate which ties are to be removed before successive dips in different colored dye, the men use various colors of plastic tape. The process of dyeing, drying, untying some of the remaining tapes, dyeing again, and so on, is continued until all the colors are produced. Some factories make *endek* with five or six colors, some with only one.

Once the dyeing is complete, the tapes removed, and the thread dry, the threads are separated and wound onto spindles. Remember that when the woman first tied up the frame of weft threads, she drew her thread from 20 ganged spindles. So this entire piebald and colored skein is really just 20 threads. At this point in the process, these 20 threads are separated out. The operator takes one end of the skein, finds the 20 thread ends, and passes them through a frame with 20 openings. These thread ends are then spaced out, top to bottom, on a huge rotating drum. When the drum is turned, the threads are deposited in 20 separate coils. These, by turns, are pulled from the drum using a spinning device made from a bicycle wheel. The thread ends up where the tire would be. From here the thread is transferred to a spindle compact enough to fit into the shuttle of the loom. All twenty spools of weft thread are collected in this way.

MEANWHILE, THE WARP IS PREPARED. Warp thread is purchased pre-dyed and already wound on spools. To load this on the loom, the thread must first be laid out in a smooth sheet on a large drum, like the one that was used to separate the dyed weft threads. The average thread count for the *endek* made in Bali is 25 threads/centimeter (63 threads/in.); since the finished cloth is 110 centimeters (43 in.) wide, 1,450 threads must be laid on in a sheet on the drum. To accomplish this, 100 spools of thread are ganged and the thread is laid out in tight, 100-thread ribbons on the drum. These are, in turn, transferred to another drum to yield a smooth sheet of all 1,450 strands. The thread is then ready to be strung onto the loom. Stringing the loom, as one might imagine, is an extremely tedious process. The threads must be passed into a wire frame and constantly attended to to avoid tangles. It may take two women all day just to string the warp for one loom.

The horizontal wooden hand looms used to weave *endek* are of a type that has been used for centuries in Europe. The warp threads run from their drum through a device called a shedding harness. When a foot pedal is depressed, the shedding harness raises alternate threads of the warp, creating a space, called the shed, between the elevated and the depressed warp. The weft thread, in its shuttle, is run through the shed, propelled by a rope that is attached to a second pedal. The weaver then beats the new weft tight with a hinged frame. This completes one crossthread. She then steps on the shedding harness pedal again, raising the opposite threads, and kicks the pedal to shoot the shuttle back the other way. Back down with the frame to beat it tight, and on and on.

As the shuttle with the weft thread makes its way back and forth, the tied pattern reappears. For the first ten passes of the shuttle,the pattern of the material remains the same—five loops on the tying frame—and on the eleventh pass, a new and slightly displaced pattern appears. It continues for 10 passes, and then a new one. This continues until all 800 passes of weft thread, one complete cycle of the pattern, are laid down. This cycle, given the thread count, produces about 32 centimeters (13 in.) of pattern. Then another of the 20 identical spools of warp thread is taken up, and an identical 32-centimeter pattern is woven. The finished product is just over six meters (20 ft.), with 20 repetitions of whatever pattern the men tied into the tying rack.

The pattern can be made more fine by using fewer windings for every ribbon laid out on the tying frame. For our description here, we used five wraps, but it could be just two or three. Of course, the rack would have to be twice as high and there would be twice as many rows for the men to tie. This kind of fine work gets very expensive. Sometimes you will see *endek* with a mirror image pattern. This is accomplished by tying up the weft strands on a rack that is only half as wide as the loom. This actually saves work, by producing a symmetrical pattern with only half the labor of tying. There are twice as many crossings of the weft on the frame as compared with a full width frame. That is, the ribbon of 20 threads is wrapped ten times around the frame for each row instead of just five. Each tie covers 400 threads instead of just 200, cutting the number of ties in half.

The weaving rooms of the *endek* factories are crowded and noisy places as the shuttles clack-clack back and forth and the shedding harnesses clatter. As many as 20 or 30 looms may occupy one room, with only enough space to squeeze in and out left between the looms. An experienced woman can weave two to three meters of cloth each day.

ENDEK IS MADE OF EITHER RAYON OR COTTON, or a blend of the two. A really expensive *endek*, not widely available, is made of silk. The Balinese prefer rayon because of its sheen and because it is softer than cotton and drapes nicely into folds. Foreigners often like pure cotton, since it is cooler than rayon and takes a press—at least for a while. In the tropics the air is so humid that carefully pressed in, knife-edge creases can last just moments. (On the plus side, the wrinkles produced by hand washing are just as fleeting.)

The colors and designs of *endek* are almost unlimited in variety. The Balinese like the geometric patterns; the tourists prefer faces and masks. If the basic colors of the weft and warp threads are close, but slightly dissonant, the hue of the cloth will appear to change color as the light shifts, yielding a pleasing shimmery look. Some of the rayons can be almost iridescent. Blues and reds are particularly vivid, and there is a vibrant coral color that is especially favored by the Balinese. In recent years the *endek* factories have experimented with alternating the colors of warp thread, adding another element to the pattern.

People in Bali buy the *endek* for *sarung*s, a waist wrap worn by men, and for *kamben,* a cloth worn by women and, on ceremonial occasions, by men (see CHAPTER 17). The *sarungs* and *kambens* don't have to be made of *endek.* Batik is widely used as well—perhaps even more widely than *endek.* Most cloth in Bali is sold in sheets, hemmed on all four sides, that are sized for *kamben*s—just over a meter wide and about two-and-one-half meters (8.2 ft.) long (a *sarung* may be one of these lengths sewed into a tube, but is often wider and shorter, and has a differently colored panel sewn into the middle). Both *kamben* and *sarung* can be tied in an variety of attractive, untraditional ways by Western men and women.

Visitors prefer to buy *endek* that is made into shirts, blouses, and dresses. The material is very comfortable, and the colors are reasonably fast. But *endek* shrinks, even though it has been dyed in hot water, and it is important to determine if the material has been washed before purchasing a ready-made garment. Likewise, if you buy *endek* fabric, be sure to wash it before you cut it out. Single-dyed *endek* sells for about Rp 7,000 per meter, and multicolored patterns cost a bit more. There are many tailors in Bali who, for a very modest sum, can produce excellent shirts and dresses to order in a day or so. Tailors can easily make shirts and pants for men, but they are not always the best dressmakers. They can skillfully copy anything that you bring in, though, so you can have a dress reproduced in *endek* or you can bring dress patterns from home.

In recent years *endek* made from mercerized cotton has become very popular. It is more expensive than the usual coarser cotton, but its surface is smooth, and it has a texture almost like that of rayon. It has the feel of rayon and the coolness of cotton. Another innovation, unfortunately, is the introduction of machine made, fake *endek.* Thus far the fakery is rather crude, and anyone with any experience can easily distinguish between real and imitation *endek. Endek* that is similar to that made in Bali is also produced by Balinese people who live in Lombok, the next island east of Bali in the Nusa Tenggara chain. *Ikat* materials are also produced in other areas of Indonesia, each with its distinctive style.

There is a very rare, and sought-after type of *endek* still produced in a few places in Bali called *geringsing*. This is a double *ikat* weave, with both weft and warp threads tie-dyed. The material comes from a tiny village in northeast Bali called Tenganan. Villagers here, and at a few other remote outposts in North Bali, call themselves Bali Aga, and claim descent from the original ancient inhabitants of Bali, instead of the Javanese migrants who arrived during the 12th–14th century Majapahit dynasty. The method for making this material is so time-consuming that very little is made anymore, and, if any can be found for sale, it is almost prohibitively expensive. It is often woven of silk and even a small *geringsing* belt made of the material can cost hundreds of thousands of rupiahs. It is not unusual for a single *kamben* to take several *years* to make. Some is sold in Tenganan, and some shops in Klungkung and Denpasar sell it also.

ENDEK WILL DOUBTLESS BE BALI'S "OTHER FABRIC" until such time as it is merchandized in the slick and attractive way the big Javanese batik manufacturers sell their product. Bali has many well-located, modern batik shops, staffed with English-speaking workers trained to understand Western tastes and styles. *Endek* is still sold mostly in the crowded village markets and at the remote factories where it is made. Shopping for the fabric can be an adventure. The materials are not well displayed, and the employees do not generally speak or understand much English. They expect you to bargain, of course, which is difficult if you cannot speak Indonesian or Balinese. But the material is so inherently attractive that your efforts will be handsomely rewarded.

PART V

Pastimes

CHAPTER 19

Cockfighting

A LIVELY, RAUCOUS SPORT

THIS CHAPTER IS NOW PRETTY MUCH HISTORY. When I wrote it, it was not. Cockfighting is a very old tradition in Bali, and before the Indonesian government banned gambling in 1981 the sport attracted huge crowds to the public *wantilan* arenas. Gambling was a large part of the attraction, but not the only one. Cockfights have a ceremonial purpose, and the government's ban includes an exemption—three rounds of a cockfight may be carried out for the purposes of ritually spilling blood, an important appeasement of the demons that accompanies Hindu temple festivals.

A cockfight is not just *allowed* at every Balinese temple festival or religious ceremony, it is *required*. The blood is an offering to the hungry forces of evil, the *butas* and *kalas*. Since religious ceremonies are almost daily affairs all over Bali, and since Bali is a rather small island, one still has an excellent chance of seeing a cockfight, if he arrives at the right place and at the right time.

The Balinese call the cockfights for ritual purification *tabuh rah,* "pouring blood." Of course it is illegal to bet on these three matches. But the law is not easy to enforce, given the ancient traditions of betting on cocks and the predilection of the population for this sort of thing, plus the remoteness of many of the ceremonies and accompanying cockfights. Theoretically the cockfights at temples, called *tajen telung seet,* consist of only three matches—*telung* means "three." This rule was (and still is) generally ignored. The Balinese can't resist continuing, often until sunset.

Cockfights used to be held on non-religious occasions. Sometimes a village might need money to renovate a temple or improve a public building. It could make quite a bit of money by staging a cockfight, because the house took a cut of the betting pot—often as much as 25 percent. The biggest non-religious cockfights in Bali were held three days a week at a big public arena in downtown Denpasar. The gambling there was intense and serious, and amateurs knew they had best stay away. Permission for a village to hold a cockfight had to be granted by the police. But the big, public cockfights are permanently gone. Since this chapter was first written before the gambling ban, I shall maintain its use of the present tense instead of turning it into an historical article.

There is no point in worrying or preaching about the blood and guts aspect of cockfighting. Although such activities may shock our sensibilities, there is never any sense of guilt among the Balinese about this, or any notion of such treatment being "inhumane." The Balinese are not known for spoiling their animals, except, perhaps, their cows and water buffalos. To them, the death of a chicken in the cockfight arena is in no way different from its demise under the knife in the kitchen.

THE COCKFIGHT ITSELF, called either *tajen, meklecan,* or *ngadu,* is only part of the scene. Everywhere you go you see men handling their *siap,* the fighting cocks. The birds are fondled, massaged, plucked, bathed, deloused, and fed the choicest mixtures of corn, rice, egg, and proprietary strength-building ingredients. It is said that a mixture of chopped grilled meat and jackfruit leaves thickens the blood and prevents serious bleeding when injury results in the fight. No child is as spoiled as a fighting cock. Whenever two or more cock owners gather there are impromptu mock fights in which the birds are released to confront each other. But no blades are used on their legs, and no injuries result. A common late afternoon scene in any village is a group of squatting men, chatting with each other, and playing with each other's animals. In this idle pastime, *megecel,* the men ruffle the feathers, pull the bills and combs, feel and press the birds' muscles, and frequently hand each other the cocks they are handling. This may go on for hours on end, and the scene is endlessly repeated in village after village. It goes on even today.

No women are ever involved in any aspect of cock handling or fighting. Balinese society involves no sex discrimination in daily activities, although there are some jobs that are basically for women, and others for men. There are, however, no prohibitions against men making offerings or women hoeing rice fields. Women just don't go to cockfights and have nothing to do with husbanding cocks.

Every road is lined with rows of bamboo cock cages, *guungan siap,* which are shifted regularly to give their inhabitants the proper balance of light and shade. The cages are placed near the roads to accustom the animals to noise, people, and activity. This way, when put into action in the arena, they will not shy from the spectators or run away. Hanging on the outside of the cage is a coconut shell dish, with which the bird is watered and fed his special mixture. The going price for a young, untried cock was about Rp7,000 to Rp10,000 in 1980. The offspring of a good blood line, like the offspring of a good horse, are highly prized and considerably more expensive. Cocks are generally not fought until they reach a year and a half old, and a cock is considered to be at his fighting peak at three years. The animals can live seven years, but occupational hazards almost always prevent this.

As with many other Balinese rituals, the lore and law of cockfighting is written in sacred palm leaf books called *lontars*. The writings are unbelievably intricate and detailed. There is a mind-boggling classification of cocks by color, shape, configuration, neck ruff, and other characteristics. Certain colors of cocks should fight cocks of other colors only during specific phases of the moon, on specific days, at specific times of day, from specific directions in the ring—and so on. This is the subject of endless discussions when men exercise their birds in the cool of the evening.

The larger temples generally have a permanent cockfight arena, a *wantilan*, which is outside the temple proper, but near its entrance. It may or may not have a roof. The arena itself is about 15 meters square, enclosed almost completely by tiered seats. At the smaller temples, an area for the fights is roped off nearby and a row of benches set up just outside the "ring." There is often a huge banyan tree nearby for the little boys to climb and from which they get a good view.

MOST COCKFIGHTS BEGIN IN THE AFTERNOON. Only the larger temples have morning starts. But people begin to collect long before starting time. The push cart vendors sell their hot noodle snacks. Ladies set up stands and sell rice cakes, *saté,* fruit, and shaved ice with sweet, brightly colored syrups. Men play cards and shoot dice. Today, vendors hawk plastic buckets, photographs, calendars, stuffed animals, and squeaky whistles for kids. You can tell long before you arrive that a cockfight is being held. There are huge jams of bicycles, motor bikes, pedestrians, push carts, and various forms of public transportation. Getting there early is important, because there is never enough room, and once the fights have begun the crowd is impenetrable, even in the biggest *wantilans.* At the larger fights a small admission is charged, perhaps Rp 100 to 200.

The cocks are brought to the arena in small, flexible bamboo cages, called *kere* or *kisa,* their fluffy tails protrude and it is impossible for the birds to move around. The cages are lined up around the edge of the arena, inside the barricade, and their handlers squat behind them. It is a noisy affair, with the crowing of the cocks, the cries of the food vendors, and the raucous laughter and chatter of the crowd.

At the appointed hour a white-clad *pemangku,* a lay priest, advances to the center of the arena and presents offerings on the ground to the *butas* and *kalas,* chanting over them, ringing his bell over them, and finally pouring rice wine on the ground. Then he makes similar offerings to the gods in a shrine built up off the ground at a corner of the arena. Blood is on the way. Although the actual fighting is still a long way off, now the action begins.

The men who handle the cocks before and during the fights are not the owners. They are professional handlers, *juru kembar*, hired by the owners to manage the animals. A skillful handler is of great importance to an owner. The winning cock is the one that last manages to stay on its feet, even if it is mortally wounded and drops dead seconds later. A good *juru kembar* has a large bag of tricks to revive a seemingly lifeless cock and instill enough spirit in him to return to the fray. He plucks, massages, and ruffles the feathers. He has salves and medicines. He may breathe on the cock's mouth, or even put the cock's whole head inside his mouth— anything to enable the wounded bird to get in there and land one more blow. One good stab is often all it takes to turn an apparent winner into a future feather duster—the fate of losing cocks. Sometimes, if the handler is a gambler himself, he may seek out owners of cocks that he thinks he can make win.

After the *pemangku* has finished his prayers, a dozen or so cocks are brought out into the arena by their handlers. Usually a miscellaneous crowd of bystanders collects too. The handlers are seeking opponents. After much wandering around and talking, quite time-consuming, a potential opponent is usually found. The two handlers squat down, face each other and, still firmly holding their birds, allow the cocks to glare at each other and get in a peck or two. Ruffs flare, and the animals get very excited. Then the handlers exchange birds by simultaneously handing the bird with the right hand and receiving the other with the left. Their oppo- nent's muscles are felt and its strength tested. When a match and the amount of the bet are agreed upon, the handlers signal the owners who are seated in the audience. Owners may veto the match, but they usually abide by the decisions of the handlers. Three or four such pairings consti- tute one set of matches, called *mbakan*.

The next step is to affix the blade, the *taji*, to the cock's leg. The per- son who does this is usually a specialist, a *pemasang taji*, or *pekembar*. It is the *taji* that gives the cockfight its name—*tajen*. A *taji* is a tiny, razor- sharp dagger, 11–15 centimeters (4–6 in.) from tip to tip. The blade is thin, and diamond-shaped in cross section, and terminates in an unsharp- ened, roundish handle which is attached to the bird's leg. There are almost as many stories and as much lore about *taji* as about the powerful kris daggers. Menstruating women may not look upon them or touch them. They may only be sharpened at the dark of the moon. They must be forged with charcoal from a tree that has been struck by lightning—and some say they may be forged only when there is lightning going on outside. They must not be touched by a member of a family in which there has been a recent death. The prohibitions and lore are end- less, and endlessly variable. A good *taji* may cost up to Rp 10,000 (in

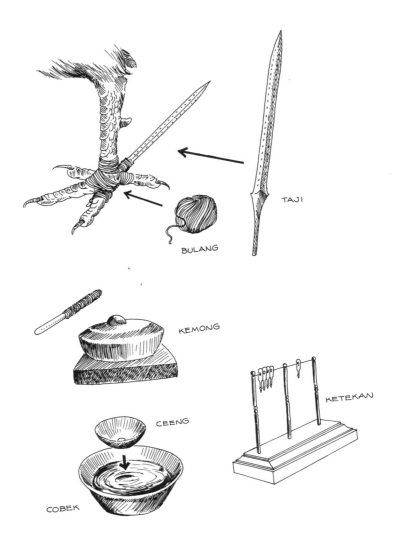

TAJI

BULANG

KEMONG

CEENG

COBEK

KETEKAN

THE ACCOUTREMENTS OF A COCKFIGHT

1990, Rp 20,000). There are usually 10 or 15 *pemasang taji* around to be hired for Rp 500 or so to affix the blades. Sometimes the handler has his own *taji*. They are carried in a little wooden or leather wallet, called a *kupak*, which contains half a dozen or so different sizes of the little knives.

A single blade is attached, normally to the left leg, by wrapping twine around the leg and handle of the *taji*. This is an extremely important part of the preparation. If a blade is improperly fastened, the cock will be at a great disadvantage. If the bird is small, the *taji* is attached to the outside of the leg; if large, to the inside. The angle of the *taji* is also critical. A good *pemasang taji* is very important. Sometimes, when one cock clearly outweighs the other, the heavier one is handicapped by modifying the attachment of the blade. But this is never done unless both owners agree. While the blade is being attached, the cock is held by the assistant, the *saya taji*. A firm grip is important. The blade is very sharp, and if the bird gets loose, the handler or a spectator could be critically injured.

When the cocks for the first set of matches are ready, the arena clears out, and the first match, *sehet*, begins. The handlers of the first two cocks meet, with their birds, in the center of the arena and give the pot for the central bet, the *toh dalam*, to one of the referees, the *saya*. The wager was agreed upon when the match was made a few minutes earlier. It is always even money—no odds. If necessary, as indicated above, the birds are handicapped with the *taji*. The money is provided by the owners, who usually get contributions from family, friends, and backers in the crowd. This bet may be considerable. Even at the small matches, a central bet of Rp 100,000 is not unusual. And at the really big cockfights as much as Rp 1 million (U.S. $600) is often bet. Considering that the 1981 per capita income in Indonesia was U.S. $415, this represents a sizable risk.

There are always several referees in the arena. But the chief judge, the *juru dalem,* is the man in charge. A casual visitor might think the timing official is most important, because he is most visible. But the Balinese know who the *juru dalem* is. He must be a man of impeccable honesty and reputation, and he must have no relationship to or interest in any of the owners, handlers, or cocks. His word is undisputed law in the arena. If he is tainted in any way, people will not fight their cocks under him.

The *juru dalem* signals the amount of the bet to the time keeper at his table overlooking the arena. This is of interest to all, because it indicates the confidence that the owners and handlers have in their animals, and thus will influence the amount of the side bets, the *toh kesasi*—bets between members of the audience or between them and the cock owners or handlers. To the uninitiated, this phase of the proceedings is utter chaos. Bettors yell at each other, wave money around, stand up and gesticulate wildly, and make unfathomable signals with fingers and hands. But to the aficionado, this is all a very intricate, and carefully structured series of events. It is as if one were betting on a horse race and there were no ticket windows or pari mutuel machines.

ALTHOUGH THE CENTRAL BET IS ALWAYS EVEN MONEY, the side bets are never even money. One of the most fascinating aspects of cockfighting is the way in which odds are set. First the favorite, *kebut,* and the underdog, *ngai,* must be established. The first shouts of the betting are generally made by the experienced, more or less professional bettors. These are the men one sees at almost every cockfight. They follow the fights around and have no regular jobs except gambling. They quickly assess the two cocks, using their considerable knowledge and experience, and decide which is the favorite. And then they start shouting its color. The shout is a staccato repetition of the color name. For example, *bieng* means red and white. So if a red and white cock is being pushed as favorite, one hears: "Bieng, bieng, bieng, bieng, bieng, bieng" in rapid fire succession. Color is classified in a variety of ways. Some examples: *putih*, white; *barak*, red; *buik*, speckled green and black; *selem*, black; *brumbun*, black, red, and white. These colors generally refer to the color of the cock's collar or ruff and not to the overall body color. If two cocks have the same color, some other differing aspect will be called out—the size of the tail, the size of the body, or even the side or compass direction of the arena that the cock is located in. The latter is done either by shouting the direction name or waving with the hand, palm toward the cock that the bettor is backing.

The less experienced bettors listen carefully to the first calls and generally follow their lead. But one must pay strict attention because the favorite may change, depending upon the opinions of the bettors and the overall sentiment of the crowd. If more people yell one color name than the other, and do so more vigorously, the former will replace the latter as the temporary favorite.

After the first color shouts, made to establish the favorite, those who wish to bet on the underdog start yelling the odds they want. The color shouters are the backers of the favorite and the odds yellers are backing the underdog. The object is for two of these opposing bettors to find each other in a crowd when they are separated by a distance as great as the width of the arena, packed so tightly together that even standing up is difficult, and walking around is impossible. This is done, however, with great efficiency and ease. There are names for the various odds, as follows:

10 : 9	dapang
5 : 4	gasal
4 : 3	cok
3 : 2	teludo
5 : 3	telewin
2 : 1	apit
5 : 2	ngelimin

If a bettor shouts "Balu!" or "Sapih!" after the odds he wants, then he wants to win in the case of a draw—a rare event. The first four on the above list, the shortest odds, are by far the most common. The backer of the underdog tries to get the longest odds possible, and the favorite backer tries to get the shortest. The underdog backers usually start at about 3:2 and are forced by lack of takers to work down to 4:3 or 5:4. The favorite backers look for shouters of low odds, but, if there are none, have to settle for worse odds. Both types of backers usually indicate the amount they want to bet by holding up fingers.

Curiously enough, the monetary unit of betting is not the Indonesian rupiah, the standard of currency for the entire country, but, the *ringgit,* an obsolete unit used during Dutch colonial days. Nowhere in Bali will you hear a price quoted in *ringgits* except at a cockfight, and there nothing but *ringgits* are used. Since there is no *ringgit* currency in Indonesia, debts are paid in rupiahs—but they are always wagered in *ringgits.* It is rather like the way the guinea is used by the British in transactions with high snob appeal. The number of fingers held up indicates the number of thousands of *ringgits* being wagered, unless the bettor indicates by his shouts that it should be interpreted as hundreds of *ringgits.* The conversion rate for Balinese cockfight *"ringgits"* is always one *ringgit* to two-and-one-half rupiahs. Two fingers means 2,000 *ringgits* (Rp 5,000), an average side bet at a medium size cockfight.

Favorite and underdog backers scan the crowd quickly, looking for someone to take their bets. The backers of the favorite stand and wave toward their choice, while the underdog backers wave rupiah notes, not to indicate the amount they wish to bet, just to attract attention. When eye contact is made with a likely looking prospect, the two exchange a complex and rapid series of signals to make sure each understands the nature of the bet. Palm waving indicates the favorite. Finger extension indicates the bet size. Lip movements reinforce the signals, because the din makes oral communication impossible at a distance. If the bet is agreed upon, the two men signal the fact by touching their heads or pulling at the fronts of their shirts. If there is disagreement, they break eye contact and look elsewhere. If someone shouting odds cannot get a bet, he lowers them one notch on the scale and keeps trying, getting closer to, but never attaining, even money. The handlers also bet, spurring the crowd to back their cocks by holding them aloft and walking around the arena. During this phase of proceedings, confusion and noise reign supreme. The sound is deafening, as the odds criers yell: "Cok, cok, cok, cok!" or "Gasal, gasal, gasal, gasal!" The backers of the favorite shout his colors in a frenzied patter.

While the betting is taking place the handlers carry the cocks to the center of the arena and incite them to fury by pushing them at each other, plucking their combs, and bouncing them on the ground. As fight time approaches, the frenzy of betting reaches a state of pandemonium.

THEN THE TIME KEEPER SOUNDS HIS GONG. The match is to begin. Last-minute bets are sealed and the crowd becomes quiet. The chief referee and the judges squat down in the corners, and the handlers release their charges from opposite sides of the arena. At this point, anything can happen. Usually the birds flare their ruffs, extend their necks, and, after a preliminary glare, have at each other in a fury of feathers and flying feet, so quickly that the eye can hardly follow the action. The crowd groans and shouts, almost as one man, following the action with their bodies. Pretty soon one cock lands a solid blow with its *taji*. At once its handler signals the head referee, who signals the time keeper to stop the first round, or *elebaan*. This is to prevent the two animals from making further contact—at this point the aggressor's instinct is to move in and peck his opponent to death, but the wounded bird, at such close range, could easily stab him with his *taji*.

When the birds are pulled apart, the time keeper starts his clock, called the *ceeng*. It is a half coconut shell with a hole in the bottom, placed, large side up, in a bucket of water. It sinks in about 10 seconds, or one *ceeng*. The time keeper's gong, the *kemong*, is sounded once after each *ceeng*. The cocks are allowed three *ceengs* to recoup between rounds.

During the break, the handler of the wounded cock works frantically, trying all of his tricks to revive the bird's fighting spirit. He is often quite successful, and the injured animal, seemingly indifferent to its wound, sails right at his opponent. At the end of the third *ceeng*, both cocks have to be put on the ground immediately. Failure to do so forfeits the match. Round two starts. If the wounded cock cannot stand, and if the other one can stand for one *ceeng*, the match is over. If the two birds start fighting, the match proceeds as in round one, until one or the other is struck. The gong is sounded again, a three-*ceeng* period is allowed for the revival of the injured animal, and the fight continues. If both cocks are still going strong after five rounds, the match is declared a draw. This seldom occurs. The time keeper keeps track of rounds on a counter called a *pengetekan*, a wooden frame with a horizontal wire. Five wooden strips are suspended vertically from the wire, sort of like the beads of an abacus. The timer pushes one counter aside after each round.

Often the wounded cock loses its appetite for fighting. Or, in some cases, a cock may not have any desire to fight at all right from the beginning, and tries to escape from the arena. The crowd scatters quickly because a wild, flapping cock with a lethal dagger strapped to its leg could cause great harm. One or another of the spectators grabs it by the neck and returns it to the ring. The handler has nine *ceengs* to get his animal back into action or he forfeits the fight.

Another rest is signaled if the cocks stay in the arena, but do not start fighting. During this time out, the handlers of the reluctant cocks try to urge them on. In the next round, if the cocks still do not clash, the *pemeruputan* is ordered. This is an ordinary bamboo cock cage without a bottom. It is the tie breaker—the finisher. The word *mruput* means "to fight in a surrounded place." The two reluctant cocks are placed on the ground under the cage, and the referee brings it down quickly and leaves it down for one *ceeng*. The head referee watches carefully from close up. Victory goes simply to the aggressor. It need not kill or even wound the other cock, although it frequently does. It merely has to display aggression. But if the two cocks—now face to face with no retreat—start to fight again, the cage is pulled off and the fight continues as before.

As soon as the winner is declared, money starts to fly. Side bets are paid in cash—at once. No I.O.U.'s. Those who are wedged into the crowd wad up their bills and throw them at the person who won their money. If the money misses or lands in the arena, someone always forwards it to the rightful owner. There is remarkably little bickering and dispute over who owes what to whom. I have been told of an increasing number of gamblers who bet with no cash on hand. These men are quickly grabbed by the police. And, if they cannot raise money from friends on the spot, are hauled off to jail and sufficient of their property sold so that the debt can be paid.

The owner gets the entire pot from the main betting, which has been watched by the referee during the fight. From this money he pays the handlers and the *taji* man, gives the house its cut, and distributes the winnings to all those who contributed to the bet. He also gets the body of the losing cock. He always gives the *taji* leg to the *pemasang taji*. The lower part of the leg is chopped off and placed, with *taji* still attached, on the time keeper's table. The owner retrieves it, unwinds the string, puts the blade back in stock, and looks for further work.

The match itself has lasted only a few minutes. Immediately the second match of the set begins. The cocks have already had their *taji*s attached. Their handlers carry them into the arena, the central bet is quickly made, and the side betting begins just as before. There is no connection at all between the separate matches. One set consists of four or five matches. When they are over, the handlers and hangers-on come out into the arena and start looking for opponents, just as they did before the first set. This goes on until dark, the crowd never thinning until it is all over. Many temple anniversary festivals last three days, and so does the cockfighting.

Some cockfights actually take place inside temples. It is not an especially common event, but it does happen. I recall one such instance at Eka Dasa Rudra, the once-a-century exorcism that took place at Bali's mother temple, Besakih, in 1979. It was considered important to spill blood in the actual temple itself, since the ceremonies concerned themselves largely with the exorcism of evil spirits. The cocks were handled only by the *pemangku*s, who told the spectators not to bet because of the sacred nature of the offerings. But the urge was irresistible, and money changed hands as usual during the three brief *tabuh rah*.

Cockfights are regularly held at the ceremonies performed in family house compounds when it has been determined that the grounds are unclean and in need of some sort of purification. At such times a very large offering, called a *caru*, is made inside an enclosure of coconut leaf mats, and the *butas* and *kalas* are placated. Word of the cockfight gets around fast, and villagers from all over come to help stage an impromptu *tajen* right inside the family house compound. Some temples regularly have their obligatory three *tabuh rah* inside, but these are conducted rather quickly and unceremoniously, so that the outsider will be unlikely to be able to see them.

GAMBLING ON COCKS has been responsible for the dissipation of a good many Balinese fortunes, large and small. Many a raja of old lost his palace, wives, and treasure by being "cock crazy," as the Balinese call an habitual bettor. I have heard from many of my Balinese friends how their fathers or grandfathers were reduced to poverty by this addicting habit. There are now even troops of professional gamblers who go from fight to fight, pooling their financial resources to back a favorite in the central bet. Stories are told of wild rages and uncontrolled fury displayed by those who lose large sums of money. Countless friends have told me that they really should stop betting. But they never did.

Fighting cocks, cockfighting, and wagering on the fights have been popular obsessions with the Balinese for generations. The tourist who could worm his way into the sweating, jostling, noisy, gesticulating crowd of men and join them, standing around an open arena, watching the proceedings, might have wondered if he had stepped into a different country. Are these the graceful, deferential, dignified people whom he has seen in his hotel? Are these the same individuals who carry the offerings to the temples and pray with such heart-felt fervor? The boisterous crowd was a sight to behold. As it suddenly quieted down and the action began, the fast and furious flurries of engagement were punctuated with the "Ooohs" and "Aaahs" of the audience.

This opportunity is no longer available, and although this is probably beneficial in the long run to the Balinese people, it unfortunately transforms rather routine studies and photographs of cockfighting into irreplaceable historical documents. I hope that this discussion has given a taste of these wonderful events to the visitors who are now deprived of the privilege.

Cricket Fighting

TICKLERS AND CHOPPED GECKO

HAVE YOU EVER SEEN a grown man tickling crickets? I don't mean just for the fun of it, but seriously? People the world over indulge in bizarre practices in order to satisfy their gambling urges. Races, fights, casino games, sports contests—all of these are common outlets. Wagering on pork bellies or September wheat, and playing the stock market are favorites in the developed countries. In the United States you can bet your insurance company that you will get hit by a chunk of falling satellite, or that your health or life span will defy actuarial tables. But what do you do if your resources are severely limited? Suppose you don't like the sight of blood, can't afford veterinary bills or broker fees, yet still like to gamble? In Bali, you go to the cricket fights.

Cricket fighting, *jangkrik mapalu,* is the ideal sport for the poor man. Crickets are free. You catch them yourself. You can make the bamboo cages yourself. The insects are delighted with a few grains of rice a day. They don't bite, scratch, or kick, or make a mess on the floor. And they chirp you to sleep at night. A cricket fight is a nice way to spend an idle afternoon, chatting with friends, bragging about your champion, enjoying the brief excitement of the fray, and winning (or losing) a little money. You can carry your whole collection of fighters (what would you call it—a *stable?*) in a small box, which is not only convenient, but which allows for a fast getaway in case the authorities come.

Gambling has been illegal in all of Indonesia since 1981, But, since the amounts bet on crickets are minuscule compared to those that used to be bet in cockfights, and since the cricket fights are generally held well away from the eyes of those who might object, nobody worries too much about the vice.

A TYPICAL CRICKET FIGHT in Bali may begin about noon. It is usually in a rural, shady clearing, well off the beaten track, away from prying eyes. Or perhaps it is held on someone's front porch, concealed in a labyrinth of narrow alleys in the city. Fights are regularly scheduled, usually alternating days between two different places in the same locality. They are hard for the outsider to find. After the Indonesian Government outlawed gambling people take no chances. Everyone involved knows where and when, but it may be hard to extract the information. The first time I attended a cricket fight it took me several hours to find out details, asking a dozen people, and I only succeeded by paying a three-year-old boy to lead me two kilometers through brush and forest on foot.

The fighting arena is a rectangle, about two by four meters (6 by 12 ft.), bordered by a very low row of bamboo poles. The poles are cut lengthwise and mounted with the concave side up—this forms a trough to hold the round cages. Men straggle in for an hour or so (the devotees are all men or boys). There is no hurry. A cup of coffee, a rice cake, or a clove cigarette can be purchased at a little *warung* (food stand) set up nearby for the occasion by some enterprising woman. Small fights may involve only 10 or 12 cricket owners. Larger ones may have as many as 50. Each brings his 10–15 cages in a little box, sits down on the ground or squats on his haunches behind the bamboo barrier, and unpacks his cages. There are at least as many onlookers as cricket owners, and they delight in second guessing the experts and participating in the excitement.

The cricket cages are lengths of bamboo, about 15 centimeters long and 5 centimeters in diameter. There is often a piece of glass set into one end, the other end plugged with a round piece of coconut husk. The top half of the cage has a half-dozen slots running almost the whole length, allowing light and air to enter. (See illustration opposite.)

There are two species of crickets in Bali, called *jangkrik kalung*, and *jangkrik kalian*. Only the *kalung* is fierce enough to fight. It comes in three different varieties, distinguished by wing color. Yellow, called *jangkrik gading*, is considered to be the prettiest, but there are brown and black-winged *kalung* as well. Only the males are collected, and they can be distinguished by their rougher bodies and wings. These crickets are larger than those we are used to in the West, being about as big as a man's thumb.

Collecting crickets is best done after the rice is harvested and the wet fields allowed to drain—about six months out of the year. Farmers are too busy and the crickets are too scarce when the fields are wet. Crickets are always hunted at night, and the collectors locate them from their chirping. The hunter has to be very stealthy—if the creature hears an unfamiliar sound or senses the vibration of the ground under the hunter's feet it stops singing. Having located the source of chirping, the hunter digs out his prey and pops it into a little bamboo tube, plugging the end with a

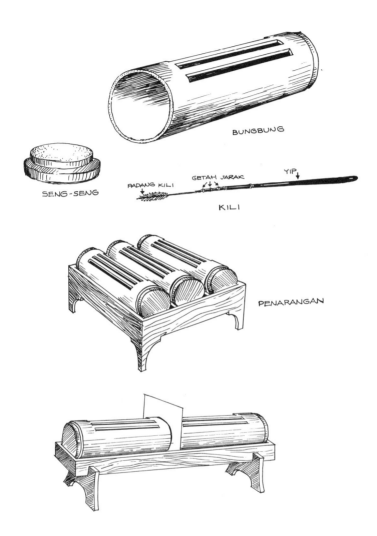

BUNGBUNG

SENG-SENG

PADANG KILI GETAH JARAK YIP

KILI

PENARANGAN

THE CRICKET FIGHTER'S TOOLS

wad of folded leaf. Hunting is often done with a torch, but today flash-lights are more popular. The hunter doesn't have to dig more than a dozen centimeters (5 in.) or so. No shovel is necessary in the soft soil.

Newly captured crickets must be exercised regularly by suspending them from a thread or hair tied to one of their rear legs. They thrash about and struggle, and this makes them fierce and strong. A friend of mine once had twenty or or thirty of his little charges so exercising, a mobiling mobile of crickets. After the crickets get their exercise they are bathed by placing them in a shallow bowl of water into which a bit of the juice of the betel pepper leaf has been squeezed. This period of exercise and bathing is very important and must be repeated at three-day intervals.

Fighting crickets are most often just fed a few grains of wet rice and a frangipani petal or two every day. To make them fierce however, they are fed the chopped up remains of any two animals (within reasonable size) that have been seen fighting—perhaps a pair of geckos. Puree of aggressive gecko, although it increases ferocity, will shorten a cricket's life to about 25 days. On white rice and flower petals, an average cricket is good for two months (but won't be at his fighting best).

A cricket fight enthusiast has to catch a new warrior every three days or so in order to maintain a sufficiently large fighting stock. Sometimes he will feed his charges a herbal elixir, called *sadek,* a variety of the *jamu* that he himself uses for strength and health. (See CHAPTER 25.) Sometimes he puts tobacco juice on the cricket's head to make it fierce. Needless to say, there is an enormous lore surrounding the care and feeding of crickets, with so much local variation that generalizations are difficult.

AS THE MEN GATHER AROUND THE ARENA, their first task is to try to find suitable matches for their crickets. When one owner proposes a contest, he will hand over his choice in its cage to the owner of the opponent. This man holds the two cages in his left hand, takes off the stoppers, and looks into the open ends, comparing the two candidates. Body size and size of mouth are considered of prime importance. Most important, however, is aggressiveness. No cricket owner comes to a match without his *kekili,* or tickler. This is a very thin stick of stiff palm leaf rib, about 20 centimeters long, to which has been tied a tuft of grass heads. The owner sticks the *kekili* into the cage from either the open end or through the slots to see how the animals behave when disturbed. If his own cricket is sluggish compared with the other one, he will decline the match, making a mental note to take this lazy one home for more exercise, baths, and puree of gecko.

Cages are passed back and forth between the men as they examine, tickle, laugh, frown, and compare. The near-sighted have an advantage in this activity. This preliminary haggling and examining may take several hours—far longer than the fights themselves, and even longer than the preliminaries to a cockfight. There is no rush. If not today, then tomorrow, or the next. There are cricket fights almost every day somewhere in the neighborhood. When a match and the amount of the bet are agreed upon, the cages of the two opponents are set aside in pairs; after four or five pairs have been decided, the actual fighting begins.

Like cockfighting, there are two kinds of bets. The central bet between the two owners is always even money and is placed on the ground next to the cages. Bets are quite modest compared with the cockfights. The usual central bet may run from about Rp 5,000 to Rp 10,000. Cockfight bets often run into the millions of rupiahs, and there are tales of gamblers losing their homes and possessions backing an unsuccessful cock. This never happens in cricket fights. Fun is more important than money. And the most one might lose is a week's cigarette money.

The other wagers, the side bets, are made between spectators and cricket owners whose animals are not fighting at the moment, or just between the spectators themselves. Sometimes the owner of one of the crickets that is fighting makes side bets with spectators in addition to his central bet. These bets always involve odds. Those who want to bet on the favorite, as yet not established, call out the direction—west or north, for example—of the side on which their choice's cage is located, or they gesture with their hands in that direction. Those who want to bet on the underdog call out the odds they seek. The favorite is established by consensus among the first group.

The betting procedure for side bets is a subtle and difficult phenomenon for the outsider to determine. Odds seekers, backing the underdog, call out the odds that they wish, using the same terminology used in cockfight betting. For example, odds of 3:2 are called *teludo,* 4:3 are called *cok.* The underdog bettors chant out long strings of "Cok-cok-cok-cok-cok-cok!" and wave bills of the amount that they wish to bet, looking for a taker among the group of those backing the favorite. These men keep waving and yelling the direction of the cage of their choice. If there are no takers, the odds close up a bit. Since there is quite a din, wagers are sealed with signals. A wave of the hand makes it clear which cricket is being backed. The number of fingers shows the number of thousands of rupiahs bet. A tap or pull on the head indicates that the bet is sealed. No money changes hands yet. It all happens very fast in a seemingly confused way, but there is method to all the madness, although this is hard to detect until one studies the betting procedures carefully.

Now the bets have been placed, and the first fight will begin. The stoppers of the cages of the two opponents are removed, the two open ends placed together, separated by a thin sheet of wood or metal, and the pair of cages is placed on a low wooden stand, a half-cylinder of bamboo raised about 20 centimeters (8 in.) off the ground. The two cages, being cylindrical themselves, rest in the concave groove of the support. The betting reaches a frenzy of yelling and waving because once the fight begins, all betting is closed. Then the crowd quiets down and attempts to see what is going to happen.

When all is ready, one of the men slips the divider out from between the two cages, and the crickets are free to have at it. If they are reluctant to fight, their owners tickle them through the cage slots with their *kekilis.* No tickling is allowed once the crickets start to fight, but it is permissible to get them started. Spectators crowd in close. It is impossible for anyone who isn't right on top of the cages to see what is going on, but one can get a fair idea: the backers of the losing cricket groan with outrage and disappointment while those backing the winner are all smiles and cheers.

Unlike a cockfight, a cricket fight is not adjudicated and managed by a bevy of officials. There is no need for any of this. No fight lasts more than a minute or two. The loser is simply the cricket who runs away and gives up, retreating to the far corner of his own cage. Seldom does the winner kill his opponent—perhaps only one such event occurs in an afternoon of 50 different matches. Since only those in the immediate vicinity of the cages has any idea of what happened, the word is passed quickly, and it soon becomes apparent which one is the winner. The winning owner picks up all the money on the ground, and the side betters toss money to each other to satisfy their obligations, which are seldom more than a few thousand rupiahs. The disgraced cricket will fight no more. Its glory days of gecko steaks, baths, and exercise are over. It is usually released or given to the children to play with, who generally pull off its wings.

There are never any excuses made, I.O.U.s suggested, or outright reneging. Payment is expected in cash, on the spot. If not, the bettor who defaults will not only be unwelcome at tomorrow's cricket fight, but his reputation will haunt him for a long, long time. I have never seen any arguments over these matters. All is very clearly understood beforehand, and the money settlements are quickly made.

The winning cricket is returned to his cage, taken home, exercised and bathed, and perhaps given an extra ration of mashed lizard. And, of course, the reputation of said winner and his owner are greatly enhanced. Crickets look indistinguishable to the novice, but these same people will meet again tomorrow or the next day, and they well remember who won, what his cricket looked like, how it behaved, and how much money its owner made. And they will adjust their betting accordingly when the same animal shows up for competition once again, in a day or two.

I ASKED A FRIEND OF MINE, an avid cricket fight devotee and a recognized authority on the sport, why he preferred cricket fights to cockfights. Cricket fighting, he said, requires a lot less money. He can do everything himself. He doesn't need handlers, specialists, trainers, referees, judges, and so on. And there is no house to take a cut of his winnings. He also said he found it more exciting than cockfighting. Furthermore, crickets look good to him, he said. (Up close they do look like little armored warriors.) Cockfights, he said, are too serious.

How many years had he been at this game? "Twenty-four." How profitable? He grinned: "I've lost more than I've won, but it has been fun. And I still have my house and farm. If I had bet on cocks I would have lost everything."

CHAPTER 21

Betel Chew

ASIA'S POPULAR QUID

It's easy for a traveler to tell if he is in betel chewing country. Look for bright red lips, dark-stained teeth, and the telltale streaks of red saliva that stain the rural countryside, city streets, and even the marble floors of mosques and museums. Betel, the world's most popular quid, is chewed regularly by an estimated 400 million people—one tenth of the earth's population. Chewing betel is an ancient petty vice. The first European to document the practice was Herodotus, in 340 B.C. But the chew is more than a pleasant diversion; it has vast social, medicinal, industrial, and ritual importance.

In parts of South India, it would be considered the height of rudeness for a host to neglect to offer betel to his guests. Importing betel ingredients is big business in India, which can't grow enough for local consumption. In China, betel is a specific for tapeworm in both humans and animals. A doctor friend of mine who lives in Java still recalls seeing the navel of his new-born younger sister disinfected and shriveled by application of the red betel sputum—the midwife spat on a hot roof tile and the powdered sputum was applied to the navel. Some betel ingredients are widely used in industry for tanning leather, fermentation, and dyeing. And in Bali, it would be unthinkable for a woman to make any sort of religious offering without including the ingredients of the betel chew.

The betel chew has three ingredients: areca nut (often, mistakenly, called betel nut), betel leaf, and lime. Very often a fourth material is added, gambir. And in some parts of Asia still other aromatic flavorings are added. A sliver of the areca nut is the essence of the chew, the betel leaf provides an aromatic wrapper, and the lime is necessary to release the active ingredients of the areca nut. *Gambir,* when used, is said to improve the taste.

The areca nut (pronunciation stress is on the first syllable) is the fruit of a tall, thin tropical palm, *Areca catechu.* This lovely tree probably originated in Malaysia and now grows wild and on plantations in well-watered tropical lowlands from East Africa to the Pacific islands. Areca palms reach up to 30 meters (100 ft.) in height, with a thin trunk topped by a crown of feathery leaves. The nuts grow in bunches at the crown, and each is about the size of a hen's egg. A single tree may produce 300–1,000 nuts every season. As the nuts ripen they turn from green to yellow and finally to red. They are harvested green in some areas of Asia, whereas in India the fully ripe, red nuts are preferred.

Harvesting the nuts is no small problem, considering the dizzying height of the tree and the fierce ants that like to crawl on its trunk. In some countries, specially trained men rope their ankles together and shinny skillfully up the trunk to the nuts. If the trees are close together, as in plantations, the men can jump from one tree to another. In Malaysia, trained monkeys are sometimes used to harvest the nuts. In some places men use long bamboo poles with sickles tied to the top.

Each nut is like a miniature coconut, with a fibrous husk surrounding the nut meat. In season, the nuts may be used raw, and they are husked and cured—sun dried or smoked—for use in the off season. The cured nuts are stored in pits in the earth or in big water-filled jars. A friend in Sumatra told me that he still recalls the terrible smell in his home when he was young because his father worked in the areca nut business.

Lime for the betel chew is obtained from the coastal areas of the island where quicklime is produced by calcining coral in wood-fired kilns. When water is added to quicklime, ordinary slaked, or shell lime is produced. Most of this is used to make mortar for building. For the betel chew, specialized lime makers buy small amounts of the kiln output, take it home, and purify it. The building grade lime is purified by stirring it in water, and allowing the impurities to settle out. The process is repeated several times and then the slurry is scooped out and dried in white blobs 4–6 centimeters (1.5–2.5 in.) in diameter.

These two ingredients, areca nut and lime, are called *buah* and *pamor* in Balinese. These are theoretically the only ingredients necessary to produce the desired effect. But they are almost never chewed alone. The universal practice is to wrap them in a betel leaf. The leaf is from *Piper betle,* a pepper plant closely related to the species from which we get common black pepper. It is called *base* in Balinese. It is a slender, creeping climber or shrub that reaches a height of 3–4 meters (9–13 ft.) and produces an abundance of sharply pointed, oblong leaves, up to eight by 15 centimeters (3 by 5 in.). The vines grow wild in tropical rainforests, but they are usually domesticated by transplanting cuttings to the base of a tree, often an areca palm, and allowing the vine to climb the tree. The leaves are usually used fresh, but in some places they are bleached and softened by packing them tightly in banana leaves and keeping them in the dark for several days.

Since the betel pepper leaf is an important, and usually the most obvious, part of a chew, Europeans who first observed the practice named the nut (the active ingredient) after the wrapper of the chew. Thus "betel" may refer to just the betel leaf, to just the areca nut, or to the whole quid. The name of the pepper leaf itself—*base* in Balinese and *sirih* in Indonesian—is also used in Bali to refer to the entire quid—the combination of leaf, nut, lime, and other adjuncts. But it is incorrect and confusing to refer to the nut alone as "betel nut."

Another frequent accompaniment of the betel chew is a pale, earthy substance called gambir (gambier, pale catechu, or terra japonica). This product is obtained by boiling in water the leaves of a tropical shrub, *Unicaria gambir*. (Gambir, as a colloquial name, is also applied to *Acacia catechu*, a legume that produces a dark gambir used primarily in the tanning industry.) The extract is thickened over heat, poured into molds to solidify, and then cut into cubes the size of bouillon cubes. The gambir cubes are chocolate-colored on the outside, but the interior is a pale tan. The cubes are the consistency of dried mud, and break and crumble easily.

Betel users say that the quid smells bad unless they put gambir in it. There may be other adjuncts of the quid, varying from area to area. Usually these are sweet-smelling substances, such as cinnamon, cardamom, camphor, nutmeg, or turmeric. Sometimes the chew, wrapped in a betel leaf, is pinned together with a clove. In Bali, the only ingredient that is regularly used in addition to *buah*, *base*, *pamor*, and *gambir* is a wad of chewing tobacco.

ALTHOUGH IN SOME CULTURES a special, highly decorated purse or box is used to store the betel ingredients, the Balinese use a small wooden box or, in many cases, just an ordinary plate. To make a quid, a betel leaf is selected, a sliver is cut from an areca nut, and it, a pinch of lime, and a crumb of gambir are placed in the leaf. The leaf is then folded or rolled tightly, and it is ready for chewing. For those who are toothless, the wad may be pre-mashed by placing it in a metal tube and working it with a plunger. When the ingredients are well mashed, the plunger is removed to the other side and used to push the ready-to-chew wad back out. In Bali this device, which looks like a slightly down-sized bicycle air pump, is called a *panglocokan* or *penyokcokan*. Betel chew ingredients are commonly sold fresh in all tropical Asian markets. For those in a hurry, ready-made wads of the four usual ingredients are available. One can buy a week's supply of materials for about the equivalent of half a U.S. dollar.

A copious flow of saliva results as soon as the wad is put into the

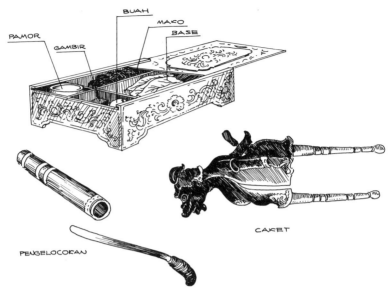

A BOX WITH BETEL INGREDIENTS AND IMPLEMENTS

mouth, forcing the user to spit repeatedly. The sputum is blood red, and darkens upon exposure to air. The chew produces a persistent stain, both on the ground and on the lips of the chewer. The teeth of habitual users are usually stained dark brown or almost black. Some attribute the red color of the saliva to the gambir. But the combination of areca nut, lime, and betel leaf alone produces a red sputum. If gambir is added, the sputum reddens and darkens even more when the air hits it. The lips of the chewer are a bright red during the chewing, as if the chewer were using gaudy lipstick. After a minute or two the saliva stops flowing so rapidly. At this point the habit in many countries, including Bali, is to wipe the teeth with a small wad of tobacco. The tobacco is often retained along with the betel quid in the traditional spot between the lower teeth and the lip.

In Indonesia, betel chewing is pretty much confined to the rural, older generation—and there mostly to women. Young Indonesians, seeking a modern image, look upon the practice as somewhat crude and unenlightened—certainly non-Western. In some parts of India and Nepal, however, all classes use betel, and it would not be unusual for an upper class professional man to be offered an after-dinner chew by his host. Hospitality in the West dictates offering one's guests tea or coffee or—although this courtesy is fast disappearing in the United States—a cigarette after a meal. Betel chew serves the same purpose in Asia. If a musical or dance group is hired to entertain, a plate of the betel ingredients is handed around and a bowl provided for expectorations. Many older Balinese chew betel. And it is almost invariably present at social or religious events, when a group of people meet to rest or talk. But it has been my observation that, as the years go by, fewer and fewer people use it at such gatherings.

IN BALI, *BUAH, BASE,* AND *PAMOR* are used in offerings to symbolize the Hindu triad—Brahma, Wisnu, and Siwa; creator, preserver, and dissolver of life. Color and directional symbolism are extremely important in Balinese religion and Brahma's color is the red of the *buah,* Wisnu's is black, or green, like *base,* and Siwa's is white, like the *pamor.* As symbols of the Hindu Trinity, the betel chew ingredients provide the places for Brahma, Wisnu, and Siwa to occupy, serving much the same function as a shrine. No Balinese offering does without them.

Used in an offering, the betel ingredients are usually inconspicuous. Generally a tiny smear of lime and a minuscule bit of areca nut are rolled or folded up in a betel leaf, enclosed in a coconut leaf, and skewered with a sliver of bamboo. This combination, called a *porosan,* is placed in the bottom of a small square coconut leaf box, about 10 centimeters (4 in.) on a side, and covered with bright flowers and other necessary materials so that the *porosan* is not visible. This offering, called a *canang,* is the most widely used of all offerings in Bali and is invariably placed on top of the elaborate high offerings women carry to temple ceremonies. Every market in Bali has *canang*s for sale. You see them everywhere—even on the dashboard of your bus or taxi, as the driver's offering to god to maintain balance, order, and safety. There is another type of offering, called *pesucian,* in which all five of the betel quid ingredients are present. But this serves an entirely different purpose from the *porosan.* It represents an offering to the gods of man's everyday needs, one of which is betel, not a place of occupancy.

In Malaysia and Indonesia the word for the areca nut is *pinang.* And the word for proposing marriage to a girl is *meminang,* meaning "to give *pinang*" to someone. This comes from the ritual, observed in parts of Malaysia and Sumatra, wherein a marriage proposal is accompanied by an offering of betel chew to the family of the girl. In Java, an important part of the traditional marriage ceremony involves the bride and groom throwing rolled betel leaves at each other. The bride is usually advised not to take direct aim as this would indicate to the guests that she will have the upper hand in their future life together. In West Java, the young areca nut, called *jambe,* is rolled with several ingredients and offered by the groom to the father-in-law. In some other parts of Indonesia, ceremonial etiquette demands the honored guest be offered prepared betel chew in gilded wood or brass boxes, presented by dancing maidens.

Many Hindus, especially in India, wear a red spot on their foreheads. Its distinctive shape indicates whether the wearer is a follower of Shiva or Visnu, to use the Indian, rather than the Balinese, spellings. Its presence acts as a "third eye" to give power. In the past this spot was applied using the red sputum resulting from chewing betel.

In addition to these ceremonial uses (which would fill a book) people chew betel because it is refreshing to the mouth. Almost all the Asian doctors to whom I spoke said that the effects of betel are purely local—in the mouth. Yet in the literature, such as it is, betel is called a stimulant and exhilarant, much like tobacco smoking, and one pharmacology text calls it a euphoric. Most people who use betel feel a sense of languor when deprived of it. Many say that they don't feel hungry if they chew betel, even if deprived of regular meals. Several doctors told me that betel chewers have an abnormally high incidence of cancer of the lips and gums. The almost invariable response in support of chewing is that betel "strengthens" the teeth. Some people say that they swallow a little of the betel saliva so as to aid digestion and prevent stomach aches.

The areca nut itself has been used for centuries as a specific cure for tapeworm. It is also taken to sweeten the breath, strengthen the gums, and improve the appetite and taste. Burned and powdered nuts are used as a dentifrice. The nuts are applied to ulcers, bleeding gums, and as a lotion to the eyes. I have a list of 31 different symptoms and diseases for which betel leaf alone is claimed as a remedy, ranging from adenopathy to venereal disease. My Balinese assistant, Budi, tells me that he and his family always stop nosebleed by plugging the afflicted nostril with a betel leaf. A doctor from Surabaya told me that, although his mother seldom took baths, she always smelled like a flower because she rubbed betel leaves on her body. Crushed betel leaves are widely used on cuts and burns. I even saw a friend washing his pet bird using the leaves as a kind of soap. *Gambir* is used for the treatment of diarrhea, burns, lumbago, and sciatica and as a gargle for sore throat. *Gambir* is used in industry to prepare dyes of browns, reds, and drab colors. These are sometimes used on batik in Indonesia. The dyes develop an intense color as they oxidize on the material when exposed to the air. *Gambir* is also used as a material for tanning leather.

THERE IS VERY LITTLE MEDICAL INFORMATION in the West on betel chewing. But by searching the database of the U.S. Department of Agriculture's Economic Botany Laboratory in Maryland I was able to glean some pharmacological data on the betel ingredients. Areca nut contains a significant amount of the alkaloid arecoline and closely related alkaloids. Arecoline is a drug that stimulates the parasympathetic nervous system in the human body. This system is that part of the involuntary, or autonomic, nervous system that regulates nutritive, vascular, and reproductive activities. Stimulation of the parasympathetic nervous system constricts the pupils of the eyes, dilates the blood vessels, slows heartbeat, and increases the activity of glands and smooth muscles of the digestive and reproductive organs. Arecoline also produces an arousal or activation response in the cortex of the brain. That is, it is also a central nervous system stimulant. Arecoline cannot normally penetrate the mucous membrane of the mouth because it is ionized in the normal acidic environment of the mouth. If a base, like lime, is added to change the environment to an alkaline one, arecoline changes from its ionic to its molecular form and is readily absorbed into the bloodstream through the mucous membrane. This same principle, by the way, explains why South American coca leaf chewers put lime in their quids.

Betel leaf contains no alkaloids, but it does have a significant concentration of sugars and several phenols, including eugenol and cineole. Phenols are often powerful germicides. Eugenol is the principal ingredient of clove oil and is used by dentists as a local anesthetic for tooth decay. Cineole makes up about 70 percent of oil of eucalyptus.

Gambir is especially rich in tannins and is reported to contain small amounts of three alkaloids, one of them reputedly an aphrodisiac. It also contains the dye catechu-red, which deepens in color upon oxidation (which is why *gambir* cubes are much darker on the outside than on the inside). Areca nut also contains a large amount of tannin or tannic acid. Tannin is an effective astringent that shrinks body tissue and precipitates proteins on the surface of cells. It was formerly used in the treatment of burns because of its astringent properties. The high tannin content of some unripe fruits, such as persimmon and banana—and areca nut—causes an unpleasant "sappiness" or puckery sensation when they are eaten. The tannin content reduces dramatically as the fruit ripens. It is said that this serves to dissuade animals from eating the fruit before the seeds are ready to be disseminated.

Such are the chemical and pharmacological facts. Betel is essentially a mixture of a powerful alkaloid, tannin, lime, sugars, two aromatic oils, phenols, and a red dye, followed by a wad of tobacco held in the mouth. It would seem that the betel chew is much more than a simple mouth freshener. The presence of arecoline and lime, the latter allowing the arecoline to be quickly absorbed into the blood stream, plus the known parasympathetic and central nervous system stimulating effects of arecoline, strongly suggest that it is, among other things, a physiological stimulant that would cause arousal, a physiological "lift" like tobacco, stimulate flow of saliva and other glandular secretions, stimulate the intestines, and lower blood pressure by dilating blood vessels. The astringent tannin would cause a stimulating tingle in the mouth, aided by the warming effects of the eugenol and cineole, since they are mild irritants. These would also produce a fresh, aromatic taste and odor and would help the sugars mask the bitter taste of the tannin and alkaloids.

The catechu-red dye, gradually oxidizing, would stain the teeth and mouth, as would the tannin. Tea drinkers have this problem. Smokers know full well how tobacco can stain the teeth. So the tooth stain could have multiple causes. Astringent tannin would tend to strengthen the peridontal membrane of the gums, but lime is an irritant, and its effect would be to destroy and irritate this membrane and would probably be more destructive than the tannin would be constructive. I am aware of no scientific study dealing with the effect of betel upon mouth cancer. But the fact that tobacco, a known carcinogen, is usually kept in the mouth for a long time after the chew would lead me to suspect it, not the betel chew, as the cause of mouth cancer—if, indeed, there is even a cause and effect relationship.

It is difficult to evaluate claims by users that betel chewing strengthens the teeth and those by doctors that it corrodes and ruins teeth. By "strengthening" teeth, I suppose that what is meant is preventing tooth decay. It is true that some of the betel ingredients are germicides. But the human mouth is normally so full of germs that it seems unlikely that an occasional betel chew would have more than a transitory effect upon the germ population. Further, dental caries normally develop under a layer of plaque, coated on the teeth, which the germicides of the chew could not reach anyway. One dentist suggested that any lessening of tooth decay due to betel chewing might simply result from the fact that many people who are not educated in the principles of dental hygiene don't ever brush their teeth. At least betel chewers wipe their teeth with tobacco, and this may take the place of brushing.

Many of the other claims of folk medicine are explainable on the basis of the known chemistry of the system. Tannin is widely used for tanning leather. Germicides are great for cuts. Astringents can stop bleeding. Stimulators of the intestine can expel tapeworms, and the very same alkaloids are known to paralyze worms so that they drop off. Often a system of drugs acts synergistically. That is, one drug can enhance the effects of the others. One of the amazing features of folk medicine is how sometimes a sophisticated chemical result has developed apparently from experience with trial and error. The betel chew is a perfect example.

Clove Cigarettes

INDONESIA'S PERFUMED SMOKE

THE SEARCH FOR SPICES launched the Age of Exploration, and cloves were one of the most coveted export products produced by what is now Indonesia. Today, however, Indonesia consumes all of her own clove production—and then some. Although throughout the centuries cloves have been used for perfume, embalming, relieving tooth pains, sweetening breath, and, of course, spicing food, they are most popular today in the unique clove cigarette. With a pleasant smell almost of incense and a sweet, cool taste something like a mentholated cigarette, clove cigarettes are Indonesia's favorite smoke. Your first greeting when you land in Indonesia is a whiff of sweet and spicy cloves as you walk past the airport customs gate.

Indonesians call the cigarettes *kretek,* an onomatopoeic word that suggests a crackling sound. A leisurely drag on a clove cigarette produces a faint sort of popping sound, like that of a distant forest fire, as the volatile clove oil is released from the spice within. Although brands vary in the proportion of cloves to tobacco, a *kretek* cigarette is about 30–50 percent cloves. Although American plain tobacco brands are also popular, *kretek* are by far the preferred smoke in Indonesia. In recent years, the scented cigarettes have even made small inroads into the U.S. market, cropping up at specialty tobacconists.

Since an average cigarette contains approximately one gram of cloves. Although precise figures are not available, a good estimate is that well over 100 million *kretek* cigarettes are manufactured in Indonesia every day. That means that over 100,000 kilograms of cloves are used daily, or about 40,000 metric tons per year, with a value of about U.S. $120 million. Indonesia has to import about 120,000 tons each year and has set self-sufficiency as a target. This is big business. It is estimated that some 80 percent of Indonesia's tax income—20 to 25 percent of its *total* income— comes from tobacco taxes.

Kretek cigarettes aren't cheap. A single stick of one of the better brands costs about Rp 50. That is a considerable fraction of the average daily income of a Balinese, who might expect to earn somewhere in the neighborhood of Rp 1,000. This does not dim the popularity of *kretek* cigarettes. It is not uncommon to see people purchasing single cigarettes rather than buying them by the pack.

Cloves are the dried, unopened buds of a tree that is a member of the myrtle or eucalyptus family. There is general disagreement among botanists about its proper genus and species. References are made to: *Eugenia aromatica* (the genus being named after Prince Eugene of Savoy, a patron of botany and horticulture), *Eugenia caryophyllata, Caryophyllus aromaticus, Jambosa caryophyllus*, and *Syzygium aromaticum*. The tongue twister *caryophyllus* comes from the Greek word for the clove tree, *karyophyllon*, from *karyon*, "nut," and *phyllon*, "leaf." The closest the French could get to this was *girofle*, which is their name for the clove tree. The English had trouble with the French word and changed it to "gilly flower." The French considered that cloves looked like nails. The French word for nail is *clou* so, in French, cloves are *clou de girofle*, from which our "clove."

Cloves were used to relieve the pain of tooth cavities even in ancient Egypt—and still are. Clove oil, which makes up about 16 percent of the spice by weight, is over 90 percent eugenol, a chemical closely related to phenol or, as it is commonly called, carbolic acid (phenol is used in disinfectants, for example, Lysol). Eugenol, named for the commonly used species name, has antiseptic qualities and acts as a local anesthetic, counter-irritant, and anti-inflammatory. It is widely used for root canal filling and for temporary fillings for cavities. It also finds a use in microscopy and in the synthesis of the important flavoring vanillin.

Although cloves are still used to stud Christmas hams in the West, and are very popular in Indian cooking, their use as a spice in Indonesian food is minimal. Some cloves are used in Indonesia to season food, but their most popular use, other than in cigarettes, is to make an analgesic ointment. They are not common or plentiful in the spice markets.

THE LEGENDARY SPICE ISLANDS, which prompted centuries of trade and domination, were at one time the world's only source of cloves, nutmeg, and mace. Today the Spice Islands are the Indonesian province of Maluku, popularly known as the Moluccas, a large group of islands located between Sulawesi on the west and New Guinea on the east. Cloves are native only to the tiny volcanic islands of Ternate and Tidore and a few even smaller islands to their south, along the west coast of the large island of Halmahera in the north Moluccas. The nutmeg tree, producing both

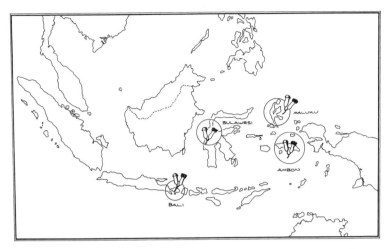

INDONESIA'S CLOVE-GROWING REGIONS TODAY

nutmeg and mace, is native only in the Banda Islands, a tiny group of volcanic islands in the Banda Sea south of Ambon and Seram. Mace, the
dried outer covering of the nutmeg seed, is sold separately from nutmeg,
and commands a higher price.

The earliest mention of cloves in history occurs in Chinese books of
the Han period, dating from the third century B.C. References are made
in these books to the use of cloves by court officials to sweeten their
breath while addressing the ruler. Arab, Malay, and Chinese merchants
sold Moluccan cloves all over Southeast Asia. Europe's supply was shipped
from the Moluccas to Persian Gulf ports. From there Arab traders carried
them overland by caravan to the Mediterranean, and they were distributed from Alexandria and Constantinople by the ships of Venice. Each
exchange of ownership resulted in a doubling of the selling price, and by
the time the spice reached the markets of Europe, it had increased in
value at least ten-fold. This provided a strong encouragement for the governments of Europe to find a way to bypass the middlemen and find a
route to the source themselves.

A serious deterrent was that until the end of the 13th century, nobody
in the West knew just where the cloves came from. Those involved in the
spice trade wisely kept their secrets—and their monopoly. It was the
Venetian, Marco Polo, in his travels in Asia from 1271 to 1295, who first
brought back a description of the spice producing areas. The results of his
explorations were studied with great interest by seafaring nations. For the
next 200 years Europe actively sought a sea passage to the Spice Islands.

The Portuguese led the Age of Exploration. Spurred on by the efforts
of Henry the Navigator, Vasco da Gama was the first to sail around Africa
and reach India by water in 1498. Afonso de Albuquerque conquered the

strategic port of Malacca, commanding the approaches to the Moluccas from the West, in 1511. In that same year, Antonio de Abreu reached the Spice Islands. These achievements brought on the era of foreign domination of the Indies, an era that did not end until after World War II.

In the de Abreu party was young Ferdinand Magellan. His own expedition, minus the leader, was shortly to reach the Moluccas from the other direction—east. Magellan, sailing under the flag of Spain, was killed in the Philippines in 1521, but his crew reached the Spice Islands, with one ship remaining, and returned to Spain with a load of cloves. Emperor Charles V of Spain rewarded Juan Sebastian de Elcano, the captain of the ship that finally reached Spain, with a coat of arms—emblazoned with two crossed cinnamon sticks, three nutmegs, and twelve cloves.

All the major European powers were getting into the act. Sir Francis Drake, in the *Golden Hind*, stopped by for a load of cloves in 1579. And then, in 1599, the Dutch arrived. In 1602 they founded the infamous United East India Company, Vereenigde Oostindische Compagnie, or V.O.C. The Dutch were the best organized and the most ruthless. By the end of the 17th century they had eliminated Spanish, Portuguese, and English competition and had established complete domination over the Indies. They owned the entire clove trade for 200 years thereafter. In order to keep prices high by limiting supply the V.O.C. systematically destroyed all the clove trees in the North Moluccas and concentrated clove production in area around the island of Ambon.

But the developing French empire became envious of the clove monopoly. In 1770 M. Pierre Poivre, governor of the French island of Mauritius east of Madagascar in the Indian Ocean, sent a smuggling expedition to a remote part of the island of Seram, near Ambon, but hidden from the prying eyes of the V.O.C. His men brought back seeds and seedlings which were planted in various French controlled areas including, in 1818, Zanzibar, just off the coast of East Africa. Today Zanzibar is the largest clove grower in the world, and Indonesia, thanks to her population's huge appetite for *kretek*, imports large amounts of cloves from the recipient of her smuggled treasures.

CLOVES ARE STILL BIG BUSINESS IN INDONESIA. But the principal clove growing area is now Sumatra, not Maluku. Clove trees are starting to appear all over the highland areas of Bali now, especially in the hilly country. Not many of the Balinese trees are very large yet, but it may be that cloves will become an important cash crop in the years ahead. North Sulawesi is also an important producer of Indonesian cloves. But Indonesia cannot begin to grow enough for its own manufacturing use. And their only important use in Indonesia would be absolutely unbelievable to those famous explorers who risked their lives for the fabulous profits from spices.

Harvesting cloves today in their birthplace, Maluku, isn't much different than it was hundreds of years ago. One of the more productive islands is little Saparua, one of the Lease Islands, just east of Ambon. The harvesting season begins when the rains stop in November and continues through January. The population of this rocky, hilly island swells at harvest time, as Indonesians from all over swarm in to help harvest the crop, which must be hand-picked. There is a movie every night in the main village during harvest, but none at all the rest of the year.

The clove orchards are located on the tops of the rolling hills. The pickers climb the 15-meter (50 ft.) trees with baskets and ropes, and are swallowed up by the thick foliage. Some skill is required because breaking branches, although the easiest way to get the cloves down, damages the trees. Full baskets of cloves with attached leaves and twigs are lowered to the ground where they are packed into large sacks. Ladies scour the area below the trees for loose cloves. A man can pick about five kilograms a day; a mature tree, on average, yields about 15 kilograms a season.

The clove farmer must watch the trees carefully. The clove is actually a bud, which must be picked before it opens. They turn pink, beginning at the base, and must be picked before the color reaches the top. Otherwise the petals open, the clove oil content decreases, and the market price goes down. If allowed to mature, the petals quickly drop off, the dozens of fuzzy stamens produce pollen, and a single seed is produced in the ovary. This swells to a fleshy fruit, about four centimeters long and a centimeter or two across. The mature fruit has no value as a spice and is used only to propagate the plant.

The day's pickings are carried home from the hills, and the family spends the evening separating twigs and stems from the cloves. Stemming is done by pressing the bunch against the palm of the left hand with a slight twisting motion. The buds snap off if this is skillfully done, and no stems remain. Everybody, young to old, participates. The huge heap of cloves is piled onto a mat, and the family sits on the ground around the heap. The green cloves are dried in the sun for a minimum of three days. As they dry they turn the familiar rich cinnamon brown. They must be taken in at night and turned over several times during the day. This is done on mats spread on the ground. During harvest, drying cloves can be seen in backyards, fields, and in and on the streets of town.

On market day everyone brings his cloves to Saparua village. Small boats from the nearby island of Nusa Laut drop their passengers off on the tidal flats, and they wade ashore with their cloves packed in anything from huge burlap sacks to small plastic bags. Sometimes they bear a branch from a clove tree, like a flag, as a gift for friends. They and the Saparua islanders swarm into the little shops of the buyers, who are usually Indonesians of Arab or Chinese background. The sacks are weighed on a steelyard by the shop owner, and he calls out the weight of each to his paymaster. He dumps the contents onto the floor and gives it an expert examination for impurities, opened buds, seeds, moldy cloves, leaves, cloves without the ball, and twigs, and other points that would detract from its value. If it passes inspection the seller is paid in cash on the spot, the cloves are shoveled into the corner, and the next customer steps up.

Prices vary wildly, depending upon the size of the harvest. When I was in Saparua in 1980 the buying price in town was Rp 6,500 per kilogram. But just before the main harvest it was double that. The Indonesian government attempts, rather unsuccessfully, to stabilize the price. The cloves are then shipped in 70 kilogram sacks to Ambon, where they are stored in large warehouses and to be shipped to the *kretek* factories in Java.

THE CLOVE CIGARETTE INDUSTRY BEGAN as a small home industry in Kudus, in central Java, about 1916. The first *kreteks,* called *klobot,* were conical in shape and wrapped in a maize leaf, on the principle that a paper wrapper comes apart if profusely sweated upon by a laboring smoker. *Klobot*-type cigarettes are still made (with paper wrappers), but most *kretek* cigarettes are filtered and look just like American cigarettes.

Today there are about 400 *kretek* factories in Java employing more than 100,000 workers. There are four huge factories, in Kediri, Malang, Kudus, and Surabaya. The others are small by comparison. The manufacturing process is very labor-intensive. Although the big Western tobacco companies produce their wares in highly automated factories, in Java every step, except shredding the tobacco and cloves and printing the cartons, is done by hand. To a country that seeks to provide jobs for large numbers of unskilled workers, a booming cigarette industry is a great asset.

The giant Gudang Garam factory in Kediri, East Java, is typical of the large establishments. The name, interestingly enough, means "Salt Warehouse," and the label of each package of cigarettes shows the warehouse that used to exist near the home of the company founder, Sunya Wonowijo. Gudang Garam employs 27,000 workers in its six separate units at Kediri. Most of the employees are women who work in the rolling rooms. In these cavernous areas several hundred women sit in long lines, rolling cigarettes by hand. They spread the clove-tobacco mixture into the paper wrapper held in a small trough in a cloth belt. A little glue goes on one end, and a quick pull of a handle spins the layers into a cylinder. The women are paid by the piece and, as with many Indonesian workers, the pay is partly in rice. Other women trim the cigarettes to the proper length with scissors. The last step, packaging and placing the rolled cigarettes in cartons, is also accomplished entirely by hand.

Other than the printing presses that produce the cartons, the only machinery in use is for chopping the cloves. Gudang Garam has 22 warehouses for cloves, each holding six tons. That is a total of a six days supply. The cloves are soaked in large concrete vats filled with water, to which has been added various flavorings—oils of cherry, banana, pineapple, and other fruits. Men stir up the vats with large boards, then drain off the liquid and rake the cloves into thin layers to dry in the sun to the proper degree of dampness. Forty-eight chopping machines chew up twenty tons of cloves a day. Every month, Gudang Garam uses 30 to 40 tons of paper.

The chopped cloves are bagged and taken to the mixing room. Here the various varieties of Javanese tobacco are weighed, mixed thoroughly, and spread out in a layer about 8 centimeters (3 in.) deep on the concrete floor. The proper number of bags of cloves are dumped on top of the tobacco, covering an area of several hundred square meters. Then a gang of three men crawl barefoot on their hands and knees through the clove-tobacco layers, mixing the ingredients with their hands, legs, and feet. It is quite a scene, and the sweet odor is overpowering.

At the rather small Panamas cigarette factory in Denpasar, Bali, this mixing was done a little differently. (I use the past tense because, although I saw the factory in action in 1981, the Denpasar plant is now closed.) Here an enormous cylinder was built up on the floor by alternately dumping baskets of tobacco and cloves in a circle 10 meters or so in diameter. Between layers, the flavorings were sprayed on with portable, hand powered sprayers. When the pile was big enough for the next day's rolling, it was broken apart and mixed thoroughly with shovels.

The cigarette factories package their products in units of 10, 12, 14, and 20 cigarettes per pack. A package of 10 is the most popular size. There is considerable export business to Asian countries, and in the last few years, the clove cigarette business has really caught on among young people in the United States. A short while ago nobody had heard of them unless he had been to Indonesia. Now they are common in tobacco shops.

The large *kretek* manufacturing companies are mostly owned by Indonesian citizens, and most of these of Chinese ethnic background. In contrast, the factories that produce regular, non-clove, cigarettes, called *rokok putih* ("white cigarettes"), are mostly foreign owned.

THE CIRCLE OF HISTORY HAS BEEN HALF TRAVERSED. The fabulous Spice Islands, goal of world famous explorers, now produce less than 10 percent of Indonesia's cloves—not to mention the world's. When the well-known American historian Samuel Eliot Morison visited Ternate in 1971, he had trouble finding just one clove tree for a photo. So well had the V.O.C. exterminated the spice from its original home. Maluku, once the richest area in the Indies, is now an economic and cultural back eddy. The action, political power, tourists, and money are in Java and Bali. Refrigeration, chemical synthesis, and modern medicine have diminished the demand for cloves from their early and original uses. But the demand in Indonesia is great, although da Gama, Albuquerque, Magellan, and Drake would be astonished to learn what it is.

CHAPTER 23

Tuak, Arak, and Brem

BALI'S WINE 'O THE COUNTRY

THE BALINESE ARE NOT, as a group, heavy drinkers. Imported drinks are expensive, and the average Balinese, if he drinks at all, will consume a little Indonesian beer or, even cheaper, one or another of the three main varieties of "home brew"—*tuak, arak,* or *brem. Tuak* is palm beer, a sudsy and quite mild elixir brewed from palm tree sap. *Arak* is palm brandy, distilled *tuak,* and it is stabbing and potent—definitely an acquired taste. *Arak* is used in traditional medicine and most Balinese spice it heavily or avoid drinking it altogether. *Brem* is a very sweet rice wine.

Fermented palm tree juice is consumed everywhere in the world that palms grow, including all of tropical Asia, Africa, and America. The Balinese didn't invent the idea. The British called the drink "toddy," a butchered version of the Sanskrit *tari.* The British controlled Indonesia for only 15 years, however, and the term has not caught on here. In both Indonesian and Balinese, the word for the drink is *tuak.*

TUAK IS PRODUCED by fermenting the sap of the flower bud of any of a number of species of palm. In Bali, the coconut tree, called *punyan nyuh,* is most often used because the trees are quite common. In areas where sugar palms, *punyan jaka,* grow, their juice is used. Sugar palms produce not only the widely used dark brown sugar, but also a strong black fiber, *duk,* used for thatching the roofs of shrines and a white fruit, *beluluk,* which is mixed with syrup and other fruits and served on ice as a desert or snack. In Malaysia and Thailand, *beluluk* is packed in syrup and sold as "toddy palm fruit." To produce palm sugar, the same sap from the flower bud used to make *tuak* is simply boiled until the water evaporates; the sugar is allowed to solidify in round molds. In North Bali, the *lontar* palm, called *punyan ental,* is used for *tuak.* The problem with *ental,* how-ever, is that the leaf-bearing branch of the tree is full of thorns.

Cocos nucifera, the most well-known of all the palm trees, grows best in low altitudes, in sandy soil, near the sea. It will grow in other environ-ments, but nut (and *tuak*) production is limited under other than ideal conditions. If the growing conditions are favorable, about a dozen com-pound flower stalks are produced during the course of a year. Each flower stalk appears at the base of a leaf stem, at the crown of the plant. When it first appears, the stalk is covered by a soft, green sheath. The stalk, with its enclosing sheath, is called *danggul*—the Balinese have a rich vocabulary of very specific coconut tree terms—and looks for all the world like a giant corn cob inside the husk. If allowed to mature without cutting, the sheath of the *danggul* hardens into a wood-like cover, or spathe, called *keloping,* which is widely used for firewood. As the *danggul* matures, the *keloping* splits open, and first the male, pollen-producing flowers develop and later the female flowers—which exude a honey-like, sugary liquid upon which the pollen falls. This sap is a magnet for ants and other insects, and it soon ferments and spoils, producing an odor close to the tree that is quite unpleasant. The task of the *tuak* maker is to harvest this sap before the sheath opens. He has from two weeks to a month, or a bit more, to do it.

The sap harvester selects a *danggul* that is just one month or so away from opening. He bends the bud so that the tip points down, and cuts an incision through the not yet hardened sheath into the flower stalk itself. The cut must be made with a backward motion of the knife or the slit will have rough edges, which is bad. Then a container is tied to the *danggul* to catch the draining sap. Each bud will, on average, fill one coconut shell with sap each day. The standard volumetric unit for measuring produc-tion, consumption, purchase, and sale of *tuak* is the "beer bottle," *botol bir.* And *tuak* lovers take heart—a standard Bintang brand beer bottle holds 620 milliliters (about 22 fluid ounces), which is a healthy portion. At the *warungs*—roadside and village food stands—where it is sold, *tuak* is almost always put into an empty beer bottle. Sometimes the *tuak* is put in larger bottles, scrounged from stores or hotels, such as originally con-tained gin or whiskey. In this case the container is said to hold two, or one-and-one-half *botol bir.* A good tree will produce four or five "beer bottles" of *tuak* a day. A malingering tree might yield half that.

The *danggul* has to be bent just right so that the sap drains into the container without leaking elsewhere. The open mouth of the container is covered with *tapis,* a natural material—it looks like burlap— that covers the base of the leaf branches. The *tapis* keeps out rain, dirt, and insects. The yield of *tuak* for a given tree does not depend upon the season, wet or dry, but rather varies according to changes in the weather. If it is the rainy season and the tree is producing well, the yield will drop dramatical-ly if it suddenly stops raining and turns sunny for a short period.

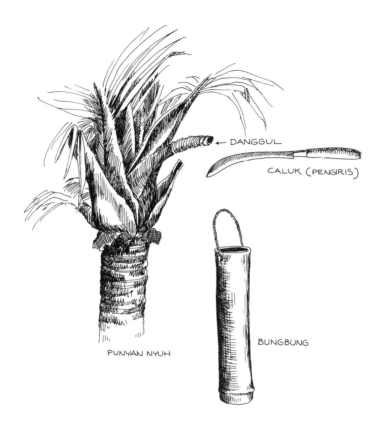

← DANGGUL

CALUK (PENGIRIS)

BUNGBUNG

PUNYAN NYUH

TOOLS FOR GATHERING TUAK

Harvest practices vary considerably from village to village. In the Denpasar area the containers are usually sections of bamboo, called *bung-bung,* the bottom closed by the natural node of the culm. In many other areas the containers are made of coconut shells. Some *tuak* makers harvest the liquid twice a day, others only once. Harvesting, of course, involves climbing a very tall tree—perhaps 15 or 20 large trees. To facilitate this daily routine, the owners cut steps in the trunk. They use no special climbing gear—usually not even a belt. To gather *tuak* from the sugar palm, a ladder must be used because the trunk of the *punyan jaka* is very rough and cannot be climbed like that of a coconut tree. One *danggul* can be repeatedly incised and the sap gathered daily or twice a day for from two weeks to two months, depending upon local conditions. Of course, if you take *tuak* from a *danggul,* it will produce no coconuts. It is an either or proposition.

There are two kinds of *tuak—tuak manis,* "sweet," (sometimes called *nguda,* "young") and *tuak wayah,* "old." The difference between the two is in taste and alcohol content, with *tuak wayah* being "dryer" and more potent. *Tuak manis* is fresh from the tree, and it has a fairly high sugar content because the fermentation process has not gone on very long. Most connoisseurs avoid *tuak manis* because it causes stomach problems, flatulence, and diarrhea. But it does have a following. The preferred drink is *tuak wayah.* It has a much stronger taste than *manis,* with a definite alcoholic flavor, somewhat sour, and not unlike heavily hopped beer. Like beer, it is an acquired taste. But an awful lot of Balinese seem to have acquired it.

The sap begins to ferment immediately, and one could make a fairly strong *tuak* simply by collecting the sap and letting is sit for 12 to 14 hours. But the preferred method is to "seed" the collection containers with a small bit of yeast and some already fermented *tuak.* Yeast is collected by hanging a dry coconut husk near the roof of the kitchen for several months. This husk is pounded up into fibers, and a bit of this fiber and a splash of *tuak* get the brew started. This way, when the tuak is collected at the end of the day or the next morning, the product is already *tuak wayah,* ready to drink. In fact, it has a much better taste than the *tuak wayah* produced by letting the fresh *tuak manis* age. All serious *tuak* drinkers consume this variety of *tuak wayah,* which is called *wayah baru*—literally "old new."

Both varieties of *tuak* produce bubbles constantly, because fermentation is still going on, and one of the products of fermentation is carbon dioxide. *Manis* has thicker bubbles than *wayah* and more of them. A narrow mouthed container of *tuak* will bubble and foam as if it contained soap suds. It cannot be sealed, of course, or it would explode. These days the favored receptacle for *tuak* is a plastic *jeriken,* or "jerry can." *Tuak* gets stronger as the day goes on. If produced in the morning, you can drink it that evening, or even for two or three days after that. Then it turns to vinegar. Most people drink it fresh. *Tuak* will keep for a long time in the refrigerator, but few individuals have refrigerators. No *tuak* is prepared and bottled in large factories for sale in stores. All *tuak* is collected and fermented by individuals or small groups of individuals who market it very locally.

Tuak nyuh, tuak from the coconut tree, is a pale tan color with a kind of musty odor. Because of the high concentration of suspended solids, the beer is translucent, even opaque. No attempt is made to filter the drink. And the continuous production of carbon dioxide bubbles contributes to its opacity. *Tuak jaka,* from the sugar palm, has more of a pink or reddish color. Old and new *tuak* both look exactly the same.

Tuak drinking is quite a social affair in Bali. There are innumerable small *warungs* scattered all over the island where men come to sip a glass, have a snack, and chat in the heat of the day. Usually some sort of rice dish is served, wrapped in a banana leaf—*nasi bungkus.* The owner has a couple of dozen bottles of all shapes and sizes lined up on the table, each filled with foaming *tuak wayah baru,* right from the tree. A beer bottle full costs Rp 100. It is never consumed from the bottle, but always from a glass or a short *bungbung* of bamboo. There is no hurry. The table is in the shade in front of the little *warung.* There are benches all around, and few are the topics that are not covered. I have never seen a woman at such a place, except if she is the owner of the *warung.* A man generally drinks only one bottle of *tuak* and then leaves to go about his business. Since *tuak* has about the same alcohol content as beer, there is virtually no drunkenness. As the day goes on, the *tuak* gets a bit stronger, and the price may rise to Rp 200 a bottle.

The Balinese love to participate in *seka* (or *sekehe*), which are roughly equivalent to clubs or social groups in the West. There are *seka* for harvesting coconuts, *seka* for religious ceremonies, fishing *seka,* and harvesting *seka.* And in my village, as in many others, there is a *seka tuak.* Every evening, just after sundown, about a dozen members of the group gather in front of the home of the head of the *seka,* squat or sit on woven coconut leaf mats on the ground, and just talk and drink *tuak.* A big plastic *jeriken* of the drink is bought from a man who makes it in a neighboring village. Attendance is mandatory, and there is a Rp 25 fine for not being there—no excuses. Visitors may partake for Rp 100 a bottle. Again, no women. The session may go on for several hours, but I have never seen anyone get rowdy. It is just pleasant talk. It is quite a jolly, pleasant group, and the members have a strong feeling of camaraderie. You will find *tuak* for sale on a smaller scale at most of the night markets and as an incidental beverage at the most popular food stalls—for example the enormous *be guling* (roast pig) eatery in Gianyar. But it is quite unusual for a man to bring a bottle of *tuak* home to drink in private. *Tuak* is something to be enjoyed with much talk and many friends.

ARAK IS DISTILLED TUAK, and as such it has a much higher alcohol content. *Arak* is clear and colorless, and has a very sharp, biting taste. Since there is no fermentation going on, it can be bottled—in beer bottles, of course—capped, and sold in almost all stores that the Balinese patronize. Tourists have discovered that it is powerful and cheap. *Arak* does not have a pleasant taste, however, and the Balinese prefer to drink it, if at all, mixed with spices to kill the sharpness. Spiced *arak* is called *arak mabasa.* Tourists often drink it mixed with rice wine (*brem*).

Arak is more than a liquor, however. It is widely used for medicinal purposes, both internally and externally. Balinese traditional medicine involves an enormous number of preparations that are rubbed on the skin, not only to relieve aches and pains, but also to effect cures of more serious problems. And *arak* is universally used in Balinese Hindu religious ceremonies. Typically it is poured from a bottle into a kind of ladle made from banana leaf, called *tapan*. Holding the *tapan* in his left hand, the worshiper or Hindu priest wafts the essence of the *arak* with his right hand, often with a flower held between the fingers, towards the gods in a gesture called *ngayabang*. Then, shifting the *tapan* to the right hand, he grasps his right elbow with his left hand and pours the *arak* on the ground, as an offering to the *butas* and *kalas*. This second act is called *matabuh*, which refers to the spilling of any liquid on the ground as an offering to the lower spirits. The substance poured is called *patabuh*, the noun form of the word.

For use as a *patabuh*, high quality *arak* is not needed, and it is usually purchased in village *warungs* specifically for use as an offering. As a liquor, *arak* will keep indefinitely. A good size ceremony, say a fairly elaborate temple anniversary, might require a dozen or more bottles of *arak* just for *patabuh*. Since religious ceremonies are important and frequent, the consumption of *arak* as a *patabuh* is quite great and there are areas where *arak* making and selling is the principal occupation. But the liquor is also distilled in small batches at home stills.

The initial product of the still is high quality *arak* with a large alcohol content. As the process continues, the distillate contains correspondingly less alcohol and more water. Some *arak* makers divide each batch into three products, using the first distillate for higher-priced beverage-grade *arak*, and the middle and end of the run for various grades of *arak patabuh*. Others just collect what they can, mixed together, and sell it for any use the buyer wishes.

In the cottage industry distilling operations, *tuak wayah* is purchased as the raw material for *arak* from a nearby maker. The boiling vessel is often a big broad-bottomed clay pot with a flared rim, called a *payuk tanah*, or *jun*. The maker may buy 24 beer bottles of *tuak* for a day's production at a cost of about Rp 1,400. The *tuak* is delivered in the afternoon. Next morning, half of the *tuak* is put in the *jun* and covered with a clay cover. A brick is put on top of the lid to keep it from being dislodged and, more likely than not, an offering will be found here. A copper tube, sealed into the clay lid, leads to a single coil immersed in a nearby clay pot full of water. The tube emerges from the side of the cooling pot, and from this end drips the distilled *arak*.

The vapor from the boiling *tuak* passes through the tubing, into the cooling coil where it condenses into *arak* and drips out the end. One batch takes about three hours to distill, and 12 *botol bir* of *tuak* will yield about two-and-one-half bottles of *arak*. Since two batches can be run per day, the total daily yield is about five beer bottles. It is sold in the home for about Rp 1,000 for a bottle of the best quality, and Rp 400 or Rp 300 for a bottle of the two lower qualities. Normally the three grades are mixed for sale. But if only the finest grade is desired, only about two bottles can be produced per day. The residue is fed to the pigs. But there is no special joy for them, since the alcohol has been distilled off.

The center for the large scale production of *arak* is an area north and a bit east of Klungkung, between Klungkung and Sideman. All told, there are about 500 stills in this area, located in and around the village of Talibeng. Each is run by a *seka* of perhaps five men who carry out the process of gathering the *tuak,* fermenting it, distilling it into *arak,* and taking it to the market at Talibeng. Methods here differ significantly from those in areas where the main product is *tuak*. In this area very little *tuak* is made for sale, and the whole process is geared toward making *arak*.

Each of the five members of the *seka* owns and climbs about 15 coconut trees. If there is no other work to be done they start about 4:00 or 5:00 in the morning, taking the full coconut shell reservoir down and putting a new one in its place. At the same time the *danggul* is cut. This gathering and cutting is repeated 12 hours later, in the afternoon. The yield is about two shells of *tuak*—about four *botol bir*—a day for each tree. The five members of the seka, together bring in maybe 300 bottles of *tuak manis* each day. It is *manis* because, so far, no yeast has been added and no old *tuak* has been placed in the shells.

The day's batch is poured into a very large clay container and part of a pounded up, aged coconut husk is added for yeast. The batch is loosely covered and allowed to ferment for four or five days in the shade. On the day before distillation the old yeasty coconut husk is removed, squeezed out into the batch, thrown away, and more is added. Next day it is ready to be distilled.

The still, called *bingkil nira,* is made from the hollow stump of a coconut tree and is shaped like a truncated cone. The bottom part is steel, shaped like a wok, and this is fastened to the coconut stump with a glue made of Balinese palm sugar and clay. The stump sits on top of a brick stove that is about four meters square and one meter high. Three bamboo tubes, each about five centimeters (12 in.) in diameter, extend radially outward from the stump-boiler, each sloping upward slightly. The tubes end in a node, and a smaller bamboo tube extends from there straight down into a large pottery vessel. The three tubes come off at equally spaced intervals around the perimeter of the boiler. A low wood fire is kept burning under the still. The top of the coconut stump still is capped by a wooden disk sealed with the white fuzz of the kapok tree and clay. In the wooden top of each jug is a small hole, and from time to time a thin stick is thrust into the jugs to determine the extent of the distillation. *Arak* is quite flammable, and the workers have to be very careful with it around the still. It is not uncommon for a still to burn.

The still holds about 80 bottles of *tuak,* so the men run off two, sometimes three batches a day. Their total production is about 24 bottles of *arak* a day. In this area all the *arak* is mixed together—the three grades are not kept separate—unless they get an order for top grade *arak*.

Every market day (every three days) they bring their *arak* to the big market in Talibeng. There is a very large parking lot on the west side of the road and a big *wantilan* for the market on the east side. The *arak* is carried and sold in *jerikens,* each of which holds 12 bottles. Each market day they take two *jerikens* to the market, which normally sell for about Rp 6,500 each. This is essentially a wholesale market, and buyers from all over Bali come here to buy bulk *arak,* which they bottle, mix with water and other substances, and sell to the *warungs.* The price for ordinary grade bottled *arak* in Denpasar is about Rp 900, but there are expensive brands costing twice as much, as well as low grade quality that costs half as much. Some is imported from Jakarta.

BREM IS RICE WINE. The correct pronunciation is to make the word rhyme with "drum." As with *tuak* and *arak,* there is a booming home industry in which small amounts are made for home use or for sale in small quantities. But there are also large commercial factories that make the *brem* from rice, bottle it, and wholesale it. Like *arak, brem* is, in addition to being a beverage, a necessity for *matabuh* in almost all religious ceremonies. Very large quantities of it, perhaps even larger than *arak,* are made and used for that purpose. This is usually low grade, homemade *brem,* and it is often mixed with water. The bottled product, which costs about Rp 2,500 a bottle, is far too expensive to use as a *patabuh* and is sold mostly to tourists in stores, restaurants, and hotels. Foreigners like to drink it over ice or mixed with *arak,* to take the sharp edge off the latter. I find *brem* far too sweet for my taste, but *de gustibus non disputandum.*

Brem is made from glutinous or "sticky" white rice, called *ketan* in Balinese, and a smaller amount of Indonesian black rice, *injin.* Both *ketan* and *injin* are less commonly used in cooking than the common white rice, *baas.* Glutinous rice is sweeter than the staple *baas* and is used in rice cakes and desserts. The black *injin,* for example, is made into a delicious traditional dessert by cooking and serving with brown palm sugar and coconut milk. Since *injin* is rather expensive, only enough is used in *brem* to impart the desired final color.

A typical individual *brem* maker who sets out to brew the wine for sale locally or *patabuh* starts out with about a kilogram and half each of *injin* and *ketan.* The rice is soaked in water until it is very soft, about two hours, and then steamed in the usual way. After about one hour, the rice is removed from the steamer and stirred in hot water. This keeps the rice from drying out and is a normal procedure when steaming any kind of rice. It is then returned to the steamer and cooked for another hour or so. The cooked rice is then dumped out into a shallow, woven bamboo box, in which it is allowed to cool. Yeast, *ragi,* purchased in little cakes, is broken up and sprinkled on top of the rice.

Finally the damp mixture of rice and yeast is transferred to a hemispherical bamboo container about half a meter in diameter, lined with banana leaves (*penyaipan*). Fermentation takes place over the next three days, and the *brem* drains out through the loosely woven bottom of the container into a pan. Three kilograms of rice yield about two bottles of *brem*. The solids remaining are called *tape* and sold at the market.

The commercial *brem* factory presents quite a contrast to the cottage industry. The closest such factory to the tourist areas is in Sanur, just west of the By-Pass Highway, a few dozen meters south of the road that leads to the telegraph office and the Sanur Plaza. This factory, and another in the Singaraja area, are the biggest *brem* factories on the island. It is known as "Perusahaan Brem Bali Cap Dewi Sri; Fa. 'Udiyana.'" All of this means that its product goes by the trademarks "Dewi Sri" and "Brem Bali" and that it is a privately owned company (Fa.) owned jointly by several individuals and by the village of Sanur. The factory in Singaraja uses the dangerously close trademark "Bali Brem." There are four other *brem* factories in Bali, but the rest are considerably smaller than Perusahaan Brem Bali, the daily output of which is about 400 large bottles (*botol bir*), and about 1,000 small bottles. The factory employs about 25 people.

The Brem Bali factory uses about 100 kilograms of 70 percent *ketan*/30 percent *injin* a day. The rice is first cooked for about three-and-one-half hours in the factory's two large aluminum cookers. Each holds 50 kilograms of rice and 50 liters of water. Usually the white *ketan* and *injin* are cooked and fermented separately, because only enough *brem* from the black *injin* is added to achieve the desired color. The taste of the resulting *brem* is the same for both. After cooking the rice is spread out on shelves to cool.

Then the yeast is added by powdering it up and sprinkling it on top of the cooled cakes of rice, which are then cut up into smaller pieces and placed in cylindrical aluminum sieves. These sieves are then put inside covered aluminum containers to ferment. Each of these containers holds a kilogram-and-one-half of must. The combined output of each larger covered container, after five days of fermentation, is about one liter. This liquid is collected, and the must is squeezed in a hand operated press to extract the remaining liquid. The resulting cake, called *ampas,* is sold as an animal food.

The new *brem* is placed in 20-liter glass bottles that are covered with plastic film which keeps the dirt out, but allows the carbon dioxide to escape. The *brem* produced by the white rice is lemon yellow; that from the *injin* is brown. After about two months in the smaller bottles, the *brem* is transferred to large, 1,250 liter, fiberglass tanks. Care is taken in the transfer to leave any sediment behind in the glass bottles. The Sanur factory has 45 of these large aging tanks, each with a conical bottom. They too are vented so that gases can escape. The minimum aging time is six months in the holding tanks, for a total of eight months storage after fermentation. The longer the aging the better the product.

The *ketan* and *injin brem*s are then blended to produce a product with the desired color. The mixture is transferred to 20-liter glass bottles and sent to the bottling room. Here it is siphoned from the glass bottles into the glass bottles in which it is sold, which are then capped by a hand operated capping machine, using metal caps like those used on beer bottles. Finally the paper labels are glued on. The small bottles are packaged in units of three in palm leaf baskets. The large size bottles are packaged singly in cylindrical baskets. The price at the factory is Rp 2,200 for one package of three small bottles or for one large bottle. The price is higher, of course, in retail stores.

The product is periodically sent to Bogor, Java for analysis. It typically runs 7–9 percent alcohol by volume, and 23–25 percent sugar. No sugar is added during the process, but the final product, as mentioned earlier, is quite sweet. The alcohol content, of course, depends upon how long the *brem* is aged. Compare this with *arak*, which is typically anywhere from 20 to 50 percent by volume alcohol, depending upon quality, and which contains no sugar at all. *Tuak*'s alcohol content is quite variable, but it averages about the same as that of beer—around 5 percent.

In 1979 some of the factory's product was exported to Japan and Germany, but this is no longer done, as no great demand materialized. *Brem* too requires some acquisition of taste, largely because of its extreme sweetness. If served on ice, this becomes less obvious. And if mixed with *arak*, the best of both beverages is enhanced, and the worst of both are minimized.

PART VI

Food

CHAPTER 24

Rice and Ritual

DEWI SRI'S GIFT

ONE CAN ONLY USE SUPERLATIVES to describe the beautiful irrigated rice fields of Bali. Cut into the walls of the steep slopes and valleys of Bali's many volcanoes, the terraces, often only a few meters wide, tumble down from the ridges like lines on a giant contour map. After planting, the yellow-green of the young rice begins to appear above the silvery pools of water and the seedlings are reflected as if by a giant mirror. Two months later the terraces are deep, rich green and a little later the rice matures to a golden yellow. After harvesting the straw is burned leaving ashy stubble and dried-out, cracked ground.

The rice paddies are also marvels of hydraulic engineering. Streams are dammed far uphill from the fields, and the water is directed by hand-built aqueducts to fields far away from the dams. Weirs and smaller dams divide and re-divide the streams, settling basins allow the silt and sand to drop out, and finally the water reaches the highest terraces.

Oryza sativa has been under cultivation for six or seven thousand years, and rice is the staple diet of one-fourth of the world's population, including the 2.5 million Balinese. In Bali a complex governmental and village infrastructure organizes and supervises rice growing and irrigation, and a large body of religious observations, prayers, ceremonies, offerings, festivals, and obligations penetrate all aspects of Balinese rice farming. Rice and rice ritual occupy a major portion of the time, energy, and money of the people of Bali.

WHEREAS WESTERNERS do fine with just one word for rice, the Balinese need at least four. *Padi* is both Balinese and Indonesian for rice on the stalk, whence the English word, "paddy," which can mean stalk rice or an irrigated rice field. *Jijih* is the Balinese word for unmilled rice that has been separated from the stems (*gabah* in Indonesian). *Beras* is the High Balinese word for milled, uncooked rice (the Indonesian word is the same). The Common Balinese word is *baas*. And cooked rice is *nasi*. So important is rice in the Balinese diet that most people just use the word *nasi* to mean food—any kind of food—assuming, naturally, that the meal will consist mostly of rice. This habit applies to other Indonesians as well. Another term that is sometimes used for rice is *merta*. This comes from the Sanskrit word, *amertha*, meaning "not dead," and the letter *a* was later dropped and the meaning changed somewhat to refer to "that which is essential for life"—rice.

Rice is further classified as *ketan*, if it is sticky, glutinous rice, *injin* if it is black, and *barak* if it is red. These are the only colors of rice that grow in Bali. But white, red, and black represent only three of the four sacred colors—yellow is missing. The story is that Siwa, God as dissolver of life, brought rice to the Balinese from heaven through the agency of a bird. He brought rice of the four sacred colors, but the manifestation Batara Wisnu Sangwerti ate all but a little of the yellow rice. Wisnu planted what was left under the eaves of his house, and it grew into the turmeric plant, which the Balinese call *kunyit*. When the Balinese need yellow rice, as they do for many offerings, they have to dye the white rice yellow, *kuning*, using turmeric. Yellow rice is most important in offerings to be given on the day Kuningan.

As RECENTLY AS 1970 economists were concerned that Bali's burgeoning population would cause a crisis in the food supply, since all the available agricultural land was already under intense cultivation. At that time Bali had to import 10,000 tons of rice each year. But the crisis has not come to pass. Starting in 1969 the International Rice Research Institute, an international organization headquartered in Los Banos, The Philippines, began to introduce new, high-yield, disease- and insect-resistant strains of dwarf rice. Further research was conducted by the Indonesian agriculture department at Bogor, Java. Now, 15 years later, almost 90 percent of all Balinese rice is of this new "miracle" variety. Despite a population growth of 300,000 in the last ten years, Bali is now a net exporter of tens of thousands of tons of rice annually.

In a purely emotional sense, the introduction of the new rice to replace the old *padi bali* is a pity. *Padi bali* is a beautiful plant, about 140 centimeters (55 in.) high, almost as tall as a man, with a graceful, nodding head. When harvested, the old style rice is tied into bales and carried to the home rice storage barn, *jineng*, on the heads of the women who cut it. It is a picturesque sight, and the harvest rituals, to be described subsequently, culminate a traditional series of practices that are beginning to die out as the new dwarf rice spreads.

The new strains are usually noted IR, standing for International Rice Research Institute, or PB, *peta baru,* referring to the Indonesian strains developed in Bogor, or by the symbol "C." In all cases, the letters are followed by numbers indicating the particular strain. At the moment IR36 is the variety recommended most strongly by the Department of Agriculture. The Balinese call it *tiga nam* (simply, "36"). There is an even newer variety appearing now, named Beras Sedani. The Balinese say it doesn't taste very good. It is an aesthetic disaster compared with the old style *padi* Bali. It is short and stumpy—only about 65–70 centimeters (25–30 in.) high. Because the stems are short and the grains are easily dislodged, the rice must be threshed when it is cut. Its superior yield and resistance to pests, of course, far outweigh these superficial criticisms. It also has a much shorter growing season than the old rice—about 120 days, instead of the 150 days required for *padi bali* to mature.

Assuming peak farming efficiency, 4 tons of *jijih* per hectare (1.6 tons/acre) is the maximum yield that can be expected for *padi* Bali. By contrast, the average yield of the new rice in Bali, using the method called *intensifikasi,* which includes proper fertilization, choice of good seed, and so on, was 5.6 tons per hectare (2.3 tons/acre) per crop in 1981. In 1979 one group of farmers, Subak Rejasa, in the district of Tabanan, South Bali, averaged 11.8 tons of PB36 per hectare (4.8 tons/acre), which made them the number one producers in all of Indonesia. Their record was shattered in 1981 by a nearby village that produced almost 15 tons per hectare (6 tons/acre).

How good is the Balinese average compared with that achieved with Western technology? In the rice growing region of California, everything is done by machine: lasers are used to precisely level fields, airplanes sow the seed and spray and fertilize the crop, and enormous, electronically-controlled machines harvest the rice. In 1979 California averaged 7.23 tons per hectare (2.9 tons/acre). California, with one crop per year, out-produced Bali (two crops per year), on a crop-by-crop basis, but the reverse is true on an annual basis. Labor-intensive Bali requires somewhere around 740 man-hours per hectare per crop, whereas California needs about 17.

In 1979 Bali produced 766,000 tons of rice on 160,000 hectares of land, an increase in production of 43 percent in 9 years. This figure represents so-called "wet" *jijih,* that is, rice directly from the rice plant. There is a shrinkage of about 13 percent when the grain is dried, and a further shrinkage of about 38 percent in the milling process, so that the total figure becomes 410,000 tons of *beras,* ready to sell and cook.

I visited the Indonesian record-holding Subak Rejasa in 1980. It is a very efficient and energetic organization. I asked I Gusti Latih, the head of the *subak,* the irrigation association, how he won his distinction. He offered five principles: regular irrigation; high grade seed purchased from the government, not just saved from a previous crop; fertilizer; and regular use of recommended insecticides. No members miss meetings. They are proud of their accomplishment. They want a repeat of their 1979 achievement. No wonder. Latih showed me a photo of President Suharto awarding the members their prizes in Jakarta: Rp 5 million, a Toyota pick-up truck, 20 breeding bulls, two fertilizing machines, 2 radio-cassette players, one television set, three books, and, to top it all off, the government paved 20 kilometers of the road to their village. As with most Balinese farmers of the new rice, this area raises just two crops a year, allowing the land to rest in between or planting a legume like soybeans to rejuvenate the soil.

BECAUSE OF BALI'S DRY SEASON, from about April through September, rice fields have to be irrigated. The mountainous geography, deep gorges, steep slopes, and rugged terrain of the upland areas made it impossible in the old days for an individual to provide irrigation for his own fields all by himself. So, groups of neighboring farmers banded together and cooperated to tap the water sources to bring the water to all of their fields collectively. Present day *subak* organizations are the descendants of those who originally tapped these sources.

A *subak* is a group of rice farmers having adjacent fields, *sawahs,* that share a common water supply. *Subak*s control irrigation, repair aqueducts and dikes, and prevent theft of water and the inevitable problems that arise among neighbors. Today there are approximately 1,200 *subak*s in Bali, averaging 200 members each, with an average field area of about 50 hectares. Everyone owning land within the *subak*'s area must become a member. Members vote periodically (the period varies from 5 to 10 years) for a head, called *pekaseh,* or *kepala subak.* The position is unpaid, except that the *kepala subak* is usually given extra water for his fields and sometimes even extra land. Meetings are held periodically, at which attendance is compulsory. If a meeting is missed a fine of up to Rp 250 is levied.

The head of the *subak* has several assistants, among the most important of which are the *pengliman,* who is in charge of work projects, and the *kelian munduk,* who oversees water distribution. There is a standing joke that the best man to pick as *kelian munduk* is the one who owns the lowest rice fields, since he will see to it that he gets his share of water, and thus everyone in between will get theirs too.

The *subak* decides on all matters pertaining to dates of planting and harvesting, appropriate times for and kinds of offerings, ceremonies to be held, control, cleaning, and repair of dams, canals, and weirs, proper times for fertilizing and using insecticides, and the amount to be used, and where to procure seed for the next crop. And every *subak* maintains its own small temple out in the fields where the principal rice ceremonies are held and where the deities associated with rice reside when invited to earth. There are always many other small shrines and temples scattered throughout the *sawah* areas and almost always near dams and weirs. But these are individual shrines, or at most, are erected and used by small groups of farmers.

The practices vary considerably, but some *subak*s are themselves associated into still larger irrigation groups which perform the proper ceremonies at the sacred mountain lakes which the Balinese farmers believe to be the ultimate sources of their water. Perhaps the most important of these is Lake Beratan, near Bedugul. The famous temple on the shores of the lake, Pura Ulun Danu Beratan, is the focus of important pan-*subak* ceremonies designed to insure a steady supply of irrigation water. Some *subak*s make regular pilgrimages to this temple just before the irrigation season begins.

Indonesian agriculture ministry officials work with the *subak*s, but the two are careful to maintain separate identities. Each of Bali's eight districts, *kabupaten*, has an official from the department, the *sedahan agung*. Under the *sedahan agung* are several men, called *sedahan yeh*, who oversee irrigation matters. The department also maintains a staff of field and extension agents, and agents in charge of buying rice in the fields to guarantee floor prices, and in charge of transporting, milling, and storing rice for government stocks. Generally speaking, the government and the *subak* organizations get along efficiently and with a minimum of friction.

No Balinese deity is better loved and more frequently and fervently worshiped than Dewi Sri. She is the female aspect of rice, and as with all other things in the Balinese universe, she is both male and female. Her dual image, usually called Dewa Nini (*nini*, "grandmother"), is invariably present in the *sawah*s at harvest time and adorns every rice barn. The figures are made out of rice stalks right in the field. Fifty-four stalks for the female figure and 58 for the male are tied together to form the two figures, so that the rice stalks form a conical skirt. The tie point is the pinched waist, and above the waist the ends of the stalks are formed into a triangle and decorated as a face. In the fields of new rice the figures are made from cut stalks. But in the *padi bali* fields the Dewa Ninis are made from stalks still rooted in the earth.

This double triangle or hour glass figure is called *cili*, from the word *cantik*, "beautiful," or *benda kecil*, "small thing." It is repeated endlessly in Balinese offerings of every imaginable sort, and in paintings, statues, wood carvings, and every kind of decoration. Woven of coconut leaf, painted, plaited, chiseled, or hammered into metal, the *cili* is the symbol of Bali. (See illustration opposite. The symbol opening each chapter in this book is also a *cili*.)

Rice is more than just a useful crop. It is life, *amertha*, and, as such, an enormous and complex set of rituals accompany every stage of its cultiva-

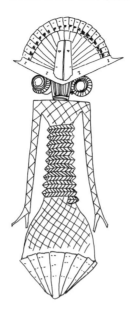

A CILI FIGURE

tion. These may vary from the tiny offerings, *penampeh,* placed in the corners of a field to keep animals away, to a huge, village-wide, multi-day temple ceremony, *ngusaba nini,* involving weeks of preparation, thousands of elaborate offerings, and hundreds of people. No hospital patient in intensive care is watched more carefully than rice as it develops, and no effort is spared to nurture and protect the crop.

The rice farming cycle begins about 25 days before planting. An auspicious day is chosen according to the rather complex systems of Balinese calendars, both the 210-day Pawukon cycle and the Hindu-Balinese Saka, a lunar calendar. The first event is the hoeing of the *sawah,* called *ngendag,* "opening up." Before the *tambah* (a hoe with tines like a rake) is used to break up the dry ground and stubble of the old crop, a small offering, *peras tulung,* is carried into the field on a tray. The offering, called *kewangen,* contains plaited coconut-leaf shapes, a Chinese coin, and the ingredients of the betel chew. After a prayer, the essence of the offerings is wafted toward the field with a small basket, called a *saab.* The offerings are placed on the ground and sprinkled with holy water. And always a bit of rice wine and palm brandy are spilled on the ground for the evil spirits, the *butas* and *kalas.*

Only then can the hoeing begin. When this is completed the *sawah* is flooded with five to ten centimeters of water and plowed with a wood and steel plow, *tenggala,* pulled by one or two cows. Water buffalos aren't often used in Bali, but one does see some gasoline-powered tractors nowadays. If weeds are a problem, the plowed fields may be dragged with a scraper, called *lampit*. This may be a special steel device or sometimes just a banana log impaled on the tines of a hoe.

If there is a pilgrimage to be made to Lake Beratan or one of the other sacred lakes to present offerings for a good supply of irrigation water, it takes place at this stage. Not many farmers in the Denpasar area do this any more, but it used to be common. Sometimes a ceremony, called *mapag toya* is held when the first irrigation water comes into the *sawah,* but I did not witness this.

Meanwhile, a seed bed, *pemulihan,* is prepared by enclosing a few square meters of the irrigated field with dikes and surrounding the area with woven coconut leaf or bamboo mats to keep animals away. Practices differ in preparing the seedling nursery. With *padi bali,* the seeds of rice used are left attached to the stalks and are laid by hand, one by one, on the moist ground, which is later flooded. With dwarf rice the seeds are broadcast by hand into the already flooded seed bed. In either case, the seeds are soaked for two days prior to planting in order to start germination. And in both cases a small offering is planted in the seed bed before the seeds are laid down. The soaked seeds, called *binih,* are brought to the field in a bamboo basket.

The planting of the seeds ceremony, *ngawitan ngurit,* is accompanied by an offering called a *suyuk,* and a small *kewangen,* similar to that described in the hoeing ceremony. The more elaborate *suyuk* is a small tray containing flowers and plaited offerings made from coconut leaf, with some colored rice and rice cakes. As with the hoeing, a favorable day is always required for starting the seed germination.

The seedlings are allowed to grow for 20 to 25 days in the nursery. Three days before they are transplanted, the fields are fertilized with trisodium phosphate (TSP), and then, just before planting, with urea. Transplanting the seedlings is a group activity, again occurring on a favorable day. A team of men pull the seedlings from their nursery bed, *ngabut,* place them in bunches on round bamboo trays, and carry them to the nearby field that has been flooded, smoothed, and fertilized. Before any seedlings are planted, a ceremony called *ngewiwit* is performed. Offerings are placed in one corner of the *sawah,* prayed over, and then nine seedlings are planted next to the offerings, one in each of the cardinal directions, one in the center, and one in each of the intermediate directions. This symbolism of the nine directions, *nawa sanga,* occurs in a great many religious ceremonies.

Now the entire team starts the planting proper, *ngeberan.* The trays of seedlings are set upon the slippery mud ooze and pushed from place to place as the barefoot men thrust two to five seedlings into the same hole that they poke into the mud with their fingers. Holes are spaced one handwidth apart and are lined up in neat rows. The planters are usually hired for the occasion. At one planting I visited 10 men worked one-half day and were paid Rp 700 each, plus food.

At one of the *sawahs* I visited, a special and unusual *pengulapan* cere- mony was held right after planting. The previous crop was small because of an insect infestation, so the owners of the *sawah* decided that a more elaborate ceremony than usual should be held to prevent a recurrence of the disaster. A white-clad lay priest, or *pemangku*, officiated. Seated on a narrow dike between flooded and seeded fields, he faced a bamboo altar upon which three sets of offerings had been placed: *sayut pengastawan, pemerascitaan,* and *tetebasan.* These rather elaborate offerings were dedi- cated to Dewi Sri with prayers and sacred mantras, the whole event accompanied by incense and the ringing of the priest's bronze bell. It was a colorful sight. The *pemangku*'s reflection in the still pools of water was broken only by the tiny seedlings, planted just a few hours before.

During the first month after planting, ceremonial practices vary consid- erably. Some farmers make a small offering called *pecaruwan pengulapan suang-suang* before the rice is 17 days old and another small one called *bubuh tabah* at the age of 17 days. Others make a small *peneduhan* offer- ing at 20 or 21 days. After 35 to 40 days another urea fertilization is rec- ommended.

The Balinese call a period of 35 days a *bulan,* which is usually translat- ed into the English "month." But this is kind of confusing, because they have another word, *sasih,* that means a lunar month (See "Balinese Calendars" in *S&N Vol. I*). At the end of the first 35-day "month" a major offering called *nasi warna* is made, consisting of the four colors of rice. Some *subaks* require a 42-day offering called *esan,* usually just a woven coconut leaf decoration planted in the field. At 55 to 60 days the last urea fertilization is made. At two months, at a ceremony called *sayut nagasari,* an offering called *bulayag* is carried to the fields. This consists of rice cooked in a small woven container of coconut leaves, plus the usual flowers, rice wine, and holy water.

Now the rice begins to ripen as the grains start forming on the heads, *padi leg.* The rice is said to be pregnant, *beling,* as the ears fatten. And this calls for renewed vigilance and care, for it is now that the birds and mice constitute a threat to the crop. Scarecrows, *petakut,* are erected. Bamboo poles are stuck into the ground all over the rice fields, and long strings are fastened to them. Then plastic bags, bits of old clothing, anything that flaps in the wind, is fastened to the strings so that, from a distance, the fields look like masses of vibrating trash. Sometimes the strings are all run to a little elevated enclosure in the rice field in which a small child sits. He pulls their ends, animating the dance of a thousand plastic bags. Older men and women walk through the fields shouting. Many of them use a bird scaring device called a *kekepuakan,* which is a meter-long section of

ANGGAPAN

DEWA NINI

IMPLEMENTS USED IN RICE GROWING

bamboo cut almost all the way through longitudinally. When held by the uncut end and waved, the two halves clap together, producing a loud, hollow noise. Windmills whir, often activating ingenious noise makers of bamboo that bang and clatter as the blades revolve. I have even seen children snapping huge bull whips—anything to protect the rice.

Usually small offerings containing lime, called *penampeh,* are placed at the corners of the fields to keep out animals and insects. Modern farmers spray on insecticides and rodenticides. The brown rice hopper, *wereng,* is an especially dangerous pest and can ruin a crop almost overnight.

Now the new rice is starting to turn yellow as harvest time approaches,

but the *padi bali* still has another month to go. A three-month ceremony
with offerings, called *miseh*, is usually held, but its importance is dwarfed
by the upcoming harvest rituals. Two weeks before harvest, irrigation is
stopped, and the fields are allowed to dry up. Just before harvest almost
all farmers hold the *mabiukukung* ceremony in the fields. The name
comes from the offerings of coconut leaf that are woven into shapes that
look like bananas, *biu*, or the cylindrical beehives, *kungkungan*, that are
common in Bali. This ritual is more elaborate than any thus far.

THE RICE HARVEST, *manyi*, or *gampung*, involves a lot of work by a
large group of people. The two different kinds of rice require two very
different techniques. Dwarf rice cannot be moved from the field because
the grains fall off the heads. Traditional rice is always baled and carried
home, to be stored in the rice barn and threshed as needed.

Padi bali is cut stalk by stalk by a crew of a dozen or more men and
women, chattering noisily as they work under their huge bamboo hats in
the shoulder high grain. From a distance all you can see are the hats. The
rice knife for *padi bali* is called *anggapan*. It is almost concealed in the
right palm—they say that this is done so that the rice will not be frightened by a big knife. The slightly curved metal blade, about 4 by 10 centimeters (1.5 by 4 in.), is held in a small horshoe-shaped wooden frame. A
small bamboo stick that is perpendicular to the plane of the blade and
frame fits next to the palm to steady the knife. The knife itself is held
between the index and second fingers of the right hand. To cut the rice, a
stalk is grabbed by the thumb and index fingers above the blade. Then, by
rotating the wrist counterclockwise, the knife edge is brought into contact
with the stalk, and the third, fourth, and little fingers below the blade
wrap around the stalk as it is severed from the lower part. In this way each
stalk can be cut with one hand only. The cut part is about 50 centimeters
long. It is transferred to the left hand, and the process continued until the
left hand is full, making a bundle called a *cekelan*.

A roving gatherer takes the handful and combines it with nine more,
making a *tengah*. This is handed to a nearby man who is in charge of making the lovely round bales, called *suwun*, or *depukan*. The baler collects
10 *tengah* to make a total weight of about 10 to 12 kilograms, ties a bamboo string around the bunch below the heads, and pounds the stalk ends
with a wooden paddle, the *penatapan*, until they are even—the stalk ends
being up, heads down. The bales and the ever-present Dewa Nini are carried home at the end of the day on the heads of the ladies. Men carry two
bales at a time suspended from the ends of a flat bamboo stick, *tegen*. The
harvesters are either paid in cash or are given one out of every ten bales.

The new rice, on the other hand, is cut close to the ground by the
handful, using a sickle-shaped knife called an *arit*, the handles of which
are often seen stuck in the back of the pants of rice farmers. A canvas

sheet is spread on the ground nearby, on top of which a board, *penata-pan*, is propped up in a frame. The board is long enough to accommodate several threshers at once. Women grasp bundles of rice at the bottom end and whack them down over the board. Three or four whacks are usually enough to dislodge all of the grains in the handful. The grains fall in a pile beyond the board, the straw is discarded, and a new bundle is threshed. The straw is piled up and burned, which returns valuable minerals, especially calcium, to the soil. In rice harvesting season the slopes of the mountains are enveloped in smoke for days.

Unless the resulting *jijih* is to be used for home consumption it is usually sold right on the spot, often to government buyers. Thus, although there are always Dewa Ninis nearby, there is no picturesque carrying home of the bales, nor are any of the interesting procedures carried out that have to do with blessing the rice barn and storing the newly cut *padi bali* therein. These will be described subsequently.

The largest *subak* rice ceremony, *ngusaba nini*, is held in the *subak* temple in the fields. Some groups hold it just before harvest, some just after. It is a thanksgiving to Dewi Sri for the gift of herself. Sometimes *ngusaba nini* is a village-wide ceremony, held rarely and requiring months of preparation and involving hundreds of people. I witnessed one of these at Gulingan, Mengwi, in late September, 1980. All villagers in the area brought Dewa Ninis to one of the village temples. There were hundreds of them. Then there was a cleansing procession to the sea, a huge demon sacrifice, called a *caru*, a complex and beautiful set of offerings in the temple, long processions, and decorations throughout the village.

Most *ngusaba nini* ceremonies are not nearly so elaborate. Sometimes slightly more elaborate ones are alternated with rather small ones, just as is done in the case of temple anniversary festivals, *odalan*s, in many areas. One of the more interesting *ngusaba nini* ceremonies that I saw was held just before harvest at Subak Dukuh in Tabanan. The organization had erected a large shrine, *sanggah cucuk*, just in front of the gate of the *subak* temple. Offerings of plaited coconut leaves, colored rice, flowers, rice cakes of every hue and shape, fruits, roast ducks, and suckling pigs and rice wine and palm brandy were placed in the shrine and on mats in the temple. After God has partaken of the essense, the *sari*, of the food, the people are free to eat the offerings, and always do. The most dramatic offering was a meter-high cone of white rice.

When all was ready, a *pemangku* sat down on the mats behind the offerings inside the temple and invited God to descend and receive thanks. Then he dedicated the offerings to God's pleasure, wafting the essence of the offerings toward the many shrines with the usual basket. He did not forget the *butas* and the *kalas*. Rice wine and palm brandy were spilled on the ground for them too. And smoldering incense helped the prayers travel to God and His various manifestations to whom the shrines within the temple were dedicated. Members of the *subak* sat behind the priest, and all prayed in the Balinese fashion, thumbs against the forehead, fingers of both hands pressed together in front, a flower held between. Then the women carried some of the offerings around to the various shrines, placed a few in each, and sprinkled holy water on the shrines. Finally, all the men paraded around the inside of the temple carrying the big rice cone and shouting loudly in thanks. The cone was returned to the ground, and it and the suckling pig were cut up for distribution to the *subak* members.

THE FINAL CEREMONY OF THE RICE CYCLE, *mengetam,* is only performed in areas where *padi bali* bales are brought home to be stored in the rice barns. A rice barn, *jineng,* has a very steeply sloping roof and is always built far up off the ground on pillars to prevent access by rodents. The little door is reachable only by a long bamboo ladder. The storage area is, so to speak, the second floor, and the space below is nice and shady and is often used for lounging, storage, or other purposes. There is almost always a horizontal structure built between the posts that can be used as a sitting area or a bed.

When the rice bales and Dewa Nini are carried home the bales are left out in the sun in the house compound to dry, and the Dewa Nini is kept in a safe place until all is prepared for the storage ceremony. First the bales are lifted up into the *jineng* on the end of a long bamboo pole. A man impales a bale on one end of the pole, places the other end in a special socket in the ground, and then "walks" his hands down the pole as the bale is lifted to a second man inside the barn.

Now the rice barn is elaborately decorated. A tall bamboo pole, *penjor,* is set up nearby, with coconut leaf decorations on top and an offering on the end. Plaited palm leaf plaques, *lamaks,* and colorful pieces of cloth are hung from the rice barn door. Baskets of offerings, called *soda anyar,* and *peras pengambian,* are prepared for the inside of the barn storage area. And some small triangular offerings, called *segehan,* are made for the *butas* and *kalas.* Then the Dewa Nini is carried up to the barn door on a lady's head and handed to another person inside, who places it beside her sisters, left over from previous harvests. The offerings are spread out on top of the newly cut rice bales, and prayers of thanks are offered.

There is not as much straw in *padi bali* fields as in dwarf rice fields, because some of it is carried home to the barn. But the *padi bali* fields are burned too, often enveloping the rice growing areas in an impenetrable smog for weeks on end. Although three crops of new rice could conceivably be raised per year, experience dictates that the fields should be allowed to rest for a few months, or else a legume crop such as soy beans is planted to enrich the soil. The growing season for *padi* Bali is too long to permit more than two crops per year, sometimes only one.

LIKE MOST RICE-EATING PEOPLE, the Balinese insist upon having their rice white, with husk and germ removed—and with them, almost all of the fat, protein, and vitamin B1 (hence the prevalence of pellagra here some years ago, caused by vitamin B1 deficiency). With *padi bali*, removal of the brown parts is usually, but not always, done at home by removing a small bundle, *sepingan*, from a bale, and pounding the rice, *nebuk*, with a two-meter-long pole. The rice is either put on the ground or, if the family has one, placed in a long wooden trough, the *lessung*. A wooden pole with a steel bottom is used first, the *buntar*, followed by an all wooden pole, called a *lu*. The pole is pounded alternately with the left and right hands in a rhythmic cadence until the husk and bran are stripped off. Then the pounded rice is put on a large bamboo tray and winnowed by tossing it into the air and letting the wind blow off the chaff.

Most new rice, and some of the traditional rice, is milled in a factory called a *slip*. There are 1,448 of them in Bali, so one is never very far away. The *slip*s buy rice outright, mill it, and sell the resulting *beras* in 100 kilogram sacks. Alternatively, an individual may bring in his own *jijih*, wait in line, and have it milled on the spot for about Rp 5 per kilogram. The mill usually has a large concrete area out in front upon which the rice is sun-dried before milling.

The mill itself consists of gasoline or diesel powered counter- rotating wheels with special abrasive coatings that wrench the outer parts off the seed while doing a minimum of damage to the white part. The rice passes through the wheels and then falls through a stream of air as it descends into shaking screens below. The screens and the air separate the products into four parts. The large, light husks are blown through a big pipe to the outside of the mill. They are good for nothing but fuel. Inside the mill, three streams emerge from the machinery. One is the white rice, *beras*, ready for the pot. A second contains the very light, feathery bran and attached germ. This material, called *oot alus*, is widely used as a pig food. The third stream consists of somewhat coarser fragments of the bran and the finer fragments of husk. It is called *oot pesak*, or *oot kasar*. It may be used for pigs if one cannot afford the better *oot alus*. Often it is burned or just thrown away.

Beras bali can be easily distinguished by sight from grains of PB or IR *beras*. *Beras bali* is a short-grain rice, while the newer dwarf rice is long grained. *Beras bali* usually sells for a premium price because it is some-what scarce and because people prefer its taste. In 1985 *beras* Bali cost about Rp 400 per kilogram, with the dwarf varieties selling at around 50 to 100 Rp per kilogram less. Very little black rice and glutinous rice, including the red variety, is raised, compared to ordinary *jijih*. These sell for even higher prices. But they are always available in the markets because they are needed for offerings of all kinds. Black rice is used to make rice wine, *brem*, which is a very popular drink, both among tourists and Balinese. The latter often mix it with a bit of *arak*, the distilled brandy made from palm beer, *tuak*.

The Indonesian Government subsidizes the price of rice in order to keep it affordable. Huge rice storage warehouses have been built on the outskirts of Denpasar. The Balinese call them *dolog*. All government employees are paid partly in rice, or, to be more accurate, in coupons that can be exchanged for rice. If an employee marries, his or her monthly ration is increased. If he has a child it is increased again. But, to encourage family planning, this increase does not go on indefinitely. At the moment, allowance for three children is the maximum. Some private companies pay partly with rice also. But a good many people I know don't like the taste of this rice, which may have been stored for quite some time, and so they sell their coupons to others and buy *beras bali* or fresh IR or PB with the money.

THE BALINESE COOK RICE in a great variety of ways, but the most common methods are steaming and boiling. The rice is always winnowed first, to remove bits of dirt and husk. This is accomplished by putting the required amount in a round tray and tossing the contents lightly up into the air, letting the breeze blow away impurities. The Balinese are very finicky about dirt or other impurities in their *nasi*. Then the rice is washed in cold water, so as to remove the chalky exterior of the grains.

To make steamed rice, which is called *nasi kuskus,* the cleaned rice is placed in a loosely woven bamboo container that is in the form of a cone, especially made just for steaming rice, the *pengukusan*. I have seen many a tourist mistake the *pengukusan*s for hats at the markets and buy them for that purpose, much to the mirth of the sellers.

The bamboo steamer with *beras* in it is placed in the upper, funnel-shaped part of the *dangdang*, an hour-glass–shaped metal pot, into which it just fits. A hole is made in the rice with a wooden stick, the *siut*, to allow the steam to penetrate all the grains. The boiling water fills the lower part below the constriction or waist of the pot, and the steamer with rice in it fits into the upper section, above the waist. Then a special clay bowl with a handle, the *kekeb*, is inverted over the top of the rice in the steamer to keep the heat and steam from escapingr.

Steaming takes place for about half an hour. Since this tends to dry the rice out, it is removed from the steamer to a clay container, the *pane*, or *gembor*, and a little hot water is added. After 15 or 20 minutes the rice, having soaked up the water, is returned to the steamer and steamed for another half hour until done.

Alternatively, the housewife may elect to prepare boiled rice, *nasi jakan*. This is simple and fast, but most Balinese prefer their rice steamed. To boil the rice, cleaned rice is stirred into water boiling in a clay pot, called a *payuk*, or a metal pot, the *panci*. A wooden stirring stick is used to mix up the contents until the water boils again. Boiling is allowed to continue for about half an hour. Inevitably a little of the rice in the bottom burns a bit and forms a kind of browned cake, which is a favorite of the children of the family, who take it out and munch on it all day long.

The Balinese cook rice twice a day, in the morning and in the evening. It is never reheated, but it is often kept in a large insulated container until it is ready to eat. They do not mind if it is cold, which it almost inevitably is by the time it is eaten. Rice is never kept over until the next day, because the taste deteriorates rapidly without refrigeration. Although Japanese-made electric rice cookers are now available in Bali, I have never seen a family use one in the village in which I live, even though there is electricity and even though the appliances are not very expensive.

Another very common way of preparing rice is by making one of the several varieties of *ketipat*. A *ketipat* is a kind of box woven of coconut leaves, made very loosely, but not so open that the rice grains fall out. *Beras* is put inside, through one of the spaces between the leaves by prying an opening apart. The *ketipat* is then put into the rice steamer, or boiled in the pot. The rice swells to fill the container, and the result is a package of rice that the husband can take to the field for a snack or the kids can take to school, or that can be used as an offering.

Rice cakes, *jaja*, are characteristic of most of Indonesia, but Bali has more varieties than any other area that I have seen. I have photos and recipes for over 60 different kinds of cakes, each with a different name, and each serving a specific purpose. Many are made for offerings, and the markets are overflowing with them when important religious ceremonies are imminent. But lots are consumed daily for snacks, and they are delicious. They are so numerous and are made in so many different ways that it would be folly to try to attempt a dissertation of *jaja* in this essay.

BUDI, MY BALINESE ASSISTANT, lived with my wife and me in America for two years studying English. Every day he cooked his supermarket-bought, California rice in an electric cooker made in Japan. Every day he also put a little pinch of the cooked rice on each of three leaves. Then he offered a silent prayer, wafted the essence of the rice toward God, and put one offering on the rice cooker, one in his room in front of the holy water that he had brought from Bali, and one outside the front door.

He never forgot.

CHAPTER 25

Jamu

INDONESIA'S HERBAL FIX

JAMU IS THE JAVANESE WORD for any of a great number of traditional Indonesian herbal medicines and health concoctions. Almost every culture has its powdered antlers, sassafras tea, or Rolaids. And reliable estimates indicate that about 80 percent of Indonesia's population—well over 100 million people—takes *jamu* every day. There are about 100 *jamu* recipes in use, but only a dozen or so are really popular. *Jamu* is not in the same league as the quack potions that made the rounds in the United States during the previous century. The recipes for a given mixture—to cure hemorrhoids, say—are more or less consistent from vender to vendor, from the local girl selling it in the villages by the glass, to the huge commercial *jamu* factories in Central Java.

Jamu had its origins in the royal court of Solo (today sometimes called Surakarta) in Central Java in the 17th century. This area has historically been the cultural and political center of Indonesia. And *jamu* is just another one of its products, which include classical music and dance, philosophy, literature, and President Suharto. One of Indonesia's patriotic songs describes its island chain as stretching from "Sabang to Merauke." The former is a little island off the northwest coast of Sumatra. The latter is a city in extreme southeast Irian Jaya, 5,000 kilometers from Sabang. This is a span of one-eighth of the earth's circumference. *Jamu* is found in Sabang, Merauke, and all intermediate points. But the makers and the sellers are almost always Solonese.

JAMU IS COMPLETELY AN INDIGENOUS PRODUCT. Although most of the commercial aspects of the industry are controlled by Indonesians of Chinese ethnic origin, that is only because these people form a kind of business class, not because the *jamu* traditions were rooted elsewhere. *Jamu* recipes originated empirically. The ones that did what they were supposed to were carefully recorded and handed down through families. I had occasion to buy some *jamu* at a Chinese-run shop in Denpasar recently. The young owner took out a worn notebook he said belonged to his great grandfather, from Solo, and proceeded to formulate my *jamu* from a recipe therein.

What are *jamu*s supposed to do? Some of the more sensational claims that one reads about in magazines and hears on the radio highlight the effect of *jamu* on sexual prowess. But this is just one of many reasons for the use of *jamu*. Most people to whom I talked said they take *jamu* regularly to stay or become strong, healthy, and beautiful. Some use *jamu* for the relief of fatigue. Some *jamu*s are intended to restore beauty and shape after pregnancy. Some are externally applied powders, salves, and oils. Some are for the relief of gas pains, headaches, colds, or hemorrhoids (a separate mixture is required for each of these). And some *jamu*s claim cures for kidney stones, dysentery, malaria, and flu.

What do they contain? Indonesia is a botanical treasure house. About 150 species of plants, from acacia to zingiber are used in *jamu*s. Each formulation has a name widely known to its users and contains one or several species of plants or plant parts that are "known" to produce the intended effect. These plant parts may be leaves, seeds, bark, roots, rhizomes, stems, or any other part of the plant in which the efficacious material is located. Since many of the *jamu* mixtures are sold as powders to be stirred in warm water and drunk, and since many of these plants look, smell, and taste awful, cinnamon, fennel, mint, turmeric, and the like are always added to make the concoction palatable.

People who possess the recipes for *jamu* often just make it themselves. The plants for the more popular formulations grow in every rural back yard, and it is easy to pluck the proper leaves, dig up the specified roots, powder them, and stir them into a glass of water. Urban dwellers can buy the proper raw materials, already mixed in proper proportions, neatly packaged in a plastic bag at a nearby *jamu* store. Jakarta's largest department store has a big *jamu* counter in its basement, and it does a land-office business. Whenever I leave Bali to go to some other island, my friends beg me to bring them back some leaves or roots or oil of so-and-so, because they need it for a *jamu*. And even in the course of my travels around Bali, Budi, my assistant, is forever stopping and picking some leaves or plants, or begging some bark from people who live up in the hills where such plants grow, since we live down near the shore. When we get home he or his wife makes up some *loloh,* an infusion of the plant material boiled in water, and he drinks it with great enthusiasm.

In every Indonesian city, of whatever size, one finds the *jamu gendong.* The word *gendong* means to "carry on the back." Early each morning,

THE JAMU GENDONG

well before dawn, a young girl, perhaps 15 to 20 years of age, and almost invariably first- or second-generation Solonese, (and, I might add, almost always very pretty) prepares several liters of three or four different kinds of *jamu* in her home, having purchased the ingredients from a local market, or having had them sent by her relatives in Central Java. She measures out the plant materials, grinds them on a stone mortar and pestle, mixes them with water, and pours them into empty plastic Aqua bottles, puts the bottles into a large round bamboo basket, hoists the basket on to her back, and sets off on her regular *jamu* route. She carries a plastic pail of water to rinse out her glass between customers, as well as a wad of change wrapped up in the knot of her shoulder cloth.

Each *jamu gendong* has a regular route. She begins at dawn, visiting her steady customers on foot, although she might have to take a *bemo* to get to her area (a *bemo* is a kind of small bus or van or truck used for public transportation). These customers may be *becak* (pedicab) drivers who, after tossing off their fatigue-relieving tonic, joke familiarly with the pretty girl. Customers include shop keepers, house servants, restaurant customers, and just private people in their homes. The *jamu gendong* charges about Rp 20 to Rp 25 for each glass. Often her route is several kilometers long. Some girls favor the residential areas, other the crowded markets. Wherever they go they do a good business. Within a few hours she has pocketed Rp 2,000 or so, and, her plastic bottles empty, trudges home. Tourists don't often see the *jamu gendong* girls because they generally finish their routes rather early in the morning. But they are as characteristic of Indonesian cities as rice for breakfast (and lunch and dinner).

One is seldom out of sight of a *jamu* shop in Indonesia, whether in teeming Jakarta or in a little village in upland Sumatra. The aggressive commercial manufacturers have blanketed the country with their gaudy billboards, awnings, painted store fronts, magazine advertisements, free samples, pamphlets, free movies on village soccer fields, and, in short, all the gimmicks of modern advertising. No little village *warung*, however small, is without at least one or two of the most popular kinds of *jamu*, and many stock an amazing variety. There are three giants in the industry and dozens of smaller companies. Together they produce somewhere around 200 million packets of *jamu* each year, worth around U.S. $15 million. But this is still only a small percentage of the entire *jamu* industry, which has a gross value of somewhere closer to U.S. $1 billion. This latter figure, of course, counts the *jamu gendong* and the market sellers of *jamu* ingredients.

One interesting commercial use of *jamu* is a beauty shop, Mustika Ratu ("King Jewel") in Jakarta. Run, naturally, by Solonese ladies, the shop has its own factory for manufacturing beauty products from natural plant materials, and it runs a school for beauty operators who want to open their own "natural cosmetics" beauty shops. Mustika Ratu has a clientele of elegant Javanese ladies, and even tourists go there for the usual gamut of beauty treatments. In recent years, other *jamu*-type beauty shops have opened, capitalizing upon the worldwide craze for things that are "natural." At a conference on *jamu* and native medicinal products held recently in Surabaya, at least half a dozen beauty product manufacturers claiming the benefits of cosmetics made from natural plant products had erected elaborate displays, plastered with advertising hype, and staffed by pretty saleswomen.

THE BIG THREE *JAMU* PRODUCERS are located in Central Java. Air Mancur (the name means "Water Fountain") runs several big plants in and around Solo. Cap Jago ("Rooster Brand") and Nyonya Meneer ("Mrs. Meneer") are located just north of Solo at Semarang, on the north coast of Central Java. Their *jamu*s are typically marketed in small packets containing about 7 grams of the finely powdered product that is to be stirred into a glass of warm water for taking internally, or in cakes for the skin, or in oils for the hair.

The *jamu* packets are imprinted with interesting advertising materials. Cap Jago people tell me that their *jamu*, the cheapest of the three, is intended for the average man. Their packets, costing about Rp 250, usually just have the contents and name of the *jamu* printed on the front (but often there is a pretty girl on the back). Nyonya Meneer, the most expensive of the three at Rp 300 per packet, considers itself the elite *jamu*. Charles Ong, Nyonya Meneer's grandson, received his degree in economics from Miami University in the United States. He has switched the package display material away from the traditional portrait of his grandmother toward a somewhat abstract representation of the effect that the *jamu* within is designed to produce. For example, Nyonya Meneer Jamu No. 3, Jamu Pria Jantan, "He-man Jamu," has a muscle man drawn inside the biological symbol for male, the circle and arrow, and the man is shooting the arrow with a large bow. Air Mancur goes in for pictorial representations of the symptoms of the ailments that their *jamu*s are intended to relieve, with well-known movie and TV stars in various postures of physiological agony.

The commercial *jamu* factories use enormous quantities of raw plant products. Air Mancur, for example, uses 5,000 kilos a day and raises many of its own plants on a large plantation near Solo. So popular have traditional native medicines, particularly *jamu*, become, that some medicinal plants are in real danger of total depletion in Indonesia (and in other countries as well). This has led the Indonesian National Institute of Biology to list 36 native medicinal plants that are in danger of extinction. The Indonesian health minister now recommends that commercial *jamu* producers either own their own plantations or cooperate with the forestry department to grow the critical medicinal plants they require.

The other two big *jamu* manufacturers buy the plant materials that they need—an operation that needs to be carefully controlled. Exact identification of plant material is often a big problem. As a result, each company maintains an elaborate herbarium and good facilities for gross and microscopic examination. Further, samples of a given species of plant will vary greatly in their potency depending on the age of the plant at harvesting, rainfall, soil type, temperature regime, and so on. Thus, to maintain some degree of uniformity, *jamu* manufacturers have to stockpile raw materials and blend them. Still, the potency of even the same manufacturer's *jamu* will vary batch to batch.

Grinding and mixing of the raw plant products is the only machine operation in the commercial *jamu* plants. The Indonesian government strongly discourages the use of machines to displace hand work, and thus jobs, in a country where the middle class is just now beginning to feel its strength. Commercial enterprises are, quite rightly, encouraged to be labor-intensive. The *jamu* factories employ enormous numbers of girls who spoon the powdered *jamu* into individual packets, seal, wrap, and pack them by hand. The average pay for the unskilled workers was about Rp 35,000 per month. Some of the pay is in the form of rice, And 10 percent is always put into the bank for the worker.

The commercial *jamu* manufacturers have lately taken to packaging some of their products in the form of pills and capsules on the theory that this will be attractive to consumers as a "modern" way to take medicine. Drs. Z. Arifin, head of the Air Mancur laboratories, claims that the capsules contain an extract of the active ingredients of the *jamu*s, hence the capsules or pills, which are the usual small size, are just as effective as the much larger packets of powder. (Others claim that since nobody knows exactly what active ingredients should be "extracted" to go into the capsules, that all they contain is the same powder that has always gone into the packets.)

All *jamu* manufacturers maintain testing laboratories. Air Mancur has a particularly elaborate one, complete with white rabbits, who are given the *jamu*s and tested for such things as blood sugar, metabolism, toxicity, and so on. Some assay work is done on the raw materials and *jamu* products. But much of the analytical work concentrates upon toxicity tests. It is virtually impossible to assay a complex plant chemical without a great deal of very sophisticated, modern, laboratory equipment, and neither this equipment nor the skill to use it is at hand.

The big three are experimenting with exporting their products. Regular shipments already go to Holland, where there is a large Indonesian minority, and to Malaysia, Singapore, and Australia. The U.S. Food and Drug Administration has extremely strict regulations regarding the importing of such materials, and so far *jamu* has not been allowed into the United States.

THE GOVERNMENT OF INDONESIA attempts to regulate the commercial *jamu* industry. The ministry of health has a branch of food and drug control, and this branch has a directorship of traditional medicines. The former head of this organization told me that though it had been operating since 1975, it is still quite in its infancy. For example, it has a field staff of only 14 inspectors for all of Indonesia. Still, each of the 300 or so commercial *jamu* manufacturers is now required to file with the health department a list of all the ingredients used in each of their products. The government checks them carefully to insure that no narcotics or dangerous drugs are included. And the law now requires ingredients listings on each package of *jamu*. The ministry has sponsored symposia on *jamu*s, the protection of endangered species, and the conservation of medicinal plants, and has published a series on Indonesian medicinal plants.

Dr. Mien Rifai of the National Biological Institute in Bogor told me that one of his big concerns is that spores of the mold *Aspergillus flavus* have been found in random samplings of commercial *jamu*s. The spores of this mold are of no special concern. Indeed, they are found in many plant products that are in close contact with the soil—for example, peanuts. But, if the spores germinate, the resulting fungus produces a potent chemical called aflatoxin, the most powerful cause of liver cancer known to man. Germination results from moisture penetrating the *jamu* packages, and so the manufacturers try to remove old merchandise from store shelves, since humidity is high all over Indonesia and since the packages are not air-tight or waterproof.

DO *JAMU*S "WORK"? Do they perform the preventative and curative functions that they are widely advertised and believed to perform? Are these formulations of the "snake oil," medicine show variety, or is there at least some basis in scientific fact for their claims?

Opinions on this cover the spectrum of course. My very good friend, Dr. Suwidji Wanamarta, head of the Department of Surgery at Airlangga University in Surabaya, tells me that "*jamu* does no harm to a healthy person," provided that its use does not prevent him from seeing a doctor. The former head of the branch of the Ministry of Health that controls *jamu* manufacturers admits to taking his nip of the *jamu* called Beras Kencur every morning. Prof. N. Zaman-Joenoes, Head of the Department of Pharmacology at Airlangga University, told me that the only way that she could rid her face of "cold sores" was with *jamu*. You get a different answer from almost every person you ask, even those who are in the medical and pharmaceutical professions.

It is very easy to be skeptical and dismiss the whole phenomenon of *jamu* and all other so-called traditional medicines as a fraud. But that is not a very intelligent reaction or evaluation. Consider that a very cursory perusal of a pharmacopoeia or a textbook of pharmacology reveals that a large number, approximately 40 percent, of our modern medicines are either the raw plants themselves, or are derived from plants, or are synthesized to resemble the active ingredients originally found in plants. For example, digitalis, used to increase the force of myocardial contraction, is extracted from the leaves of the foxglove. Quinine is still produced from the bark of the cinchona tree to treat malaria. Ergot, a fungus, is a treasure house of drugs used, for example, to stimulate uterine smooth muscle and to produce LSD. The plant *Rauwolfia* yields reserpine, useful in the treatment of hypertension. Castor oil is an effective cathartic. Curare is a neuromuscular blocking agent. And let us not forget that the active ingredient, salicylic acid, in our favorite over-the-counter drug, aspirin, gets its name from the bark of the willow tree, *Salix alba,* which was prescribed for patients with headaches to chew centuries ago. Dr. Thomas Burks, head of the Department of Pharmacology at the University of Arizona, tells me that the Mexican yam, *Dioscorea,* is the principal source of birth control hormones. A chemical obtained from the wild rosy periwinkle is effective in the control of leukemia. The list is enormous.

Dr. Burks also tells me that a synergistic effect is often demonstrated with plant products. That is, a combination of chemical substances present in a raw plant product can often be more effective than a single chemical synthesized from or made to resemble one of the combination.

Generally speaking, *jamu* enthusiasts—commercial producers and users both—never make wild claims of instant cures. Their advice is to take the *jamu* over long periods of time. Then and only then will its effects, whatever they are, become noticeable. No miracles are claimed. It is obvious that the pharmacologically active ingredients in plants are often not present in large concentrations, or are present in such form that they cannot be readily absorbed into the body without some chemical modification. It is my impression that the *jamu* business, or most of it, is in a different class from the frantic TV hucksters that would have you believe that taking their magic can cause instant relief, loss of pounds overnight, and so on. That isn't the way *jamu* works, and nobody claims that it does.

What is my own personal attitude toward *jamu*? Well, of course, I am not a doctor. I have not the training or interest to spend the necessary years analyzing and testing and investigating. But my attitude has actually changed a great deal since I became interested in plants and plant products from one of skepticism to one of cautious belief. Less than one percent of the world's 250,000 species of flowering plants have been systematically studied. Considering the invaluable medicines that have already been found in this one percent, I am willing to believe that the other 99 percent may very well contain chemical substances that are equally or even more useful than those already known. In other words, I will not sell short the *jamu* phenomenon.

CHAPTER 26

Food and Spices

TRADITIONAL BALINESE CUISINE

MOST BALINESE EAT VERY SIMPLY at home. Rice is cooked early in the morning and left, covered, for anyone in the family to help himself when the spirit moves. The rice may be kept in an insulated container, but as often as not it is just left in a covered pot, so that it is probably cold when eaten. It is consumed, along with a few side dishes of vegetables, and perhaps a small morsel of chicken or fish, and a very spicy chili seasoning called *sambel,* which is made fresh daily. The other principal spice for cooked food has the confusing (to a Westerner) name of *kecap,* pronounced "ketchap." But *kecap* is what we call "soy sauce," not our familiar tomato sauce. It comes either sweet, *kecap manis,* or sour, *kecap asem.* Although there are hundreds of spices used in Balinese cooking, everyday food is often quite simple.

The Balinese eat very little meat in their everyday meals, deriving most of their protein from soybean products. *Tahu,* which we would call "tofu," is often fried and eaten with rice. Another soybean product called *tempe* is prepared by fermenting shelled soybeans. A special yeast is used which grows white tendrils throughout the soy beans, forming a kind of flat cake, which has a delicious, nutty flavor when fried. Nobody in Bali is far from the sea, and so fish is another source of protein. The favorite variety, or at least the cheapest, is dried or salted fish, if one lives away from the sea. And even those who live near the sea generally purchase and eat rather small fish, only 10 centimeters or so long, and eat them whole.

Never is protein served as a "main course." There isn't any main course. The meal is rice and side dishes. The rice is the "carrier." One mixes up a bit of the scanty side dishes with the plentiful rice, rolls the combination into a wad, and pushes it into his mouth, using various techniques. One is to pop the wad in with your right thumb. At any rate, it has to be the right hand. (The left hand, as elsewhere in Southeast Asia, is considered unclean.)

Mealtime for the Balinese is not a social event. They prefer to eat quickly, silently, alone if possible, and whenever they feel like it. The wife prepares the rice and side dishes in the early morning, and husband and children can eat whenever they wish. Usually hands are the only utensils, and likely as not a banana leaf is the biodegradable plate.

The Balinese are compulsive between-the-meal snackers, and the little village food stalls and traveling push carts find ready customers, from young to old, for their rice cakes, peanuts, brightly-colored iced syrups, noodles, soups, beans, and fruits. The jam of food carts at public events and at the beaches on weekends is a sight to behold.

The food the Balinese eat every day is not the kind of food that most foreigners would probably even want to taste, let alone eat for any length of time. It is usually filling, starchy, contains little protein, is often prepared under less than the sanitary standards that the visitor is accustomed to, is often eaten cold, and with the hands. And it is often very spicy.

A STANDARD SPICE MIXTURE is used in Bali in cooking a great many meat and vegetable dishes. Every housewife has a box of the ingredients around the kitchen. The Balinese call it *basa genep,* which means "complete spices." The most familiar ingredients in *basa genep* are *uyah,* a coarse sea salt, and pepper: black pepper (*mica selem*) and white pepper (*mica putih*). The pepper is sold as pepper corns, and both varieties are rather similar in appearance except that the black variety has wrinkled spheres. Both come from the same plant, *Piper nigrum,* the only difference being that white pepper, somewhat milder, comes from seeds that have had the outer hull removed.

Also included will be *tabia,* the general word for what are called chilis in English. These are *lalah,* "spicy hot." Chilis come in all shapes and sizes. Their degree of spiciness seems to vary according to their size—the largest chilis, *tabia gede,* are about as "spicy" as our bell peppers. Like all chilis, *tabia gede* are green before maturity, turning red when ripe. The Balinese don't use them much because they have little flavor. The Balinese do not like to eat the seeds of the *tabia* and carefully remove them before using them. The medium chilis, about 12 centimeters long, are often called *tabia Jawa,* and the small ones are called *tabia cenik.* The very smallest, *tabia kerinyi,* are by far the spiciest and must be used with caution. It is difficult for a foreigner to distinguish between a small *tabia cenik* and a true *tabia kerinyi,* but the Balinese have no problem. Typically a Balinese family will have a chili bush in its front yard, because they grow very easily and with little care.

Tabia for seasoning are mashed up and blended into *sambel* using a

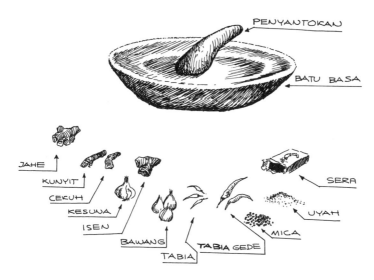

TYPICAL BALINESE SPICES

shallow round mortar made of black stone, called *batu basa,* and a peculiar stone pestle. The mortar, *cantok,* has the shape of a cone but bends at
right angles near the flat, grinding end, so that the operator holds the
handle parallel to the mortar and rolls the flat end back and forth over the
mixture to be made into a *sambel.* It is more of a mashing motion than a
grinding motion. *Tabia* are the standard ingredient in the many different
varieties of *sambel.* One favorite kind involves mixing thin slices of *tabia
kerinyi* with salty soy sauce.

Also in *basa genep* is *bawang barak,* literally "red onion," but more like
what we would call a shallot. This onion is small, with reddish-purple
skin. There is a strong onion odor, but the tears do not flow as copiously
as with our larger onion, some of which are now being raised for the
tourist trade in Bali. These are called *bawang* Bombay. *Bawang barak* are
widely grown in Bali, and the tops are sometimes sold separately as vegetables called *don bawang.*

Garlic (*kesuna*) in Bali comes in very small cloves. They do not differ
appreciably from those in the West, except they do not seem to be as
strong smelling. Their small size makes the Western fashion of garlic using
rather difficult. Instead of peeling and sectioning the garlic and onions,
most Balinese cooks just slice them, skin and all, before chopping or
mashing with mortar and pestle.

A very common and important spice is fermented shrimp paste, called
sera. It is sold at the markets in small, rectangular cakes. It has a very ripe
smell. It can be easily cut with a knife and is often mashed up with the
other spices in the mortar. It is never eaten raw, but always incorporated

into the fried spices that are used with vegetables, meat, and fish.

Basa genep includes four common rhizomes, only one of which is well-known in the West. Ginger, which the Balinese call *jae,* is familiar. Turmeric is known to Western cooks as a bright yellow powder. The Balinese call it *kunyit,* and it is always sold fresh. Turmeric is a large rhizome with bright orange-yellow flesh. *Kunyit* has a faintly sharp smell, and it stains anything it touches—a *kunyit* chopper is marked for days after the act.

Cekuh is another root, known occasionally in the West as lesser galangal. The skin is very thin, and the inside is white. *Cekuh* has a faint, spicy smell. Its leaves can also be used as a green vegetable. *Isen* is known elsewhere as *laos* or greater galangal. *Laos* powder is a standard spice in import shops in the United States. Unlike most other Balinese or Asian spices, it has a rather subtle taste. Inside, the spice is a dull white, and it is not as moist as the others. It has only a very faint odor.

Very important to add a sour taste to foods is *celagi* (also *lunak*), or tamarind. Tamarind trees are very common in the dryer sections of Bali. They are very tall, spreading trees with peculiar, irregularly shaped pods. Inside the pods is a mass of large flat seeds, imbedded in a stringy, gooey, black or brown mass of flesh. *Celagi* is sold as the entire interior of the seed pod packed in plastic. For use, it is soaked in water and the resulting solution is used for imparting the sour taste. The seeds and stringy parts must be removed.

Tingkih, or candlenuts, are also included in the *basa genep.* These are large nuts that, in the shell, look like overgrown pistachios. Most often they are sold without shells, and the meaty nuts look like they are made of yellow candle wax. The nut itself is quite soft and can be easily crumbled or cut with a knife. Candlenuts do not have a very distinctive taste, but the Balinese use them at every opportunity.

Gula, sugar, is always on the shopping list. Coffee or tea is simply not palatable to a Balinese unless it is about 50 percent sugar. Two kinds of sugar are available. Familiar white sugar is what the Balinese call *gula pasir*—*pasir* is Indonesian for "sand." Cheaper and more popular is *gula barak,* a dark brown palm sugar. *Gula barak* is sold in round cakes, and it has a richer taste than *gula pasir.* A syrup made of it is a popular topping for fruit and ice dishes and is an invariable accompaniment to certain types of *jaja,* or rice cakes.

Another important ingredient in *basa genep* is *ketumbah,* the familiar whole coriander seed. So is monosodium glutamate, MSG, which is sold in little packages, just big enough for the average pot full, in almost all *warungs.* Aji-No-Moto and Mi-Won are the most widely available brands. The Balinese call it *pitsin.*

Add to the above list the ever-present *lemo,* and you have *base genep.* *Lemo* is a very small green citrus. The Balinese use them in quantity for seasoning, putting the whole rind into some of their dishes. It is not generally intended to be eaten because the taste is quite strongly citrus-like. But, the unwary chewer can get a mouthful very easily and regret it.

THE MOST ELABORATE BALINESE dishes are prepared only on special occasions: weddings, tooth filings, and cremations, where many guests must be fed. And special food is usually prepared on important religious holidays, the most most important of which are Galungan, occurring once every 210 days, and the anniversary of the local temple.

The special meal that is most loved by the Balinese and least known to foreigners is called *ebat,* meaning "chopped up." The preparation of *ebat* is a truly Herculean task, often involving dozens of men, unlike the simple daily meals that are always cooked by women. Since there is no refrigeration, the food, especially meat, spoils quickly in the hot, humid climate. So, cooking usually begins shortly after midnight, is finished by dawn, and the food is eaten before noon.

Near the coast, where sea turtles, *penyu,* are readily available, their meat is the preferred choice for *ebat,* whereas, inland, pigs are usually used. Bali is a Hindu enclave in the middle of predominantly Muslim Indonesia, so no prohibitions against eating pork exist here. First an offering is made to the turtle, begging its pardon for what is about to happen. Then its throat is slit, the preferred method of killing animals in Bali. The blood is carefully saved and kept from coagulating with a little lime. In a huge, steaming cauldron the liver, intestines, stomach, lungs, and carti-

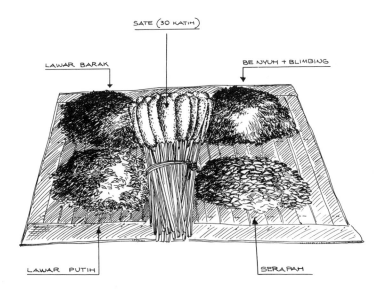

A TRAY OF EBAT

lage of the turtle are boiled. The meat is used raw, but first it must be "mebatted" and then pounded in a large mortar, like that used for pounding rice, until it is reduced to almost a paste.

But before the cooking, mountains of spices must be chopped up. This procedure, called *ngeracik basa*, generally starts about 6 or 7 P.M. the evening before the ebat is to be prepared. Several days before that representatives of the family must go to the market to buy the spices. And since the quantity involved is often considerable, those who live near Denpasar go to the huge Pasar Badung, where prices are lower than in the smaller village markets. The amounts are rather staggering. On one spice buying trip I attended, the shopping list was as follows, for 85 *karang*s (a large tray) of *ebat:*

QUANTITY	SPICE	COST
8 kg.	kesuna (garlic)	Rp 24,000
16 kg.	bawang barak (shallots)	6,400
5 kg.	cekuh (lesser galangal)	2,250
5 kg.	isen (galangal)	3,000
3 kg.	jae (ginger)	2,700
2 kg.	kunyit (turmeric)	200
7 kg.	tabia (chilis)	7,000
2 kg.	tingkih (candlenuts)	4,800
4 kg.	gula barak (dark sugar)	400
3 pkg.	mica selem (black pepper)	1,800
4 pkg.	sera (shrimp paste)	1,800
3 pkg.	ketumbah (coriander)	2,700
75 pkg.	basa wangen	4,500
	Total cost (1984)	Rp 64,550
	Total weight	52 kg.

Now, that is a lot of spice. Assuming that the 85 *karang*s could feed, say, 700 people, it figures to about 100 grams of spice per person. The women in the market generally give a couple of small bags of *basa genep* to the buyers as gifts, so that they will remain steady customers. There is usually a member of the family who knows his spices well, and he is the leader of the spice buying expedition.

Mounds of coconut must be grated by hand. Baskets and baskets of the *basa genep* spices have to be chopped—*mebat*. It may take 25 men just to chop spices, which are usually not peeled, although some of the loose, outer parts may be removed from onions and garlic. Five or six men grate the coconut, some grated fine to make coconut milk, some coarser to be used in one of the five dishes. Five or six men chop up the meat, and several more must be present to mix and tend the materials in the boiling pot. The chopping is done with heavy knives, almost cleavers. The Balinese called them *belakas*. The chopping blocks are sections of tree trunk. Generations of *mebat*-ing have caused the center to become depressed a bit, which keeps the ingredients from running over the edges. You can hear the preparations going on blocks away, as the steady rhythm of the rapid chopping shakes the stillness of the night.

Most of the grated coconut is then used to make coconut milk by mixing it with hot water and squeezing repeatedly. The coconut milk is then heated with turmeric until it just starts to thicken, producing what is called *kekalas*.

After four or more hours of chopping, grating, pounding, boiling, and grinding, the several dozen workers put their products in big baskets from which the chief cook takes great handfuls and assembles each of the five main dishes, mixing them with his hands. *Lawar* is any food that contains a substance cut into long, thin slivers, called *tataban,* and usually mixed with uncooked blood, making it red. Usually, some sort of meat is added for taste. With *lawar penyu,* turtle *lawar,* the *tataban* is cut from the boiled cartilage. Meat may not be used, in which case the *tataban* may come from melons of different sorts, unripe mango, or coconut. I have eaten a delicious *lawar* made from bee larvae, with its *tataban* made from unripe papayas.

The second dish of *ebat* is *jejeruk,* made from coarsely grated coconut mixed with *kekalas*. The third is *geguden,* made from the pounded turtle meat, *kekalas,* and the boiled leaves of the starfruit tree. Fourth is *serandu,* made from the pulp leftover from making the coconut milk, blood, meat, and spices. And the last of the five main dishes is *urab,* consisting of ground coconut, meat, and *kekalas*.

Usually side dishes are also prepared. The boiled viscera are skewered and grilled to produce *serapah*. *Komoh* is a soup made from spices and blood. Spiced boiled banana stem, *ares,* is a usual accompanying vegetable. And an almost invariable companion is a special *saté* called *saté lembat*. Most Asian *saté*s are made by skewering small pieces of meat on a sliver of bamboo and grilling them over charcoal. Balinese regularly eat this sort of *saté* too. But, *saté lembat* starts out as a thick paste, almost dough-like in consistency, made of pounded raw meat, grated coconut, coconut milk, and spices. Thick sticks of bamboo are prepared, diagonally cut on one end, flat on the other. A small chunk of the dough is scooped up and shaped onto the flat end of the bamboo stick, forming it into a pear shape, about the size of the end of one's thumb, tapering down to the diameter of the stick below. A piece of banana stem is cut, several of the sticks are thrust into it, hence their sharp ends, and the banana stem serves as a holder as the *saté lembat* is grilled over the charcoal until a golden brown.

When everything is finished, the family of each of the workers gets its share of the five main dishes and optional side dishes, which are placed on a tray of woven coconut leaf. (See illustration page 311.) This placement is not done at random. To the Balinese, food is a gift of God, and important directional and color symbolism always accompanies ceremonial foods. The number five represents the four cardinal directions land center, each, in turn, representing one aspect of God, each aspect with its symbolic color. Thus, the green *geguden,* representing Wisnu, is placed at the top of the tray, which is oriented toward the north; the red *lawar,* the color of Brahma, is placed at the bottom, south; the yellow *urab,* at the left, west, represents Mahadewa; the white *jejeruk* at the right, east, symbolizes Iswara; and the multicolored *serandu,* symbol of Siwa, is at the center. The food, always eaten cold, is exceedingly spicy. Even the Balinese break out into profuse sweat when eating it, and most Westerners cannot handle it.

If the *ebat* is prepared for a ceremony that celebrates some sort of rite of passage, the ingredients are carefully parceled out, arranged on coconut leaf trays, and each section of the extended family has its portion carried to his own house compound by one of the workers. By now all the workers are exhausted, it being well after dawn, and they have worked most of the time since midnight. There is some temptation nowadays just to buy the *ebat,* as there are several factories in the Denpasar area that make it on a regular basis.

ON PAR WITH *EBAT* as Bali's most popular dish is pig roasted on a spit. The Balinese call it *be guling,* or just *guling,* meaning "turned," in the sense of a rotisserie. Tourists are told that the word is *babi guling* and that it means roast suckling pig. But, *babi* is an Indonesian, not a Balinese word, and the pigs are invariably long past the suckling stage. *Guling* can be prepared on a less grandiose scale than *ebat.* Commercial kitchens turn out quantities of *guling* in the larger cities for sale in street food stalls and night markets. Sometimes a family will make *guling* at home just for the pleasure of it.

The pigs vary from 3 to 6 months old and weigh from 4 to 6 kilograms. After they are slaughtered by cutting their throats, they are dehaired in boiling water and the viscera are cleaned out. Then the body of the pig is rubbed with turmeric to make the final color a deep golden brown, and the abdominal cavity is stuffed with more or less the same *basa genep* that is used with *ebat,* and then sewed shut. A long wooden pole is thrust through the pig, and it is turned by hand over burning coconut husks and wood for two to three hours, depending upon the size of the pig. Someone has to fan the flames with a long paddle-like object, so it takes at least two people to cook the meat.

Balinese pigs are a breed unto themselves, with enormous protruding pot bellies that literally drag along the ground, like a drooping sack slung between two poles. As a result, the *guling* is extremely fatty, generally too much so for Western tastes. But the Balinese love it, and they consider the golden brown, crispy skin the best part.

There is a famous *be guling* food stall in Gianyar village, northeast of Denpasar. Here a constant stream of Balinese taxi and truck drivers, farmers, children and locals consume 6 or 7 big pigs by the individual plate every day. The standard plate costs about Rp 600 and is heaped with *guling*, pig *lawar,* rice, boiled jackfruit, cooked blood, and sausage made from pig intestines. The nearby kitchen is operated by a single family. The group of around 15 or 20 workers starts work at 3:00 A.M. for the benefit of those who go to market early. The food is delicious.

ANOTHER POPULAR BALINESE DISH for special occasions is called *betutu bebek,* duck stuffed with spices and vegetables, wrapped in banana leaf, and cooked in hot ashes or a rice steamer for three or four hours. This is probably the only one of the three special Balinese dishes that can come close to pleasing the uninitiated palate, and it is surely the only one that can be cooked in modest proportions.

Some of my own favorites cannot be called strictly Balinese, because they are found in other areas of Indonesia as well. One is *be tambus.* You will note the recurring use of the word *be,* which can mean in Balinese any sort of meat or fish or even such things as soybean foods, depending upon the circumstances. It must always be used with some adjective that indicates what kind of protein food is being referred to. *Be tambus* is often made from fish by mixing it with grated coconut and spices, wrapping it in a banana leaf and grilling it on embers or a piece of hot metal.

Another favorite is *tum,* ground beef or pieces of fish wrapped in a banana leaf, skewered with a bit of bamboo to hold the leaf tight, and steamed in a rice cooker. Some *basa genep* must be added before the ingredients are wrapped up.

A great favorite of the Balinese is *rujak.* This is always made with some sort of unripe fruit that is not full of tannin. Tannin produces the astringent, puckery feeling in the mouth, such as when you eat an unripe banana or persimmon. Many tropical fruits do not contain tannin, but are merely sourish before they ripen. *Rujak* is a kind of "sweet and sour" fruit. It is made with slices of the fruit—mango or papaya are favorites—*sera,* sugar, tamarind, chili, and salt. Pregnant women seem to crave *rujak.* It is quite good. If you add meat to *rujak,* plus some other spices, you have a dish called *cinggur,* a favorite in Java. If you add the water in which you have boiled some salted fish you have Javanese *petis.*

THE BALINESE FOOD WITH THE GREATEST VARIETY are rice cakes, *jaja.* I have photographs and recipes for 67 distinctive types of *jaja,* with every shape and color imaginable, and I'm sure my collection is quite incomplete. There are two general varieties—those that are made for everyday consumption, and those that are used first as religious offerings and then eaten afterwards. The latter are generally brightly colored with commercial food colorings and may be intricately designed. The former taste better, but they are not much to look at. The standard Balinese breakfast may consist only of coffee and *jaja*. The cakes are made very early in the morning and are available in the village food stalls by dawn, still warm. *Jaja* are the usual snacks that the Balinese love to nibble on all day long and are available in every food stand in every village, large or small. They don't keep overnight, so they're always fresh.

Most *jaja* are made with a dough of rice flour mixed with water, then steamed, baked, or fried. They are usually eaten with palm sugar. Either sticky, glutinous rice or ordinary rice may be used, depending upon the recipe. If steamed, the *jaja* are generally wrapped individually in pieces of banana leaf to keep them from sticking together. Many *jaja* are served covered with grated coconut and palm sugar syrup. They are always eaten with the fingers, served on a bit of banana leaf. My favorite is *kelepon*. It looks like a green olive because the dough is colored with the juice of a green leaf. Inside, in place of the pit or pimento, is a dab of palm sugar that may be so juicy that it squirts out if you bite unwarily. A close second on my list is *jaja laklak,* round cakes baked on top of the stove in a clay container that has individual holes formed into its top and a little cover for each hole. *Jaja lapis* features layers of different colors. *Bulung* is a brown, jelly-like cake made from dried seaweed containing agar-agar. Some *jaja* contain beans. Some are made with manioc, some with pumpkin. Another one of my favorites is *sumping,* sweetened rice dough steamed in a banana leaf, with a little slice of banana inside the dough.

THE *JAJA* FOR SPECIAL CEREMONIAL OFFERINGS are not always available except in the biggest markets where they are sold in special stalls, spilling over a cascading rainbow of colors. Many of these cakes are made with glutinous rice grains stuck together and molded into various shapes, rather than from rice flour. They are used as offerings in an integral part of the Balinese-Hindu religion.

Food offerings take various shapes. In their simplest form they may be merely small baskets of fruit or *jaja,* with flowers, and always with the three ingredients of the betel chew, betel pepper leaf, *areca* nut, and lime—the symbols of the Hindu Trisakti: Brahma, Wisnu, and Siwa. At the other extreme, food offerings may take the form of gigantic towers of fruits, meats, eggs, and cakes, all skewered with bamboo sticks onto a central stem of a banana plant. In some situations and in some villages these high offerings, *banten tegeh,* may be two or more meters high. They are usually made at home and carried on the heads of the women who made them to the temple, to be blessed by the *pemangku* in charge, offered to

God and his manifestations as deified ancestors, and left there for a brief period in order that the deities accept them as thanks from those who made them.

Once the temple priest has blessed the offerings and sprinkled them with holy water the people pray, and then the offerings are carried home and eaten. Priests and some *pemangkus* do not eat offerings. But the average Balinese does so with relish.

The Balinese save their most beautiful, delicate, and decorative cakes for these high offerings. *Jaja uli* is a favorite. It is made with steamed glutinous rice dough and palm sugar, usually wrapped in a cylindrical bundle in coconut leaves. When it is finished, the cook cuts off slices with a thread of bamboo. The round slices may be folded over, dried in the sun, decorated with other kinds of cookies, or just used as is. Sometimes the cylinders are not cut at all, but just incorporated into the tall offering. *Jaja gipang* is often seen on high offerings. This is one of the types that is made by shaping sticky rice grains together without making flour out of them. The grains are usually colored and are often shaped into something that looks for all the world like round ash-trays. *Jaja gegodoh biu* are often used. These are the familiar fried bananas, dipped in a batter of rice flour before frying in coconut oil. *Gerinda* is an interesting *jaja* that is very decorative. A flat cake of rice dough, usually colored, is rolled out, cut into a square, and three diagonal cuts are made part way through the square. The square is then folded, the cut parts sticking out like ribs, and then fried until hard so that it maintains its shape. *Jaja matanai* means "sun cake," and it is a round, red, fried cake, decorated and cut to look like the sun. *Sirat* is a very lacy cake, looking for all the world like a tangled string. *Bantal* is a long, thin cake that is wrapped with a spiral of coconut leaf. Still another, *jaja apem,* is very similar to a cupcake.

On very special occasions, cookies are made of colored rice dough into symbolic religious scenes, and these are fried and attached to huge rattan or bamboo frames, making symbolic representations of the Balinese universe, showing the earth borne on the back of the world-turtle, all done with cookies. These *sarad* are never eaten, because the huge creation usually remains within the temple for many days.

RELIGION ALSO ENTERS into the preparation of everyday food. After food is cooked, even if it is only steamed rice, a tray of little offerings is made, each with a speck of the recently cooked food on a leaf, and these are taken to the various house shrines and presented to God before the family eats. These are called *banten jotan.* Small offerings of food are always put on the ground to placate the demonic forces that live there. Before a Balinese will drink his rice wine or brandy, or sometimes even his tea or coffee, he spills a little on the ground as an offering.

Three Pillars

BAMBOO, BANANAS, AND COCONUTS

IT WOULD ALMOST BE POSSIBLE for a civilization to subsist on just four plants: bamboo, bananas, coconuts, and rice. Indeed, the Balinese, in common with most Southeast Asians, make remarkably thorough use of all these resources.

Bamboo is eaten as a vegetable and is a versatile building material for houses, plumbing, furniture, storage boxes, drinking cups, and musical instruments. The banana plant, in addition to producing a nutritious fruit, provides leaves and a thick, spongy stem that have countless practical and ceremonial uses. The coconut produces a quenching drink, oil, strong wood, fiber for ropes and string, and leaves which are woven into everything from floor mats to offering baskets.

BAMBOOS ARE GIANT TREE GRASSES, members of *Bambusoideae*, the most primitive family of the grasses. One tends to think of the bamboos as tropical plants, but they grow at latitudes as high as 45°N and 45°S, and at altitudes up to 4,000 meters, where they are covered by snow at least part of the year. There are 60 genera of bamboos and perhaps as many as 1,500 species. Although native to Asia, they are found on every continent, either as native or introduced species.

Although there is great variety, it is not difficult to discuss the many characteristics that bamboos have in common. The part that one sees, the "stem," is more properly called a culm. New culms emerge from underground rhizomes and emerge looking for all the world like giant asparagus tips. The new shoot grows very rapidly, often as much as one meter per day, and reaches full height in just a few weeks. In true equatorial climates, shoots emerge all year round. But in regions with a pronounced dry season, like Bali, new shoots emerge only when the wet season is at hand. *Embung* is the Balinese word for bamboo shoot.

In tropical countries the young shoots are cut and used as a vegetable. Many are cooked, canned, and shipped to areas where there are no bamboos. One factory in Taiwan currently cans 150 tons of shoots daily. Young shoots of some bamboo species contain lethal amounts of cyanogens and may be toxic to cattle. But humans always cook them before eating, which destroys these substances. One bamboo clump can produce about 40 shoots per year, each of which may weigh 3 or 4 kilograms.

Bamboo culms are usually, but not always, hollow. Transverse walls, at the nodes, separate the culm into segments. Much of the usefulness of the plant stems from this hollow, cylindrical form. A hollow cylinder that is flexible is an ideal structural member. It resists crushing because of its circular cross section. It will bend because the long fibers run parallel to the culms, but these fibers are so strong that the culm breaks only under extreme stress. Although the fibers have great tensile strength,they are held together only rather loosely. This makes it easy to split the wood, producing regular strips, slices, or even individual fibers that can be twisted into very strong string or twine. The strips can be used for grilling meat (*sate* sticks), or for supporting plants, for clothes pins (by cutting a stick longitudinally, almost in half), or even toothpicks. Long, flat slices are woven into baskets, mats, and even whole walls. The nodal divisions can be knocked out with a rod or removed with a knife from the outside, producing a length of pipe. It is not uncommon to see bamboo water pipes several kilometers long.

The Balinese word for bamboo is *tiing*. Thin bamboo strips made from the variety that the Balinese call *tiing tali* are the common ties for almost every purpose (*tali* is Balinese for "string," or "thread"). *Tiing tali* holds lids on baskets, lashes scaffolding together, holds decorations on to their supports, and serves to fasten myriad other devices. It looks easy to tie something up with *tiing tali,* but it takes a bit of practice. The strip of bamboo is placed around the object to be tied and twisted in a practiced way. There is no knot. *Tiing tali* is also made into a true thread or rope by separating individual fibers and twisting them together. This produces an extremely strong rope used for everything from fishing lines to kite strings. Dried *tiing tali* is also used as a kind of skewer to fasten together the plaited coconut leaves that are made almost daily for offerings, large and small. The person who is making the offerings places the layers together that she wants fastened, slips a thin stick of bamboo into and out of the layers like a single stitch, and then breaks off the bamboo.

The mechanical properties of a somewhat flexible, hollow cylinder are ideal for construction. The usual scaffold of a new building or a building under repair in Asia is made entirely of bamboo culms laced together with bamboo twine or strips. These structures may be enormous—dozens of

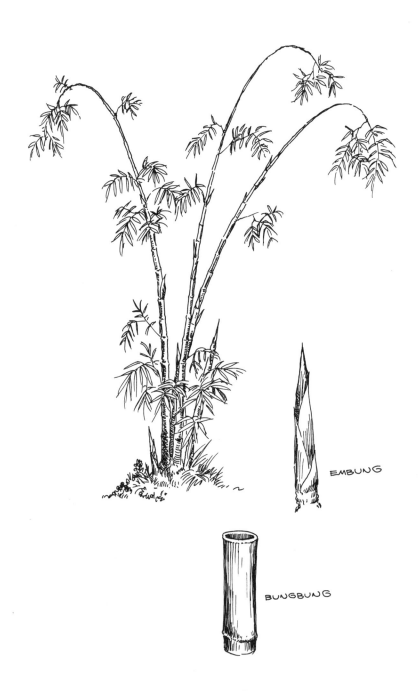

EMBUNG

BUNGBUNG

BAMBOO

stories high and hundreds of meters long, as in the large apartment build-ing projects in Hong Kong and Singapore. For the same mechanical rea-sons, bamboo culms make perfect fishing poles, either natural or laminated. Research has also indicated that culms make quite satisfactory replacements for steel reinforcing rod in concrete.

Bamboo makes a durable and waterproof roofing material. One method of construction involves splitting bamboo culms in half. A row of half cylinders is laid down, concave side up to form the base. On top of this comes a row concave side down, the cut edges resting in the troughs of the first layer. Many alternating layers are thus built up, assuring a waterproof and long lasting construction. You don't see many bamboo roofs in the lowlands, because the heat of the sun cracks bamboo quickly. But there are lots of them in the highland villages.

Bamboo furniture is a very popular item in Bali, as it is elsewhere in Asia. The village of Bona, near Blahbatuh, specializes in the manufacture of all manner of chairs, tables, and containers of various sorts. The spotted bamboo, *tiing tutul,* is the most popular variety used, but, lately, there has been a drift toward using a so-called black, actually more or less chocolate colored, bamboo imported from Java. I have a list of 15 differ-ent Balinese bamboos, each with its specific uses and functions. Tiny *tiing buluh* makes fishing poles. Strong *tiing ampel* is the material of choice for scaffolding and for *saté* sticks. One of my favorites is *tiing gading,* the culms of which are bright yellow.

A short length of culm from a large diameter bamboo is often made into an interesting crab trap. The material forms a stout cylinder with one open end which is slotted and fitted with a trap door. The door is held open by a string that is attached to a trigger inside the culm near the closed end. The trap is baited with coconut meat and placed over a crab hole in the sand. When the crab crawls into the trap and grabs at the bait, the trigger is tripped, and the trap door slams shut and prevents escape.

The bamboo box is the standard all-purpose container of Asia. Boxes, mats, woven walls, screens, fans, and hats are all made from flat strips of bamboo about one centimeter wide that are peeled from culms with a knife. An experienced weaver can produce a sturdy box in only an hour or two. Whole villages in Bali specialize in such cottage industry, taking their raw material from outside their front doors and their finished products to markets far from home. In Bali the square bamboo boxes without lids are called *sok,* which is really a name for any open basket that is woven. If it has a top it is called *keben.* They come in all sizes up to almost a meter square and are surprisingly cheap, considering their durability. There are different qualities, so, if you are tempted, be sure to get a sturdy *alus,* "fine quality" one. The standard Balinese *pengukusan,* a rice steamer, is a loosely woven cone of these same flat bamboo strips. The apex of the cone is a bit more loosely woven than the sides, and it just fits down into the hourglass-shaped metal or clay water boiler.

Of course, bamboo makes an ideal ladder, since it is both light and strong. And culms of the larger bamboos, such as *tiing petung,* are used as outriggers for the small boats that dot Balinese beaches, both for tourists' pleasure and for fishing. Boatmen are generally careful to shade the bamboo or remove it to the shade after use because direct sunlight will quickly crack bamboo. Incidentally, bamboo just does not hold up in a dry climate. I live half the year in Arizona, where it is not unusual to have the humidity less than 10 percent. Every single bamboo article that I have brought home from Bali has cracked within days of arrival, even though I was careful to paint them with several coats of varnish.

Bamboo is made into a wide variety of musical instruments. The hollow culm requires only a few finger holes and a mouthpiece to produce an excellent flute. In Java and Bali, lengths of culm are used as resonators below the bronze keys of xylophone-like instruments called *gangsa*s. The resonators must be adjusted precisely in length and diameter so that they will reinforce only the desired note and make it "sing." A popular instrument that makes up whole orchestras in Bali is the *tingklik.* This is also like a xylophone, except that the keys are themselves made of bamboo and have no resonators. The sound is a mellow, liquid, hollow one, in contrast to the harsh, bright notes of the metallophones. A length of bamboo representing one node and an internode, open at one end, is called *bungbung* in Balinese. Thus the *tingklik* is made of *bungbung*s, and the dance that it is commonly used to accompany, a kind of social flirtation dance, is called *joged bungbung.*

Bamboo makes a sounder to scare birds away from the rice fields. This device sometimes takes the form of a one- or two-meter piece of culm that is cut lengthwise almost in half. Some of the culm walls are cut away, leaving a handle by which the device is shaken. The two halves bang together, producing a great hollow noise. The Balinese language is full of onomatopoeic words, and this is a good example. They say that the sound it makes is *"puak, puak, puak,"* so the bird scarer is called a *kekepuakan.* Alternatively, the bird scarers may be wind operated via an ingenious mechanism whereby a sort of sail attached to a string pulls the two halves of the bamboo apart, the device being suspended on a long pole. The springy bamboo then claps back together. Still another variation makes use of a small windmill (made of guess what). Attached to the shaft is a hammer that bangs the culm as the blades revolve. Some of these are made with multiple hammers that strike tuned sections of culm as they revolve, producing a nice but rather monotonous melody. They are called *pindakan* in Bali.

In Bali every important religious celebration requires each family to erect a tall bamboo pole, *penjor,* on the street outside his home and and attach decorations to it. *Penjors* have two functions, as do most Balinese offerings. One is to beautify the area when the deified family ancestors are invited to descend to the family or village temples. The second function is as an offering to the gods. *Penjors* symbolize the rivers that bring the life-giving water to the Balinese. The arch of the *penjor* is the peak of the mountain. The graceful tail that hangs over the street is the tail of one of the sacred dragons that provides man with his material needs. Along the pole are the fruits of the fields through which the rivers wind on their way to the sea. The bottom of the *penjor* is the head of the dragon. And here one always finds a temporary shrine in which offerings are placed as long as the *penjor* remains standing.

An integral part of many exorcism ceremonies in Bali requires bamboo firecrackers. The Balinese call this arrangement, onomatopoeically, *keke-plugan*. Three sections of green bamboo are cut so that each piece has a culm node at each end. They are sealed tubes. The three are tied together, and a fire is built underneath. There is sufficient moisture inside so that, when heated, the tubes explode quite satisfactorily and safely, the long fibers preventing pieces from shattering and flying all over the place.

THE BANANA IS ONE OF THE WORLD'S MOST IMPORTANT FRUITS. The annual world commercial production is about 8 million tons, worth about U.S. $2 billion. But with the exception of The Philippines, there are no huge banana plantations in most Asian countries. Problems of transportation and distance from markets in the non-industrialized world prohibit operations on such a scale. But there are plenty of bananas raised for local use. These are often called in the trade "backyard" bananas, implying that they are grown on a small scale for local consumption, or possibly for occasional sale in nearby markets.

There is an incredible variety. At least 100 kinds of bananas are known, but there is considerable confusion because different names are usually used for the same variety in different places. Botanists assign the banana to a genus, *Musa*, but do not bother listing any species. The many varieties are simply called cultivars. The name "banana," of limited use worldwide, is of East African origin. There are about as many names for the plant as there are areas where it grows. The Balinese call the banana *biu*, or *biyu*, but that won't get you too far because there are so many kinds of *biu* that you will immediately be asked which one you want.

The fruit of the banana plant is a berry, botanically speaking, and the plant is properly called an herb, not a tree. The fibrous "trunk" is properly named the "false stem," or "pseudostem." The Balinese call it *gedebong*. This *gedebong* is made up of successive layers of leaf bases. A plant generally has about 10–20 mature leaves, each of which may be up to three meters in length. Under favorable conditions, leaves emerge at the rate of one every week or two.

Bananas are propagated by planting sections of rhizome. About 7 to 9 months after the rhizome is planted the flowering process begins. At this point, no more ordinary leaves are produced. Instead, there grows upward from the rhizome in the center of the pseudostem the stalk, sometimes called the stem or shoot, which will bear at its end the flowers, and eventually, the bunched fruit. The shoot emerges at the crown of the plant, carrying the last leaves with it, remains briefly erect, and then usually bends over because of its rapidly increasing weight..

At the tip of the inflorescence is a very large maroon bud, called *pusuh biu*, "banana navel" by the Balinese. As the inflorescence develops one of the bracts lifts up, revealing a double row of 12–20 female flowers with short-lasting yellowish-white petals. The bract soon drops to the ground and the female flowers swell into the familiar fruit. Bananas, unlike many plants, will produce fruit even if the flowers are unpollinated. Thus very rarely does one find seeds in a banana. If they are present, they are small and stone-like and represent a considerable hazard to the unwary biter. There is a variety in Bali called *biu batu*, ("stone banana") that is full of seeds—a favorite joke in Bali is to give a foreign friend a *biu batu* to chomp on. It is difficult to tell the difference on the outside, and the shock is considerable, after years of seedless bananas.

After the bunch of fruit forms, the *pusuh biu* is often cut off and eaten as a vegetable. Cutting off of the bud while the fruit are maturing is thought to produce a more vigorous bunch. When the fruit has been produced, the entire plant dies—except for the rhizome. If left alone, the rhizome produces many suckers that grow up from the ground into a dense clump. Most of these are cut away and only the hardier ones allowed to grow. After the oldest plant has produced fruit and dies, one of these suckers is allowed to grow to maturity. A single rhizome can produce many generations of bananas.

The uses of backyard bananas in Bali are almost too numerous to mention. There are red ones, called *biu udang*, meaning "shrimp bananas." There are delicious tiny ones, no longer than the length of your finger, called milk bananas, *biu susu. Biu kate* plants are dwarfs, but the fruit is normal size. *Biu gadang* are still quite green when ripe and ready to eat. *Biu mas* are of a deep golden color. *Biu raja* comes about as close as any to resembling the bananas of commerce that we get in the United States.

Bananas are similar to potatoes in nutritional value. They contain about 70 percent water, 20 percent carbohydrate (sugar in sweet bananas and starch in plantains), and are rich in vitamin C.

Bananas can be dried and pounded into flour. This may be sweet or starchy, depending upon the original banana, and may be substituted for all the uses of rice flour. A favorite way to eat bananas all over Asia is fried—*gogodoh biu*, they are called in Bali. Pieces of the peeled banana are dipped into a batter made of rice flour and water, and are fried in coconut oil until golden brown. Starchy bananas are usually steamed, boiled,

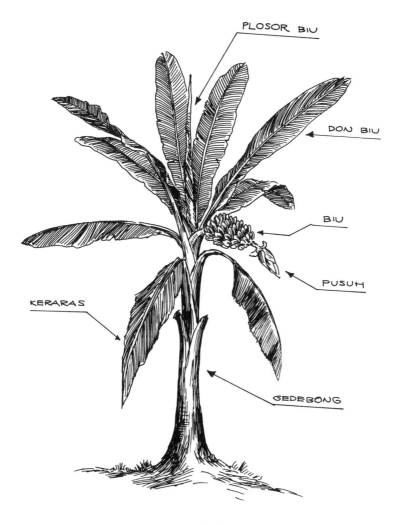

BANANA

roasted, or baked until the starch is more palatable.

Bananas are sliced into chips and dried in the sun, in which form they will keep for a long time. Or, if the bananas are brown and over-ripe when sliced, the dried form is soft, sweet, and sugary and is sometimes called banana fig.

Boiled banana stem with spices, called *ares,* is served as a vegetable. Standard pig food in Bali is sliced up banana pseudostem mixed with water and rice bran. The starchy stem fattens the animals quickly.

The banana leaf is the original disposable, biodegradable, plate and wrapper of Bali and all of Asia. *Saté* is sold on banana leaf plates. Food stalls sell their snacks wrapped in them. All sorts of rice cakes are steamed in them. The leaves are also used to mold rice cakes into conical and cylindrical forms by pushing the soft paste of the rice dough into the shaped leaf and peeling it off when the mold is full. Most food bought at the market, if it is wrapped at all, is wrapped in banana leaves, and each stall has a stack of squares, just as a Western market would have a roll of plastic bags. Food is almost always eaten with the fingers, so that when the meal is over, there is nothing to wash. I once went to a very fancy banquet held in the spacious home of an Indonesian friend in a large city. The catered meal for 50 was served on banana leaves—on the floor.

In Bali bananas are frequently used in offerings. Four days before Galungan, the most important Balinese religious holiday, a special day, Penyekaban, is set aside for the ripening of green bananas so that they will be ready for the many required offerings. Unripe bananas and green leaves are placed inside a tall clay jar, and the lid is sealed with mud. A coconut husk fire is kept burning on top of the lid. Three days later the jar is opened, and the ripe bananas are ready for the pleasure of the visiting spirits. After the bananas have been offered the makers of the offerings eat them.

Cremation is a very important final rite of passage for every Balinese, for it is only in this way that the spirit may be released from its body to join the family's deified ancestors. At Balinese cremations, the body is usually placed inside of an animal effigy made of wood, and the fire is built under this effigy. The fire is prevented from spreading by a rectangle of low walls built of banana pseudostems. These *gedebong* contain a high percentage of water and are efficient at containing the intense heat.

At Balinese cremations a flowering banana plant is cut and tied to a temporary shrine, the *sanggah ragung,* in which offerings are placed. The banana flower is a symbol of Surya, the manifestation of God as the sun.

In Bali the *gedebong* also serve as the central support for the high offerings that are such an important part of every temple festival. A one- or two-meter section of *gedebong* is thrust onto a long iron rod affixed to a special offering plate, shaped to be carried on a woman's head. The offerings consist of colored rice cakes and cookies, fruits, whole ducks, parts of roast pigs, and sweets. They are impaled upon bamboo skewers, which, in turn, are thrust into the upright pseudostem, covering it completely and transforming it into a tower of colors and smells. The offering, called a *banten tegeh,* is carried on a woman's head to the temple.

One of the most popular forms of night entertainment in Bali and Java is the *wayang kulit* shadow puppet play. Leather puppets are displayed behind a translucent screen, illuminated by an oil lamp. The puppet master, or *dalang,* acts out with his puppets the enormously popular stories of the ancient Hindu epics, the *Ramayana* and the *Mahabharata*. There are dozens of characters, and only a few can be displayed at once. The ones not being used are held on each side of the screen by thrusting their supporting handles into a long section of banana pseudostem.

Logs of banana pseudostem are sometimes used by rice farmers to smooth their irrigated rice fields before the rice is planted. A section of *gedebong* is impaled on the tines of the rake that is used to break up clods of dirt, and the log is dragged up and down the flooded *sawah* as one might use a push broom.

Banana pseudostem makes a clever candle chimney. Recall that the pseudostem is just a cylinder consisting of concentric layers of cylindrical leaf bases. A section of the desired length is cut from the pseudostem, and one of the outer layers of leaf base is peeled off, much like a layer of onion. Its corrugated inner surface is scraped smooth, producing a translucent membrane with a lacy texture. A piece measuring about 15 by 50 centimeters is cut off and wrapped into the form of a cylinder, held in place by a bamboo skewer. When placed over a candle it keeps the wind from blowing out the flame and forms a screen upon which the flickering flame plays.

PROBABLY A NATIVE OF SOUTHEAST ASIA, the coconut tree has been spread throughout the tropics by man as well as by natural causes. The nut, actually one of the world's biggest seeds, floats readily, and it can maintain its viability for several months in the sea before being washed up above high tide, and taking root nearby in its preferred habitat, the sandy lowland environment of the areas near the shore. Sometimes these floating seeds ferry other small plant and animal life as they drift, and are thought to have been responsible for the spread of some species, even between hemispheres.

There are about 300 named varieties of coconut, but botanists classify all of them in a single species, *Cocos nucifera,* the most important of all the many palms of the world. The word "coconut" comes from the Spanish and Portuguese who penetrated to Southeast Asia in the 16th century. They took the name from the Spanish verb *cocar,* meaning "to grimace or make a wry face." The grimace is provided by the three "eyes" on the end of the coconut's shell. Most tropical cultures have their own, very different, words for the plant and its fruit.

The generic Balinese name for coconut is *nyuh.* But my Balinese dictionary lists twelve different varieties of *nyuh,* based upon the color of the nut and the size of the tree. *Bungsil* is very young coconut. *Bungkak* is older, but still not ready to eat. *Kuwud* is a young mature coconut, the best age for drinking the water and eating the soft meat. *Nyuh* is a fully mature coconut, the stage at which the nut is used to make coconut milk, coconut oil, and copra.

Coconut palms grow best near the sea, but they can survive, although producing fewer nuts, at altitudes up to about 600 meters. The trees are

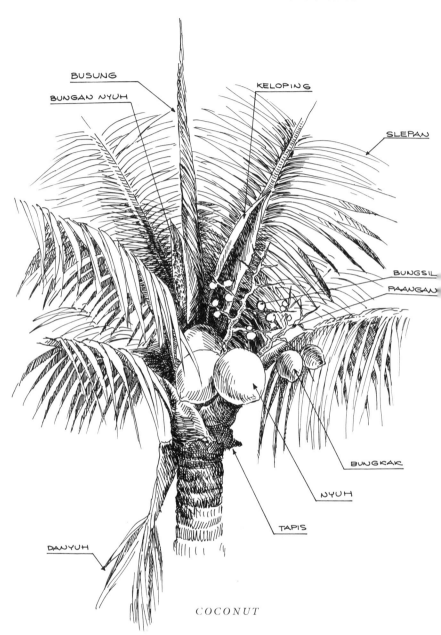

BUSUNG

BUNGAN NYUH

KELOPING

SLEPAN

BUNGSIL

PAANGAN

BUNGKAK

NYUH

TAPIS

DANYUH

COCONUT

propagated from the mature nut, preferably cut from the tree. The nuts are in nursery beds close together and covered with damp soil. Within 90 to 125 days roots break through the husk. A sprout appears, called *entik nyuh,* or *pujer.* Within 6 to to 10 months the seedlings are big enough to transplant to open areas where they are spaced farther apart. A coconut tree can be expected to produce profitably for about 50 years.

If coconut trees are located near homes, as many are, the owners are careful to cut the older nuts on a regular basis. A heavy coconut falling from the top of a 30-meter (100 ft.) tree can cause lots of damage to life and property. In fact, in Bali, there are teams of nut cutters who go around to trim the trees near homes and hotels, keeping a percentage of the nuts cut as their pay.

Coconut flowers do not have showy petals. In fact, they are rather inconspicuous, being wind-pollinated, and, in most species, appear so high up that you can't see them anyway. Before opening the flowers are protected by a woody spathe (*keloping*). When dry, the *keloping* makes excellent firewood. Young boys are assigned to climb the trees to collect them. If not cut after they open, they fall to the ground and are eagerly collected. Flowering commences when a tree is about five years old and continues throughout the life of the tree. Fruits require about one year to ripen, but production is more or less continuous, since there are many nuts, and they ripen at different times. About 50 mature nuts per year is considered to be good production, but as many as 100 can be produced.

FEW NATIVES OF THE TROPICS eat the meat of the mature nut. It is considered inferior to the much softer, pulpy coating that lines the cavity of the young nut (*kuwud*). The young nut also contains more and sweeter watery liquid than the old nut. This liquid is correctly called coconut water, not coconut milk. For a cool drink and snack, one need only find a *kuwud*, and cut it with a few strokes of one's *arit*, a sickle-shaped knife. You can tell if the nut is *kuwud* from the color of the husk. If it is green, it is probably good; if it is yellow it is too old. The husk, *sambuk,*of a young coconut is not nearly as fibrous and tough as that of a mature nut. A few cuts with the *arit* makes a flat place in the husk so that the nut can be set down without rolling. The husk is sliced away revealing the rather soft shell, almost full of delicious coconut water—*yeh kuwud*. The water is drunk straight from the shell by cutting a thin slice of husk and inserting it like the mouth of a pitcher into the hole in the coconut. Once the liquid is drunk, the hole is enlarged and the creamy pulp is scraped out and eaten with another, larger slice of husk, used like a spoon.

Such young coconuts are sold all along the major highways of Indonesia, a welcome and inexpensive thirst quencher for the traveler. Some people climb the trees to get the nuts, but if the tree is not too tall, a knife tied to a length of bamboo makes the chore easier. When a tree is climbed regularly, notches or steps are often cut into the trunk. Sometimes the climber ties his ankles together to keep his feet from slipping apart. One hazard invariably encountered are the red ants, *samangah,* that live in the trees and attack anyone that invades their home.

Coconut water is sterile and contains about 5 percent sugar, with a food value of up to 240 calories per liter. Thus it occurred to an American surgeon (who happens to be my brother, Dr. Ben Eiseman) that coconut water would make an ideal intravenous solution for use with patients in areas where sterile solutions for intravenous feeding are impossible to obtain. A series of experiments performed in the 1950s indicated that the method worked quite well and that no untoward effects were observed.

De-husking a mature coconut is a standard chore around the Balinese home. To do it, the coconut is impaled on a long steel stake called a *pangesan* or *linggis* that has been embedded in the ground. If it is done skillfully, the fiber can be separated from the nut with a neat twisting motion in just a minute or two. The husk fiber, called *sambuk*, is always saved. It makes an effective, if smoky, fuel. Its fibrous nature makes it a pretty fair abrasive dish cleaner, or brush, called *sepet*. In industry,the fiber is used to produce a commercial product called *coir*, from which a great variety of brushes, brooms, mats, and ropes are made.

Once the fibrous husk is removed, the hard shell, *kau*, of the nut is whacked with something hard to split it open. The water of the mature nuts is generally wasted, being inferior to that of the *kuwud*. The split nuts may then be allowed to dry for some days in the sun, or the meat may be pried out to use for cooking. The meat adheres quite firmly to the shell, and, for this purpose, a steel tool called a *penyeluhan* is used, a kind of miniature tire iron. The meat can be loosened by heating the coconut gently in a fire, but a skilled person doesn't require this step.

If the meat is to be made into coconut milk, it is grated and then squeezed with warm water, producing a creamy white liquid used in cooking many tropical dishes. The Balinese call it *santen*. If the familiar grocery store "shredded coconut" Westerners use in cooking desserts is to be made, either the meat, or just the opened nut is dried in the sun. The shell is never thrown away because it makes an excellent charcoal, *adeng kau*, that is preferred for grilling *saté*. Cut in half, the shell also makes a useful dipper, bowl, or measuring cup.

Local people make their own coconut oil by boiling coconut milk, and ladling off the oil that rises to the top. But a large international trade has developed in copra, dried coconut meat, and the oil derived from it. In the middle 19th century, northern Europe was faced with a shortage of dairy fats. Experiments showed that the oil obtained from copra made a perfect substitute for such fats. So began the great coconut oil industry. The oil is obtained by either solvent extraction or by pressure. The residue cake makes a good animal feed. Coconut oil is a white material that melts at about 23° Celsius (73°F). Thus, in the temperate zone, except in the summer, it is often a soft solid. From it and its derivatives are produced enormous quantities of soap, margarine, and cosmetics. Coconut oil used to be the only oil used for cooking in the tropics, although palm oil and vegetable oils are now widely available.

Copra has been exported from the Indies to Europe for decades. One of the greatest ports of Southeast Asia was Makassar, now called Ujung Pandang, on the southwest tip of Sulawesi (formerly the Celebes). Makassar exported more copra to Europe than any other port in the archipelago. The coconut oil pressed from the copra was sometimes called Macassar oil and was widely used as a hair pomade. When a fashionable man leaned his pomaded hair back onto his chair a grease spot was produced—hence the invention of the antimacassar.

Coconut wood is very hard, strong, decay resistant, and makes excellent building timber. It is exported and sold as "porcupine wood," so called because of the dark and light banded appearance of the fibers. It is the preferred wood in Bali for the construction of rafters and roof beams. It takes on a lovely, mottled appearance with age. Coconut stumps make wonderful chairs. They are so massive and heavy, however, since they are cut from a single piece of wood, that they are very difficult to move. Coconut wood is not used in making woodcarvings because it is too hard and grainy to carve in any detail. If a tree is cut for lumber, the bud or "palm cabbage," called *empol*, is eagerly eaten.

Whole coconut leaves, *don nyuh*, are a standard material from which to make woven mats. The mats are used for everything from just sitting on to containers for food, to temporary roofing or walls, coverings—any purpose that requires a quick, cheap, and easily made flat object. Gangs of men go out into the coconut plantation areas with bamboo poles, *arits* tied on the end, and, with one or two quick cuts, remove one or two of the older, bottom leaves from selected trees. Once the ants are shaken off, the leaves are trucked or hauled home, and fashioned into woven mats in very short order. The leaves on one side of the branch are folded over and interwoven with the leaves on the other side. Several patterns are possible, depending upon the use of the mat, as a shade for a temporarily roofed over area or a container or a wall. Any Balinese man can convert a coconut leaf into a mat in five minutes.

WHEN THE YOUNG LEAVES of a coconut tree emerge they are tightly folded along the central spine in a long, straight bundle. These young leaves, called *busung*, are much in demand as the principal part of most "sewn" offerings, the sort that the Balinese call *jajaitan*. The *busung* are made into literally hundreds of different kinds of offerings, and containers for offerings, ranging from simple square containers to giant, elaborately cut extravaganzas. The *busung* are stripped off of the central spine running between them and are cut and skewered together with short splinters of bamboo. The spines, called the *lidi*, are often saved until a bundle has accumulated, and are then tied at one end into a broom, called a *sampat lidi*. The young coconut leaves are for sale in all village markets.

A kind of dwarf coconut tree that produces yellow nuts is much sought-after on the island. These yellow coconuts are used in a large variety of ceremonies as containers. In the tooth-filing ceremony that every Balinese must undergo, he must spit his saliva into a yellow coconut that has arcane symbols inscribed on the outside. Yellow coconuts are also used as containers for holy water, and in certain ceremonies the water within them is used to sprinkle offerings.

One of the most important of all Balinese offerings is the *daksina*. It consists of a cylindrical basket, made of coconut leaves, within which are placed a variety of leaves and fruits, rice, and other symbolic materials, but the featured ingredient is a coconut that has been specially shaved and cleaned for the purpose. There is even available a special plane, like a carpenter's plane, for shaving the hairy fiber off of the outside of the coconut so that it can be used in the *daksina*. *Daksinas* are one of the few offerings that are left in shrines or temples for a long time.

When the bundle of young leaves unfolds and spreads out, the individual leaves turn green. At this point they are called *selepan*. And they too are often used in offerings—usually as bases to contain or support other materials within. The *lidi* from *selepan* are stiffer and better for brooms than those from *busung*. The sheath at the base of each leaf is covered with a network of interwoven fibers, and this is often removed and used as a kind of strainer, especially to purify and separate coconut oil from the milk.

So useful and important is the coconut tree that the Balinese make special offerings to the tree once every Balinese calendrical cycle, which comes around every 210 days. The day is always Saturday of the 7th week, Wariga, of the 30-week Pawukon religious cycle, a day called Tumpek Uduh or Tumpek Bubuh, or, sometimes Tumpek Nyuh, Tumpek Wariga, Tumpek Pengatag, or Tumpek Pengarah. *Bubuh* is a kind of rice porridge that is put inside of offerings that are attached to the tree. The word *uduh* means "to command," and each tree is commanded to produce lots of coconuts in the years ahead. *Pengarah* means "announcer," again indicating that the person in charge announces to the tree that the ceremony is going to occur and asks for a fruitful year. *Pengatag* means "encouragement," referring to the same thing.

Many offerings are made to the trees. In my village, Jimbaran, representative trees are dressed up in traditional Balinese clothing. At head height is wound a headband, *udeng*, exactly like those that all men wear to temple ceremonies. Below that is a batik or woven waistcloth, the *kamben*. And on top of the *kamben* is the scarf-like *saput* that all Balinese men wear on religious occasions. Special offerings are attached to the trees. When the prayers are about to be made, the person in charge knocks three times on the tree with a decorated hammer, to notify the tree of what is going to happen and sort of wake it up. Then the prayers are said, and the tree and offerings are sprinkled with holy water.

PART VII

Industry

CHAPTER 28

Garment Industry

BACKBONE OF THE EXPORT ECONOMY

Since its modest beginnings in the middle 1970s, the growth of the garment industry in Bali can only be called phenomenal. In 1976 the industry produced a few thousand garments per month; in 1986 Bali exported 6.25 million garments with a value of almost U.S. $22 million. Garments make up well over half the value of all of Bali's exports—greater than all the others combined, including handicrafts, coffee, and vanilla. Kanwil Departemen Perindustrian, the Bali office of the Department of Industry, estimates that more than 20,000 Balinese are employed in the garment industry. Operating on the island are 30 licensed clothing exporters and about 200 factories, ranging in size from those that employ a few dozen workers to giants with more than 2,000 employees each.

This industry does not involve traditional fabrics, like *endek* (see CHAPTER 18) and batik, or traditional Balinese clothing. It is an export industry, with Balinese seamstresses hired to execute designs provided by Western distributors. These Western style clothes are sewed from ordinary mill-manufactured textiles such as cotton, rayon, and mixtures of the two, as well as knitted fabrics. The textiles are manufactured in Java and shipped in bulk to Bali for cutting and sewing. Almost all of these garments are decorated for the Western market. Garments like T-shirts are usually silk-screened. Women's apparel is generally embroidered.

The center of garment manufacturing is in the Kuta–Sanur–Denpasar region, although there is one large factory in Singaraja. Some of the factories have retail outlets in the tourist centers. And some maintain small shops next to the factory that sell production overruns. But almost all of the merchandise is exported.

When a few Americans brought their clothing patterns to Bali in the middle '70s, they found an ideal environment for the workers they sought. Compared to the United States, labor in Indonesia is extremely cheap, and many Balinese girls learn to sew at an early age. The old-fashioned foot treadle sewing machine was already a fixture in many Balinese living rooms. These are inexpensive, easy to use, and quite reliable.

ALMOST ALL THE DESIGNS PRODUCED by the clothing industry are created by foreigners to suit the demands of their local markets. There is nothing "traditional" about the techniques used or the garments themselves. The large majority of the factories are owned by local people, but most of the companies work very closely with representatives of their customers, who supervise the work and check quality. Little of the work involves cutting out the material for the garments. This is done in bulk, often with simple machinery. The vast majority of the people employed by the industry spend their time sewing the garments together and decorating them with embroidery.

Almost all the employees are women. With a large staff of trained young women it would seem that the management of a factory is in a precarious position with respect to job turnover. Women get married and have children. But if this happens the woman, if she wishes, can go right on working at home. In fact, most of the employees do just that. Paid by the piece, they pick up cut and marked material at the factory, and at the same time deliver the last batch of completed garments. The larger factories have regular receiving and dispensing windows for this purpose. The completed garments are inspected on the spot, and the worker is credited for her work. She then receives a bundle of material and goes home to continue. If a worker lives too far from the factory to bring in finished garments and get new material, no matter. The factories employ collectors, *pengumpul,* who go from village to village to gather up the completed garments and distribute new raw materials.

Many of the garment factories do have large rooms full of machines run by workers who prefer not to do the job at home. A typical factory room has one hundred to two hundred foot-operated machines fairly close together. Although the setup is reminiscent of 19th century New York garment district sweatshops, the difference is that the factories are airy and open, and popular music blares from a powerful speaker, drowning out the hum of the sewing machines.

MUCH OF THE WORK INVOLVES *BORDIR,* "embroidery." The designs are produced by hand, the seamstress following a pattern that has been silkscreened onto the fabric at the factory. The garment factories sell in very large quantities to big foreign importers. An order might consist of several thousand identical garments, differing only in size and color. Strict uniformity is the rule. A women often embroiders the same pattern over and over again on thousands of identical garments. Some of the sewing machines are electric, but most are the foot treadle type that have been used for a century all over the world. The machines do not have automatic zig-zag devices. The common technique is to bind the material in an embroidery hoop and apply the decoration free-hand, jiggling the hoop and material back and forth.

The industry distinguishes eight standard types of *bordir*:

kecek pinggir	zig-zag edging
kecek susun	zig-zag double edging
bordir pasir	a branched zig-zag pattern
bordir jalan, or *bordir searah*	relatively straight lines
bordir melingkar	little circles and dots
bordir sembur	filling in outlines
bordir kerawang	lace work
aplikasi	appliqué

SOME DEFINITIONS:

kecek—zig-zag sewing
pinggir—edge
susun—row, series
pasir—sand
jalan—road, path
searah—one direction
melingkar—circle
sembur—sprinkle, pour out
kerawang—openwork

It takes about three months to train a worker in these techniques. Although training is normally done in the factory, the Indonesian Department of Manpower, Departemen Tenaga Kerja, maintains vocational training schools all over Indonesia. There are five schools in Bali, in Denpasar, Karangasem, Tabanan, Singaraja, and Negara. The schools are called Balai Latihan Kerja (BLK), literally "Building for Work Practice," and are equivalent to American vocational-technical schools. The schools offer training in a variety of trades, ranging among plumbing, commercial secretary, drafting, fishing, and embroidery. Bali's BLKs are among the best in the country and have received special recognition from the Minister of Labor for their excellence. Everything is free, no matter what the financial status of the individual, but most students come from poor rural families. The emphasis is upon placing the student in a paying job. These vocational schools have existed for a long time in other parts of Indonesia, but were begun in Bali only in 1982. In addition to the five main schools there are two mobile units that travel to the more remote villages to provide education in some areas.

MAKING BORDIR

The average pay in the garment industry is low by Western standards, about Rp 1,500 (just under U.S. $1) for a seven-hour day. Most factories work seven hours a day, six days a week. If the employees work at home, their hours are their own, and they are paid by the piece. Depending upon the intricacy of the design, it takes two to eight days to complete one dress. In Denpasar, a typical worker gets Rp 6,000 for a simple dress that takes two days to make. The pay varies somewhat, and some factories provide housing and meals for their employees.

Some factories sell only to one customer per country, thereby insuring that the designs are exclusive. In many cases that customer will have provided the designs and even the labels. Current designs are rather jealously guarded from the eyes of those who could copy. This is obviously a bit hard to do if the sewing is done in the villages. Other manufacturers sell to anyone who wants to buy. Overseas customers come to the factories to place their orders. They often send their representatives to oversee the work and make sure that the quality is as specified. Some manufacturers have their own quality control personnel.

Huge factories, most of them in Jakarta and Bandung, West Java, provide the the cotton and rayon material, which comes woven and as jersey. This is the raw material for almost all of the garment manufacturers in Bali. Most of the goods are bought already dyed, although some manufacturers purchase white cloth and dye their own, as needed. Accessory materials such as sequins and buttons are usually imported from

Hongkong, Taiwan, and Japan. Decorations of leather, shell, and wood are made in Bali or Java.

Almost all of the garments are exported. However, a few of the larger factories maintain showrooms for walk-in customers. These are usually stocked with production overruns, and there is often not a complete selection of sizes and colors. Bargains abound, however, and tourists are welcome. Based on personal experience, I can recommend the following three stores:

MAMA AND LEON. This is the largest garment manufacturer in Bali. The main factory and show room is on the main street of Sanur, Jalan Tandjung Sari, on the west side, not far from the Pacto Travel Bureau, south of the Hotel Tandjung Sari and north of the Bali Hyatt.

SARI BUSANA. This is on the west side of the By-Pass highway, north of Sanur, just south of the Tohpati Y, where the Jalan By-Pass joins the road from Denpasar to Batubulan. It is the biggest of the show rooms that I have seen and has a wide selection.

BALI GARMENTS (P.T. Bali Busana). This is a small shop on the second floor of the factory that is located behind the Segara Village Hotel in Sanur. The hotel and the factory are under the same ownership, so the best way to find out how to get there is to ask at the front desk at the hotel. Segara Village Hotel is just west of the Beach Market in Sanur.

IT IS ONLY NATURAL that the production of these factories is a function of the demands of their customers, which, in turn, is a reflection of the fashion trend of the times. Sequins are big in some years, absent in others. The garments are obviously designed for warm weather use. Most are blouses and skirts and dresses. They range from those with a minimum of decoration to highly ornamented creations full of lacy designs. Prices in Bali are almost ridiculously low by Western standards. If one divides the annual export value of the garment industry by the number of garments exported, the quotient is about U.S. $3.50. Most of the garments sell in Bali for U.S. $3 to $25.

Of course, by the time the garments reach their destinations, the cost is many times the Bali price. Part of this is the cost of air freight. Almost all of the goods are sent by air. Five dresses weigh about one kilogram, which costs about U.S. $4 to send by air. Thus, the air freight is about 10 percent of the cost, if an average dress costs about U.S. $8. Duty at the port of entry is normally no less than 20 percent depending upon the item. Shipping within the country of destination and markup of the retailer must all be figured in.

Some of the bigger companies are Government licensed exporters and can ship their own production overseas. There are 30 of these in Bali. All other manufacturers must deal with a licensed exporter. About half of all garment exports from Bali go to the United States.

CHAPTER 29

Fishing

TRADITIONAL HARVEST FROM THE SEA

THE BALINESE HAVE NEVER taken to the sea as have the Polynesians, whose long inter-island voyages, guided by stars, waves, and ocean currents, are legendary. There is no history of oceanic exploration or maritime trade—except with nearby Java to the west and Lombok to the east—among the Balinese. Trade did come to Bali, but it was others who came and did the trading—Chinese, Malays, Buginese, Indians, and later, the Europeans.

This lack of a seafaring tradition is at least partly the result of the island having few sheltered harbors and anchorages. Most of Bali's coastline is relatively straight and unprotected. Coral reefs line many of the beaches, allowing only small boats to penetrate, and sheer, wave-cut cliffs dominate in other spots. This is one reason why the Dutch, who came to the East Indies at the beginning of the 17th century, left Bali pretty much alone until the 19th and early 20th centuries. Even today tourist cruise ships must anchor at Padang Bai, between Klungkung and Amlapura, far from the principal tourist attractions of Bali. It is the only accessible deep-water anchorage in Bali.

A common misconception is that the Balinese consider the sea to be impure and profane. This derives from the Balinese directional axis that leads from holy Mount Agung (*kaja*) to the sea (*kelod*). It is true that in Balinese rites and ceremonies, and cosmology, *kaja* is "pure" and *kelod* is "impure." But *kelod* is a direction, not a place. It does not follow that the sea is impure. In fact, the sea plays an extremely important part in Balinese culture, both in secular and in religious affairs. The sea purifies the spirits of the dead before they go to heaven, *suarga*. Holy water made from the sea is regularly used for purification and prayer. The Tirtha

Amertha, the holy water of immortality, was churned up from the sea in a very famous Hindu-Balinese legend.

Because the sea does have these mysterious powers, it is generally regarded with a certain amount of respect and awe—the same that the Balinese extend to any object that is obviously charged with magical power. Few Balinese can swim. Bali's lovely beaches are fine for family picnics, football games, and horseplay, but the shallow water areas inside the coral reefs and the huge breakers on the unprotected beaches are not ideal places for swimming. The public beaches are jammed on Sundays, but mostly people just wade or splash around a bit.

Throughout the island, small-scale fishermen wade out onto the coral reef at low tide to fish with long bamboo poles, or use kerosene pressure lanterns to attract small sea creatures in the evening, scooping them up with small dip nets. If the tide is low in the early evening you see their lights bobbing and weaving in ceaseless, random patterns offshore. Singaraja and Kusamba have groups of fishermen who catch a small harvest with trolling lines and throw nets. But the most important and largest fishing and fish processing port is located in Pengambengan, in the *kabupaten* (county) of Jembrana, along Bali's southwest coast, 10 kilometers southwest of Negara, and at least an hour-and-a-half drive from Denpasar. And the second-largest is Jimbaran Bay, just south of the International Airport.

THE MAIN FISHING VILLAGES of Jimbaran Bay are Tuban, Kelan, and Kedonganan, whose fishing activities are grouped together at Kedonganan, and Jimbaran itself, the most southerly of the four and the largest. Together, these villages produced about 2,000 metric tons of fish in 1983, with a value of about Rp 220 million, roughly U.S. $200,000. The total harvest and its value are probably at least double these figures, which come from the area fish auction facilities. Pengambengan produced almost 12,500 tons of fish in 1983, worth about Rp 625 million—one-fourth of Bali's entire annual fish harvest.

Although Pengambengan harvests six times as much fish as does Jimbaran, the value of its catch is only three times that of Jimbaran. This is because the Pegambengan fisherman catch mostly sardines, while their peers in Jimbaran Bay pull in larger, and more valuable, species.The total Bali harvest of ocean fish in 1983 was 51,000 tons, worth almost Rp 9 billion, or about U.S. $9 million. This represents an industry growth of about 17 percent a year since 1979, attributable to bigger boats, better technology, and more fishermen.

Ninety percent of the fish caught in Bali are ocean fish, and one single species represents 70 percent of the ocean catch. It is the Indonesian oil sardine, *Sardinella longiceps,* called *lemuru* in Bahasa Indonesia and nicknamed *kucing,* "cat," in Bali (although it does not resemble a catfish in any way). *Kucing* average about 20 centimeters (8 in.) in length. On a good day at the height of the season 250 tons of them may be brought ashore at Pengambengan and about 100 tons at Kedonganan. Vast numbers of sardines are found in the area of the Indian Ocean between Java and Bali known as the Bali Sea, and they migrate irregularly in this triangle of ocean. Some of the best fishing areas are along the south coast of Bali from Tanah Lot west to the coast of Java, and in the large mouth of Selat Bali, due west of Jimbaran. The sardine fishing grounds are at least two hours by motorboat from Jimbaran Bay, so only the large powerboat owners, mostly from Kedonganan, catch *kucing.*

Twenty percent of the ocean fish harvest in Bali consists of tuna and mackerel, and these are the specialties of Jimbaran's fishing fleet. The most important of the large fish are the frigate mackerel and the eastern little tuna. In Indonesian these are both called *tongkol,* although the Balinese make a distinction between the former, *awan,* and the latter, *bangkuk.* The other important species of tuna are the skipjack, called *cakalong* in Indonesian, and *suwat* in Balinese, and the yellowfin tuna, called *madidihang* in Indonesian, and *bengkones,* or *kenyitang* in Balinese. These are not really big varieties of tuna and mackerel, as commercial fish go, averaging about 3 to 5 kilograms. They range in length from about one-half to one meter, the yellowfin being the largest.

The remaining 10 percent of the sea fish catch consists of sharks and coral fish. The sharks are mostly of two varieties, Balfours sharks and hammerhead sharks. Sharks are called *kakia* in Balinese and *cucut* in Indonesian, Hammerheads are *kakia subeng* in Balinese and *cucut martil* in Indonesian. Many of the sharks are babies, but an occasional monster weighing 200 kilos (440 lbs.) or more is brought to shore. The coral fish are mostly red snapper, grouper, hairtail, and other minor species, including a few of the large shrimp and spiny lobsters.

Most of the larger fish are caught in gill nets by both some of the large *prahu*s and the smaller one- or two-man boats, locally called *jukung.* There are three sizes of *jukung*s, but all are small enough to be hauled up on the beach after the day's fishing. *Jukung*s are quite narrow, about a half meter wide, and are five or so meters long. Because of their narrowness, they use a bamboo outrigger for stability. The outriggers are always removed from their supports and stored in the shade when not in use, since the sun cracks the water-soaked bamboo. The favored wood for *jukung*s is called *punyan ganggangan,* more because it is readily available than because it is particularly durable.

The smallest *jukung,* which can accommodate only one person, is called a *penunggalan;* the two-person craft is called a *pemelasan;* and for three or more, a motorized *jukung, mesin gede,* is used. The smaller two *jukung*s are propelled by paddle or sail, the latter by outboard motors of small size, often using kerosene as fuel.

SARDINES ARE HARVESTED using a purse seine, a very large net that is used to surround a school of fish, and then is pulled up tight from underneath with a kind of drawstring, thus trapping the fish. Locally called *jaring selerek,* purse seines are made of twisted nylon cord. Net size in Bali is measured by a unit called *depa,* which is the distance between the tips of the fingers when both arms are outstretched at the sides. Purse seines are 35 to 50 *depa* deep (about 60 meters), and about 90 to 150 *depa* long (135 to 225 meters). Mesh size is measured in a somewhat arcane unit the Balinese call *in.* Of course, this is the English inch, which is how the nets are sold—most purse seines have a mesh about one inch on the diagonal. The purse seine is buoyed up at intervals by red floats, and the bottom of the net is held down with lead weights. Large rings are attached at intervals of two *depa* along the bottom, and through these a rope is passed.

The use of a purse seine requires two *prahus,* called a *unit,* and a crew of 14 to 20 men. One *prahu* is smaller, and is decked over. It hauls the net. The other is much wider abeam and has no deck so that the fish can be stored directly inside or in cold boxes. Each *prahu* carries one to three long shaft marine diesel engines for propulsion. These are attached to the gunwales, usually on one side only so not to interfere with the handling of the net.

When a school of sardines is sighted the smaller boat drops its net in a circle around the fish as quickly as possible. When it gets back to the larger boat the ends of the net are joined. The line passing through the rings at the bottom of the seine—the drawstring—is fastened to the larger boat which then roars off at a tangent to the circular net, pulling the bottom of the "purse" closed and trapping the sardines inside. Then the two boats come alongside each other with the net in between. Crew members dip the sardines from the seine into the large, open *prahu,* using dipnets called *serok.* The empty net is then pulled in, and the boats head home.

The equipment is not cheap. A single purse seine alone costs about Rp 6.5 million (U.S. $4,000). A complete *unit,* two *prahus,* net, and engines costs almost Rp 20 million (U.S. $12,000). Thus these outfits are group owned and operated, with the members sharing in the profits and work. The Pengambengan *prahus* use larger diesel engines than those in Jimbaran Bay—often as powerful as 240 horsepower. This gives them a considerable advantage over the smaller Jimbaran *prahus* which pack a maximum of 130 horsepower. The Pengambengan fishermen brag about their boats being larger and able to range farther afield, but the Jimbaran fishermen say that the sardines are closer to their home base than to Pengambengan and so they don't need large engines.

If the catch is so large that the *unit* cannot handle it by itself, they seek help by radio. Each *prahu* can haul about 5 tons of fish. A catch of several times that is possible during the best fishing season, and neighboring *prahus* can be called in or new ones dispatched from home base if radios

PENCAR

SAU

CEKOT

A VARIETY OF FISHING NETS

are carried, as is standard practice in Jimbaran. In 1984 there were 63 purse seine *units* at Pengambengan, 23 at Kedonganan, and 4 at Jimbaran, although these four used the landing facilities at Kedonganan rather than those at Jimbaran itself.

Sardine fishing is a year-long activity at Pengambengan, whereas the Jimbaran Bay fleet is inactive during the rainy season, from about November or December to April. The heavy winds blow straight in from the west, unattenuated by any land mass. Pengambengan, though on the coast, is close enough to Java to enjoy protection from the seasonal storms. Thus the Jimbaran Bay fishermen beach their *prahu*s in November or December or send them off to fish along the Java coast. The rainy season months are used for *prahu,* net, and engine repair, and perhaps a temporary job nearby. This short season is partly responsible for the smaller number of *units* stationed in Jimbaran Bay, which, of course, results in a much smaller catch than at Pengambengan. In April, the prevailing winds reverse and blow from the East, the waters of Selat Bali are calm, and the Jimbaran Bay fleet puts to sea once again.

Pengambengan sardine fishermen observe a practice of not fishing during a ten-day period called *bulan terang,* meaning "bright moon," extending from about three days before full moon to six days afterwards. They claim that the sardines can see the net clearly when the moon is out and swim away from it. And the reflection of the moonlight on the water makes it hard to see where the sardines are in order properly to deploy the nets. This rest period is used for net, boat, and engine repair. Most Jimbaran Bay sardine fishermen do not observe a *bulan terang* rest period, claiming that, since they fish in shallow waters along the coast, the sardines cannot swim deep enough to escape their nets. A few Jimbaran Bay fishermen stop for a period of three or four days at full moon, but almost none stops for as long as ten.

GILL NETS, *JARING,* (meaning any sort of net) are made of monofilament nylon, with mesh sizes ranging from 1.5 to 4 *in,* the thickness of the filament depending upon the type of fish being sought. A typical single fisherman in a *jukung* uses a gill net that is about one meter wide and 150 meters long. The length varies, depending upon the number of nets attached end to end. *Prahu*s use much bigger gill nets, perhaps 25 *depa* (35 meters) wide. Each section of net is 35 *depa* (50 meters) long, and a single *prahu* can handle up to 25 nets strung together, a total length of over 100 meters. A gill net can be set to any depth, according to the judgment of the fisherman. Floats are attached to a thick nylon rope at the top of the net, and small lead weights hold down the bottom. A rock at each end serves to sink the net to the desired depth above the bottom, and a plastic foam float attached to one end of the top line allows the net to be found and retrieved. A single length, 90 meters, of small boat gill net costs about Rp 25,000 without floats or sinkers.

A gill net, as the name suggests, is simply a barrier into which the fish run and get entangled by their gills. When the net is retrieved the fish are simply picked out of the meshes, either in the boat or on shore. Much larger fish than the mesh size of the net are often caught because once they strike the net they thrash around and become entangled. Almost every day a large shark or two, a swordfish, or a sailfish is hauled ashore, sometimes requiring two men to carry it on a bamboo pole.

The fishing practices of the small boat operators vary greatly depending upon the season. During the rainy season they fish close to shore, seldom more than half a kilometer away. In the late afternoon, when the temperature has cooled down a bit, they sling a carefully wrapped net or two on a paddle, and, carrying this over a shoulder, walk the few hundred meters down to the high tide mark on the beach where their *jukung*s are kept. They take the coconut leaf cover off the boat, attach the bamboo outrigger, and drag the little craft backwards down to the water's edge, turning it around to face the sea when they arrive.

If the wind is onshore and the waves large it can be a problem to get out past the breakers without upsetting. Long experience tells them the safest moment to shove off. Paddling out to the desired depth, they deploy the net by throwing the rock attached to one end of the top line into the water and paying out the net with both hands as they move the boat backwards, using one foot for propulsion like a scull. This takes no more than an hour.

If fishing is very good they may remain all night, pulling in the net at intervals to remove the struggling fish, since these scare away others. But, in the rainy season, when the water is rough and winds strong, they just come back to shore and go home, leaving the net out all night. Next morning at about 4 o'clock they retrieve their nets. Their wives carry big metal tubs out to the beach to carry the catch home on their heads and take it immediately to sell in the Jimbaran market, only one kilometer distant. The men gather up the nets and carry them home, after pulling the boats up to a safe level above the high tide line and removing and storing their outriggers.

Most of the morning is spent repairing the gill nets. The sea bottom near the Jimbaran beach is full of sharp coral that tears the thin line, and larger fish often rip up the nets when they become entangled. Several hours each morning are spent patching. The nets are suspended by their top lines from bamboo poles in the shade, and the entire family sets to work repairing torn spots.

Sometimes a big sea turtle is hauled in with the more sturdy nets. These have a ready market in the Jimbaran area where turtle meat is the main ingredient of the meal, commonly called *ebat,* that all South Balinese people prepare upon special ceremonial occasions. Large shrimp and lobsters are also prized because they bring a premium price—up to Rp 4,000 per kilo, compared with the Rp 200 to 500 per kilo for the usual tuna and mackerel.

Gill net fishermen are not bothered much by the moon. Small mesh nets are made of very fine monofilament and don't scare the fish at night. But the waves and wind limit the gill net fishermen, with their small craft, to localities near the bay. Starting about the end of March, when the winds begin to shift to the east and the dry season commences, the small boats venture forth as far northwest as a place they call Soka, near Tanah Lot and Yeh Gangga, shoreward of the village of Tabanan, 17 kilometers away. Or they may venture south as far as the Pura Luhur Uluwatu cliffs, 13 kilometers away. The ocean currents south of the Bukit are too strong for any of the small boat fleet. The sea is very deep here, since the north edge of the Java Trench, one of the deepest ocean trenches in the world, is just south of Bali.

FISHING IN INDONESIA is under the jurisdiction of the Ministry of Agriculture. The head fishery office in Bali is Dinas Perikanan in Denpasar, and it supervises fishing throughout the island. In turn, each of the 8 *kabupaten* (districts) of Bali has its own fisheries office which is responsible for activities in its local area and which reports directly to Dinas Perikanan. There have been established throughout the main fishing areas of Bali ten locations called TPI, Tempat Pelelangan Ikan, literally "Places for the Auction of Fish." In the Jimbaran Bay area there is a TPI office on the beach at Jimbaran itself and another, larger, one at Kedonganan. These two TPI offices are under the supervision of KUD, Koperasi Unit Desa, cooperative.

TPI does not set or control the prices, but it makes the prices public, and TPI employees witness the transactions, weigh the fish, and record the name of buyer and seller, the kind of fish, weight, and price. It also sells ice and salt to fishermen and buyers. Although Jimbaran is a major producer of sea salt in Bali, it is too high quality to be cost-effective for salting fish. Instead, TPI trucks in crude, yellow, chunky salt from Madura and sells it at Rp 50 per kilo. Ice sells for Rp 700 per 25 kilo block. For its services, TPI takes 5 percent of the sales price—paid on the spot. TPI offices also encourage fishermen to help in fish conservation, particularly to keep from over-fishing the valuable sardine grounds, and it rents space in some of its facilities to those who wish to make fish meal.

All of the big sardine *prahu*s at Kedonganan operate under TPI, as do some of the gill netters. Nobody is required to join TPI, however, and many of the small fishermen prefer to save the 5 percent fee and sell on their own. Sometimes these transactions take place at the Jimbaran TPI, and sometimes the fishermen have regular volume customers who come to the beach to buy for restaurants, other inland markets, and hotels.

Different fish reach different destinations. Almost all the sardines go to canneries. There is one in the Denpasar area, in Suwung, and there are three canneries right on the beach in Pengambengan. But sometimes Pengambengan sardines end up in Denpasar, and sometimes Kedonganan sardines end up in Pengambengan, depending upon the sizes of the day's catch. If the catch exceeds the capacity of the canneries in Bali, or if Javanese buyers out-bid those from the Balinese canneries, the sardines are packed in ice and salt and shipped off in huge trucks to the canneries in Muncar on the east coast of Java. They may even end up farther west in Java—at Probolinggo, or even Jakarta.

Most canneries buy whole sardines in Kedonganan. But, one, Indo Bali, rents facilities from TPI at Kedonganan and processes the fish right on the spot. A team of women behead and gut the fish in a shed only a few meters from the scales. The fillets are packed in ice and salt and shipped at once to the Pengambengan cannery. The heads, guts, and any rotten, spoiled, or broken fish are boiled briefly, then strained and sun dried. The result is a product called *gaplek ikan,* a coarse fish meal, worth about Rp 300 per kilo. This is used as chicken feed. In addition to sardines, the Pengambengan canneries produce fish oil and *petis,* a salty fish sauce that is popular all over Indonesia and Asia.

The canneries export a great deal of the product, of course, since the Balinese don't buy or eat canned fish when they can get the fresh product right in their own markets. Most of the cans have Japanese labels, and, indeed, some of the canneries are Japanese owned. The cannery at Suwung, Bali Raya, also cans tuna and mackerel, and even corned beef from Bali cattle. It produces 15 to 20 tons of canned fish each day and employs 450 people.

The small-scale, independent gill net fishermen, who may catch only one or a few bucketfulls of fish—tuna, mackerel, or snapper—may sell their fish directly in the Jimbaran market. The gill net fishermen who use *prahu*s may catch up to 100 kilos of large fish per day, and they often have regular customers from restaurants, hotels, or sellers from the big Pasar Badung in Denpasar. These last come down to meet the arrival of the catch and bargain for the fish, usually icing and salting them in their own trucks before departing.

Some of the fish, especially the sharks, are purchased by companies for salting. The fish are soaked in big concrete vats of salt water for three days, then cleaned and dried in the sun. The fish is sold principally in Java. There are big salting tanks just south of Kedonganan, back from the beach a hundred meters or so. Whole sardines are also salted for sale in the more remote markets. They are first boiled and then packed in brine in a large metal can. Prepared this way the sardines are called *pindang kucing* and will keep for months.

In Benoa, a government-owned fishing company called Perikanan Samudera Besar (PSB) operates a fleet of deep sea fishing boats that range over the Indian Ocean towing trotlines. The yellowfin tuna, big eye tuna, albacore, and marlin they catch average 35 kilos with occasional 600-kilo monsters. The trawlers are large and are propelled by 360-horsepower diesel engines. The ships have refrigerated holds and the PSB maintains a refrigerated warehouse that can store 900 tons of fish. It also has an ice plant that can make 10 tons a day, which is sold to smaller fishermen and buyers. PSB sells all of its fish to Japan and Italy, which regularly send refrigerator ships to Benoa.

THE BEST TIME OF THE YEAR TO VISIT the Jimbaran Bay fishing activities is at the peak of the dry season, June through September. The best times of day to come are either shortly after sunrise, no later than 6 or 7 A.M., when the fish are being brought in from the boats, or around 3 or 4 in the afternoon, when the *prahu*s and *jukung*s are preparing to shove off.

Early in the morning, as the small craft approach the beach, the waiting wives and family come down to the water's edge to meet them, metal tubs balanced casually on their heads. The boatman waits just beyond the line of breaking waves for a clear space, then paddles furiously to shore, jumping out to steady the boat on the beach as the fish are loaded into the tubs and carried on the women's heads to the scales at the inland, shady edge of the beach. After buyer and seller agree on a price, the TPI employee shouts out and records the price, as well as the weight and type of fish. The seller then pays his 5 percent, and the fish go to waiting trucks where they are iced and salted and quickly sent on their way. Many women bypass the scales and carry their own fish to market, or sell them to their steady customers who are already waiting on the beach. Buyers hover around in the shade waiting for the little boats to come in.

The larger gill net *prahu*s anchor offshore and are met by small *jukung*s into which the usually large catch is loaded. It may take a half dozen women to carry the fish to the scales when the *jukung*s land. These *prahu*s have regular customers too, and the catch is often sold even before it is weighed. An occasional large shark or billfish may require two men to carry ashore and weigh on the small platform scale.

Meanwhile, the *jukung*s are dragged up above the water line and the nets removed. Smaller fish still sticking in the nets are picked out and thrown into the empty boat. Then the boats are dragged up above the high tide mark, propped up on coconut log chocks, covered with mats, and the outriggers removed. By mid-morning most of the work is done, the fish iced down and disposed of, and the beach is deserted except for those few fishermen who use hand nets.

Hand nets are of two kinds. The *jala* is a large round throwing net, perhaps three meters in diameter, with small weights on the periphery and a long line attached to the center. The fisherman wades out into the shallow water and, when he spots a group of fish, throws the net in such a way that it hits the water spread out in a circle, flat side down. He then carefully pulls the center line. The weights pull the outer edges down and together, and the net is hauled in and opened.

Another shore net is the *sau*. This is a large V-shaped wood frame that holds a triangular net about as tall as a man. The fisherman holds the apex of the V and pushes the wide, open end along the sandy bottom near the shore. These nets are for *nener*, a tiny fish that is now being grown commercially in saltwater ponds in South Bali. *Nener* are almost invisibly small, but they grow to quite a large size, called *bandeng*, in captivity, and are then sold in Java. There are also a few hook-and-line fishermen who fish from small boats. But these shore fishermen contribute only an insignificant amount to Jimbaran Bay's catch.

IF YOU GO TO KEDONGANAN EARLY IN THE MORNING of a good sardine day, you will find the chaotic scene there which provides quite a contrast to the relatively slow and quiet proceedings at Jimbaran. On a good day 100 tons of sardines may be hauled ashore. The beach at Kedonganan slopes much more rapidly than at Jimbaran, and the big *prahu*s can come to within a few meters of the water's edge. Their sardines are scooped by dipnets into large baskets. Laborers, who are paid Rp 5,000 per ton, wade out into the chest-deep water with thick bamboo poles. Each basket, loaded to overflowing, is slung on a pole between two men and carried to the TPI scales. Little boys jostle the baskets on the way to the scales, causing a few fish to spill out, and quickly pick them out of the sand and plop them into pans or plastic bags for a free meal or a quick sale, as the laborers helplessly scold them. There may be 25 or more pairs of men carrying the dripping baskets, waiting in line to have their baskets weighed.

Meanwhile, in the TPI office, the *prahu* owner and the buyers haggle over the price. As soon as they agree, the price is hollered out on the very loud public address system. Prices may change quite rapidly as the quantity and quality of the day's catch appear to be more or less than expected. On a good day at the height of the sardine season in August there may be as many as 90 large trucks lined up in front of the TPI office, as 30 or more buyers bid for their share.

Next to the scales a team of 50 or more girls work feverishly over piles of sardines in a shaded pavilion. Heads and guts go onto the floor, from where they are shoveled off to the fish meal production facility right next door. The cleaned filets are put in small pans and quickly packed into cold boxes on trucks with salt and ice to be shipped off to the Pengambengan cannery. If the catch is too large to be processed immediately the basket carriers are directed to dump their baskets into large concrete vats inside the adjacent warehouse rather than onto the cleaning tables. Salt and ice are put in the vats and the fish kept until there is room to process them.

Inside the warehouse employees are bashing sacks full of block ice with heavy pipes, crushing it and then dumping it on the arriving fish. In the fish meal area a long row of split steel drums bubble away as the leavings from the cleaning tables are shoveled in. Each batch is allowed no more than 10 minutes, whereupon it is scooped out with a large strainer and dumped on the fish meal drying pile, where other workmen turn the material over periodically to allow it to dry thoroughly. The fish oil that rises to the tops of the tanks is scooped off and is used to fuel the fires. The floors are slippery with water, oil, ice, and fish parts. The smell is strong—very strong.

Meanwhile other buyers direct sardine basket carriers from the scales to their waiting trucks. Then a boat load of tuna and mackerel comes in. Baby sharks are dumped on the beach and quickly bought up by restaurant owners who may sell them under various exotic names. There is mass, but orderly, confusion. A medicine show is going on in a nearby tent, as a local huckster praises his cure-alls, alternating his pitch with deafening music. Small food stalls, *warungs,* do a brisk business in snacks and drinks. People are yelling and shouting, little boys run about, and fish baskets swing everywhere. Puddles of goo seep from the fish meal vats, and always the smell.

And then, by about 8 A.M., it is all over. The catch is sold and processed. The purse seiners pull the nets over the booms of their boats to dry and pull away from the beach to anchor beyond the big waves off shore. Then they come ashore and go home or rest in the shade. Kedonganan lapses into its usual somnolence.

Around 3 or 4 P.M., as the heat of the day wanes and the shadows start to lean, the fishermen return to the beach. The small boat fishermen have been gazing out to sea all afternoon, looking for signs that only they can interpret after long years of experience, and they assess which size net to take along. When they have dragged their *jukungs* down to the water's edge a daughter or wife puts an offering on the prow, asking Baruna, the controller of the sea, for safety and a bountiful catch. And off they go for another try. If the wind is right a forest of sails sprouts up as the little boats head off. It is a colorful scene

The *prahu* owners who use large gill nets bring them down to the beach, if they are not already on board, lay them out, and attach the sections together. Then two men pull the long nets into small boats, which, in turn take them out to the *prahu*s anchored offshore. The sardine fishermen pile into large *jukungs*, six or eight men to a boat, and ride out to their *prahu*s. Their seines are left on board all season long unless repairs are needed. If the surf is up it can be a problem to get a big boat load of men through the breakers. There may be several tries and upsets, amidst much laughter from onlookers.

Then, as the boats move off into the sunset, the evening's soccer games begin on the beach. Villagers come down to watch the sun sink into the sea or disappear behind the mountains of Java, depending upon the time of year. The joggers finish their last laps. The kung-fu practicers and the gymnasts are out in full force. Some people dig in the sand near the water's edge for *imis,* a little cockle, for soup. By 6 P.M. it is dark. Twilight doesn't last long in the tropics. The beach is deserted.

CHAPTER 30

Salt-making

HARVESTING SALT FROM THE SEA

NEXT TO CHILI PEPPERS, salt is Bali's most important condiment, and there is a thriving cottage industry devoted to its production from seawater. There are seven coastal areas where the industry is concentrated: Suung, or Suwung, in South Bali; Jimbaran; Kusamba, a few kilometers northeast of Klungkung; Yeh Gangga and Kelating, near Tabanan one the southwest coast; and Pengeragoan, halfway to Gilimanuk from Denpasar, on the main road running along the south coast of the island, and along Bali's north coast east of Singaraja.

The basic salt-making process is the same at each of these areas. Seawater is carried in buckets to nearby sand flats and allowed to evaporate in the sun. The dry, salty sand or mud is collected in a big container, leached with seawater, and the effluent evaporated to produce salt. But each area has developed its own particular techniques. What is perhaps most interesting is that each of these small producers has solved some of the rather difficult technical problems involved in producing table salt from sea salt—without the benefit of modern chemical theory, and using only very crude equipment.

CULTURES THAT HAVE SIGNIFICANT amounts of milk and raw or roast meat in their diets do not need to salt their food. There are still areas in Central Africa where salt is little used or needed, and it is so expensive that it is confined to the rich. But those who live mostly on grains and vegetables—which are very low in salt—require at least 200 milligrams of added salt per day. The same is true for eaters of boiled meat, since boiling removes most of the salt.

Meat is an expensive luxury in much of Asia, where rice is the staple and protein comes largely in vegetable form, such as soybeans. The Balinese consume very little meat, usually adding a few tiny morsels of chicken or fish to their rice for ordinary meals and saving up to splurge during festive occasions. Even fish is rather expensive. Thus extra salt is much more essential to them than it is to those who live in, say, the United States. Excessive salt intake, linked to hypertension and heart disease, has even become something of a problem in the United States. This is not the case in Bali.

To some the saltiness of the sea is its most undesirable quality. It is undrinkable, useless for watering crops, and highly corrosive. But seawater is an inexhaustible storehouse of chemicals, the most important of which is table salt. From the earliest times, salt has been used as a preservative and for the curing of meat, fish, and hides. In the industrial world, it is the source of many of our most basic chemicals—soda ash, baking soda, lye, hydrochloric acid, baking powder, bleach, chlorine, and magnesium, to name just a few. All of the salt found in the world originally came from the sea. Inland deposits of rock salt, such as those mined in the United States, are merely relics of ancient seas.

To a chemist, "salt" is a generic term that can mean any of a large class of compounds in which the hydrogen of an acid is replaced by some metal or a group of elements that acts like a metal. Most people, however, use the word salt to mean just a single member of this class—table salt, sodium chloride (NaCl). There is table salt in the sea, but there are many other dissolved substances as well, most of them also salts. If seawater is evaporated to dryness, the result is a grand mixture of many substances. Seawater varies slightly in its dissolved solids content, but averages about 3.5 percent by weight. Each liter of seawater holds about 37 grams of salts in solution.

In seawater the salts exist in ionic form, that is the table salt does not exist as the compound NaCl, but as free Na+ and Cl- ions. Although 73 of the 92 naturally occurring chemical elements have been found in seawater, only 67 ions make up more than 99 percent of the total:

chloride	Cl^-	55.04 percent
sodium	Na^+	30.61
sulfate	SO_4^{--}	7.68
magnesium	Mg^{++}	3.69
calcium	Ca^{++}	1.16
potassium	K^+	1.10
carbonate or bicarbonate	CO_3^{--} or HCO_3^-	.41
TOTAL		99.69 percent

When the water is evaporated, negative and positive ions combine, the least soluble pairs coming out of solution as solids first, while the remaining ions remain in solution. If all the water is evaporated, a mixture results, composed chiefly of the salts listed below:

calcium carbonate	$CaCO_3$
calcium sulfate	$CaSO_4$
table salt	NaCl
magnesium sulfate	$MgSO_4$
magnesium chloride	$MgCl_2$
potassium chloride	KCl

Of course, most of the mixture, almost 80 percent of it, would consist of table salt, NaCl, because most of the ions present are sodium and chloride ions. But there would be significant concentrations of the other salts—traces of calcium sulfate and calcium carbonate, as well as 9.4 percent magnesium chloride and 6.6 percent magnesium sulfate. These latter are violently bitter substances. Magnesium sulfate is commonly known as Epsom Salts, a very effective laxative. The presence of even small amounts of these magnesium salts would be unpleasant, to say the least. The problem for the salt-maker is to achieve a product that is as high as possible in sodium chloride content and as low as possible in magnesium salts.

Obviously if the salt-maker just evaporated off all the water, the resulting product would be unsatisfactory. Fortunately, however, the two magnesium salts are about twice as soluble in water as table salt, and magnesium and sulfate are present in much smaller concentrations than sodium and chloride. So the technique must be to evaporate just enough water from the solution to cause the sodium chloride to precipitate, but not enough so that the magnesium salts form. Of course, there are no sharp dividing lines, and some contamination is inevitable.

In industry, elaborate techniques are used to effect this so-called fractional crystallization. In Bali it is done entirely by rule of thumb, tempered with long experience. Unfortunately, calcium carbonate, a form of chalk, and calcium sulfate, a form of gypsum, are much less soluble than even table salt. They precipitate before the table salt does and necessarily contaminate the product. But these are white, tasteless, harmless substances that lend only a slightly gritty texture to the table salt.

A second problem facing the salt-maker in Bali is the sheer volume of water that must be processed. Say a salt-maker produces 25 kilograms per day. The volume of seawater that contains 25 kilos of salt is about 1,000 liters. It would require an unreasonable amount of time and fuel to evaporate off all of that water, to say nothing of hauling a metric ton of water. This is why a preliminary concentration is effected by hauling the water only a short distance to the beach and allowing the sun to evaporate the solvent. The rest of the process consists of recovering the salt from the beach material and purifying it.

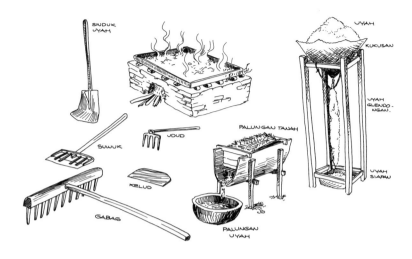

SALT-MAKING IN BALI is strictly a family activity. There are no companies or cooperatives. In each of the areas named, ten to 20 families work independently to produce the salt, storing the product in and selling it from their private homes.

The eastern side of the isthmus on which Jimbaran lies is a broad tidal flat with an earth bottom, bordered by mangrove trees. At dawn each salt-making family first spreads on its allotted six to eight hectares the soil from which the previous day's salt has been extracted. Then they begin innumerable trips carrying water from nearby sinks dug into the mudflats to the spread-out soil. Some still carry the water in clay pots, slung in pairs from a shoulder yoke, but one sees more and more plastic buckets. Everyone participates in sloshing the water from the buckets onto the soil, using a coconut shell dipper. The soil is then allowed to dry for about six hours. Around noon the soil is turned over with a rake and allowed to dry further until about 3 P.M. Then the family rakes the salty soil into long rows and scoops it into bamboo baskets, which they carry on their heads to the storage hut higher up on the edge of the flats.

When the storage hut is full of salty soil, the leaching process begins. Each family maintains two leaching tanks, usually made from part of the hollow log hull of an abandoned outrigger. Dry soil is loaded into the tanks by the basketful, and seawater is poured on top. It trickles through the soil, dissolving the salt, and is caught in buckets below. The buckets of thickened brine are then carried to the salt kitchen, several hundred meters back from the beach. The spent soil is emptied—to be spread on the flats first thing next morning—and the leaching is repeated until all the stored soil has been used up.

The evaporating-gathering activity can only be carried on for a one-week period during the neap tides of first and last quarter moon. The spring tides of full and new moon inundate the flats and make work impossible. And almost all work must cease during the rainy season from about November through March.

The salt kitchen is a dark, smoke-filled, soot-stained shelter with a tile roof and woven bamboo walls. In the center is the evaporator, a shallow, rectangular metal tray about two meters square. Saltwater from the leaching tanks is stored nearby in huge tanks carved from coconut stumps. Each evaporator batch consists of about ten buckets, approximately 300 liters, of saltwater. The fire below the evaporator is fueled with whatever wood is available, which has to be purchased because there is little firewood in the Jimbaran area. Coffee wood from the mountains is a favorite, but even dry cow dung may be used. After several hours of simmering, two more buckets of water are added to the contents of the evaporator. When the salt starts to form, the most interesting operation begins.

Near the evaporator is a large, loosely woven bamboo basket held about two meters off the ground by four stout poles. A string dangles from the bottom of the basket to the ground. Some families use a big rice steamer—a cone of woven bamboo—instead of a basket. The operator shovels the mush from the evaporator into the basket with a big, long-handled ladle. The liquid runs off the mush and trickles down the string to the ground. Here is the fractional crystallization. The least soluble salts started precipitating out in the evaporator. The more soluble salts start to form on the string and, in time, build it up into a white stalactite that may reach 20 centimeters in diameter and a meter long. The Balinese call it *gelendongan*. This stalactite drips, as more water from the basket runs down, and a cake of salts, called *siapan*, forms underneath in a tray on the ground. These, of course, are the most soluble of the salts. By this crude method, three grades of salt are produced. The *uyah* in the basket on top is the purest sodium chloride and commands the highest price. The magnesium salts, being more soluble than table salt, start to precipitate on the *gelendongan*, making it more bitter than the *uyah*. And the *siapan* contains a high percentage of bitter salts and is the cheapest.

A family can manage three boils per day, each producing about 50 kilograms of *uyah*, which is then stored loose in a nearby room. In Jimbaran the *uyah* is wholesaled to regular distributors who come to the salt-makers' homes and buy the product by the basketful. Each 25-kilo basket sells during the dry season for about Rp 2,000. The *gelendongan* and *siapan* are much cheaper, the latter used chiefly for salting fish. The cost may double during the off season when evaporation is difficult and supply short. The distributors take the salt to the various markets in South Bali, especially to the large Pasar Badung in Denpasar, and retail it in small plastic bags.

Benoa salt-makers follow a process quite similar to that of the Jimbaran people, since their coast is also a tidal flat. Some of the Benoa flats lie inland far enough that solar evaporation can be accomplished even at periods of extra high tide, at full and new moons. In the Benoa area the product is not purified by making *gelendongan*s and *siapan*s. The product is just scooped out of the evaporators and allowed to drain from baskets into large plastic jugs. These jugs of brine are sold to makers of bean curd. The Benoa product is considerably more bitter than Jimbaran's salt, because of its higher magnesium salt content.

Kusamba salt-making is different still. Here there are no mud flats, but rather, a sparkling black sand beach of volcanic debris, weathered from the rocks of Bali's sacred mountain, Gunung Agung. The beach at Kusamba is well above even the highest spring tide level so that salt-making can proceed all the time except during the rainy season.

In Kusamba water is carried from the warm sea in two unusual yoked buckets made from the protective sheath that surrounds the base of the leaves of the *areca* palm, *Areca catechu,* from which the nuts, often incorrectly called "betel" nuts, are produced. The gatherer wades out into the sea, fills his two buckets, and climbs the gentle slope of the beach to the flattened evaporation areas. Here, by expertly jiggling his shoulders and pushing with his hands, he sloshes the water evenly onto the raked sand. Wetting the entire family spread of seven or eight hectares takes about two hours and many, many trips to the sea.

Turning and drying and gathering of the sand is done in about the same way as in Jimbaran. But in Kusamba the salty sand is packed directly into a huge wooden vat inside the family's beach hut. As more sand is hauled in, more boards are added to the sides of the vat. These vats are leached directly with seawater, without transferring the sand to secondary leach tanks. And in Kusamba the final product is produced by solar evaporation instead of a wood-fueled fire.

Inland from the beach hut, each family has several dozen long hollow troughs made from coconut logs, set on low wooden platforms in rows. At about noon, each is filled with several centimeters of brine from the leach tank. Just before sunset enough water has evaporated to form a salt slush. Using coconut shell scrapers, women scoop up the slush and pile it into conical rice steamer baskets. The liquid, containing most of the more soluble magnesium salts, runs back into the trough, and the sodium chloride is retained on the loosely woven strainer-basket. Here again a sort of fractional crystallization occurs, because the salt-maker knows from experience at just which stage of evaporation to scoop out the mush, leaving magnesium salts in solution. If she doesn't wait long enough, she will get purer table salt, but not much of it. If she waits too long, she will get more salt, but it will be bitter. The troughs are periodically drained, since the bitter salts accumulate from day to day.

Each family in Kusamba makes about 25 kilos of salt each day. Most of it is wholesaled at Rp 25 to Rp 50 a kilo to distributors who take it to the nearby markets of Klungkung and Amlapura where inlanders come to buy it. Some of it goes to the nearby offshore island of Nusa Penida.

The salt-making areas on the southwest coast of Bali combine Kusamba and Jimbaran practices. Their beaches are sand, like those at Kusamba, but they use firewood-fueled evaporation as in Jimbaran, only in much smaller trays than are common in Jimbaran.

THESE VARIATIONS in salt-making processes produce differences of opinion on the quality of the various regions' product. The Jimbaran people think that Kusamba and Benoa salt is horribly bitter and refuse to use it. Used to their own product, the advocates of Kusamba salt say that the Jimbaran salt tastes strange and that Benoa and southwest Bali salt is crude and bitter.

These debates mean nothing to Western health food faddists who crave Bali's salt because it is "natural," whatever that means, and because it contains so many other substances than our presumably unnatural supermarket product. One problem with all salt in Bali is that it cakes badly in the humid climate. Salt shakers are useless.

Because of the seasonal nature of the industry, the Balinese salt-makers have to supplement their incomes with other activities. More often than not this is fishing, since they all live on the sea. But there is usually enough salt in their storehouses to sell all during the rainy season at premium prices, and this tides them over until once again they can haul seawater to the shore.

The Jimbaran Bay area is the second largest commercial fishing port in all of Bali, and much of the fish must be salted and iced en route to market. But the Jimbaran sea salt is never used for this. It is so pure and (comparatively) expensive that it is cheaper to import crude, yellow sea salt from the island of Madura, off the northeast coast of Java. This is a kind of coals-to-Newcastle story, but it is also true that the fine quality Jimbaran salt is not produced in anywhere near the quantity required to satisfy the fishing industry.

CHAPTER 31

Seaweed Farming

FROM BULUNG TO CARRAGEENAN

COLLECTING WILD SEAWEED for food and various food additives has gone on for so long that its origins cannot be determined. Even in Bali, those who live along the coasts have collected seaweed since ancient times. But an innovation on the island in the past few years has been treating seaweed as a crop—planting, tending, and harvesting the seaweed from offshore "fields."

The Indonesian word for seaweed is *rumput laut,* "sea grass." In Balinese it is called *bulung.* Of course, "seaweed" refers to an enormous diversity of plants of many genera and species. All of these are algaes, and range in size from microscopic unicellular plants to 45-meter (150 ft.) strands of giant kelp. Seaweed has historically been most important in the preparation of *agar-agar,* called simply "agar" in the West. This is a clear vegetable gel—usually extracted from the red alga *Gelidium*—which has some uses in the West but is used quite frequently in Asian cooking as a thickening agent. Most agar comes from Japan, where its production is a flourishing cottage industry, and Balinese sea coast dwellers have been gathering *Gracilaria gigas,* locally called *bulung sangu,* to sell to exporters and their agents for shipment to the Japanese agar producers.

The Balinese have also historically gathered the smaller wild seaweeds, *Gelidium* sp. and *Hypnea* sp., called *bulung bulun ayam* (chicken feather seaweed), and *bulung merak* (peacock seaweed). These are used for making the popular snack called *jaja bulung.* This is nothing more than sweetened agar, and is sold in the markets as a brown, somewhat firm gel cut into wiggly squares. These algae are gathered, dried, washed in lime water, and dried again into pale brown, lacy mats. In this form the seaweed stores indefinitely, and is merely shredded up into boiling water to produce the tasty cakes.

But the most useful—and valuable—extract from seaweed is a material that was originally produced from a seaweed called Irish moss, *Chondrus crispus,* a purple-red alga found on the rocky shores of North Europe and North America. This extract—carrageenan, has been used for years as a solidifying agent in jams, jellies, lotions, and medicines. This somewhat unusual name comes from an Irish town, Carragheen, near which the seaweed was plentiful. About 15,000 metric tons of carrageenan are produced annually in the world. Most of it is used in food products as a thickener and jelling agent and stabilizer, normally in very small concentrations. Carrageenan gives the smooth feel to ice cream, the desired stiffness to toothpaste, the body to jams and jellies, and the ability of liquid salad dressings to keep their spices in suspension. It adds creaminess to cottage cheese, stabilizes iced lollipops, glues the fruits on to fruit cake, prevents cream cheese from exuding water, and thickens milkshakes. In short, carrageenan is a virtual necessity in the modern food industry.

Demand was so great in the late 1960s for carrageenan that seaweeds were harvested in a totally uncontrolled fashion. Companies paid good prices, up to U.S. $630 per metric ton, and at that time almost all of the wild seaweed was harvested in Sulawesi, Maluku, East Nusa Tenggara, and in nearby islands. Some was produced in the western islands, such as Bangka, but these areas have never been major suppliers.

Carrageenan is marketed in commercial quantities by two large U.S. multinational corporations, Hercules Incorporated and FMC Corporation. Since carrageenan is an important article of commerce, these companies, and others, have been active in exploring potential sources of raw materials, and pioneering scientific methods of aquaculture so that the seaweed could be harvested on a regular, self-sustaining basis—thus maintaining a dependable supply.

Early experimental work in commercial seaweed farming was carried out along the coast of Belize, formerly British Honduras, and then attention shifted to Micronesia. But the politics of these areas were not deemed conducive to long term capital investment. Seaweed culture experiments in Indonesia were started as early as 1967 in the Pulau Seribu ("Thousand Islands") area, a group of islands in the Java Sea just north of Jakarta. The project was halted when its director passed away. Unsuccessful attempts at sustained farming were made in 1975 at Samarinda Island off Sulawesi, and in 1976 and 1977 in the Riau Islands off the east coast of Sumatra.

IN 1978 SOUTH BALI BECAME THE FOCAL POINT for experimental work in seaweed farming. The Copenhagen Pectin Factory Ltd., a subsidiary of Hercules Inc., which did the early work in Sulawesi, chose the Cape Geger area of South Bali. This beach is about 2 kilometers south of the Nusa Dua tourist area. The alga *Eucheuma spinosum* was chosen as the most suitable to the area. About four hectares of *E. spinosum* were farmed from 1980 through 1983 with reasonably good results, producing 30 to 75 metric tons a year. But, although the tonnage was considered good, the product was inferior in carrageenan content, apparently because the Cape Geger area was so good that the alga grew too rapidly. The sponsoring company was thus unwilling to increase production at the Cape Geger site.

Meanwhile, the same Copenhagen Pectin Factory established a very successful *spinosum* farming facility in the Philippines. So successful was the project that the market was flooded, prices fell, and the market collapsed, with a great deal of *spinosum* remaining unsold in 1980 and 1981. But the political instability of the Philippines led the companies to focus their attention once again upon Indonesia, in particular, Bali.

The Cape Geger area was too limited for a large scale operation, and the Indonesian tourism department felt that the seaweed farming area was too close to the Nusa Dua tourist hotels. Sites picked as having potential included the coast just west of Tabanan, the Pengambengan area south of Negara, the area around Gilimanuk, the north coast just east of Pulaki, and most of the southeast coast between Karengasem and Sanur. Preliminary experiments were carried out by various companies and Indonesian government agencies at Pengambengan and Gilimanuk. But by far the most attractive site proved to be the narrow strait between Nusa Lembongan and Nusa Ceningan off the northwest coast of Nusa Penida, and the stretch of coast between Nusa Lembongan and Sampalan, along the north coast of Nusa Penida.

By January, 1984 *spinosum* seedlings from Cape Geger had been distributed to fishermen at Lembongan village on Nusa Lembongan. Conditions on the reef between the two small islands proved to be excellent. Within five months of the start monthly production was almost double that of 1983. And by the end of 1984 production had reached 400 metric tons. As of this writing about 900 families are involved in seaweed farming on Nusa Penida, about 35 families at the Cape Geger operation, and about 30 families in a newly developed area on Pulau Serangan, "Turtle Island." The fisheries office in Denpasar estimates that about 9,000 Balinese are involved in this new industry.

There has been some effort to establish a different strain of algae, *E. cottoni*, which has yielded good results in The Philippines. The reasons for this change of emphasis are two-fold. Food additive producers are demanding more of the firmer-setting *kappa* carrageenan, of which *cottoni* is the better source. And *cottoni* has proved to be far superior to *spinosum* in its ease of farming, particularly in its disease resistance. But in Bali, unlike The Philippines, *spinosum* has been the traditional seaweed, and it is difficult to convince the seaweed farmers to replant. Farmers are currently being paid Rp 225 for a kilo of sun-dried *spinosum*, compared to Rp 450 per kilo of *cottoni*.

Growth rates of seaweed in Bali are about double those achieved in The Philippines. But, as mentioned above, this is a mixed blessing, because carrageenan content has to date been only about 70 percent that of the Philippine seaweeds. The companies feel that agronometric practices in Bali are not good, mainly because the farmers have not been taught how to go about their business properly.

WILD *EUCHEUMA* SEAWEEDS are found in the intertidal zones where there are sandy bottoms and a litter of coral fragments, usually with many other species of sea plants. Selecting a good site involves finding a spot where the conditions match those preferred by the wild strains. An ideal spot would be a lagoon inside a coral reef, where the salinity is stable at around 33 parts per thousand, where there are reasonably strong currents, and where water temperatures will not get too high. The crop can be easily damaged by wave action, so the protecting reef is a necessity. And the depth has to be such that the plants are still below water level at low tide, yet not so deep at high tide that the sunlight cannot reach them.

Most seaweed farming in Bali is done with the so-called stake, rope, and line method. Bamboo stakes are driven into the sandy bottom to form the corners of a rectangle roughly 2.5 by 5 meters. The water is usually waist to shoulder high, depending on the tide. Plastic rope is tied between the pairs of stakes at the far ends of the rectangle, and from these

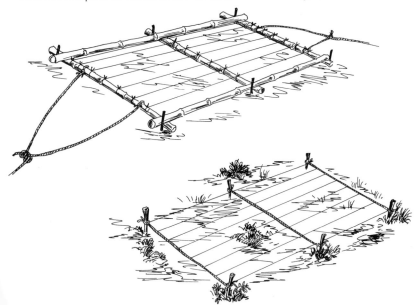

SEAWEED FARMING FRAMES

12 lines of rope are strung lengthwise. Usually another pair of stakes is placed in the middle of the rectangle and a crosswise rope is tied between them in order to support the 5-meter span of lengthwise ropes. Each unit holds about 400 seedlings. Fifty units, each with an area of 12.5 square meters, make up a square, and there are 16 squares per hectare. Thus one can raise about 320,000 seedlings per hectare. The seedlings are placed about 20 centimeters (8 in.) above the bottom. If there is a problem with disease or abrupt changes in the temperature, the damaged seedlings are placed in bamboo rafts to recover and then later replanted. Fish nets are placed around the growing area to prevent the escape of strands that have been broken off because of wave action.

An average family of five can tend a minimum of about one quarter hectare, or 80,000 plants. On an average bed, this area produces about 20 metric tons of dried seaweed per year, which gives the family a gross annual income of about Rp 4.5 million or about Rp 375,000 per month—well above average for a Balinese family. If production were primarily *cottoni,* this income would approximately double. From this, of course, would have to be deducted the cost of seedlings, rope, and so on, most of which is either a one-time expense, such as seedlings, or reusable, such as rope.

The term "seedling" is used in the trade even though algae do not produce seeds. After tying them carefully on the lines, all the farmers have to do is wait. After two weeks they harvest the crop by wading out into the water and picking off the long trailers, leaving a substantial amount on the lines for future growth. the seaweed is gathered in bamboo baskets equipped with plastic foam floats, brought ashore, and spread out on the beach to dry in the sun. This last action upsets the buyers and processors because it means that a quantity of sand is included. It would be better to dry the seaweed on nets above the sand, but nets are expensive.

In some of the seaweed farming areas, for example at the Geger beach, the farmers live in small shacks of woven bamboo mat right on the beach. Many of them have homes elsewhere, but they prefer to be near their crop. At Geger there are about 25 houses spread out along about one kilometer of beach. From the shore, the farming area looks almost like any other stretch of beach, since the crop is submerged. All one can see are the tops of some of the stakes. The farmers prefer to work early in the morning when it is cool, because it takes a lot of work to rid the crop of unwanted weeds, re-tie broken seedlings, and repair wave damage. When work is being done there is again little to see, just bobbing heads and floating baskets.

SOME THOUGHT HAS BEEN GIVEN to the construction of carrageenan processing facilities right in Bali. But the consensus is that this would not be feasible. There are only five such plants in the world, two in

Copenhagen, Denmark, owned by subsidiaries of Hercules and FMC. These are the destination of all of the E. *spinosum* grown in Bali. These extraction plants are highly automated and employ relatively few people. Furthermore, the extraction of carrageenan from seaweed is carried out while the seaweed is wet. That is, extraction involves chopping up the seaweed in water suspension. Since a considerable part of the price of the seaweed involves payment for time spent drying it for export, having an extraction facility on the spot might even result in fewer jobs, since this part of the operation would be eliminated. Also, to insure consistent results, the Copenhagen factories use a blend of seaweeds collected worldwide. So the processing plants have to be located in places that are central to world production, not just local production.

Exact export figures are difficult to come by, but Indonesia exported an estimated 2,300 metric tons in 1984. Denmark, Hong Kong, and Singapore were the major recipients of the crop. Bali's export of seaweed in 1983, the last year for which complete figures were available, was 413.3 metric tons, of which 370 tons was farmed. This crop was worth U.S. $15,283. This is an insignificant fraction of Bali's U.S. $20 million in total 1983 exports, but the industry is young—some 1,200 hectares in Bali are suitable for seaweed farming and only 169 of these are currently being farmed.

CHAPTER 32

Coffee

GROWING KOPI BALI

"JAVA" IS STILL A NICKNAME for coffee in the United States, and the world's first commercial cultivation of coffee east of Arabia began on the island of Java in 1699, 61 years before coffee was planted in Brazil—the leading producer of coffee today. With its neighbor Java, Bali shares a climate hospitable to coffee growing and the industry is the island's second-largest cash producer. Every year Bali produces 5,000 metric tons of coffee beans, some U.S. $10 million worth, and an estimated 13 percent of the island's population earns at least part of its income from the industry. Although the value of coffee growing in Bali is second only to the burgeoning garment industry, Bali's contribution to the entire production of Indonesia is small—4 percent. As a whole, today Indonesia ranks third, behind Brazil and Columbia.

Most of Bali's coffee finds its way to the export markets in the United States and Europe, although the Balinese are great coffee drinkers. Balinese style coffee is not for the faint of heart. They prepare it by putting a spoonful of finely ground roast coffee—not instant—right into the cup. This is stirred up, and a large amount of sugar is spooned in. The result is more of a thick suspension than a solution, and is muddy and opaque. It quickly produces a deposit in the bottom of the glass, so it is stirred occasionally to keep the powder in suspension.

COFFEE DRINKING BEGAN in the valleys of what is now Ethiopia where *Coffea arabica,* the most important of the commercially valuable species of coffee, grows wild. Arab traders who encountered the practice in the 13th century took the habit back home with them—among other places to the important Red Sea port, Mocha. Mocha, in what is now Yemen, is another place that has become synonymous with "coffee." The coffee drinking custom spread to Egypt, Syria, and Persia, and Mocha became the great emporium for coffee trade in the Arab world. Mocha's location, just across from Ethiopia in the narrow strait between the Red Sea and the Gulf of Aden, gave it a great geographical advantage in the early coffee trade. Venetian traders brought the coffee drinking habit from the eastern shores of the Mediterranean to their home port in 1615, and from there it spread quickly all over Europe. The first coffee house in London was established in 1652.

Coffee plants were introduced to Java in 1699, and Bali's neighbor dominated the world markets until the middle of the 19th century. The Dutch administrators were ruthless in insisting that all available land be devoted to coffee growing. By the time the Englishman Sir Stamford Raffles—later to found Singapore—became lieutenant governor of Java in 1811, coffee production was so widespread that the production of food crops was dropping off dangerously, a practice that Raffles quickly stopped.

Coffee growing had spread to Ceylon, now Sri Lanka, at about the same time as it had come to Java. Ceylon's industry did not furnish much competition for Java until the middle of the nineteenth century. But the Ceylon groves proved disastrous, not just to Java, but to the entire coffee growing industry in Asia. In 1869 *Hemileia vastatrix,* a fungus that produces leaf rust, appeared on the coffee trees in Ceylon. It appears to have spread there accidentally from its native habitat in Africa. In twenty years it destroyed the entire coffee industry of Ceylon. It continued to spread, reaching Java in 1869, Mauritius in 1880, and The Philippines in 1890. It wiped out the *Coffea arabica* groves.

After this disaster, many of the coffee growing areas of mainland and peninsular Asia were turned over to other crops such as rubber. And during this same period, at the end of the 19th century, the coffee industry of Brazil rapidly grew to its present preeminence in the world. But coffee growers still sought a type of coffee that would be resistant to leaf rust. *Coffea liberica,* native to Liberia, was tried in 1873, but it held its own for only a decade before it too succumbed to leaf rust.

By 1900 the surge of Brazilian production had dropped the price of coffee to such a low level that even *liberica* plantations in many parts of Asia were abandoned in favor of rubber trees. But coffee growing in Java had never been completely abandoned, as it had in places such as Malaysia. Javanese growers continued to search for a disease resistant strain. By about 1900 they were achieving success with strains of still a third species of coffee, *Coffea canephora,* various cultivars of which today are called *Coffea robusta.*

It was discovered that disease resistance was often related to the altitude at which coffee grew. Experiments with *robusta* indicated that it grew very well at altitudes from 400 to 800 meters above sea level and was sufficiently disease resistant in this range to warrant large developments. On the other hand, the *arabica* variety seemed to be much less susceptible to *Hemileia* and other diseases when grown at altitudes above 800 meters. So this has been the direction taken by coffee growers in Indonesia—*robusta* at lower elevations, *arabica* at higher elevations. *Robusta* is by far the dominant crop in Indonesia, making up a total of 90 percent of the coffee grown and 95 percent of the coffee exported. The situation is just the opposite in Brazil, where 85 percent of the coffee production is *arabica*.

Arabica fetches a somewhat higher price and is in greater demand in the coffee importing countries. *Robusta* coffees are somewhat more mild than those from *arabica* strains. Indonesians describe the taste of *arabica* as *asam*, "sour," but Westerners usually describe *robusta* as being relatively tasteless. Most of the *robusta* exported in the world is used to make so-called "soluble" or instant coffees, for which it seems to be more ideally suited than *arabica*. Overall, about a quarter of the world's coffee is picked from *robusta* bushes.

THE COFFEE PLANT is a small tree or a large bush related to the gardenia and the cinchona tree, which produces quinine. Wild varieties commonly grow to three or four meters and occasionally reach 10 meters in height. The hybrid plants that produce the best coffee are trimmed to an ideal height of just under two meters to increase production and facilitate picking. The oval leaves are dark green and shiny, and come to a sharp point. Robusta leaves are 20 centimeters long and half that in width; *arabica* leaves are slightly smaller. The tree needs shade, and in Bali it is usual to plant some fast growing tree like *dapdap* to cover the coffee trees and protect them from the sun.

In Bali the fragrant white flowers appear first in April and then remain dormant until at least a little rain has fallen, usually in September or October. Then the blossoms develop fully and produce seeds—*robusta* by cross pollination and *arabica* by self-pollination. Green berries form, grow to spheres about the size of small grapes, and finally turn red and are ready for harvest. From flower to harvest takes about 10 months.

The ripe fruit of the coffee tree is very much like a small cherry, and, in fact, is sometimes called just that, although it is less plump and somewhat elongated. The fruits are green when first formed, gradually changing to a bright red when fully ripe. The red outside covering is a thick pulpy skin, inside of which is a yellowish, sweet, "jelly." This surrounds the two beans or berries—coffee beans grow in pairs, and are hemispherical in shape. The beans vary in color from pale tan to pale, mottled green. They only turn to the rich "coffee" brown after roasting. Each of the two beans in a cherry is enclosed in a membrane called the "parchment," which becomes brittle when the cherry is dried. Inside this layer, surrounding each individual coffee bean, is a delicate seed skin, commercially called the "silver skin." The preparation of coffee for either roasting or for export in a green state consists of removing the juicy layer, the parchment, and the silver skin, and then drying the bean itself.

The method of preparation used on the large coffee estates of East Java is called WIB, for West Indische Bereiding, Dutch for "West Indian Preparation." The process originated in the Caribbean. The beans are picked only when completely red. This means that the trees have to be picked at regular, frequent intervals and it involves a good deal of labor. The beans are first placed in a large vat of water—the red beans sink while the defective ones are skimmed off and saved for another process. The red beans are then sent through a pulper that breaks them open and squeezes the beans right out of the pulpy skin. The beans then go to large tanks where they are allowed to ferment for a day. This loosens the glutinous "jelly" and allows it to be washed off. The beans are spread out in the sun to dry, which may take several weeks, during which time they must be turned over regularly. In some areas mechanical heaters are used. When the beans are thoroughly dry they are put through hulling and polishing machines which crack and remove both the parchment and silver skins.

In Bali the usual preparation is done via a dry process, called OIB, for Oost Indische Bereiding ("East Indian Process"). This is a much simpler method, but it produces coffee that is of a lower quality than WIB. The beans are picked when about 70 percent red, 20 percent green, and 10 percent yellow. The pulping and fermenting stage is skipped. The beans are washed to remove dirt and other impurities, then spread out under the sun to dry. They are then sent through fanning and hulling machines that remove the hulls, the pulp, and the skins. In Indonesia the average yield is about 400 to 500 kilograms of dried beans per hectare per year, which is not very good by international standards, which are almost double this amount.

Coffee trees are usually started from seedlings obtained from government nurseries. Coffee trees need good shade all during their productive lives. In Bali a farmer planning to plant coffee will plant some fast growing tree like *dapdap* two years before the first seedlings are planted. A coffee orchard or plantation produces a great deal of cover, and the soil underneath it is protected from erosion by the dense growth of coffee trees, cover trees, and other surface vegetation. In recent years clove trees have been edging out coffee in Bali. Twenty years ago there were hardly any cloves in Bali. Now one sees them along the roads and in the forests everywhere. They have been popular because of the premium market price and because the crop requires little work to bring to harvest. But clove trees require total open sunlight and a clear ground surface between trees. This clearing of the land has resulted in severe erosion in several places and has led to worries about the future quality of the water supply in some areas. Strict laws have now been passed governing the cutting of trees. The recent falling price of cloves has also helped discourage this practice.

Coffee trees can also be grown from seed. *Robusta* cross pollinates and is not best when grown from seeds. It is usually grown by grafting on to resistant stocks. *Arabica* is self-pollinating and can be grown from seeds. Seedlings can also be produced by bending down the lower branches of the tree and burying the tops in the earth. After about four months roots form and the new growth starts. A coffee tree may continue to yield profitably for 30 years or more, although about half of that is average, and growers prefer to insure high yields by replacing older trees at intervals of about 12 to 15 years. An old tree can be cut to ground level, and, if left alone, will branch and produce again. New trees are set out in a grid, each plant three meters from the next. A coffee tree produces a big crop only in alternate years, although proper pruning will even out these fluctuations.

COFFEE GROWING IN BALI began in the 1750s with plantings of *Arabica*. These thrived for about 100 years, finally being destroyed, along with their Javanese neighbors, by leaf rust. Coffee production on a large scale did not resume until the introduction of strains of *robusta* in 1912. All eight districts in Bali produce some coffee, but Buleleng, Tabanan, and Bangli exceed all others by far. These are the data for the 1987 harvest:

KABUPATEN	METRIC TONS
Badung	168
Bangli	841
Buleleng	3,079
Gianyar	91
Jembrana	256
Karangasem	43
Klungkung	7
Tabanan	885
TOTAL	5,370

About one-third of the coffee plantings in Bali are *arabica*, two-thirds *robusta*. The principal *arabica* growing area is north of Kintamani. Some is grown in the mountainous areas south of Singaraja. And some *arabica* is grown south of Kintamani village, but not much to the east or west. The main seedling nursery for *arabica*, the 10 hectare Kebun Induk Kopi Arabika, is maintained at Kembangsari, toward the coast from Penulisan.

Coffee farmers traditionally work in groups called *kelompok tani*. The government assists them with technical guidance and distribution of high yielding materials, and credit for seedlings, fertilizers, pesticides, tools, and upkeep costs for the first three years of replanting a crop. Each farmer is entitled to a Rp 500,000 credit. Continuing research is being done both in Bali and at the Spice Research Institute, Balai Penelitian Perkebunan, in Jember, East Java. Development of disease resistant strains is especially important. *Hemileia* is by no means the only disease of coffee. The trees can be attacked by everything from mice to nematodes.

There are two centers of production for *robusta* coffee. One is Pupuan, somewhat off the beaten tourist path, between Antosari, where the road from Denpasar to Gilimanuk turns abruptly southward at Antosari toward the sea,

THE COFFEE PLANT

and Siririt, west of Singaraja. The other is at Banyuatis, even farther off the track, reached by traveling east, starting at a junction just south of Siririt, along the Siririt–Antosari road toward the Beratan caldera. The government maintains a seedling nursery at Banjar Sai, near Pupuan. And there is a very large central coffee processing plant at Punungan, also near Pupuan. It is closed except during the harvest season.

The vast majority of Balinese coffee—and Indonesian coffee in general—is grown on small farms of less than a hectare. Bali's farms average about two hectares, slightly above the national average. Indonesian law prohibits individuals from owning more than nine hectares, and farms smaller than a half hectare are not profitable. The collection, processing, and transportation of coffee beans to buyers, users, and exporters varies considerably from place to place. Singaraja has always been the commercial center for coffee in Bali, and all the biggest buyers and exporters have their headquarters offices there. But all coffee must be hauled by truck to West Bali to be shipped to Surabaya, Java for export.

Small coffee farmers generally sell their production on site to professional collectors, called *tengkulak*. The farmer may sell his beans right off the trees or he may borrow or rent a simple hulling machine and dry the results himself. In Pupuan farmers can take their beans to the large mill for processing. Collectors then take the beans to buyers who must process the green beans. At this stage the beans must be carefully sorted into the various standard grades that have been established by the government, on the basis of the contents of adulterants such as twigs and stones, and upon the percentage of broken, immature, or diseased beans. uhis sorting is always done by hand. The price that the broker pays the gatherers is a function of the grade. These are usually cash transactions. The gatherers bring their beans to the broker's large warehouse where the load is carefully sampled and paid for on the spot. Some brokers have their own gatherers. There are many such companies in the Singaraja area, some of which also deal in vanilla and cloves.

The lowest grades of *robusta* coffee are generally destined for domestic consumption. About 80 percent of the *arabica* and a good deal of the *robusta* is exported, that part retained being of the lowest quality. There are nine exporters, all in the Singaraja area. There is some variation in their operation. Some raise coffee and export it. Some just buy. Some of their coffee comes from middlemen; some from the farmers directly. *Arabica* can be profitably exported to the United States even in competition with Brazilian coffee because the price is often lower. Bali coffee, either *arabica* or *robusta*, has a taste that is different from the South American coffees and is often sold overseas under the name "Bali Coffee." For the best flavor, the beans should be kept in storage for at least a year before roasting. All of the coffee is exported green. Roasting is done at the destination.

Indonesia is a member of ICO, the London-based International Coffee Organization, which is a trade organization for some 75 coffee producing nations. The organization sets export quotas, attempts to even out prices, smooth political relations between producing and consuming countries, and to beef up coffee's image in the consumer nations. The ICO also sets grading standards. Indonesia is not famous for the quality of her coffee, and one contributing factor is the confusion over grades, which vary from region to region. For domestic coffee, the most often used grades are SP and GB. The former stands for "Single Picked," the latter for Gewone bereiding, meaning "Ordinary Preparation." SP is of high quality. GB contains almost no whole seeds or green seeds. For exporting purposes, quality is shown by a pair of numbers separated by a slash, for example "9/12%," meaning 9–12 percent of the coffee consists of inferior beans.

COFFEE FOR THE DOMESTIC market in Bali varies considerably in quality. Except for those who roast, grind, and package coffee for the high quality domestic market, much of the coffee is GB *robusta* mixed with the lower grades of *arabica*. In places like Lombok and Madura, individuals buy the green beans, roast what they need in a frying pan, and pound it into a powder by hand. But in Bali, almost all of the coffee sold to consumers has already been roasted and ground to a powder. This is called *kopi bubuk*.

A great deal of the *kopi bubuk* sold in Bali is adulterated with corn. The corn is boiled and roasted separately from the coffee. The corn is added to the coffee before grinding. A typical small coffee roaster produces three grades of *kopi bubuk*. Grade A is pure coffee. Grade B contains about 50 percent by weight corn; and Grade C contains about 70 percent corn. The price varies accordingly, being less than half as much for grade C as for grade A. The coffees with and those without corn are visually identical. Other adulterants, such as chicory, are never used.

One of the typical small coffee mills that I visited processes about 100–500 kilograms per day, depending upon demand. Green coffee beans, both SP and GB grades are purchased in 100 kilo bags, called *karung*, from brokers. The roaster is a hollow steel sphere about one meter in diameter. The coffee is placed in the roaster and it is sealed with a large steel door. The roaster is suspended on an axis that passes through its center, terminating in a pulley. It is turned slowly over a large kerosene blast burner by a small electric motor. Three sides of the roaster are encased in fire brick. After roasting the loose skins are separated from the beans with a blower. And then the beans are ground with motor-driven ceramic disk grinders. Successful roasting is more of an art than a science. The entire aroma and taste of the product depends upon this process, which must be very precisely timed.

As with most coffee roasters in Bali, the factory I visited uses no *arabica* at all. Although it may be the world's favorite, customers in Bali are not used to the taste and consider it *kasar*, "rough" or "coarse," and bitter. It sells only to merchants. But there are larger coffee roasters and grinders, both in Singaraja and Denpasar, who sell *kopi bubuk* both in bulk and sealed in one-quarter, one-half, and one kilogram plastic packages. This coffee is more expensive than the bulk variety. Whether or not it is adulterated is hard to say. There is no reason to think that it is not. Coffee prices are notoriously variable, but at the time of writing the best grade of packaged *bubuk* sold for about Rp 8,500 a kilogram in Denpasar. At the other end of the scale, grade C bulk coffee, about 70 percent corn, sold for Rp 3,000 a kilo.

Since most of the major coffee growing areas are far from the beaten tourist trails, the chances of a visitor making a routine visit are rather small unless the there is extra time allowed for a side trip to be taken with a guide. However, there are small numbers of both wild coffee trees and small coffee plantings along the main roads in many of the areas of Bali that are several hundred meters or more above sea level. You can see coffee trees between Mengwi and Bedugul, and both north and south of Tampak Siring on the road to Kintamani, and there are a number of coffee groves along the road as it descends from the summit of the mountains as one drives north from Bedugul to Singaraja.

Index